DESTROYING THE SHADOW AGENDA

HOW GOD'S ASTONISHING PLAN WILL OVERCOME THE SHADOW AGENDA

BRUCE R. PORTER

Liberty Trades, LLC

Littleton, Colorado

This book is licensed for your personal enjoyment. If you'd like to share it with another person, please be kind enough to purchase an additional copy for each recipient. If you're reading this book and didn't purchase it, or it was not purchased for your use only, then please purchase your own copy. Thanks so much for respecting the hard work and countless hours of research required to produce this book.

Contents

A Few Reader's Voices — vii
Acknowledgments — ix
Author's Apologia — xi
Prelude — xv

Part I. Rude Awakenings

1. Day of Infamy — 3
2. Response-Abilities — 13
3. Into an Earthly Hell — 21
4. On "The Pile" — 29
5. Ground Zero Grace — 41
6. Buried in the Rubble — 49

Part II. No Fear

7. Homeland Insecurity — 59
8. America Hijacked? — 67
9. We the Sheeple? — 75
10. America Lobotomized? — 83
11. A War on "Terror?" — 103
12. A "Crash" Course — 117

Part III. Truth: Handle with Care

13. Sworn Upon What? — 131
14. Red or Blue Pill? — 141
15. Slavery, Racism, and Natives — 151
16. No Borders=No Nation — 171
17. Our Real Enemy — 183

Part IV. Who Might We Become?

18. National Destiny?	205
19. Faith of Our Fathers	215
20. America in Covenant?	235
21. Dreams From My Founders	259

Part V. The Way Forward

22. The Price of Mercy	277
23. God's Invaders	291
24. Our Bucket List	309
About the Author	329

A Few Reader's Voices

What Others are Saying About
The Shadow Agenda

"As one reads Bruce Porter's book, it is impossible not to connect the dots and see our nation, and indeed, the world in peril. It is also impossible to avoid searching your soul for clear evidence that you have done your part to prevent that danger. You will find much inspiration within these pages to commit to doing everything you can in the time you have left to save the Constitutional Republic, which our Founding Fathers, with Divine Inspiration, so artfully created."

Tom Tancredo
Former U.S. Congressman and Presidential Candidate

Feeling hopeless regarding the direction of this Nation?
Encouraging, thought-provoking, and motivating read toward hope, prayer, and action for the repentance of this nation. Well documented excerpts indicate a strong dedication of this Nation to God by many of our forefathers and, therefore, subject to God's judgment for the breaking of His Covenant…possibly begun on 9/11! BUT Comparisons drawn between the repentance of the Ninevites of the Old Testament in the Book of Jonah and our own despicable condition renew a faith and hope that God may not yet have given up on the U.S.…and may yet grant us a mercy and grace that we would honor Him again! Highly recommend!

Alfonsi, Amazon Kindle Reader

Great read!
From the book's cover to the last page is the story of an epic moral and spiritual battle. Lady Liberty isn't just under assault, she's been targeted for assassination by evil forces. Who will come to her aid? Thankfully, Bruce Porter leads the charge in rekindling the heart of fellow patriots who love liberty and our Constitutional Republic. Bruce has a battle plan to renew America. Join him on the long march forward by going back to what made America great and the men and women of faith that sacrificed so much. Then move forward with the assurance of ultimate victory against evil with the Author of all history. The battle is the Lord's, but we also are called

to action. Bruce, as a first responder and chaplain, is calling us to join him. Read his story, and hopefully you'll want to enlist too.
Bob Haas, Amazon Kindle Reader

Factual and suspenseful!

This book is both factual and suspenseful, with the author baring his soul to give us the truth we all deserve. A real page turner as facts are presented in a clear, concise and riveting manner that leaves the reader both informed and spellbound. You will be hard pressed to find a more accurately documented case for understanding the true state of our nation and why she is worth fighting for.
Glenda Howard, Amazon Kindle Reader

Learned some things!

I learned some things I didn't know about 9-11. I agree that our country has lost its Christian roots… I highly recommend this book.
David Karr, Amazon Kindle Reader

Intense yet uplifting!

We can all help in small and large ways. Thank you for reminding us of what we can do.
Melanie, Amazon Kindle Reader

Acknowledgments

Destroying the Shadow Agenda
By Bruce R. Porter

PUBLISHED BY:
Liberty Trades, LLC
Copyright © 2018

~~~~~~

My wife Claudia made quite a few sacrifices over the years it took to produce this book. Not only did she pick up the slack in our family and ministry, but she had to put up with my frequent grousing about how hard it is to write a book like this. Some of the subject matter dredged up some industrial-strength unhappy memories and emotions, and I'll admit that I wasn't always very graceful in the way it affected my mood. I also salute her courage willingness to stand with me and face the inevitable blowback this sort of book will likely generate.

Thanks also to David Riehl for the photographic images of the Washington statue at Federal Hall and the Presidential prayer booth in St. Paul's Chapel in New York City, which will be featured in the E-book version. Also, I want to give a big shout-out of thanks to Ted Kennedy, Justin and Erika Bergfalk, and Ken and Glenda Howard for their over-the-top financial support to help me carve-out the massive amount of time it took to research and write this.

Thanks also to Carla Riehl for allowing me to use her amazing music at the beginning and end of the audiobook.

Thanks also go out to my son Jesse and daughter-in-law Aubri for their help with the audio version mastering process and graphic assistance with putting the final touches on the cover design. Finally, thanks go out to all my dear friends, fellow authors, and beta-readers who offered so much sage advice, encouragement, and support.

Thanks also to Dr. Marlene Bagnul, D.Lit., for her years of kind encouragement and wonderful writer's conferences, and for granting me the high privilege of speaking on several occasions at her conferences.

Last, but not least, thanks go out to Dr. Michael McKinney, Ph.D., President of Promise Christian University and Seminary, and his gracious and lovely wife, Dr. Adelle McKinney, Ph.D., University Registrar, for the privilege of delivering the 2004 Commencement Address at Promise Christian University, and bestowing upon me the high honor of a Doctor of Divinity degree. Your

ix

x   Destroying the Shadow Agenda

encouragement and confidence in me went a long way in helping me stay the course with this project.

To read updates and various articles, or to obtain the latest news on upcoming new books. Please visit:

www.brucereedporter.com

You may also read my blog articles at:

www.brucespeaks.com

Author's Apologia

Morpheus:
The Matrix is everywhere.
It is all around us. Even now, in this very room.
You can see it when you look out your window
or when you turn on your television.
You can feel it when you go to work,
when you go to church, when you pay your taxes.
It is the world that has been pulled over your eyes
to blind you from the truth.

Neo:
What truth?

Morpheus:
That you are a slave, Neo.
Like everyone else, you were born into bondage.
Born into a prison that you cannot smell or taste or touch.
A prison for your mind.
Unfortunately, no one can be told what the Matrix is.
You have to see it for yourself.
This is your last chance.
After this, there is no turning back.
The Matrix

~~~~~~~~

First, a confession. I've struggled with writing this book for a very long time. Part of my struggle was a personal one. I didn't feel qualified. When I walk through the literal canyons of books already written and offered in libraries and bookstores on the main themes of this book, my inner voice screams; "people *already* know this stuff! Besides, what qualifies *you* to write on these subjects?!"

Directly related to my struggle—and integral to why this was so hard to write—is the Shadow Agenda *itself*. The intensity of spiritual warfare I've endured while trying to write this work nearly overwhelmed me. Thoughts of fear, despair, discouragement, and unworthiness have sometimes swept over my mind and soul like black tsunami waves from the pit of hell. Many were the times when I nearly gave up the effort. However, the Spirit of God ever faithfully brought encouragement and spurred me on to finish. How thankful I am for God's enabling grace, for I've experienced the truth of the scripture found in 2 Corinthians 12:9, quoted here from The Passion Translation.

> But he answered me,
> "My grace is always more than enough for you,
> and my power finds its full expression
> through your weakness."
> So I will celebrate my weaknesses,
> for when I'm weak I sense more deeply
> the mighty power of Christ living in me.

As so well-described by the character Morpheus in the opening quote from the film, *The Matrix*, I've become fully convinced that each one of us is profoundly influenced—for good or evil—by unseen forces that surround us at all times and in all places. As Bob Dylan of folk-poet fame once wrote; *You gotta serve somebody. It may be the Devil, or it may be the Lord, but you gotta serve somebody.* I suspect that one of the reasons that *The Matrix* film resonated with so many people is—whether they are willing to admit it or not—the haunting sense that something outside themselves is somehow manipulating, and perhaps, even controlling their lives.

I am an unashamed Biblical Christian within the Reformed tradition and my world-view is based upon the word of God, as best I can understand it. I make no claim of personal perfection, infallible theology, intellect, or logic. I'm just doing the best I can as a redeemed hell-deserving sinner who stands solely upon the grace and mercy of Christ. My hope is that whatever God has seen fit to manifest through my meager service and labors since my regeneration, it will redound *exclusively* to the honor, glory, and praise of *God alone*.

As a student of theology for over four decades, I find abundant evidence throughout the Bible—as well as in life experiences—that convinces me that there actually *is* an unseen agenda working itself out in the lives of men and nations. *Nothing happens by accident.* The *good and holy one* is God's agenda, revealed in His holy scriptures, and which will one-day triumph and manifest throughout the Earth and universe, revealing His glory and majesty. However, there is *also* an evil *shadow agenda*, which is seeking the utter destruction of all humans and even the Earth itself, ruled by the Devil and his fallen angels (demons).

As I will try to demonstrate within these pages, the ultimate victory over all evil is inevitable, with even the intrigues of evil agents acting out—unwittingly—to bring about the greater glory of God. Those who are in Christ have been granted the honor and joy of shining out the light and glory of Christ's gospel to the ends of the Earth. They will preside over the utter defeat of the Shadow Agenda, and thrill to see our Heavenly Father's foreordained agenda—foreseen and decreed before the creation of the universe—fully manifested in all things.

There are many theological distinctions among those who claim faith in Jesus and the Holy Bible. This being the case, some of what I've written here may be controversial and even offensive to those holding differing theological opinions. Unfortunately, offenses cannot be entirely avoided. All I ask is a fair hearing and prayerful consideration.

The purpose of this book is three-fold: *Information, Encouragement, and Provocation.* First, I wish to *inform* people about the nature and strategy of the sinister "shadow agenda" taking place all around us. As the quote above reveals, we are all—to one degree or another—immersed in a virtual cesspool of deception, fighting our way to the surface to breathe the fresh air of Truth.

Second, I want to *encourage* Christ's people to embrace a confident *long-range outlook* on the world and the plans and purposes of God. I believe the promises of ultimate victory in Christ are sure and reliable. Although we face many challenges and problems short-term, I intend to remind my readers that all our struggles will end in *absolute victory over all the works of darkness.*

Third, I desire to *provoke* Christians to love and good works and increased efforts to promote the Truth claims of the Judeo/Christian Bible and the Christian gospel until the whole earth is filled with His glory.

My hope is that you will find some encouraging and eye-opening concepts within these pages that will liberate you out of the fog of secular brainwashing so rampant in our time. May you be enabled and strengthened to stand "contra mundum" (against the world) and take your place as a faithful warrior to destroy the *Shadow Agenda.*

Your hand-to-hand combat
is not with human beings,
but with the highest principalities
and authorities operating in rebellion
under the heavenly realms.
For they are a powerful class
of demon-gods and evil spirits

that hold this dark world in bondage.
Ephesians 6:12
The Passion Translation

Prelude

*God has endowed man
with inalienable rights,
among which are self-government,
reason, and conscience.
Man is properly self-governed
only when he is guided rightly
and governed by his Maker,
divine Truth and Love.*
John Dryden (1631-1700)
~~~~~~~~

This book was originally released under the title: *A Ground Zero Responder Speaks on Tyranny, Deception, and Christian Liberty*. After the 2016 Presidential election of Donald Trump, and upon further reflection, I decided to make certain revisions and updates to reflect the current situation. The election of President Trump came as a surprise to many people, and in spite of vicious criticism and nearly non-stop fake news attacks against him, President Trump has wrought significant changes for the better in his first months in office. It is my hope that this election may signal a "sea change" in our nation's downward spiral into racial and societal divisions, economic ruin, and political corruption. But, there is much work ahead for those of us who desire to see America great again, morally, economically, and socially. There is much opposition, but I'm convinced that with God, all things are possible!

Don't Be Discouraged!

All of us experience times when life's circumstances seem so overwhelming, so impossible, that nothing we do seems to make any difference. That "deer in the headlights" feeling could easily apply to our present national situation. Our country is in deep crisis, and events appear to be shifting and moving so quickly, just trying to keep up with the news feels like trying to drink from a fire hose. The temptation to feel overwhelmed and discouraged is especially high because things just seem to be going from bad to worse with each news cycle.

To me, apathy and discouragement are like giant menacing trolls who rise up in our faces shouting and bellowing industrial-strength intimidation. The "apathy troll" roars his challenge: "What's the *use*? Why bother? Nobody *else* cares that America is falling apart, so why should *you*? Just mind your own business, shuffle along with the crowd, watch television, play video games, go see a movie, and stay out of trouble."

The "discouragement troll" echoes nearly the same counsel: "And just *who* do you think *you* are anyway? You're so *pathetic!* What good do you think *you* could ever do? There are *far* more educated, smarter, and qualified people out there who are "taking care" of everything. Why don't you just *sit down, shut up,* and *stay out of their way!"*

There is also a "religious" troll I must not fail to mention. *This* ogre is the perhaps the *most* devastating of the three. It is closely allied with the first two, and regularly borrows lines from them. I call it the "defeated Christian" troll. Its strength is in the *pessimistic theology* and defeatist worldview it promotes in the minds and hearts of biblically ignorant Christians. It uses twisted misinterpretations of Scripture to convince God's people that society, governments, and world events are *supposed* to crash and burn in order to fulfill "end times" prophecy so the "second coming" of Christ can occur. Those bewitched by this troll find spiritual-sounding reasons not to engage the culture aggressively or get involved in the political or educational processes. This evil pacifist philosophy allows wicked men and the forces of darkness to wreak havoc on the world nearly unopposed. *I intend to slay this troll.*

Have you ever heard those Trollish voices? I certainly have, and often. If we pay attention to these lying monsters, we will remain in the ranks of timid and ineffective people all around us who live out their lives as described by Henry David Thoreau in *Walden*:

> *The mass of men*
> *lead lives of quiet desperation*

Oliver Wendell Holmes' echoed Thoreau's thought in *The Voiceless*:

> *Alas for those that never sing,*
> *but die with all their music in them.*

Yes, We're in Serious Trouble

I can't think of a time in our nation's history when the threat of our republic's destruction was greater. Our national problems range from racial hatred and violence, narcissism, moral corruption, ethical compromise, and "envy" politics.

These issues are not mere happenstance but are being promoted through deliberate mind control.

The near-constant exposure we endure to one demoralizing crisis after another by our nation's news media threatens to sap our strength and feed a collective sense of hopelessness. Be sure of one thing; these problems are engineered and deliberate and cannot be corrected by the wisdom of men. When people forsake the counsels of God, rebel against His commandments, and mock those who hold to a biblical paradigm, things can never end well. The inevitable outcome—as history teaches repeatedly—is oppression, slavery, poverty, and death.

I believe America's *real* problems are spiritual. I'm encouraged lately that there are some hopeful signs that God is awakening His people to their duties to respond proactively against the minions of darkness who are seeking to overthrow and destroy all that is called good and holy. Our greatest challenge is to pay more attention to what *God* is saying about our times and tune-out discouraging and demoralizing voices. Demonic forces, and those under their influence, continually rage in their hatred of God and His Christ. We must always remember that compared to the awesome power of God's grace toward the redeemed of the Lord, all the minions of darkness are nothing more than toothless, annoying, barking, dogs.

An Unusual Experience on the "Pile"
I was standing on the World Trade Center wreckage in a drizzling rain watching a giant crane pull a twisted steel girder from the rubble. Parts of it glowed red-hot from the raging fires still burning underneath the debris. All of us standing around watched intently, for it was when the jangled mess was disturbed that human remains could be revealed and recovered. When we spotted remains, the work instantly stopped so we could recover whatever we could find. These were placed in a bio-hazard bag and taken immediately to a nearby tent morgue to begin the process of genetic testing for identification. Obviously, this was gruesome smelly work, and it wasn't too unusual to see a SAR (Search and Rescue) worker hunched over retching.

It was early evening on the fifth day of my service in New York City, and darkness slowly enveloped Lower Manhattan. The work would go on throughout the night. The size and scope of the destruction was almost too much for the mind to take in. Banks of bright searchlights illuminated enormous plumes of smoke and steam rising from the debris, creating an eerie, otherworldly effect to the scene. I glanced around at helmeted men and women, representing various agencies from all over the nation, as they climbed around on the pile performing various duties. A couple of ironworkers positioned high up on the rubble in a basket suspended from a towering crane cut away parts of the tangled wreckage with acetylene torches. This created multicolored fountains of bright sparks that cascaded down on the rubble below. The unspeakable horror all around me and the beautiful and ethereal showers of sparks created a weird contrast.

I stood there wondering how long the search for human remains, and perhaps even a survivor, would go on. Indeed, it would continue through this long rainy night until the dawn, and likely for many more dawnings to come. For some of these people—who lost friends and loved ones in this jumble of wreckage—the desperate search would continue at some deeper emotional level for the rest of their lives. Such scenes become imprinted upon the mind and heart and would remain with us all forever. No eraser but the grace of God could ever cleanse the mind of such terrible scenes.

In the midst of this milieu, I suddenly heard the faint electronic ringing of my cell phone tucked inside my grimy, rain-drenched turnout jacket. Groping for the phone, I finally pulled it up to my ear, only to be frustrated by my breathing mask strapped over my mouth and nose. Jerking the mask down so I could speak, I heard my voice say in a barely audible croak, "Hello?"

Over the noise of machinery, and the hissing of torches and generators, I could faintly discern a small child's voice on the phone say; " Daddy, what are you dooo-ing?" I instantly recognized the voice of my five-year-old Hannah. She was watching the live 24-hour televised feed of Ground Zero at home back in Colorado. She'd been looking for a glimpse of me there. I heard her say, "Where are you, Daddy? I can't see you." My heart melted.

Her sweet voice instantly drew me back into a much happier place that seemed now only a dim memory. She was calling out to me from her childish world where all things were good, safe, and peaceful. Her days were filled listening to Winnie the Pooh stories or watching colorful birds visit our bird feeder or staring at clouds while trying to decide what kind of animal they resembled. I ached with all my heart to be back in her world again. Her voice was like a cold drink of water in a dry and dusty desert.

Standing there in the rain, with heavy equipment clanking all around me, I struggled for several moments to respond to her question. What could I say to answer my little girl's question without alarming her? I knew that soon enough the harsher realities of this broken world would hurt her, and perhaps even break her heart. I desperately wanted to protect her and knew I had to choose my words carefully.

I could hear her breathing into the phone, patiently waiting for me to answer her question. My eyes swept over the smoldering wreckage surrounding me where untold thousands of people lay mangled in smoking rubble. Finally, I said, "Honey, some mean bad guys made a big mess here in New York City, and I'm just helping to clean it up."

There was a pregnant pause on the phone as she thought about this. Then, in her sweet, innocent voice, she replied:

"Daddy, can I bring my little broom and help?"

The power of her question struck me like a bolt of lightning. I froze, and for several moments I couldn't speak past the enormous lump forming in my throat. The emotions that welled up were like a volcanic eruption I'd held in check until that moment. Choking back sobs, I finally gained enough control to respond. I don't remember what I said exactly, but only recall mumbling something about how important it was that she use her little broom to help mommy clean up the messes there at home. It was nearly impossible to suppress my emotions. With a husky voice, I thanked her for calling and offering to help. I told her I loved her, promising to call back as soon as I could before ending the call.

Slipping the phone back into a pocket, I pulled up my protective mask back over my mouth and nose. Despite my best efforts to keep it together, my knees buckled and I plopped down in the rubble sobbing like a baby. My little girl had just expressed as clearly as human language could ever communicate what I, and most likely everyone around me, felt in this horrible place. For whatever training and willingness to serve I possessed, all I felt I'd managed to bring to this hell-hole was a "little broom." What was that compared to the millions of tons of twisted wreckage, shattered dreams, and broken hearts? The disaster was so enormous and overwhelming, nothing I did seemed to make any difference. This feeling of helplessness was especially true since we couldn't find anyone alive.

For several minutes, I battled a wave of depression sweeping over me. It felt like I was sinking into a pit of despair like a fissure opened up under me in the rubble. In this dark place, I fought for breath, for hope, and for faith. Only love held me up–the love of a little girl in Colorado who called her daddy to make sure he was okay. Her call was a lifeline of love, and I clung to it with all my strength.

At that moment of deepest depression, I desperately cried out to God. "Jesus, I'm so weak and useless, and the needs here are so great. Please help me." A powerful revelation suddenly flooded my mind. In that instant, I was reminded this situation was not the slightest bit about me. Rather, it was about the tens of thousands of brokenhearted children and parents and husbands and wives and friends in a traumatized city who were facing a long future of crying themselves to sleep night after night. It was about people longing for someone they loved, who would never come home again, ever. It was about people looking up every day at a gaping hole in their skyline, bereft of the gleaming towers, and having to relive over and over the memory of that horrible day in September.

Sometimes, when I consider the state of our republic, I'm tempted to feel the same way. Our national problems are so enormous; that it's hard to try even to respond. How can one person make any real difference? What effect can one lone voice have while attempting to be heard over the howling of so many strident societal and political voices yelling and shouting their vitriol and hatred of our nation?

I strongly suspect feelings of despair and hopelessness are precisely what the forces of darkness want us all to feel. They want us depressed, overwhelmed and paralyzed into paranoid inaction. They want us to live in fear, find a place to hide from the storm, and give ourselves to a "survivalist" mentality that clings to life in this world as if it were the only life we have. For the Christian, this is a lie leading to slavery. They know that if enough of us succumb to these feelings, we will make almost no effort to resist them and help "clean up the messes" they are creating.

In the larger scheme of things, we must remember that our present struggles are not just about us personally. It's about billions of people around the world who grope in darkness, suffering starvation, disease, violence and are feeling hopeless and abandoned. It's about little children being sexually exploited by depraved adults, and who are being indoctrinated into hatred and racial envy without any hope of future happiness or success. It's about future generations who will inherit a world filled with evil who are too uneducated to understand what is happening to them.

Our children and grandchildren and great-grandchildren depend upon our generation to maintain a nation of just laws and economic opportunities with freedom. Within themselves, people yearn for life and meaning in a world that is often harsh and cruel. Ultimately, I believe the only broom capable of cleaning up the slimy, stinking mess that Adam bequeathed to all of us is the grace and mercy of God.

The loud metallic clanking of one of the cranes dragging another massive chunk of twisted metal out of the rubble pulled me out of the debris of my dark brooding, and back into the moment. Scrambling to my feet, and feeling a little embarrassed about my emotional display, I wiped the tears from my face with a grimy glove and looked around. The guys nearby seemed to ignore me, pressing into the work at hand, but I'm sure that they understood how I was feeling and could relate. Some things don't need much explanation in the brotherhood of suffering.

I wandered back toward the makeshift tent morgue near the World Financial Center. I thought again of the medical and support teams in there who were enduring the task of processing and cataloging the body parts we were bringing in. A weeping Firefighter Chaplain would once again take his "little broom" in there for awhile, and try to comfort, encourage, and sweep away some of the mess. A "little broom," I reminded myself, can do *something* useful and make a difference when made available. Even my little girl was smart enough to know that.

> *If you wait*
> *until you can do everything*
> *for everybody,*
> *instead of doing something*
> *for somebody,*
> *you'll end up not doing anything*
> *for anybody.*
> Malcolm Bane

Within these pages, I will attempt to describe some of my personal experiences as a volunteer firefighter and Chaplain, who served for several weeks at the ruins of the World Trade Center beginning one week after 9/11. My time in New York City changed my life forever. It was hard to write this book because it dredged up some memories I'd much rather forget. However, during the extensive research required to write it, another much larger story began to emerge, and it took on a life of its own. After over fourteen years of reflection and prayer, I think I'm finally starting to grasp the enormous issues that emerged in our country and world following that attack.

While struggling to make sense of it all, I felt drawn to a study of America's history far beyond anything I'd ever learned in school. As horrifying as the terrorist attacks were—with so many thousands of lives destroyed—something evil and threatening seemed to be emerging from the smoking rubble like some kind of mythical dragon. The 9/11 attacks began to look more and more like a gigantic metaphor and "triggering event" of some sort, setting in motion ominous after-effects. In fact, since that day, I believe our nation has come under an evil, dark shadow.

The specter of increasing secret government surveillance upon ordinary citizens and the imposition of new "security" laws are threatening our fundamental freedoms under the Constitution and Bill of Rights. These infringements are troubling enough, but uber-progressive secularists, aided and abetted by a leftist-progressive media, have infiltrated into positions of political power at the highest levels and created what appears to be the "perfect storm" for America's destruction.

> *The farther back you can look,*
> *the farther forward you are likely to see.*
> Sir Winston Churchill

Churchill had a profound insight in the above quote. We cannot hope to understand our present, let alone our future, without a clear grasp of our history. History is the key to understanding the present. If we can discover where we started from as a nation—particularly related to the spiritual and normative social paradigms of early Americans—it just might be possible to find some "reset" button and retrace our way back to better times. During my research, I was delighted to discover the rich historical Christian foundations that profoundly influenced the thinking of our nation's Founding Fathers. Along the way, I found ample evidence that those foundations were not merely the product of human genius. America's founding was deeply and unmistakably influenced by the guiding hand of Divine Providence in evident harmony with principles found in the Hebrew/Christian Bible. I'm convinced that the erosion and corruption of those early foundations are the *prime reason* that 9/11 happened in the first place. Perhaps if those Biblical principles could be rediscovered and embraced by our people, they will save our future.

This book wrestles with some severe and sobering underlying spiritual and moral problems we are facing—problems that threaten to drag our country and the world down into an Orwellian nightmare.

For those unfamiliar with George Orwell's classic book, *1984*, I offer the following quote, which summarizes the central theme of Orwell's book. The central figure in the story, Winston, is suffering through a torturous interrogation by O'Brien, an agent of the State in Chapter 3.

> *If you want a picture of the future,*
> *imagine a boot stamping on a human face,*
> *forever.*

It may yet be possible to avoid Orwell's grim vision. I'm beginning to see signs that God is now stirring the hearts and minds of many others besides myself.

We're raising the alarm and calling our fellow citizens to respond to the clear and present danger we face. If this is true, then I must believe that there is hope for us, for God is arousing His people to action.

Is it Possible to Make a Difference?

Loren Eiseley, one of the great writers of the 20th century, once wrote a compelling story about a man walking along the beach who encountered a boy picking up starfish and throwing them into the surf:

Once upon a time, there was a wise man that used to go to the ocean to do his writing. He had a habit of walking on the beach before he began his work.

One day, as he was walking along the shore, he looked down the beach and saw a human figure moving like a dancer. He smiled to himself at the thought of someone who would dance to the day, and so, he walked faster to catch up. As he got closer, he noticed that the figure was that of a young man and that what he was doing was not dancing at all. The young man was reaching down to the shore, picking up small objects, and throwing them into the ocean.

He came closer still and called out "Good morning! May I ask what it is that you are doing?"

The young man paused, looked up, and replied "Throwing starfish into the ocean."

"I must ask, then, why are you throwing starfish into the ocean?" asked the somewhat startled wise man.

To this, the young man replied, "The sun is up and the tide is going out. If I don't throw them in, they'll die."

Upon hearing this, the wise man commented, "But, young man, do you not realize that there are miles and miles of beach and there are starfish all along every mile? You can't possibly make a difference!"

At this, the young man bent down, picked up yet another starfish, and threw it into the ocean. As it met the water, he said,

"It made a difference for *that* one!"

Like the enormous number of starfish on that beach, multiplied millions of people are "washed up" on the beaches of ignorance, disease, poverty, and especially, spiritual darkness. These conditions are the cause of the many problems our nation faces now. The magnitude of these challenges can seem so overwhelming that we may freeze in the face of them. The Evil Day comes, but we must not be idle, standing paralyzed in the shadow of a "Rubble Pile" doing nothing. A deer caught in the headlights usually has a short life expectancy.

Resigning ourselves to the rubble pile of a broken world is not an option for a Biblical Christian. We are on the winning team, even when it looks like we're losing. We who've read the "back of the book" know that we win! Holding onto hope in the midst of a crisis is sometimes challenging, but it is well worth it. Long-term victory is guaranteed!

However, as capable as we might think we are, it would be wise to remember that on our own we are limited and easily discouraged when problems seem too big. Our greatest strength is in recognizing that *nothing* is too big for God. Our nation's Founding Fathers understood this truth by personal experience. With God's providential aid, all things are possible.

As I see it, based on my experiences and personal study of the Bible, God is infinitely strong! His mighty power never fails or weakens in the accomplishment of His plans and purposes. It is in His strength and ability that we are enabled to join Him in fruitful labors, face and overcome the most challenging and heartbreaking circumstances, and rise above them.

Perhaps I'm overly ambitious, but within these pages, I'm also going to attempt to harmonize two seemingly opposite lines of theological thought into a practical and logical balance. I'm speaking of the responsibility of *man* compared to the overarching Providence of *God*. Theologians have always wrestled with the tension between these two seemingly opposites. I believe both are biblically justified. We who are His people are called to be people of action, and zealous for good works. At the same time, we are equally called into His *rest*, trusting God to bring about outcomes that please Him, even as we labor toward those outcomes with diligence.

I invite you to take a journey with me into Ground Zero to see what I saw, smell what I gagged on, and feel what I felt. I warn you; it will not always be a pleasant journey. I will also share what I believe is happening to our country in the wake of that fateful day, and how great and momentous changes in our nation and world are occurring right before our eyes. I will also try my best to bring all these events into perspective. I'll conclude by suggesting some practical actions to address the crisis at hand.

By "actions," I mean that I will offer some practical ideas on how we might influence our generation in every way, including governmental, educational, media, and journalistic realms. I make no apology that I am promoting a biblical Christian worldview. Let me be clear that I'm not suggesting that Christians take any aggressive physical actions that might cause bodily injury to anyone or destroy property. Violence is the historical playground of atheists, anarchists, Islamic terrorists, and leftist revolutionaries. Critics often accuse Christians of "cramming their religion down people's throats" but this is a lie. Secularists are the ones who seek to "cram" their values and worldview down *everyone else's throats*, by force if need be. Biblical Christians have *never* built concentration or "re-education" camps down through history to force the unwilling to conform.

This statement begs a disclaimer. Right away, secularists will cry; "But what about the Inquisition and all the millions of people tortured and murdered in "the name of Christ"? This is a legitimate question, but I boldly declare that the persons who did these heinous acts of cruel barbarity were *NOT Biblical Christians*. In fact, *most* of their victims were Biblical Christians who refused to bow down to an unbiblical and evil religion masquerading as Christ's church. More on this later. I will make this distinction throughout this book because it is necessary. Throughout history, there have been those who cloaked their evil deeds in the lamb's wool of Christ's flock. Jesus referred to them as wolves in sheep's clothing.

> *Beware of false prophets,*
> *which come to you in sheep's clothing,*
> *but inwardly they are ravening wolves.*
> Matthew 7:15

Christians cannot Biblically justify violence except in definite circumstances of self-defense, *lawfully* declared war, or in defense of their country, homes, and loved ones. Our enemies never tire in seeking opportunities to discredit or slander us, and we must be wise enough not to supply them with "slander-ammo." (They'll invent their own without any assistance from us.)

Our Greatest Weapon

More than anything, I want you to come away from this book with one of the greatest weapons of all—*hope and confidence in God*. I want you to be able to look at your children and grandchildren with renewed hope and optimism for their future. I want you to imagine a revived republic and government that promotes policies in harmony with constitutional principles of liberty and freedom, with, as our National Pledge affirms, "liberty and justice for all."

In our own strength, we cannot hope to a "perfect" society in this present, fallen world. However, I *do* believe that *eventually*, all the kingdoms of the Earth will come under the absolute rulership of Christ. *We* cannot humanly accomplish this, but *God can and will*. He will do a work in the hearts of men and change entire nations. We can confidently expect a future where people live out the full measure of their days in peace, enjoying the fruits of their labors without fear or want. I want you to imagine a nation where it is possible to *"…lead a quiet and peaceable life, in all godliness, and honesty"* as we pray *"…for Kings, and for all that are in authority"* as written in 1 Timothy 2:2

Throughout the book, I will endeavor to place America's history—the good, the bad, and the shameful—within the larger framework of God's eternal plans and purposes. I'll also try to spotlight the hand of Providence as it operates right in the midst of, and in the smallest details, of everything that has ever happened, is happening, or ever will happen.

Again, this is admittedly an ambitious effort. Some of what I'm going to share may cause some religious dizziness and feelings of disorientation at times. Please fasten your theological seat belts, put your seatbacks of attention and tray-tables of presuppositions into their full and upright position. Stow all your electronic gear, (unless you're using it to read this book of course), and keep yourself inside the faithfulness of God at all times. This journey began long, long ago, and we are nearing our final destination. We may experience a few bumps on final approach to that "good, and acceptable, and perfect will of God." The Captain of our soul assures all who believe that no matter how crazy this ride gets, it will end very, *very* well indeed!

PART I

Rude Awakenings

1

Day of Infamy

I feel thin, sort of stretched,
like butter scraped over too much bread.
Bilbo Baggins
J.R.R. Tolkien
The Fellowship of the Ring

~~~~~~~~

A date which will live in infamy,
the United States of America was suddenly
and deliberately attacked.
President Franklin D. Roosevelt
U.S. Congress, December the 8th, 1941

~~~~~~~~

 A rude awakening can either be a blessing or a curse. The "curse" kind is like being awakened by someone who snores, or by a neighbor's dog barking at odd times in the night. Another example might be when your next-door neighbor decides to mow his lawn at 6 AM on a Saturday morning while you're trying to sleep in.
 The "blessing" variety of rude awakenings aren't always pleasant either, but they are *necessary*. A few examples that come to mind are when your alarm clock goes off on a weekday and calls you to your duties and responsibilities at work or school. Another "blessed" kind might come in the form of a negative medical test result after a physical exam that alerts your doctor to an impending health problem in time to make corrections to diet or exercise habits. An extreme example would be a smoke or carbon monoxide alarm that goes off in the middle of the night and startles you awake with a blaring screech. As annoying as that one might be, it is a "blessing" because it offers a chance to escape a horrible death or injury. You might not enjoy these sorts of awakenings, but you're mighty grateful later because it saved your life or your loved ones.
 Ironically—at least on a national level—the terrorist attacks of 9/11 just might

have been a particular kind of rude awakening in the "blessing" category. That painful event rudely awakened many of us to the dangers we are facing as a nation, and perhaps, in the end, may prove to be an incalculable blessing. For decades far too many of us slumbered "fat, dumb, and happy" in a stupor of indifference while our nation and world burned. "Rude Awakenings" like 9/11 can also serve as a warning that we need to change our ways so that we might avoid impending judgment. The event indeed awakened me, but far too many others have hit the proverbial "snooze button" and gone back to sleep. This book is but one of a growing number of secondary "snooze alarms" that are increasing in volume with each passing day. It is high time we rise and meet the ominous challenges now facing us.

My Rude Awakening

My home is situated nearly 8,000 feet above sea level in the tranquil foothills of the Colorado Rocky Mountains, with pristine, snow-capped mountain peaks framed by dark blue high altitude skies. The fresh alpine air blowing among tall ponderosa, evergreen, and aspen trees refreshes the mind and soul. Deer, elk, mountain lions, and bears wander through our property, and it's easy to imagine on most days that all's right with the world. That perception dissolved on September 11, 2001.

That morning, I was taking a leisurely shower after a peaceful night of sleep. I recall humming a tune while enjoying my shower with the smell of scented soap wafting around me. My bliss was rudely interrupted when my wife Claudia burst into our bathroom shouting frantically. I couldn't make out what she was saying at first over the noise of the water, so I yelled back through the shower door, "Why are you yelling? What is it!?"

She'd been watching the morning news, and I could tell from the tone of her voice that this was serious. "Something horrible just happened in New York City!" she yelled. "They think it might be a terrorist attack! You'll want to see this!" Before I could respond, she abruptly spun around and ran back out to the television in our living room. My senses now fully alert, I froze for a moment under the shower stream, my mind racing. Terrorist attacks in the Middle East weren't anything new, but here in America?

Turning off the water and jumping out of the shower, I grabbed a towel and dried off as quickly as I could. Without bothering to dress, I threw on a bathrobe and ran into the living room still dripping water. As I plopped down on the couch, my gaze locked on the televised images of the World Trade Towers in Lower Manhattan, New York City. One of the buildings was belching gigantic plumes of smoke out of an oddly-shaped hole about three-quarters of the way up the side of the building. Bright orange flames billowed out near the hole. A reporter excitedly yelled that just minutes before, what looked like a commercial airliner flew at rooftop level across downtown Manhattan and slammed into the north tower.

The live video feed zoomed in and out on the North Tower. We could clearly see people leaning out of the broken windows just above and below the gaping hole, with choking smoke and flames billowing out behind them. Some of them were frantically waving what looked like sheets or coats, desperately crying out for rescue. I immediately knew help would never arrive in time for these poor souls. As a volunteer firefighter, I did a quick mental calculation as to how hot those flames were and knew that these people were being roasted alive by the radiated heat.

As we continued to watch, the TV cameras suddenly caught the distinct outline of another aircraft approaching at low altitude in the distant background out over the Hudson River. We hardly had time to gasp before this second plane screamed in at high-speed and slammed into the South Tower! Instantly, a billowing fireball and aircraft debris erupted out of the north side of the building as the plane disintegrated, and its fuel tanks exploded.

For several seconds, we just sat there in shock, staring at the television in stunned silence. As I recall, even the news anchor went speechless for several seconds as the shocking scene unfolded before the world. Any lingering doubts I might have harbored about whether or not this was a terrorist attack vanished at that moment. I remember jumping to my feet in shocked bewilderment, shouting to no one in particular, "This is a terrorist attack for sure!"

For the remainder of that day, we remained transfixed in front of the TV as frantic reporters near the scene tried to piece together what was unfolding in real-time before the eyes of the world. From the gaping hole high up on the wounded buildings, thousands of pieces of paper, ejected through the gaping holes in the towers, could be seen raining down like slowly falling snow to the streets below.

Compounding horror upon horror, we began to see something infinitely more disturbing than paper falling from the towers. Scores of men and women could clearly be seen jumping from blown-out windows as they desperately tried to escape incineration by the searing flames near the holes in the sides of the buildings.

Authorities later estimated that over two hundred people chose to jump rather than be roasted alive. It is heartbreaking to imagine the terror and desperation these people must have experienced as they leaped out of the shattered windows of the burning building to escape the flames and fell for several agonizing seconds to an instant death. Thinking about it later, I wondered what I would have done in that same situation and concluded that I would likely have done the same thing, for it was certainly an instant, painless death upon impact.

Then, at approximately 7:00 AM Mountain Time, we saw the South Tower suddenly collapse into a billowing cloud of dust and pulverized concrete. Televised images of terrified people running through the streets of New York to escape the scalding-hot, choking clouds of pulverized concrete and debris billowing out through Lower Manhattan's canyon-like streets could never be forgotten. We hardly had time to process these images when twenty-eight minutes later, the North Tower also collapsed in a nearly identical way. I recall thinking at the time how odd it was that both Towers came down in nearly the same mirror-image way, and it seemed utterly incredible that such well-engineered steel structures could collapse so quickly. I quickly dismissed the thought, concentrating rather on the unfolding human tragedy and the suffering we were witnessing. Only much later would some rather unsettling questions re-emerge about the many strange events surrounding this tragedy and how it could have happened in the first place.

As the towers fell in on themselves, a massive cloud of dust and debris blasted through Lower Manhattan, blanketing everything in a gray-white powder. Far from being a cool blast of air, however, this pyroclastic cloud was scorching. After I had arrived on-scene one week later, I saw scorched cars parked a block away with tires melted, or burned to a crisp when their gas tanks exploded. Just across Vessey Street, the plastic coating on a chain-link fence was melted from the intense heat of the blast wave. As the towers fell, a billowing column of smoke and debris shot high into the sky over Lower Manhattan and was mercifully blown eastward by the winds toward the ocean. Images of terrified people frantically running ahead of the debris cloud reminded me of an apocalyptic scene from a movie, but this was all too real. Many suffered burns and cuts; their bodies caked with the thick dust that darkened the sky and made breathing nearly impossible.

September 11, 2001, was clearly "a date that will live in infamy." Ironically, those words were uttered nearly 60 years ago by President Franklin D. Roosevelt on December the 8th, 1941. The President spoke before a special joint session of Congress in response to the attack by the Imperial Japanese Navy on Pearl Harbor, Hawaii just a day before. His words now seem hauntingly prophetic and eerily relevant to what we experienced on 9/11:

> *Yesterday, December 7, 1941, a date which will live in infamy, the United States of America was suddenly and deliberately attacked.*

On that particular Sunday in 1941, millions of our parents and grandparents stopped everything and gathered around radios in their kitchens and living rooms to hear the unfolding news of the Pearl Harbor attack. Now, in 2001, millions of Americans sat once again transfixed—this time in front of televisions—in much the same way. Like them, we hung on every scrap of news and struggled desperately to comprehend what was unfolding, and what it all might mean. Here, yet again on our soil, our nation was under attack.

Ironically the Islamo-terrorists, like the Imperial Japanese 60 years before, overplayed their hand. Instead of intimidating us, a collective emotion of outrage erupted across America, and a desire for justice. The Pearl Harbor attack became the catalyst for America's entrance into the war with Japan. So too—at least for a time—modern Americans wanted revenge against those who perpetrated the 9/11 attack.

Following the Pearl Harbor attack, Admiral Isoroku Yamamoto, commander of the Japanese Imperial Fleet that carried out the bombing of Pearl Harbor, was portrayed in the award-winning 1970 film, Tora! Tora! Tora! as saying:

> *I fear all we have done is to awaken a sleeping giant and fill him with a terrible resolve.*

I could find no solid historical proof that Admiral Yamamoto spoke those precise words as depicted in the movie. However, I did discover he expressed nearly the same thoughts in personal correspondence to Ogata Taketora on January 9, 1942.

> *A military man can scarcely pride himself on having 'smitten a sleeping enemy'; it is more a matter of shame, simply, for the one smitten. I would rather you made your appraisal after seeing what the enemy does since it is certain that, angered and outraged, he will soon launch a determined counterattack.*[1]

Admiral Yamamoto's concerns about the Pearl Harbor attack were not unwarranted. Almost overnight, hundreds of thousands of America's young men and women reported to military recruitment centers across America to volunteer. Munitions factories were rapidly brought on-line to produce weapons and ammunition. Many car manufacturing plants—with the fresh ink of new Department of Defense contracts hardly dry—rapidly retooled their assembly lines to build tanks and warplanes. My mother worked at a munitions factory in St. Louis, Missouri, and my father and nearly all my uncles volunteered for the Army. After fast-track basic training, they shipped off to the South Pacific to fight.

Some conspiracy theories have speculated that key persons within the Roosevelt administration—perhaps even the President himself—knew in advance of Japan's plans to attack Hawaii, but did nothing to prevent it. Although I'm reluctant to accept it, some of the evidence seems compelling. I've often wondered if FDR and others in his cabinet might have speculated that a dramatic attack on U.S. territory would be just what they needed to justify a formal declaration of war. This attack would motivate the American people to confront the Imperial Japanese. Military intelligence knew for some time about a growing expansionist Japanese threat. It seems entirely plausible and disturbing.

As incredible as this scenario might appear to some, historical experience certainly supports the possibility. President Dwight D. Eisenhower was deeply concerned about this very thing. In his Military-Industrial Complex Speech, delivered in 1961, Eisenhower warned us all solemnly:

> *In the councils of government, we must guard against the acquisition of unwarranted influence, whether sought or unsought, by the military-industrial complex. The potential for the disastrous rise of misplaced power exists and will persist. We must never let the weight of this combination endanger our liberties or democratic processes. We should take nothing for granted. Only an alert and knowledgeable citizenry can compel the proper meshing of the huge industrial and military machinery of defense with our peaceful methods and goals so that security and liberty may prosper together . . .*
>
> *The prospect of domination of the nation's scholars by Federal employment, project allocations, and the power of money is ever present and is gravely to be regarded. Yet, in holding scientific research and discovery in respect, as we should, we must also be alert to the equal and opposite danger that public policy could itself become the captive of a scientific-technological elite.* [2]

As far back as ancient history, national leaders have often implemented "false flag" strategies and misinformation campaigns to manipulate their citizenry into certain courses of action. It happens all the time in business and personal interactions. Why would it seem so far-fetched to any thinking person that our government and the various occupants of the White House would also utilize such deceptive ploys as well? Human nature is what it is. Most Americans are very reluctant to embrace conspiracy theories, but this mindset is changing as new and credible information becomes more readily available to the average person through the power of information technology and the internet. We must use careful discernment to wade through the vast amount of misinformation and unverifiable propaganda available on the internet, just as we should with televised and print media, for it is certainly there as well. However, through this technology—for the first time in human history—everyone now has 24/7 access to news articles, audio, and video resources from all over the world, and this is changing the way people get their news.

Regrettably, the memory of Pearl Harbor is no longer vivid in the collective consciousness of most people in our current generation. Our socialist-oriented public education system and textbooks have minimized the event to near-obscurity in history studies. In some cases, they've even gone so far as indoctrinating students that the United States itself bears the blame for the attack under a twisted rubric of "political correctness."

In the same way, some public school history teachers are teaching their students that the 9/11 attack was likely brought on by "American imperialism." These are words borrowed from a typical Marxist propaganda playbook. As the twisted leftist narrative goes, America's greedy exploitation of the earth's natural resources, such as cheap oil or minerals, has earned the contempt of the world. This includes the grievous sin of "offending" Islam!

While We Mourned, Some Danced for Joy

A few days after the 9/11 attack, some news video came to light showing people across the Middle East dancing in the streets for joy. They were ecstatically celebrating the murder of thousands of Americans while shouting praises to their moon-god, Allah. They jubilantly gave each other gifts and candy.

Initially, I had to fight strong emotions of anger and outrage when I saw this. However, I knew in my heart this wasn't the best reaction, and I also understood from visiting the Middle East numerous times that many people living in Islamic countries were not happy about what happened. It's a reality that when the news media shows up with their microphones and cameras to get soundbites for the evening news, some people will "perform" for the cameras. This is especially so if their lack of enthusiasm might be noticed by more zealous America-haters who may be watching. Middle Eastern communities tend to be very close-knit, with everyone knowing nearly everyone else. It can be extremely dangerous—especially for Christians—to express any pro-American sentiments or appear "out of step" with what the local Islamo-hotheads think.

Cry 'Havoc!'

and let slip the dogs of war.
Julius Caesar, Act 3, Scene 1
by William Shakespeare

Millions of Americans felt outraged in the wake of the attacks. Within days, tens of thousands of our young people rushed to military recruitment centers—just as our forefathers did after the Pearl Harbor attack—to "line-up, and sign-up." Many Americans wanted to unleash unholy hell against those who attacked us, whoever or wherever they were. In retrospect, however, I can't help wondering if we were all somehow being "handled." There are those who wanted us to spend our treasure, blood, and the lives of our youth fighting some idiotic "war on terror." (More on this thought later.)

On the very morning of 9/11, I was preparing to take my son to Denver International Airport on his way overseas for a Christian missions outreach. Within minutes of the attack, however, President Bush ordered all U.S. airspace closed, and in-flight aircraft were directed to land immediately at the nearest airport. No one was traveling by commercial air that day, or in the week that followed. Tens of thousands of passengers found themselves stranded at unintended airports.

We also learned that during those first tense hours, President Bush issued standing orders to patrolling American fighter planes to shoot down any aircraft failing to comply immediately with air traffic control instructions. Thankfully, we were spared the additional heartbreak of hundreds of innocent air travelers being blown out of the sky by our military pilots. I whispered a prayer of thanks that my young son was not already in the air that morning.

For the next week, the only things flying around the nation were rumors and tightly controlled emergency and military fighter aircraft to provide whatever protection they could. It reminded me of the old saying about: "shutting the barn door after the horses escaped."

News reports a short time later said the hijackers had used conventional box cutters to attack aircrews and take over the cockpits of four aircraft.

Throughout the day of the attack, the news just kept going from bad to worse. The media reported that hijacked American Airlines Flight 77 had also slammed like a guided missile into the Pentagon at 7:37 AM Mountain Time. A bit later, at 8:03 AM, United Flight 93 crashed into a field near Shanksville, Pennsylvania. According to official reports, United 93 was headed for yet another target somewhere in the Washington, D.C. area, possibly the White House or the Congressional buildings.

In the weeks that followed, we heard awesome stories of courage demonstrated by some of the passengers on United 93. According to these reports, some of the passengers learned from friends and relatives on the ground (via onboard Airfones) that several other aircraft had been commandeered and used as guided missiles against targets on the ground. Instead of passively allowing their airplane to be a suicide weapon against more innocent people, a few heroic passengers decided to engage the hijackers and try to regain control of their aircraft.

Based on in-flight voice recordings recovered later from the crash site, as well as interviews with people on the ground who spoke with some of the passengers via the Airfones, some of these passengers did not go down without a fight. Apparently, they nearly succeeded in breaking into the cockpit of their aircraft. But in the final seconds, the terrorists realized they were about to be defeated. Rather than being taken alive, they deliberately plunged the airplane into the ground at near-supersonic speeds while shouting praises to their god, Allah.

You may have noticed that I'm using the qualifying word "reportedly" in the above paragraphs. This usage is deliberate because there are many unanswered questions regarding the actual events that occurred that terrible day. Some of the "official" explanations are, frankly, questionable. I'm not going to tackle the conspiratorial elements of this event in this book for one important reason. As I already said in the foreword, it matters little what individual minions of evil did that day. What's important is that evil agents, operating in various capacities, are ultimately to be blamed. I don't believe for one moment that the Islamic hijackers onboard those hijacked aircraft were the only terrorists "on the job" that day. They could never accomplish their mission without a large "supporting cast" of trainers, financiers, and other enablers working behind the scenes. Whether or not one thinks other Americans or "shadow government" players were involved is—in the larger scheme of things—irrelevant. My primary focus is to lay the ax of Truth to the root of the source of ALL evil that animates people to commit such atrocities.

Perhaps, further investigations as to what possible role insiders within our government might have had in allowing—or perhaps even worse—participating in the 9/11 attack should be encouraged. I have no doubt that eventually, the truth will come to light, and those responsible brought to justice, in this world or the next.

Our Long Horrible Movie

Throughout the day, we watched the televised details of the unfolding attack. Our youngest was five-years-old at the time, and she wandered in and out of the living room, hardly noticed. We were so preoccupied that none of us paid much attention to how she was reacting. At one point, she came into the living room and blurted out: "Are you guys going to watch that scary movie all day?!" In her young mind, the news we were watching was some horror film. Her usual Winnie the Pooh or Barney and Friends videos were far more entertaining, and she just couldn't understand why we kept watching something so depressing for so long.

Later we noticed she hadn't made any appearances in awhile, and we became alarmed. Calling to her and looking around the house, we finally found her hiding under her bed; evidently frightened by our "scary movie." In her way, she expressed what every last one of us felt. We all wished we could crawl under that bed and hide from the nightmares of that day, and go back to the way things were before. However, we all knew there was no going back.

Life in America—as we had known it—changed on 9/11. The nation was in shock and our collective sense of security had vaporized. The world now seemed darker and far more sinister. Evil plunged a cruel knife into our republic's heart—and twisted the blade.

Notes

1. Loose Cannons: 101 Myths, Mishaps and Misadventurers of Military History, By Graeme Donald. Osprey Publishing, Jan 1, 2012

2. Public Papers of the Presidents, Dwight D. Eisenhower, 1960, p. 1035- 1040 http://coursesa.matrix.msu.edu/~hst306/documents/indust.html Video of this entire speech available at: https://www.youtube.com/watch?v=CWiIYW_fBfY

2

Response–Abilities

> Frodo:
> *I wish none of this had ever happened.*
> Gandalf:
> *So do all who live to see such times,*
> *but that is not for them to decide.*
> *All you have to decide*
> *is how to use the time*
> *that is given to you.*
> J. R. R. Tolkien,
> The Lord of the Rings

~~~~~~~~

By mid-afternoon on 9/11, I knew I had to go to New York to help somehow, and began making plans. My many experiences over the previous 20 years gave me hope that I might be able to help. I had served as a firefighter, and as a Pastor and Chaplain in my local volunteer fire department, and a Disaster Response Officer with the Civil Air Patrol. My decades of experience in pastoral counseling, as well as training in CISM (Critical Incident Stress Management) gave me a sense of duty.

I knew the SAR (search and rescue) workers already on-scene in New York City were being traumatized by all they were enduring. The unimaginably gruesome work they were facing could scar them for life. I'm certainly no superman and had some fleeting concerns for my safety and emotional health at the prospect of being exposed to such a toxic scene. However, my experiences in other trauma situations gave me confidence in the extraordinary ability of God's Spirit to sustain and heal those He calls to such service.

I don't mean to imply that my service at scenes of disaster over the decades didn't affect me, for they certainly did. I can make no claim to any personal strength or ability to withstand the effects of horrible situations, but I discovered something about God in the midst of these experiences. When I am weak, then I am strong, for God gives strength to the weary who seek Him. What we cannot do, He does with ease. I've learned that in and of myself, I can do nothing. But with God, all things are possible. I needed the support of my family and friends for some time after I came home. But the greatest source of healing, comfort, and restoration came from God alone through Christ.

Another thing that helped me cope is a theological worldview I embraced years ago that the entire world, and everyone born into it, is *fallen*. I don't cherish high expectations of this present world or people. Therefore, I'm somewhat insulated from disappointment when evil manifests or people let me down. It's not that I'm melancholy or walk around depressed all the time or dislike people. It's just that I have an inexhaustible source of hope and comfort in Christ that far transcends this present dark world. As long as I keep my gaze fixed on that "bright and morning star," I'm good to go.

I knew the on-scene work at Ground Zero would be tough and potentially dangerous, especially in this particular incident. There was no guarantee I would even be permitted by the on-scene authorities in New York but felt I had to show up and try. A verse of scripture came to mind, and I just couldn't ignore it.

> *Therefore to him that knoweth how to do well,*
> *and doeth it not, to him it is sin.*
> James 4:17

Six days would pass before helping would become possible. Because of the nationwide air transportation shutdown, commercial flights to New York were not allowed until the following Monday, which allowed me time to make preparations before departure.

My home is located near a major approach corridor for Denver International Airport. On an ordinary day, scores of planes fly over our house as they descend into Denver. It was eerie during those days to look up and not see any commercial aircraft flying overhead. The silence in the skies was broken only occasionally by the high screech of an eagle, or a fighter jet roaring overhead from nearby Buckley Air Force Base, or an occasional "Flight for Life" helicopter.

While waiting for commercial flight operations to resume, I occupied my time with preparations. I made phone calls to contacts in New York City and secured lodging. My Fire Chief was very supportive when I told him I wanted to go to New York to offer help. Images of the scene at Ground Zero conveyed the massive size of the debris field. Neither of us had any clear idea of what I might be able to do, yet we both understood that showing up at the scene of need is a responder's first duty. Somehow, everything else would be sorted out in the doing.

A veteran missionary to Central America, Wayne Myers once told me:

> *God uses the available mud, Son.*
> *Make yourself available and He may use you for His glory.*

I was not alone in my desire to help. Our entire fire department rallied. Most of the firefighters in our department would have also gone to help in New York City in a heartbeat, but their jobs and duties prevented them doing so without creating severe financial hardships for their families. However, they found other ways to help that were just as essential. Some people from our department raised funds, sent cards and letters, and most importantly of all, many prayed! Those of us who responded personally to New York could not have done so without home support. In the weeks that followed, long lines of cars queued up along our roadways to give whatever people could to our firefighters standing with fire boots held out for donations. Our small fire department raised $80,000 for families of fallen New York City firefighters. This outpouring would later prove to be a great blessing to numerous firefighter families in New York.

As a side note, the multiple displays of U.S. flags in the months following the attack were fantastic to see. Nearly everywhere you looked—on cars, homes, and public buildings—people proudly displayed the flag of the United States in an expression of national pride and unity. I've often pondered how we tend to take life's truly important things for granted until they're threatened. We are inclined to assume what we value will always be there. The 9/11 attack reminded many Americans of the value of our flag, and all it represents. This fervency has long since waned, but I suspect an even harsher wake-up call is coming soon.

Why Did I Go?
People have often asked me why I felt such a strong urge to go to New York to help. I suppose there are many good reasons someone might choose to do as I did. For me, the simplest answer is that I was available to go, and it seemed like the right thing to do.

My vocation as a pastor allowed for lots of time flexibility, and it was no major hardship on the congregation for me to take the time away. My wife serves as co-pastor of our fellowship, and she was more than capable of serving the people in my absence.

16   Destroying the Shadow Agenda

Traveling to distant places to share the gospel or do relief work has always been a core value in our family for decades. My circumstances were such that I had to think of reasons not to go—and since I was able—that seemed reason enough.

Another primary reason I went was the inspiration I received from Rachel Joy Scott, one of the Columbine High School students who died in the school massacre twenty-nine months earlier. Only seventeen years old, Rachel was a Christian girl who bravely stood up for her faith in Jesus with wisdom and clarity far beyond her tender years. I was intensely involved in the aftermath of the Columbine massacre, and I hoped that my experiences working with the survivors might be useful somehow in New York as well. (For more on that, see my previous book, The Martyrs' Torch: The Message of the Columbine Massacre.)

Martyred for her faith in Christ by two evil, depraved young men, Rachel was the antithesis of everything these monsters represented. In videos and journals they left behind, the killers vented their maniacal rage and vulgar hatred of all Christians and made particularly vile threats against Rachel personally. As a pastor to Rachel's mother, I was intimately involved in the aftermath of this terrible event and had the honor of giving Rachel's eulogy at her funeral. Millions of people around the world watched the live televised service and received inspiration from the amazing stories of her life and Christian testimony.

Rachel left behind many amazing diary entries exhibiting her faith in Jesus and her commitment to follow Him no matter what the cost. She also passionately wrote about responding to wounded or hurting people around her with the love of God and compassion. She believed that by doing so, she could make a big difference in their lives.

One of the most inspiring things Rachel left behind—discovered by her family shortly after her death—was a piece she wrote titled "My Ethics, My Codes of Life." She composed it shortly before her death. Here is an excerpt from that essay:

> How do you know that trust, compassion, and beauty will not make this world a better place? Test them for yourself, and see the kind of effect they have in the lives of people around you. You just may start a chain reaction.
> Rachel Joy Scott, "My Ethics, My Codes of Life" [1]

Rachel's brief life impacted millions of people around the world since her death. She left behind a legacy of love and faithful devotion to Christ in her diaries and essays. Some of her diary entries even seemed to predict her death with surprising detail.

Rachel unknowingly changed my life. Since the Columbine massacre, I've redoubled my efforts to respond to hurting people wherever and however I could. Her inspiring example drove me to respond to other school shooting scenes, natural disasters, and terrorist attacks around the world—including Europe, Asia, Russia, and Israel. Even this book is partially the fruit of Rachel's inspirational Christian martyrdom. Her writings and example continue to move me to try and do my part to help ignite the "chain reaction" she wrote of. Rachel's challenge to love and good works continue to inspire millions of people around the world.

The Present National Crisis, and Our Response

If our republic is to experience a new birth of freedom, we must all brace ourselves to our duties. Our challenge, as citizens of the United States, is to raise high the bright torch of liberty and be responsive to our times. Our "Uncle Sam" is critically ill and on life-support. He has a severe heart condition. It is caused, I believe, by two things. First, our republic is contaminated by the debased spiritual state of our people and the growing influence of sinister spiritual forces that deceive and corrupt our youth. Second, the cancerous tumor of dysfunctional governmental bureaucracies threatens to kill our nation like blood-sucking leeches that drain our resources and strength. The clear and present danger to our constitutional republic is very real. The United States needs brave men and women who will stand up in this critical hour.

Response carries a price. As it is often said;

Freedom Isn't Free.

If I had titled this book; "Power Principles to Overcome Everything, and Be Perfectly Happy, Prosperous, and in Total Control Every Day in Every Way,, " it might sell millions of copies. Obviously, such a title would be a cruel lie. No one has ever discovered this formula and anyone who promises such nonsense is lying. Books promoting such fantasies in one form or another are extremely popular in our times, even among some who should know better. There are "preachers" and so-called "apostles and prophets" flying around the country in their private jets making millions of dollars selling such "doctrines of demons" snake-oil.

Struggles, persecutions, and hard times are a painful part of life in this present world. If we track the lives of men and women who faithfully served Christ down through the centuries, we see an almost unbroken litany of suffering. No sane person desires to experience pain or struggles, but useful life lessons often come through such experiences. As Benjamin Franklin wisely said:

Those things that hurt instruct.

Admittedly, it is very difficult to discern God's larger purposes in the midst of painful times. When I served at the rubble pile of Ground Zero, I couldn't see the bigger picture then as I believe I do now. The same thing has proven true at the sites of many other scenes of human tragedy and suffering around the world I've served at during my lifetime. Only later, after some time of prayer and reflection, could I find the grace to look back at the tragedy or difficult experience and see the wisdom of God at work.

I cannot hope to settle the issue of suffering and evil in this short book, and would be a fool to try. However, I'm convinced we need to struggle with these matters and consider every possibility and ramification when we must face down evil. Our present enforcement battles with wicked forces seeking to overthrow our constitutional republic will, at times, be hard and painful. Knowing this ahead of time, and armed with the assurance that the struggle is worth it, we will find the grace of God to endure. I believe Biblical Christians are commissioned to resist evil, do good, and seek to eradicate ignorance and suffering wherever the opportunity arises. Successful outcomes, however, are in God's hands alone.

As President Ronald Reagan once so wisely stated:

> *You and I have a rendezvous with destiny. We will preserve for our children this, the last best hope of man on earth, or we will sentence them to take the first step into a thousand years of darkness. If we fail, at least let our children and our children's children say of us we justified our brief moment here. We did all that could be done.*
> October 27, 1964 — from "The Speech" [2] [3]

No matter what outcome may result from our efforts, I know each of us one day must stand before God and give an account of our lives and how we faithfully obeyed Him. I wish supremely to glorify and honor Him either by my life or by my death.

Each of us must respond to the ongoing struggle according to the gifts and abilities we each possess in this unceasing battle. We are fools if we think that the forces of darkness ever sleep in their campaign to enslave humanity. As we do this, we may yet see a brighter day. Defeat is not an option.

But you must remember, my fellow-citizens, that eternal vigilance by the people is the price of liberty, and that you must pay the price if you wish to secure the blessing. It behooves you, therefore, to be watchful in your States as well as in the Federal Government.
Andrew Jackson, Farewell Address, March 4, 1837 [4]

Notes

1. Excerpt from Chain Reaction, by Darrell Scott, pages 54-56

2. A Time For Choosing, by Ronald Reagan, 1964 https://www.youtube.com/watch?v=2pbp0hur9RU

3. Why Ronald Reagan's 'A Time for Choosing' endures after all this time. Washington Times Opinion, by Steven F. Hayward October 23, 2014 http://tinyurl.com/oropl8x

4. The American Presidency Project, President Andrew Jackson, Farewell Address March 4, 1837 http://www.presidency.ucsb.edu/ws/?pid=67087

3

Into an Earthly Hell

It is easy to go down into Hell;
night and day, the gates of dark Death stand wide;
but to climb back again,
to retrace one's steps to the upper air –
there's the rub, the task.
Publius Vergilius Maro
(70-19 BC)

~~~~~~~~

Commercial flights resumed on Monday, September 17, six days after the attack. My day of departure to New York City had finally come. There were tearful farewells with my wife and children. We could scarcely imagine what lay ahead or what sorts of physical and emotional challenges I would face in the coming weeks. Six days after the attack, no one knew what might happen if further attacks against our country occurred.

My son Jesse drove me to Denver International Airport, and as we approached, we encountered security checkpoints along the road several miles from the passenger terminal. Heavily-armed military personnel and police officers in full battle-dress stopped cars, looked underneath with mirrors, checked identifications, and looked into trunks. Extremely stringent security measures were in place on this first day of resumed flight operations. Evidently, the authorities were making sure another attack would not occur, further eroding public confidence in the safety of air travel.

Flying the Unfriendly Skies

Denver International Airport looked nearly deserted on that first day. Ordinarily, the nearby parking lots would be full of cars; and long lines of vehicles would be moving slowly outside the terminal entry doors, picking up and dropping off passengers. The terminal building and concourses would normally be teeming with people. On this day, however, only a few hundred people could be seen within the cavernous terminal checking in for a handful of operational flights. The whole scene was eerie.

After arriving at the passenger drop-off area and unloading my bags, I turned to my son and our eyes locked. Stepping forward, I grabbed him in a bear hug and held him for a very long time. Despite my best efforts, I couldn't hold back a sob as I clung to him.

He looked a bit uncomfortable seeing his dad cry, and it drew my mind back to another sad goodbye thirty-one years earlier when I'd seen my father weep for the first time. It was 1969 at Lambert Airport in St. Louis, Missouri. I was departing for a tour of duty in Vietnam. My dad and mom, along with my three siblings and several friends, had come to see me off to war.

As the time came for me to board my flight, we all walked together down to the departure gate. Before hijackings and terrorism radically altered air travel security, whole groups of friends and families could walk unchallenged to the departure gates to send off or greet travelers. In the late 60s and early 70s, airport security as we now know it was almost non-existent.

My departure for Vietnam that day revealed a side of my father I'd never seen before. He was typically a rather stoic man. In his generation, it was highly unusual for men to display emotions or affection publicly. When I finally turned to say goodbye to my dad before boarding the airplane, I extended my hand to shake his. However, instead of returning my handshake, he suddenly threw his arms around me and held me tightly. Convulsing with sobs, he wept wordlessly. The depth of his emotions moved me to tears too.

Looking back on that awkward moment, I suspect Dad was thinking about his war experiences while serving in the South Pacific during World War II. He knew all too well that this might be the last time we would ever see each other in this world. I'm also sure he knew how war can change someone and must have longed to spare me from learning first-hand the real horrors of war.

Now, here I was again, standing at yet another air terminal weeping over my own son. I knew he wasn't going off to war that day, but I hugged him tightly just the same because a war had come to us all. I couldn't help thinking that if the 9/11 attacks ignited a larger war he, too, might be called to military service. There were so many unknowns at that time, and none of us knew what might happen in the coming months or years. I wanted to hold him as long as possible in that final peaceful moment. I finally understood something of what my dad felt when we said tearful goodbyes at another airport so long ago.

A Tense Flight into New York City
As I walked into the terminal to check-in, I had to pass through even more

stringent security checks. Only some of the departure gates were open that morning, with relatively few people as yet traveling by air during those first few days. Most of the shops and restaurants on the concourse were shuttered and dark. Reminders of the 9/11 attack were everywhere. 24/7 news media coverage blared from TV monitors throughout the terminal, and military guards in full battle dress with automatic weapons and attack dogs patrolled in teams of two, scrutinizing everyone. The security measures seemed designed to restore confidence to the traveling public that the watchmen were "on the job." In spite of all assurances, however, the non-stop flight I was riding that morning to Newark, New Jersey had only fifteen or twenty passengers waiting to board when I arrived at the gate. Few souls seemed bold enough to travel after the terrorist attacks just one week before.

I understood that our immediate safety was a priority, but it was also about the hundreds of thousands of transportation industry jobs and livelihoods that were on the line. The sooner Americans could confidently return to their normal routines of commerce and air travel; the better off everyone would be. Although the intense security checks were inconvenient, I understood the importance of the precautions. The American people needed reassurance that it was safe to travel again.

After boarding my flight, it was evident everyone onboard was tense. No ordinary joking or mundane pleasantries passed between us. The images of airplanes slamming into buildings and the smoking rubble at New York's Twin Towers and the Pentagon were raw in everyone's mind.

As we taxied out from the departure gate, the flight crew issued strict in-flight instructions. For example, absolutely *no one* was allowed to use the forward lavatory or approach anywhere *near* the cockpit. We were instructed to use the rear bathroom only when necessary and remain seated throughout the duration of the flight. The grim faces of the flight crew showed they meant business.

Most of the passengers looked nervous, scanning each other suspiciously. I was indeed watching everyone else, even as they watched me. I'm sure any suspicious-looking passenger who acted the slightest bit threatening during that flight would likely be pounced upon by vigilant passengers. I'm sure several armed air marshals were riding along on those first flights just to be sure terrorists didn't try to pull off an encore murder spree. The tension was palpable all the way to New York.

Looking Down into a Smoking Void
Late in the afternoon, our aircraft finally began a circling approach to Newark

Airport. The weather was clear, with the sun low in the west. Everyone on board, including the cabin crew, strained and twisted in their seats to catch a glimpse of the Lower Manhattan area across the Hudson River.

We could easily see the gap in the New York City skyline where the proud Twin Towers of the World Trade Center once stood. An enormous gray cloud of smoke still rose from the ruins, and I wondered if anyone could survive being trapped six days in that pile of smoking rubble. How many people, I wondered, were dead or dying in that mass of twisted steel?

After landing and retrieving my baggage, I stepped out of the terminal and boarded the Port Authority bus that would carry me into Manhattan. During the ride, we passed several security checkpoints manned by grim-faced, heavily armed National Guardsmen and police officers. The watchmen were visibly on guard, focused on one mission; protecting people from further attacks. They did their jobs with professionalism, and I had to admire their faithful attention to duty, but it still gave me the creeps to see military checkpoints manned by heavily-armed soldiers in full battle-dress in America.

Finally arriving after dark at the city bus terminal in upper Manhattan, I lugged my gear out into the New York City streets and hailed a cab. My driver was from India, and as he weaved in and out of traffic, he told me that this day was the first he'd been able to resume his work as a taxi driver. "It is good to be back on the job again," he said in his thick accent. "My family was starting to get hungry!"

Waving his arms and gesturing, he expertly wove in and out of traffic along the canyon-like streets of downtown Manhattan and described what it had been like in the city for the past week. He recounted how he'd dropped off a passenger at the World Trade Center just moments before the first aircraft struck the North Tower.

The cabbie was shaken and seemed to need to talk and tell his story. I asked questions and listened. For the next several weeks, I would do a lot of listening as I encountered thousands of people in this city whose world was shattered by the attack.

I finally arrived at my first destination, Abounding Grace Ministries, located on the lower East Side. Pastor Rick Del Rio graciously invited me to stay in the guest quarters of his church building while I served in the city. He heard of my work following the Columbine High School massacre, so when I called from Colorado offering help, he readily welcomed me as part of his response team.

Rick was one of the first ministers to arrive at the ruins immediately after the collapse of the North Tower. Sporting tattoos and a goatee, Rick is *not* the image of your *typical* pastor. He plies the streets of New York City on a classic Harley Davidson motorcycle and fits right into the often tough image of the New York City scene. In the first minutes after the attack, Rick—a true responder with a compassionate heart for people—fired up his Harley and roared through Lower Manhattan to the World Trade Center rubble pile to help. In those first hours, he ministered to scores of survivors streaming out of the World Trade Center ruins.

Walking Among the Brokenhearted

After stowing my gear in the guest quarters, Rick and I jumped into his van. He briefed me on the situation in the city as we wound our way through crowded streets into Lower Manhattan toward Ground Zero. All along the way, I saw signs and memorials posted in the windows of homes and businesses and the walls of buildings. It was very emotional to view the seemingly endless pictures of missing people posted on makeshift walls in a central memorial area. Although they were all strangers, I experienced the profound human link we all share in suffering. Thousands of pictures of missing moms, dads, sons, and daughters were displayed by the people who loved and now mourned for them.

The pictures often depicted the smiling memories of infinitely happier times like weddings, bar mitzvahs, birthdays, and holidays, etc. The happiness many of the images portrayed only served to underscore the unspeakable horror of the situation. According to New York Magazine, 1,609 people lost a spouse or partner in the attack, with an estimated 3,051 children who lost a parent. For the victims, life in this world ended; but for their loved ones who remained behind, a nightmare had only just begun.

Rick took me to some of the Lower Downtown FDNY firehouses out of which 343 firefighters responded and died on 9/11. Flower-laden memorial shrines were set up in front of them with candles showing pictures of the fallen firefighters from that house. Hundreds of cards and posters were displayed, many of them hand-drawn by children. All these were lovingly placed in front of the firehouses to express the community's condolences.

Several of the firehouses we visited lost most, if not all, of their morning shift on 9/11. The surviving firefighters were in deep mourning and shock. Many of the firefighters were hanging out on the street in front of the firehouses talking with people who came by with many tears and hugs exchanged. With 343 of their brethren killed, the outpouring of love and support was desperately needed and deeply appreciated.

Among the firefighter community, there is a profound sense of fraternity that's difficult to describe to an outsider. It's a unique camaraderie often experienced in other life-risking services such as the police and military.

When sharing great dangers, one learns to depend on the team. They become bonded as a family and grow to care deeply for each other.

In subsequent years after 9/11, I had opportunities to meet and speak before firefighters and First Responders from all around the United States, Europe, Russia, and in Israel. In each and every case, I saw eyes well up with emotion when the subject of New York City and the losses of the FDNY came up.

Rick and I talked with firefighters standing around outside their firehouses, expressing our condolences and offering our prayers and help in any way possible. Rescuers and Responders are entirely oriented toward helping others and being the "strong ones" in stressful situations. It was awkward for these guys to admit they were hurting and in need of some comfort.

At each fire station, a bulletin board was set up with the pictures and names of deceased firefighters from that house. At one station, a few firefighters stood around the board and recounted stories about their dead friends. There were also some lighter moments. We even shared some laughter as they recalled some of the silly antics and pranks their dead brothers used to play on each other. It seemed to do them good to laugh a bit over better times. It reminded me of scenes from old war movies where soldiers would lift a glass in a toast of honor, and reminisce about fallen friends. These guys couldn't toast their friends with anything stronger than hot coffee or a soft drink because they were on-duty, and the alarms could go off at any moment. Regardless, the sentiments were the same.

Over the next few weeks, I spent a fair amount of time sharing meals with these guys, sitting with them in the firehouses and listening to their stories during the down times between fire calls. Whenever an alarm sounded, all talk ceased, tears were quickly wiped away, and they would jump up, gear up, and ride out into the night to help people. It was inspirational to see them lay aside their grief and pain to answer duty. Many times I stood by fighting back tears as I waved them out into the streets on their way to an emergency. Their commitment and devotion to their calling was deeply moving—hero hearts one and all.

Everyone needs a word of encouragement during tough times. You can almost never go wrong when seeking to comfort and encourage someone going through painful parts of our shared journey in this life. My wife recently wrote a book about the astonishing power of encouragement, and I can't help pulling a quote from it. She wisely wrote;

No one ever died

of an encouragement overdose.
Claudia J. Porter, Author

She is so right about that. During my weeks in New York City, I tried very hard to "overdose" everyone I met with encouragement, and as far as I could tell, it didn't kill a single one of them.

The Challenges Ahead

In the coming times, we will face challenges we could scarcely imagine a few short years ago. Our republic is in grave danger from enemies within and without our borders. There can be no doubt that any serious effort to rekindle our Founders' patriotic passion for freedom, faith in God, and love for our Republic will attract violent opposition. This backlash is to be expected, especially when we focus our efforts upon the minds and hearts of our young people to reacquaint them with their historical and spiritual heritage. Those who are committed to our nation's destruction know well that the future lies with our country's youth. It will be an epic battle, for many of our people are so lost in the befuddling fog of deception that they can no longer think clearly.

Duty requires that we must be willing to "march into hell for a heavenly cause." If we "stay the course," we may together share the joy of victory and realize the seemingly impossible dream of seeing our republic rise again from the rubble better and stronger than before.

This is my quest.
To follow that star
No matter how hopeless,
no matter how far
To fight for the right
without question or pause
To be willing to march into hell
For that heavenly cause.
And I know
if I only be true to this glorious quest.
That my heart will lie peaceful and calm
when I'm laid to my rest.
Man of La Mancha, by Dale Wasserman;
The Impossible Dream

4

On "The Pile"

It's a dangerous business, Frodo,
going out your door.
You step onto the road,
and if you don't keep your feet,
there's no knowing
where you might be swept off to.
J.R.R. Tolkien
The Fellowship of the Ring

The next morning, Rick and I attended a meeting of Lower Manhattan pastors and Christian ministries. It was a strategic effort to formulate a plan to help efficiently people who were emotionally, physically, and spiritually devastated by the terrorist attack just one week prior.

It Wasn't Just the Towers that Fell
Many heart-wrenching stories emerged at this gathering. Falling debris from the Twin Towers had destroyed one pastor's church building. Other pastors shared stories of church members who were missing and presumed dead, and their efforts toward grief counseling and ministry to affected families. Several congregations had members who worked in the towers. There were also several fantastic stories of seemingly supernatural escapes from the towers before they fell. Several pastors expressed frustration about restrictions on their access to the rubble site. Understandably, some of them wanted access to Ground Zero to minister to personnel working there.

As I listened, it became apparent that, with few exceptions, most of these deeply compassionate men and women had little understanding of what it meant to walk into a mass-casualty disaster scene. For them, this was an intensely emotionally issue, and their hearts were yearning to help people. Their desire to serve was highly commendable, but the potential hazards that awaited untrained and emotionally unprepared people were very real.

The authorities were trying to control access to the rubble site because of the dangers present there. The debris field was full of voids one could easily step into and be injured or killed. Unknown fumes were rising from the wreckage that could be explosive or toxic. The pile was not a place for well-meaning clergymen without prior training.

Later that morning, a group of these ministers held a "march" down to City Hall to protest their exclusion from access to Ground Zero. I walked with them and talked with several community leaders along the way. As a way of appeasing them, someone from the Office of Emergency Management arranged a briefing for them at a staging area on the corner of Chambers and 12th Avenue. From this vantage point a short distance north of the debris field, they could see for themselves the scope and magnitude of the devastation.

After a safety briefing, everyone received protective masks and helmets at a staging tent near the site. We were then escorted down 12th Avenue toward Vessey Street, to the very edge of "Ground Zero" (or "The Pile"). After walking several blocks through the dust and debris scattered along the streets, the northwest corner of the wreckage came into view. It was nearly overwhelming and seemed to stretch on forever.

From this vantage point, only a small portion of the total debris field could be clearly seen. A literal mountain of smoking wreckage met the eyes, with broken and twisted steel jutting out in every direction. Part of the lower outer shell superstructure of the towers remained standing amid a heap of wreckage piled all around.

Atop the pile and all around it, Search and Rescue teams, FDNY, New York Police, and various other helmeted construction workers were hard at work attempting to sort out the mess. Large dump trucks queued up as mechanical shovels scooped up the twisted metal and debris and dropped it into their dump beds.

Nearly everyone wore protective gear and breathing apparatus to keep the pulverized concrete, glass, asbestos insulation, and gypsum powder out of their lungs. Every movement of the rubble released another cloud of toxic, foul-smelling dust. The fumes and smoke emanating from the debris burned my eyes and nose.

The noise around the pile was nearly deafening. Because all electrical power lines leading into the area were severed or damaged, massive diesel-electric generators were running every few hundred feet to power lights and equipment. The loud clanging of machinery mixed into the milieu. Huge floodlights were spaced all around the edges of the rubble to give illumination at night because the work went on unabated 24 hours a day.

In a Rubble Pile, Watch Your Step

The massive disaster scene at Ground Zero reminded me it's unwise to stumble into a situation without first sizing it up. We don't know what we don't know until we know what we didn't know.

It's so easy to make mistakes during an emergency. Several years ago, I committed a grave error in judgment during a medical emergency call. Our fire department responded to the home of a man who was presenting symptoms of a heart attack. We brought an ambulance to his home, and some of our EMTs went in to stabilize the patient and prep him for transport to the hospital emergency room. We were short-handed, so I assumed Incident Command.

While the man was being wheeled out to the ambulance, one of our paramedics came up on the radio to ask if we needed his assistance. He was offering to come and help even though he was some distance away. All we had on-scene were BLS (Basic Life Support) personnel, but the paramedic was ALS (Advanced Life Support).

Foolishly, I stood down the paramedic, and we ran the patient into the hospital emergency room without further incident. I based my decision on the initial assessment of our patient's condition by the EMTs on the scene.

Days later, I was confronted by the paramedic. He explained the severe error in judgment I'd made. His words were hard to hear, but the facts were undeniable. During transport to the Emergency Room, our patient might have gone into cardiac arrest at any time, and his life may have depended on the presence of a Paramedic with advanced training. The fact that I had ALS available and failed to make use of it could have cost our patient his life. It was a lesson I've never forgotten.

The massive devastation in New York City would require every available resource, and by the end of my first full day there, I'd begun to see how I could most effectively contribute. The Clergy Alliance was doing an excellent job helping hurting families and planning a long-term strategy for the ongoing support of the disaster victims.

The work of recovery and ministry to those emotionally and spiritually devastated by this attack would require years of loving care by locally-based ministries. I salute the Christian leaders who have done so much in the ensuing years, and the power and effectiveness of their various services will only be fully known and rewarded in eternity.

It soon became apparent that my New York mission lay along a different path. I possessed a level of training and experience that equipped me in ways most of the locals were not. I'd come to New York with my turnout gear and was eager to be as close to those working on the pile as possible without endangering myself or others. The next day I reported for duty.

Incident Command was run by FEMA (Federal Emergency Management Agency) and the Office of Emergency Management out of the Jacob Javits Center on 34th Street in upper Mid-Town. I reported to the authorities, presented my credentials, and obtained clearance and authorization with unrestricted access to the entire disaster scene. This permission was nothing short of a miracle, as I had witnessed many others turned away who had come to help from all over the country. I took this clearance as a sign that God had foreordained that I should be there and was greatly encouraged.

As an interesting side-note, two years and eight months before the 9/11 attack, I had a strange dream. I shared it in detail in my previous book, *The Martyrs' Torch, The Message of the Columbine Massacre.* Most of the dream related specifically to the Columbine High School tragedy on April 20, 1999. Part of the vision, however, puzzled me and made no sense.

I dreamed that I was standing in a situation of great danger, confusion, and billowing smoke. At the time, I assumed it had something to do with the Columbine disaster. As the dream progressed, however, I kept hearing the words "911! 911!" over and over. This three digit code is the number people dial for help in emergencies, but somehow it just didn't seem to fit into the Columbine event.

Then, one day as I was standing out on the rubble pile of the WTC with another SAR worker, he suddenly looked at me and said out of the blue, "Isn't it wild that this happened on 911? You know, the same as the emergency number 911?" I suddenly felt as if struck by lightning. The memory of the dream leaped up in my consciousness, and at that very moment, I realized that the part of my dream with "911" in it was about the terrorist attack! It was all about my being there, in New York City, working at Ground Zero! Goosebumps rose all over me, and I realized that God was confirming that I was standing precisely on the spot where He wanted me, at the exact time in history! I can't begin to describe the effect that moment had on my life.

Time with New York's Finest

In those earlier days, FEMA was a very different organization than it appears to be today. I will deal more with that issue later on, but at the time of the 9/11 response, FEMA seemed to be doing a superb job helping people. They made sure that the search and rescue workers at the site were getting everything they needed to respond effectively. I worked on the rubble pile of the WTC for two weeks, among some of the most amazing people in the world. My turnout gear was clearly different from that of local responders. My helmet rockers announced the word "Chaplain," so I stood out, and everyone I met knew right away that I was there for *them*.

I became aware that many of these people seemed to feel more comfortable sharing their thoughts and inner feelings with someone outside their organization. In a large and highly politicized department like the FDNY, people tend to be guarded about what they share. There was a real concern among the firefighters that things they might say in a moment of weakness could somehow find its way to the wrong ears and end up on their service record. Because I was a fellow firefighter and also a Chaplain from outside their department, many seemed more at ease in seeking spiritual counseling and sharing their emotions and inner struggles.

God placed me there as a sort of "stealth pastor" to these people. To be sure, the responders represented many varied denominations and certainly, not all were Christians. Now and then I encountered an angry atheist in deep stages of grief or rage. When they spied my helmet, they would sometimes vent their anger and hatred of God by spitting out words like, "Hey Preach! Just answer me *this*! Where the *f**k* was your "loving God" when *this* happened, huh!?" A few of them nearly got up in my face, but I never took it personally. Broken and hurt people often lash out and hurt people, and this is only to be expected.

Down through the ages, people have often asked the same question about what God was doing in the midst of some terrible event, usually venting their inner hatred towards God. I've heard that question repeated in one form or another at other disaster scenes around the world in many different languages.

In times of heartbreaking grief, most people cannot even *begin* to contemplate concepts like God's sovereignty, or His infinitely greater wisdom, mercy, and goodness that spans off into the unfathomable future. These sublime divine attributes are part of God's nature, and *always* in play, even during times of suffering. However, it's foolish to try to explain deeper theological concepts at such times. Usually, when confronted by someone who is struggling with heart-breaking grief and venting rage and anger at God, I try to shift the subject by asking a sincere personal question. "Did you lose someone close to you? Please, tell me about them." In times like this, people don't want "answers" or a sermon on God's righteous judgments or goodness. They just want someone to listen to them, care about how they feel, and offer simple human compassion.

Emotions among the workers at the rubble pile spanned the gamut. Everything from anger and shock to deep grief upon the loss of friends and colleagues was in play. Some of the firefighters were also struggling with classic "survivor guilt."

For example, one guy I spoke with served in one of the Lower Downtown firehouses near the WTC. On 9/11 he had the day off from his usual morning shift. When the first alarm came in, every last one of his morning shift brothers responded to the towers, ran into the doomed buildings, and died when they fell on them. He alone survived.

In the days that followed, he had to interact with some of the wives and children of his dead friends as they came to the station where their husbands and daddies worked. The poor guy was nearly suicidal, tormented with guilt and feeling unworthy of life. He battled a deep sense of shame that he wasn't with his brothers that morning.

As we talked, I tried to give him hope and a renewed vision and purpose for his life. I told him I believed his survival was God's plan, and his fallen brothers would likely be very grateful for his support to their families as they walked out this painful chapter in their lives. My unique position as an "outsider" offered him a bit of a refuge. Had this firefighter shared his suicidal thoughts with an FDNY Chaplain or counselor, certain legal requirements might have forced department personnel to file an official report—a potentially career-ending stroke.

This conversation was only one of several dozen similar exchanges. For the next number of days, I found myself deep in conversations and times of prayer with firefighters and NYPD officers as we worked together on the Pile. I'd sit with them in rest and dining areas, and even in the makeshift morgue on Vessey Street. Some of these guys had been up on the Pile continuously ever since the attack searching for survivors and needed someone to give them permission to go home, be with their families, and rest a bit.

Seeking the Living Among the Dead
The frustration of not finding anyone alive was demoralizing to everyone on-scene. I spoke to some of the officers handling the SAR (search and rescue) dogs. Some of the dogs had bandaged paws because their feet were getting cuts from sharp edges in some of the debris. Unlike cadaver dogs, which are specially trained to find human remains, the dogs were becoming depressed because they had been trained to find survivors—and there were none to find.

The SAR dogs weren't the only ones whose spirits were falling. Looking around at the strained dirty faces of the firefighters, ironworkers, and police personnel working nearby, I reflected on all that had happened since I arrived. Days blurred into nights as the work went on twenty-four hours a day. At times, I had to fight off intense feelings of disorientation. The magnitude of the destruction was far worse than any televised images could convey. My eyes could scarcely take it all in; I couldn't wrap my mind around it; everything was surreal. Late at night, I saw some steel girders that the cranes pulled up out of the rubble. In places, they glowed red-hot, with portions melted from mysterious fires yet burning under the rubble—even weeks after the collapse. I remember wondering if the subway tunnels running under the WTC might be supplying enough oxygen to feed the fires. It just seemed weird that fires hot enough to melt steel could still be burning after so long a time.

Pungent smoke and steam continued rising from the bowels of the wreckage, burning my eyes, and throat. A pervasive smell of burning metal, insulation, and wires rose from the rubble. Another clearly discernible scent, infinitely more disturbing, also rose up now and then. It was the distinctive odor of burning and rotting human flesh. If you ever smell that, you never forget it. It is sickening to recall it.

The heroic and weary firefighters and police officers around me continued fighting desperately against time to find someone still alive in the rubble even two weeks after the attack. Although nearing exhaustion, most just couldn't seem to give up the search. Continuing the effort probably helped them process their personal grief. Some of these guys had searched for survivors since the first morning, refusing to leave the site, sleeping and eating at nearby rest stations only when they were near collapse from exhaustion.

After the second week, the entire operation began to shift from one of rescue to a pure recovery effort. I heard later that after about the third or fourth day, no more survivors were found. All hope of finding more survivors was gone.

Some of the FDNY firefighters nearly got into a violent confrontation with New York police officers when they were finally ordered to evacuate the site, go home to their families, and resume their regular duties. The firefighter code and sense of duty and honor made it nearly unimaginable to leave their fallen brothers behind in that hellish rubble. It must have seemed inconceivable that they could ever go back to anything akin to "normal." The bitter reality that all hope of finding anyone else alive was long past. This was a bitter pill to swallow.

Identification of remains was tough because we weren't finding whole bodies. Out of the 2,753 people killed that day, only 291 intact bodies were ever found. According to New York Magazine, by final count, 21,744 fragments of human remains were eventually located. Only some time later would forensic DNA testing of bone fragments or body parts reveal the identities of some of those victims. Sadly, according to the same report, 1,717 families received no identifiable remains despite the very careful forensic work I witnessed at the morgue.[1]

As time went on, I quit trying to fight back tears and learned to work and cry at the same time. Weeping was good for my eyes because the tears helped cleanse out the pulverized concrete and dust that kept blowing up in my face every time I moved around in the rubble, or the wind blew. This nasty stuff was extremely gritty and caustic, and rubbing your eyes could cause severe eye damage. I often felt so small and insignificant among these people who were suffering so much personal loss. I often prayed God would give me wisdom and grace to encourage, strengthen, and comfort them in this dark hour.

As I picked my way through the rubble from area to area, I had to be extremely cautious where I stepped. The area just off the street where the buildings once stood contained hidden voids where the underground garages had once been. The possibility of stepping into a void was very real.

Once a beautiful edifice with opulent marble halls, and a spacious atrium on the ground floor, the Towers were now reduced to a heap of smoking rubble, humbled and mournful. The facades of surrounding buildings were also heavily damaged by falling debris and the hurricane-force blast of pulverized concrete and dust that billowed out in every direction when the towers fell. Nearly all of the windows facing the Towers from the ground floor to approximately thirty or forty stories up were blown out. A toxic gray dust covered everything inside.

Nearly twenty stories up on the World Finance Building, just to the west, a massive steel girder roughly 40 to 50 feet long was impaled into the side of the building. It looked like a huge javelin thrown by some giant. Ground Zero was an incredibly dangerous site with the possibility of falling debris and broken glass from the surrounding buildings an ever-present threat to all of us working below.

Over the front of the heavily-damaged World Finance Center, a huge flag of the United States was draped. My heart swelled with pride as I beheld "Old Glory," so prominently displayed, on the rubble of the worst terrorist attack in our history. Despite the surrounding devastation, that flag symbolized something of great significance. In a positive sense, it represented the love of country and patriotism. The flag hung over the pile in silent testimony, proclaiming to any and all enemies that even though our heads were bowed in mourning, we were still standing tall for all that flag symbolizes.

Outside the Barricades

Late one night as I walked with a group of exhausted firefighters out of the Pile to get some badly needed rest, we encountered a group of people standing beyond the security perimeter. They were holding up pictures of missing loved ones to us. The pictures were of husbands, wives, mothers, fathers, children, and friends. Tearfully, they would ask if we'd seen them. These were extremely emotional encounters.

I paused for a few minutes to talk with these people and pray for them. I offered assurances that everything possible was being done to find their loved ones. Naturally, we couldn't tell them what we were actually discovering in the rubble. The human heart just isn't designed to bear such horrible burdens.

Big Hearts in the Big Apple
In contrast with the despair and sorrows, there were inspirational moments of kindness I shall never forget. I often experienced unusual generosity and hospitality from average New Yorkers. Right or wrong, New York City is often stereotyped as a rough, mean-spirited place full of snobbish, self-important people. I suppose there are people like that in every city of the world, and perhaps they're just more concentrated in New York. However, I also encountered some kind and considerate people there too.

As I traveled from my sleeping quarters down to the Pile in the morning, I'd often stop to grab a cup of coffee at a local coffee shop. Since I was going directly from my sleeping quarters to the Pile, I had to wear my turnout gear. The first time I tried to pay for my coffee, the guy behind the counter brusquely shoved my money back over the counter, grinning. In a typical New York accent, he said, "Hey Mack, take your kauwffee and get outta heya! We don't take no money from firefightas!"

For the first couple of weeks, I couldn't seem to pay for anything. The New York subway, coffee houses, and sandwich shops were all the same. Total strangers would walk up and pay for my food. Window signs announcing "No Charge for Cops and Firefighters" seemed to be everywhere. Walking along the street on the way to Ground Zero, police patrol cars would stop and ask me if I wanted a lift anywhere. The tragedy revealed a big soft spot in the heart of the Big Apple.

White-Knuckles in Manhattan
Despite the sad drama, I had some funny experiences too. One afternoon, I was invited over to Brooklyn to speak to a group of people at a church hosting an outreach effort for the police and firefighters in their community. An NYPD officer offered to provide transportation in his squad car through the heavy traffic from Lower Manhattan.

When he pulled the patrol car up to the curb outside where I was lodging, I slipped into the front seat, and we introduced ourselves. Pulling into traffic, he asked me what time I needed to arrive at the event. When I told him, he yelled, "Holy sh-t! We gotta get moving to make it on time!" It was the height of New York City's infamous rush hour, but flipping on his lights and siren, he hit the accelerator. For the next 45 minutes, we flew through the rush-hour traffic at white-knuckle speed as cars pulled over to let us through.

It was a terrifying yet thrilling ride through the streets of New York City as we veered in and out of lanes, around trucks, and blasted across the Brooklyn Bridge in record time. By the time we screeched to a halt in front of the church where the meeting was taking place, I was in a sweat and breathing hard, shaking with adrenaline.

Grinning, the officer looked over at me and asked in his thick Brooklyn accent, "Betcha nev-vah hadda ride like dat, huh?" Rattled and probably a little pale, I took a deep breath and reached over to shake his hand, thanking him for the ride. I stumbled out of the squad car on shaky knees. Amused, he just laughed and drove away. "New York's finest at their best," I mumbled to myself and walked to the entrance of the church.

Seeking to Comfort

Inside the church, several hundred people were gathered. The pastor greeted me warmly and opened the meeting. I was frankly embarrassed over the gracious introduction he gave me. Being honored is nice, but standing among people who had endured such heartbreaking tragedy is incredibly humbling. These people didn't need an "expert" or a "celebrity," and I certainly didn't fit either bill. What they needed was someone who would only listen to them and empathize with their pain.

Attempting to shake off some of my own pain from exposure to Ground Zero, and feeling completely out of my depth, I tried to share some general advice about the grieving process. I spoke some thoughts on what they might expect in the coming months as they struggled to deal with the loss and pain of so much tragedy in their lives. Everyone was politely quiet, and I'm embarrassed to admit that I was way too formal. I felt like I was dying up there, falling flat on my face, and I knew it.

When I suggested they might experience some episodes of irritability, impatience, and maybe even sleeplessness and neurotic behavior as part of their coping process, a breakthrough occurred. Some guy in the back of the room shouted, "Hey Chaplain, you're talk'n about da normal New York experience!" At that point, the whole room erupted in roaring laughter, and all tension vanished. I relaxed. I was finally among friends.

We had a great time for the remainder of the evening. I invited several people to the microphone to share some of their experiences and losses. It can be tremendously therapeutic for people to share their pain with others is such a safe environment. There were times of mutually shared tears co-mingled with other occasions of uproarious laughter.

Notes

1. September 11 by Numbers – New York, http://nymag.com/news/articles/wtc/1year/numbers.htm (accessed August 31, 2015)

5

Ground Zero Grace

Courage is found in unlikely places.
J.R.R. Tolkien
~~~~~~

In a disaster response, you find yourself working with people from nearly all walks of life. It's inspirational to see how quickly people can lay aside racial, ethnic, religious, and political differences in an emergency situation where people are hurting. As a side-thought, I think it would be a great idea to make it compulsory for every school student in America to serve in some internship capacity in community emergency response as a requirement for graduation. Interns could help in a variety of roles such as emergency dispatch, wildland fires, high angle rescue, fire and medical response. Underneath our complicated differences, we are, after all, humans sharing life, joy, loss, pain, and triumph together.

Shortly after 9/11, a series of tents with Plywood barriers surrounding them were set up in front of the World Financial Center's north-facing entry plaza off Vessey Street. A large hand-inscribed sign in red spray paint on the plywood barrier next to the narrow entrance just read; "MORGUE – Authorized Personnel Only."

As I approached, the air became foul with a sickening stench that left no doubt about what this place was all about: death. I flashed my credentials to the National Guardsman guarding the entrance to the morgue. He nodded grimly and waved me in. I entered a series of tents filled with medical equipment, desks, lockers, and stainless steel exam tables. Large ventilation fans lined one wall of the tent, laboring in vain to remove the stench that hung in the air and eventually permeated even our gear and clothing. For months afterward, I could still smell it. Washing had no doubt removed all traces of the actual odor of that horrible place from my gear, but a conditioned, associated memory seemed to surface months later when I would put on my turnout gear. I still feel like gagging when I think too much about it.

Several makeshift morgues were set up nearby to examine properly and process the human remains we brought in from the rubble pile in red biohazard bags and buckets. The grisly task of genetically identifying the victims from bits of flesh or bone fragments would occur in a forensic lab elsewhere. Each time I entered the morgue, I'd tighten the straps on my biohazard respirator mask, but even the best mask couldn't filter out the overpowering odor of putrefying human flesh. None of us who were there will ever forget that smell.

The collapse of the buildings happened so suddenly and powerfully that the bodies of people inside the buildings were, for the most part, vaporized. As a side-note, some survivors later reported hearing explosions on the floors below the aircraft impact points on the buildings. According to these reports, powerful explosions on the lower floors detonated just seconds before the towers fell. Naturally, such stories fueled suspicions that the buildings may have been deliberately brought down by demolition explosives. In any case, the massive blast of superheated compressed air rushing out from the imploding towers as they collapsed set cars afire nearly a block away. As I said before, the heat melted the plastic coating on a chain-link fence surrounding the parking lot. I saw this with my own eyes.

Forensic pathologists working in the morgue processed the remains of thousands of people. For several days, I worked closely with technicians in the exam room and watched as distraught firefighters brought in stretcher after stretcher of fragmentary remains. I never once saw an intact body.

The forensic doctors were seeking clues that might help identify the victims. It was deeply moving to witness the tender care, respect, and professionalism everyone demonstrated. Their job was complicated and extremely gruesome work. In a very real sense, it was also a labor of love, not only for the deceased but also for their loved ones. Every positive I.D. of remains would help bring eventual closure to their losses.

I could often hear the mask-muffled sobs of doctors, police officers, and firefighters all around me as we worked. Here in this place, our shared sorrow changed the ordinary way people relate to each other. Whatever differences that might have existed between us before this extraordinary "Twilight Zone" event, they were no longer important anymore. We were all, in the final analysis, Americans and human beings united in mutual pain and grief.

During breaks, I often paused and chatted with the guards for a few minutes. My "prime directive" at Ground Zero was to try to talk with and encourage everyone I met there, seeking to bring the presence and grace of Christ into this hellhole. I interacted with police, FBI, ATF, Secret Service, firefighters, paramedics, doctors, soldiers, and anyone else who wanted to chat. When they saw the "Chaplain" rockers on my helmet, they knew I was there for THEM.

I rarely met anyone at that entire scene who refused to talk with me or receive an offer of prayer.

Late one evening, after working long hours in the morgue, I went searching for a quiet place to sit and rest. Shuffling through an exit leading into the World Finance Building behind the tents, I stepped into a deserted food court in the atrium area. The power was off, and the only light came in from the giant spotlights set up outside, shining through the smashed atrium windows. A restaurant occupied this atrium space, with tables and seating out in the open, separated by big potted plants and dividers. Partially eaten food and beverages sat abandoned on the tables. Evidently, after the first aircraft slammed into the north tower, everyone ran out of there in a big hurry.

I gazed for some moments in the partial darkness at the dust-covered table in front of me. A partially eaten sandwich and a half-filled cup of coffee with dusty grime floating on the surface sat there in the gloomy shadows. It reminded me of a scene from a science fiction movie where people suddenly vanished, leaving behind everything in mute testimony of what had once been an ordinary day.

Reality is often indeed stranger than fiction. Just a few days before, this place was filled with people talking, eating, and going about their morning routines as if there would always be more days just like it. No one sitting in that atrium that fateful morning of 9/11 could have imagined the sudden disruption their lives would experience as that first jet screamed overhead and slammed into Tower One across the street. Because the dining area was in a glass-covered atrium, anyone who happened to be looking up at the right moment could have witnessed the first aircraft slam into the north tower. I could only imagine the shock they experienced as they beheld the smoke and flames high above, followed by the debris and falling bodies that began slamming onto the pavement outside.

Plopping down in one of the dusty chairs, I propped my tired feet up on another chair, closed my eyes, and tried to relax. At least, the air in here wasn't reeking so strongly of rotting corpses. There in the shadows, I could hear the muffled sounds of generators outside, the shouts of men working, and the clanking of cranes and trucks being loaded with debris. Even with my eyes closed, I could see flashes of cutting torches high up on the pile as their light shone through the broken panes of the atrium. After a few minutes, I looked around at the shifting shadows dancing across the floor as the cutting torch flashes gave an eerie, almost ethereal effect to the darkened, deserted room.

I thought about all the body parts we'd processed through the morgue and of the thousands of people that might yet be trapped in the rubble. I also pondered the inevitable emotional and psychological trauma being inflicted upon their families and friends as they awaited some word about the fate of their loved ones. My mind drifted to my family, and of how much I loved and missed them. It is sobering to consider how fragile life can be, of how we must hold one another close, never taking a single day—or a single person—for granted. God's gift of life is incredibly precious. I prayed...Hard. I prayed I would have the strength to remain useful and productive. I also prayed that God would continuously heal my mind and emotions of the psychological hits I was taking every minute I was in that place. I didn't want to take any of this stinking hellhole home with me and wound anyone with it. By the grace of God, I wouldn't.

A Divine Appointment

One particular day stands out in my memory. I was fighting exhaustion and impending nausea after working in the morgue for untold hours. It had been a long day, and I desperately needed a break.

As I stumbled out of the examination area, I spotted two young Catholic priests in an adjacent tent sitting on some boxes. Freshly arrived in their clean black clerical robes, they both looked very nervous. Hardly into their twenties, it was a natural assumption that they were newly ordained, and like all the rest of us, extremely uncomfortable with what was happening in that place of unspeakable horror. A flood of sympathy swept over me for these young men. Such emotionally toxic sites can cruelly rip out whatever might remain of youthful innocence. I'd lost mine over thirty years before in Vietnam, and compassion welled up within me for them. We were all sharing a nightmare from which there could be no awakening.

Although I have little in common theologically with the official doctrines of the Roman Catholic Church, this does not blind me to the fact that there are many sincere individuals Christians within this organization. I sensed a firm nudge from the Spirit to go over and talk with them, and encourage them. Shuffling closer, I casually greeted them. "Hi, Fathers, how are you?" Looking at each other, one said nervously; "We were sent to administer the Sacraments and bring what comfort we may." Searching their eyes, I could see that these young men were overwhelmed, and understandably so. We were all out of our depth in that place.

Glancing back toward the exam room in the next tent, I shuddered at the thought of what they were about to walk into and wondered how it might affect them. Both nearly the same age as my son, and I wished I could somehow protect them. The horrors awaiting them in the next room was something no seminary could ever prepare anyone to face.

My thoughts drifted back to the first days I had labored among the forensic and medical examiner teams in this place. I remembered a firefighter standing next to me one day who sobbed softly into his biohazard mask as the Medical Examiners unzipped a body bag revealing the partial remains of a fellow firefighter. Bits of clearly discernible turnout gear still clung to what remained of this fallen responder. I reached over and patted a gloved hand on his shoulder, and dust and grime puffed up from his gear. Glancing up at me and seeing "Chaplain" on my helmet, he wordlessly nodded his thanks through bloodshot, tear-filled eyes. No words were required. None would be appropriate.

When the Medical Examiner finished, the remains were carefully slid into a smallish red biohazard bag and laid on the center of the Stokes stretcher. The Medical Examiner looked over at me, caught my eye and said softly, "Chaplain?" Her eyes, peering over her mask, seemed to say, "We've done all we humanly can. Now we must look to God." Glancing around to see if a Priest was present to give Last Rites, or a Rabbi to say Kaddish, and seeing none, I stepped forward to the exam table.

When other faiths were present, we would each participate in ministering. It did not surprise me in the least that I never once saw an Islamic Imam among the clergy. Such a presence in the face of this scene of Islamic terrorism would be, in my mind, one of the great enigmas of our time. Without forensic evidence to determine the victim's religion, we tried to cover every possibility for the sake of the deceased's family's comfort should they ever hear of what we did.

In a repeated ritual, a U.S. Flag was unfurled, and gloved hands reached out as men stepped forward spontaneously to help cover the stretcher holding the remains of our unknown firefighter brother with its Stars and Stripes. We carefully tucked the edges of the flag around the stretcher as a parent would gingerly tuck a beloved child into bed. I then prayed out some variation of the following simple prayer, as heads bowed throughout the tent;

> *Thank you, Father, for a life honorably given while seeking to save others. In the words of Jesus, 'There is no greater love than this; that a man lay his life down for his friends.' We commit his eternal soul into your wise and merciful care.*

Mask-muffled sobs and "amens" could be heard all around.

Without a word, firefighters and police officers then moved around the exam table and carefully lifted the stretcher, acting as pall-bearers. I led the small procession out a side exit into the street toward a waiting ambulance. As the flag-draped stretcher came into view, hundreds of people working outside instantly stopped everything, and silently and spontaneously formed lines along the street. Only the sound of electrical generators broke the silence. "Hand... salute!" someone barked. We all snapped to attention facing the stretcher, and slowly and solemnly raised our hands in salute. The stretcher was gently lifted into the ambulance. We stood for several moments silently, holding our salute to our unknown fallen comrade. The ambulance doors were slowly closed, and it quietly moved away into the darkened debris-strewn streets. Finally, someone shouted, "Order salute!" We slowly lowered our salute, and after a few seconds broke ranks and shuffled off, returning to our duties.

Emerging from my reverie, I turned back to the two young priests seated before me. I felt sadness for them. I said, "your service in this terrible place is honorable." Glancing at each other again, they seemed to relax a bit as I continued. "With your permission, I'd like to pray for you." Their eyes widened a bit at this, but I could easily see these guys needed some encouragement.

"Well, thank you, yes," one finally stammered tentatively. "That would be very kind of you."

Taking a knee in front of them, I clasped their hands and began to pray. I prayed for God's grace to help them face the challenges of service there, asking the Father in Heaven to protect and help them as they reached out to bring the comfort to others. I prayed that Christ would reveal Himself to them by His grace far beyond all they could ask or imagine and that He would be glorified.

An extraordinary heavenly presence seemed to fill the tent, and I began to sob with the pent-up emotions of the previous days. Looking up, I saw that both of these young men were also weeping. Suddenly, we stood and hugged in an embrace of mutual compassion. In this place of suffering, we held together in mutual love as humans in spite of the very real theological differences we had. We could argue over those another day. Right at that moment, these young men were reporting for duty and needed all the help they could get.

Walking out into the darkness just before the dawn, I looked upward into the New York City sky and tried to glimpse the stars. Finding none in the light pollution of the city and the glare of searchlights, I whispered a prayer of thanks that even though I couldn't see them then, the stars still shone brightly somewhere far above. Turning my gaze toward the mountain of smoking twisted steel, and the billowing clouds of smoke rising from the "pile," I watched the steelworkers cut away the rubble with torches for a few minutes.

In case it isn't already obvious, my mind sees irony and allegory in nearly everything. As I stood there in the predawn twilight, it was impossible not to see a massive parallel Biblical truth in all I beheld. The contrast between that broken, stinking, sorrowful landscape all around me and the soon-coming of a new sunrise that would dispel all shadows and bring out all the dazzling colors of a fresh new day was striking. Just like the coming dawn beginning to brighten the sky above, the Kingdom of God would come gradually, yet inevitably, until all shadows of evil and darkness flee away. I knew my Father's grace would never fail and a bright new day would dawn. The promised Day Star will one day rise in the hearts of all God's elect who received God's grace and mercy.

We have also a most sure word of the Prophets,
whereunto ye do well that ye take heed,
as unto a light that shineth in a dark place,
until the day dawns, and the day star arise in your hearts.
2 Peter 1:19

6

Buried in the Rubble

*I give you
the light of Earendil
our most beloved star.
May it be a light to you
in dark places
when all other lights go out.*
J.R.R. Tolkien
*The Lord of the Rings
The Return of the King*

~~~~~

I spent time at several FDNY firehouses in the lower downtown area. When I introduced myself as a firefighter and Chaplain from Colorado, they opened their doors and hearts to me with warm hospitality, often inviting me to eat with them in the firehouse. Some of the stories they shared around the table were nothing short of amazing. One story, in particular, stood out in my memories.

A Miraculous Story of Survival
I base the following story on my recollections as well as videotapes of conversations I had with an FDNY Captain stationed at a firehouse near the World Trade Center in Lower Manhattan. He allowed me to share his story, but I will not reveal his name here to protect his identity and privacy.

The Captain had the day off and was running some errands around lower downtown on the morning of 9/11. He told me he heard the first jet fly overhead but didn't pay too much attention to it at first, even though it seemed to be flying extremely low and loud. Then, a muffled explosion echoed amid the typical sounds of the city and brought him to full alert. A few moments later, some people ran out of a store shouting something about a plane crashing into the World Trade Towers. He moved into a storefront where a TV monitor was showing the first pictures of the north tower of the WTC belching flames and massive plumes of smoke.

A short distance away just a few moments before, Battalion 1 Chief, Matthew Lancelot Ryan also heard the roar of American Airlines Flight 11 as it passed low overhead at high speed. Chief Ryan looked up just in time to see it plunge into the North Tower of the World Trade Center. Grabbing his handheld radio, Ryan called in a multiple alarm incident. For the first time in over 30 years, the FDNY issued a total recall of all off-duty firefighters. In the massive response that followed, 121 engine companies and 62 ladder companies deployed to the WTC. Just a few hours later, Chief Ryan was killed as he bravely led firefighters into the North Tower just before it collapsed on them.

Instantly realizing the magnitude of the disaster, the Captain ran out of the store just as his alert pager went off in the total recall. He sprinted to his firehouse a few blocks away to retrieve his turnout gear and join his team. However, before reaching the firehouse, everyone on duty that morning had already deployed to the WTC on the first alarm. Grabbing his gear, he ran out into the street heading toward the towers. After hitching a ride with an emergency vehicle responding to the scene, they weaved in and out of the dense New York City traffic as quickly as possible.

"When I arrived on-scene at the towers, I reported to the IC (Incident Commander) and was deployed to help get people out of the buildings," he said. "While I was approaching the north tower, a second plane hit the South Tower. I didn't see it hit, but heard the explosion and saw the smoke and fire streaming high over the towers."

He was then diverted into the South Tower to help coordinate the evacuation of people and get them to safety. He went on, "Just as I was getting close to the entrance of the building, a body landed on the street right in front of me and just exploded! It almost hit me! I looked up and could see more people jumping out of the windows higher up. I had to take cover within the framework of the tower's outer structure as several more jumpers died on the street right in front of me."

"The building fell on me!"

Ducking into an entryway, he ran up to the second floor on the now-stationary escalators, trying to catch up with his team. Just as he was about to go higher, he heard a rumble that rapidly grew louder and louder, as the building began to shake violently.

"I knew for sure the building was coming down, and I also knew I only had a few seconds to try and find a safe place to ride it out."

The noise grew thunderous. At the last moment, he threw himself on the floor against the reinforced wall of the elevator shaft just as the deafening roar reached him. Everything suddenly went black and became utterly silent.

At this point in the story, he paused for several moments and turned his gaze to the floor. His eyes welled with tears. Finally looking up at me, he said, "All I could do was yell, 'Lord Jesus, save me!' I thought for sure I was going to die." He then described what happened next in that tomb-like silence and total darkness as he began choking on the thick dust. "For a few moments, I thought I might suffocate. My SCBA mask was ripped off, and the air was so thick with dust that it seemed like trying to breathe in a bag of fine flour. I grabbed my collar and pulled my bunking jacket up over my face. That filtered some of the dust and I was finally able to gulp some air."

Moving his arms and legs one at a time, he realized he was still alive and in one piece. "I couldn't believe it at first. I was still alive! There was total silence and darkness, and I could feel that I was in a small space. It was impossible to see anything. My eyes were burning from all the powdered concrete and drywall dust." Feeling around him, he realized he could move a bit in the small void surrounding him. "I began to crawl toward where I remembered the escalator was when I ran up," he continued. "Everything was disoriented and shifted around, but I finally felt the top of the escalator. Wiggling around, I began to crawl down backward, in case I'd come to an edge and fall into a hole. Feeling my way along a few feet at a time, I finally reached a bottom. It was pitch-black, but after a bit, I finally was able to make out a faint light, which I began to crawl toward. It was a partially ajar fire exit door, and I could see some daylight through it."

The door was jammed only slightly open by the wreckage. "I had to take off my helmet to squeeze through the opening, then pull it through behind me." Outside, he could finally see the massive devastation all around him. "The South Tower was now just a giant pile of indescribable trash, but I could just make out the North Tower through the smoke and dust surrounding me." Just before leaving the door, he coughed to clear his dust-fouled throat and shouted back into the void he'd just crawled from. "Hello! I'm a firefighter! If anyone can hear me, come toward my voice and follow the light!" After shouting into the dark opening several times and listening a few minutes for any response, he finally turned away and began picking his way through the tangled pile of twisted steel girders and debris, heading north toward the still-standing North Tower.

Voice of an Angel?

At this point, he started to laugh. I was a little puzzled, but he grinned and went on. "I have to tell you a funny story here," he began. "A few days after the attack, there was a story in the newspaper about a guy who survived the South Tower collapse—same one I was in. He told the reporters that he was searching for a way out of the rubble and heard an angel's voice call to him out of the darkness. "This angel said, 'If you can hear me, come toward my voice and follow the light!" Laughing, the Captain went on, "I've been called a lot of things in my life, but nobody ever called me an angel!"

It was striking to see how some of these guys coped with the strain of their job, even during this major disaster. First Responders often deal with their jobs with what some might call "dark humor." An outsider might think them brash and uncaring, but it's a way of processing the often overwhelming stresses of running into danger instead of running away.

Often around the dining table in the firehouse, someone would start reminiscing about one of the guys who died and recalled something hilarious he had done or a prank they'd played on him. The brothers would roar with laughter for several minutes in the warm glow of a precious moment remembered. Then, after the laughter died down, everyone would grow quite in an awkward silence as the harsh reality of their brother's death sank in. A few shuffled away trying to hide their tears.

The Captain went on with his story. "I was moving as fast as I could, climbing over smashed and burning vehicles, steel girders, and crushed fire trucks," he said. "Just as I came near the edge of the rubble to the north, I heard another rumble. When I looked up, I saw the north tower coming down!" He began running as fast as he could to get away from the building before the wreckage hit him. "I had only covered a few yards when I saw three fire trucks lined up. I started to jump behind the second one, but then I heard this voice in my head say 'No!' so I kept moving and ducked behind the third rig." A few seconds later wreckage from the building crashed to the ground all around him. Massive steel smashed almost everything, including the two fire trucks parked in front of the one he took cover behind.

"Giant steel beams were flying overhead like toothpicks," he said. The hurricane-force blast of wind nearly blew him away, and the dust cloud swept over everything, turning day into night. Once again, he couldn't breathe and had to pull his jacket up over his mouth to get some air.

"As the last of the debris crashed on the street, there was a weird silence. The only thing I could hear was the chirping of the PASS (Personal Alert Safety System) devices on our bunking coats. Then I heard some guys under the truck gasping for air and choking. I yelled for them to pull up their jackets to get some air. I could hear some of them crying and a few crapped in their pants. Talk about being scared shitless!" he said with a chuckle.

The Captain described how he finally stood up and was amazed to see that the two trucks he'd just run past were utterly crushed by debris. "If I'd stopped behind that second rig, I would be dead. It was completely flattened by the wreckage."

Pulling himself together, he began to muster the other firefighters around him who could walk. "I had to get the men moving, doing something positive and start sizing up the scene. All around us, people were wounded or dying." Pulling together a group of firefighters, he ordered them to move the injured to a safer area. "We had to get to water. Our eyes and lungs were full of dust, and we were nearly blind and barely able to breathe."

Stumbling along the street with wounded civilians and firefighters, the group eventually reached a relatively clear area. By then, emergency crews from all over the city were responding in. Somebody passed out some bottled water, and they used it to wash their eyes and clear their airways.

Many of the survivors were suffering from severe injuries, including lacerations, broken bones, and respiratory distress. "I'd never imagined a disaster of that magnitude," the Captain said. "Everybody was in shock. It took several hours to get a CP (Command Post) set up and functioning so we could start figuring out how to tackle the situation."

This firefighter's story was similar to a few others I heard while visiting several firehouses. Each one was miraculous in its way and inspiring to hear. However, such stories also beg a theological question. Why did some people survive while others did not? It's an old question, but one that haunts every thinking person.

> *Your eyes saw my unformed body;*
> *all the days ordained for me*
> *were written in your book*
> *before one of them came to be.*
> Psalm 139:16 (NIV)

As a Christian man, I believe that walking in fear is a tacit denial of God's infinite power, grace, and wisdom. If we allow fear and paranoia to dominate us, we will shrink from duty when it calls us. May He grant us all that greater grace to enjoy a life of inward peace even in the face of threats or apparent danger.

How Do We Deal With…?

In our firehouse, there's a big sign displayed above the bulletin board that reads:

"You fight fires like you train." In other words, when things seem to be going to hell in a hand-basket, those who've practiced (at least mentally) how to react in an emergency, will most often succeed. Thinking ahead about all the possible things that could happen prevents our being blind-sided by the unexpected. Without forethought, we try to make things up on the fly.

Speaking of "on the fly," years ago while training as a student pilot, my instructor would often throw an emergency at me right in a moment when I was concentrating on something else. For example, during an instrument approach to the airport the IP (Instructor Pilot) would suddenly cover up some of the gauges on the panel and declare, "You've just lost electrical power! Your electrical instruments have failed! What are you going to do now?"

Approach to an instrument landing is one of the most critical phases of piloting, and I'd be wearing a hood to obscure all outside references. My life depended on what the remaining gauges told me, and with some of them gone, some quick and accurate decisions had to be made in a hurry.

Sometimes during a takeoff, as the airplane was accelerating to gather flying speed down the runway, the IP would reach over, reduce engine power, and say something like, "Your engine is losing power. Should you continue the take-off or abort?" I had to know instantly if I had enough runway to stop or was committed to continuing the takeoff with reduced power and try to limp around the pattern for an emergency landing. There were many variations of this during pilot training, and the point of each drill was always the same. I had to learn to think "outside the box" and KNOW what I MUST do in an emergency before a potential "what if?" became a "what now?"

For myself, when faced with an emergency or a situation outside the ordinary, I have tried to train my mind to instantly turn my thoughts to God and inwardly seek His wisdom for the situation. This is my personal "emergency procedure." I've seen a bumper sticker now and then that says; "God is My Copilot." This adage irritates me and stands as a reminder of how humans cling to the illusion of control. God is NOT MY copilot. He's the Captain of the ship, fully in command, and entirely in control. I rarely understand the course He sets, or the way He runs the universe, but by His grace, I trust He knows precisely what He's doing even if it doesn't look like it.

One of the most mystifying things about the WTC terrorist attack that remains is the *fact* that NEVER in all of modern history has three steel-structure buildings collapsed within a few hours of each other from a fire. There are things about the 9/11 incident that simply don't add up. I wanted to believe the "official" reports, but now, years after the fact, I've grown extremely skeptical. The problem I'm dealing with is the fact that if what I *think* happened, *actually* happened; I don't have an "emergency procedure" to respond to it. We seem to be facing a national emergency for which we have no prior training.

Even if we believed everything "officials" had told us, the outcomes and national problems we're facing would defy logic. Is it possible that such a convergence of government incompetence, political corruption, economic blundering, and the growth of our national debt to astronomical levels could just 'happen' by accident? We need to figure out an "emergency procedure" quickly. Our shared national Ship of State seems to be rushing headlong toward reefs and rocks, apparently hijacked by evil players committed to our destruction.

A guiding principle to follow is to keep our sense of fear or panic at bay. We do this mainly by training ourselves to focus outwardly on others and think in terms of: "How can I best be of service for others and do what is right?" Succumbing to fear in the midst of a crisis can incapacitate our ability to effectively address the emergency and could even make things worse. Focusing outside prevents that deadly "panic lockup" that freezes the mind. Looking to help someone else will help keep us focused. It's a truth that flows with what Jesus taught: "Give and it shall be given unto you," and, "As you sow, so shall you reap."

This principle of focusing on others––outside of self––was responsible for enabling many to escape and survive on 9/11. From stories I've heard from some of the WTC survivors, many of those who fled the buildings refused to see themselves as victims. Often, they were people focused on helping others escape––leading them through thick smoke and down the stairwells or just encouraging those around them to keep moving forward.

The firefighter who survived the collapse of the South Tower focused on moving forward, then rescuing others. The police and firefighters at 9/11 have been called heroes––and indeed, they are. But they weren't seeking to be "heroic." They were only focused outside of themselves and striving to help others.

PART II

No Fear

7

Homeland Insecurity

*Fear
is the State's psychological weapon of choice
to frighten citizens into sacrificing
their basic freedoms and rule-of-law protections
in exchange for the security promised
by their all-powerful government.*
Philip G. Zimbardo, The Lucifer Effect:
Understanding How Good People Turn Evil

~~~~~~~~

At the time of this writing, over 16 years have passed since the terrorist attacks of 9/11. For some, this subject is ancient history, for so much has happened in the world since that time. For those of us who were there, or served on the Pile in the weeks and months afterward, it is as if it was yesterday. However, since those attacks rapid and alarming changes have occurred in American society and politics. In the name of "safety" and "security," we are witnessing an accelerating growth in surveillance technology and ominously, the employment of it against our citizens. The crisis of 9/11 has become the raison d'être for a massive expansion of monitoring and data-gathering activities by the government. This effort utilizes advanced technologies that threaten the privacy and constitutional rights of every American.

Homeland Security or Insecurity?
The "Department of Homeland Security" (DHS) was hurriedly set up eleven days after the September 11 attacks. Pennsylvania Governor Tom Ridge was appointed by President Bush to serve as its first Director. On November 25, 2002, Congress passed the Homeland Security Act, and the DHS formally set up shop as a stand-alone, Cabinet-level department, opening its doors four months later on March 1, 2003. According to the official DHS website, several expansions and administrative changes over the next several years eventually

combined 22 other government departments under the direct oversight of the DHS. [1]

According to Wikipedia, the annual budget for the DHS for FY 2013 was $60.8 BILLION dollars and employs nearly a quarter of a million people. These stats include the DHS only and do not include the other massive sub-departments that DHS now oversees. [2]

Of grave concern to people who love liberty and their constitutionally limited government is the abysmal lack of congressional oversight and accountability for the DHS. Increasingly ominous reports of citizens being "detained" by various agents of the DHS and warrantless searches made of their homes, papers, electronic assets, and communications are occurring with increasing regularity.

In the early days of the DHS, Americans were given idiotic "alert status" color codes and told to watch each other on planes, trains, and in public places. The DHS was supposedly established to protect America from terrorism. However, it has morphed—as most government agencies do—into a massive bureaucracy. No matter how altruistic anyone's original intentions were in establishing this behemoth, the very presence of such a vast (and virtually unaccountable) organization operating with almost unlimited funding represents a grave threat to individual liberties.

Under the present administration, it seems to have morphed into a leftist-progressive enforcement agency that focuses most of its attention on so-called "homegrown" terrorist threats. If the DHS was focused primarily on international threats or the Islamic terrorist cells and jihadist training camps operating right here in our country, and who are plotting to destroy America, this might make sense. However, as we will see, increasingly the prime suspects in the DHS's cross-hairs are not radical Islamists, but ordinary citizens who love America and uphold the Constitution and the Bill of Rights. Military veterans, Bible-believing Christians, Conservatives and members of the Tea Party are increasingly targeted in recent law enforcement manuals and briefings as prime suspects and threats.

I've become deeply concerned that our republic is facing a clear and present internal danger that threatens to destroy our freedoms and liberties under the cruel yoke of a modern police state. I perceive a serious threat against my children, and grandchildren and their future prosperity and happiness. For the first time in my life, I believe there is a very real possibility their enslavement by an evil tyranny that would make their lives miserable and devoid of hope. Our forefathers bled and died upon countless battlefields across the world to preserve our precious freedoms. If this present generation cannot awaken in time to rise and defend those freedoms again, the blood, tears, and sacrifices of untold hundreds of thousands of our patriots will have been in vain.

The times we live in demand that each of us put aside our interests and engage in the present struggle. Our battlefield is presently confined primarily to the realm of ideas and worldviews. Upon this battlefield, we must report for duty according to the capacity we each possess. Be very sure of this, if we fail to win the ideological war, this battle could easily deteriorate into one of unspeakable violence, death, and destruction. The cries of the widow and orphan could be louder in our land than at any time in our nation's history. We must *never* allow this to happen, and my voice cries out for peaceful resolution without violence. My fervent hope and prayer is that it will be possible to stem the tide of evil with truthful information and education.

For too long, successive generations of the youth of America have been indoctrinated to believe America is an evil, racist country. They are taught that America is polluting the planet and causing catastrophic "climate change." The answers offered by the progressives always involve bigger and more powerful government under a socialist system in the name of "saving the planet" and "economic equality" and "social justice." My goal is to discredit and tear down strongholds of such twisted lies and evil nonsense, thereby setting men free—including those who now stand as enemies. It is unthinkable to me what may happen if we fail.

As painful as the 9/11 attack was in and of itself, it served to lance—like a painful boil—a long-smoldering infection deep within the heart and soul of our nation. It exposed the corruption, moral turpitude, and the shallow spiritual condition of America's churches and national character. It also revealed the best of our people, not only in the countless acts of bravery, compassion, and selfless service shown on that terrible day but also during the many months that followed. People from across the country and around the world reached out to give help and comfort to the people and civil servants who suffered.

One of America's Greatest Generals Speaks

> *Our government has kept us in a perpetual state of fear – kept us in a continuous stampede of patriotic fervor– with the cry of grave national emergency. Always there has been some terrible evil at home or some monstrous foreign power that was going to gobble us up if we did not blindly rally behind it by furnishing the exorbitant funds demanded. Yet, in retrospect, these disasters seem never to have happened, seem never to have*

been quite real.
– General Douglas MacArthur, 1957 [3]

I believe a bright light of exposure must be focused upon the sinister and dangerous forces that are moving our government toward a frightening transformation. We are changing in fundamental and critical ways—pathways that threaten our most basic freedoms and liberties. The new "security measures" that were implemented virtually overnight after 9/11—with almost no public debate—are only the tip of an enormous and dangerous iceberg. Just who is behind these dubious actions? What is driving our national leaders to adopt policies that are counter-intuitive to our best national interests? And how have we come to a place in our history that laws are being issued from the pen of a single individual presently occupying the White House or a group of unelected and unaccountable judges? Our Constitution prohibits acts of legislation solely from the Executive or Judicial branches of our republic.

The government's warnings of more terrorist attacks, fanned by a stenographer news media, spooked our people to the point that they were willing to accept blindly increasing infringements on their liberty. People desperately want to "feel" safe. Due to pervasive ignorance regarding the Constitution and Bill of Rights, they're willing to shift the responsibility for their personal security entirely to the government. Paranoia has blinded people to the fact that most of these poorly thought-out "security measures" are virtually useless in providing genuine, effective security. Too many Americans now seem eager to accept what can only be called a nanny police state in which people are "taken care of" by the government. This "safety" comes with a high price tag—personal liberty.

In the wake of 9/11, liberal politicians cynically proclaimed the American people were "demanding security from their government." Providing for national defense certainly is a legitimate function of the federal government under our Constitution. However, it is now abundantly clear that the federal government has overstepped their legal mandate. Several new laws and "Executive Directives" trample the Constitution and certain so-called "minor" liberties and freedoms in the name of safety.

Such presumptuous statements are based only upon the thinnest of polling data. Over the past 15 years since 9/11, people are beginning to grasp just how profoundly we are all being impacted by government overreach into our private lives. Increasingly, we are witnessing suspensions of certain basic constitutional protections against such things as warrant-less searches and seizures, or protection from arbitrary incarceration by the government without due process of law. There are far too many instances of heavily militarized police units in full battle-dress and brandishing military weapons conducting "no-knock" raids for relatively minor offenses. Innocent people often suffer their property destroyed or seized, or their lives snuffed out by overzealous officers.

As Benjamin Franklin is often quoted:

> *Any society*
> *that would give up a little liberty*
> *to gain a little security*
> *will deserve neither*
> *and lose both.*

Our Republic is undergoing radical and dangerous changes unparalleled in American history. The "security measures" certain officials and organs of the government implemented since the attacks should alarm every person who loves liberty and constitutionally guaranteed freedoms. We the people must become informed and educated, and demand that our government employees cease and desist, for they are causing potentially irreversible damage to the heart and soul of America.

Why do so many government employees holding political offices so actively pursue policies that are so counterintuitive to constitutional freedom? I believe there is an even higher conspiracy afoot—beyond human individuals, governments, or religions—that operates as the real "puppet masters" of this present darkness. To borrow an allegory from The Wizard of Oz fairy tale, I intend to expose the "little man (or men) behind the curtain." Those who presently trouble this world are puppets of a sinister, spiritual plot to destroy and enslave humanity. I hope to lay bare the futility of their agendas for they are already defeated but haven't yet comprehended the memo. Biblical Christians will deliver that memo in the coming times–*with attitude*. More on this later.

In the larger scheme of things related to the 9/11 attacks, it matters little who the individual human agents were, or even how they committed their crimes. We must focus our attention on the greater mission of enforcing defeat upon the underlying source of such evil, and free people from slavish tyranny spawned by ignorance. Those responsible will eventually be brought to justice—in this life or the next. Our real enemies are not merely flesh and blood human beings. This point is of vital importance to remember, otherwise we may fall into the temptation of hating people who are presently enslaved to evil. We must always remember that such were *we*, before God's grace drew us to freedom.

I realize I'm only one voice among many others who are sounding the tocsin call to battle this present darkness. I'm also fully aware that if this book should ever be taken seriously by enough people, it could put my family and me in harm's way. History has repeatedly shown that the minions of darkness take a dim view of anyone who dares resist or expose their agendas. If I ever become a target of their wrath, slander, and violence, it will only signal that I scored a hit where it hurts. When duty calls, we must respond, no matter what short-term sufferings may result. God never calls His servants by saying; "If it wouldn't be too much trouble, would you mind doing..." His command signals duty. Nothing less than obedience will do.

It's difficult sometimes to imagine how we could ever rise above the seemingly overwhelming spiritual, social, political, economic, and moral problems we now face. The present crisis is just the continuance of the ancient clash between good and evil. Nothing new to see here. Although it is manifesting in such rapid pace that it seems impossible ever to overcome, this is only an illusion meant to discourage and demoralize us. I realize I keep hammering this point, but I'm completely confident God's counsels will stand, and in the end, the evil we face will be thoroughly defeated. There is wisdom available in the writings of the Founding Fathers can help give us the clarity we need to navigate the troubled seas of our times. However, our firm reliance upon Providence will draw us on with confidence.

I am calling for a return to faithful adherence to the Constitution and the Bill of Rights. I'm also praying for a national awakening to the reality of Jesus Christ, and the wisdom found in the Holy Bible, which is the prerequisite in any civilized society.

Not a Call For a Theocracy

As a disclaimer, I am not advocating a theocracy or theonomy for America. Theonomy is the belief that the old Mosaic law can somehow be imposed by force upon a nation or individuals. I wish to cut off all opportunity to anyone who tries to accuse me of such nonsense. The transformation I envision will be in the hearts of men, orchestrated by God's Spirit. It will be gradual, irresistible, and inevitable. As a conversion of the heart, people will willingly submit to God and delight to do His will. This response cannot be forced upon people by other people. Only God can accomplish this.

I believe that eventually, all the nations of the earth will come under the

Lordship of God and Christ. This inevitability is spoken of throughout the Bible.

> *And in the days of these kings,*
> *shall the God of heaven set up a kingdom,*
> *which shall never be destroyed:*
> *and this kingdom shall not be given*
> *to another people,*
> *but it shall break, and destroy all these kingdoms,*
> *and it shall stand forever.*
> Daniel 2:44

As Christians, we live under a "new and better covenant," thus, we have access to a "New" Testament. Within this new and better covenant, we do not stone adulterers, homosexuals, blasphemers, thieves, or disobedient children (just to name a few). We certainly do not condone such behaviors, but we leave final judgment in the hands of God and pray for them. The only exceptions to this relate to what is called "Capitol" crimes, such as murder, rape, and other heinous crimes of violence. Even with these, the guiding principle of New Testament teachings is heavily weighted toward mercy and forgiveness. What I *am* advocating is the implementation of biblical principles and a progressive establishment of the dominion of Christ over all things. As I will demonstrate later, those principles were set into the bedrock of our republic's founding by men who held profoundly Christian paradigms. The return to the Constitution is not our endgame. It is only a means to an end, for, within the framework of liberty, the work of spreading the gospel can more easily occur. The minions of darkness know this well, and this is precisely why they are working so diligently to destroy our constitutional republic. (I will deal with this point extensively in the Epilogue.)

Notes

1. Http://dhs.gov

2. http://en.wikipedia.org/wiki/United_States_Department_of_Homeland_Security

3. General Douglas MacArthur, Address to the Annual Stockholders Sperry Rand Corporation (30 July 1957) Also: A Soldier Speaks -- Public Papers and Speeches of General of the Army Douglas MacArthur Hardcover – Import, 1965

8

America Hijacked?

*No matter how paranoid
or conspiracy-minded you are,
what the government is actually doing
is worse than you imagine.
Don't believe anything
until it's been officially denied.*
William Blum,
Former U.S. State Department employee[1]

~~~~~~~

Disclaimer: I shared the above quote by William Blum even though I strongly disagree with many of his other views and especially his scathing and vicious criticisms against the United States. Specifically, I stand opposed to what I perceive to be his secular-leftist worldview. I strongly suspect he would gladly burn down the entire house over our heads just to kill some rats in the attic. However, Blum's assessments serve to underscore an important point I'm going to hammer in this chapter. *Something terrible has happened to our country.* Thieves and liars have seized significant portions of power within our government, our schools, and our society. In a word, our nation has been *hijacked*!

America has endured a long (progressive) transformation in foreign and domestic policy for the past century. The nation's plunge into evil accelerated in radical ways after the 9/11 attacks. Since that time, we've moved rapidly toward some form of post-Constitutional fascist authoritarian government. Initially, this started as a seemingly desperate push for national security under President George W. Bush. However, it is now clear that our constitutionally guaranteed rights and freedoms suffered severe damage in the name of "safety" and "national security."

With the election of Barrack Hussein Obama to the presidency in 2008, the shift to greater government control of every major sector of our lives accelerated. Under the Obama administration, domestic surveillance increasingly focused attention on our *own* citizens rather than real Islamic terrorism threats. Such internally misdirected scrutiny is continually justified in the name of "social justice," "fairness," and "racial equality." In the meantime, our *actual* national security concerns are nearly ignored. There is a growing sense of paranoia among those who dare to question the policies of the Obama administration. There is increasing evidence that public criticism of Obama triggers harassing IRS audits and other retaliatory actions by agents of the government—or worse. Even our treasured freedom of speech now appears to be at risk.

A song from the 1960s titled *For What It's Worth*, by Stephen Stills of Buffalo Springfield seems to speak prophetically to our times:

> *Paranoia strikes deep.*
> *Into your life it will creep.*
> *It starts when you're always afraid.*
> *You step out of line, the man come,*
> *and take you away...*

Has America Been Hijacked?

One of the hijacked aircraft on 9/11 ended its flight in a lonely field in rural Pennsylvania. United Flight 93 was one of the four airplanes reportedly commandeered by Jihadist terrorists shortly after departure from Boston Logan Airport that fateful morning.

The passengers and crew boarded their plane that morning with plans to travel without incident to the West Coast on a routine flight. Their entire world changed 46 minutes after takeoff when four Jihadists reportedly slit the throat of a flight attendant with smuggled box cutters and gained access to the cockpit. They then murdered the flight crew and took control. The passengers and remaining cabin crew found themselves trapped aboard an aircraft no longer under the control of legitimate pilots, flying erratically at high speeds toward an unknown destination. The terrorists in the cabin subdued the passengers with threats of fake explosives, ordering them to sit quietly and show no resistance. The cockpit voice recorder captured the terrifying moment when the terrorists gained access to the flight deck. Captain Jason Dahl of Flt. 93 transmitted a distress call to air traffic control in the seconds just before he was attacked and killed. He held the microphone key open.

> *Mayday! Mayday! Mayday!*
> *Mayday! Get out of here! Get out of here!*

A few minutes later, Al-Qaeda terrorist Ziad Jarrah, now at the controls of the aircraft, made an announcement over what he thought was the aircraft intercom. Instead, he keyed the radio microphone and transmitted "in the open" to air traffic control.

> *Ladies and gentlemen, this is the 'captain.'*
> *Please sit down and keep remaining seated.*
> *We have a bomb on board. So sit!*

The cabin crew at the rear of the airplane called airline dispatch using in-flight phones to speak to people on the ground. Apparently, the terrorists didn't know how to disable the Airfone system. Several passengers also made calls from their seats, contacting relatives and friends on the ground to gather information about what was happening. (They did *not* use, as some erroneously reported, *cell* phones, which will not operate at high altitude.) They learned about news reports of other hijackings and the use of those aircraft as missiles against targets on the ground. The horrible truth finally began to sink in. They were all prisoners aboard a doomed airplane, and unless they did something very soon, even the slightest hope of survival would be lost.

A handful of passengers became convinced that their only hope would be to rush the cockpit and try to wrest control of the aircraft away from the terrorists. They probably knew that their chances were slim to none, but there just didn't seem to be an alternative. If they did nothing, and sheepishly obeyed the terrorists, they were all dead. On the other hand, if they fought back and tried to regain control, they might die anyway, but at least they could go down fighting. According to a report filed by Glen Johnson of the Boston Globe on November 23, 2001, one of the passengers, Todd Beamer, spoke to a relative on an Airfone. He was overheard saying to a small band of travelers who decided to take action, "Are you guys ready? Let's roll!"

Grabbing up fire extinguishers, jugs of hot water, and whatever else they could use as weapons, they shoved an "assault" service cart violently down the aisle to the front of the airplane. They finally subdued the jihadists guarding the cockpit door and broke in. The Allah-praising terrorists in the cockpit realized their defeat was imminent and suddenly plunged the aircraft into the ground before the passengers could regain the controls. Their courageous act of heroic resistance to terrorism inspired nearly everyone who learned of it.

Something about that particular incident intrigued me because, within the story, I believe I've discovered a powerful allegory. This allegory may provide some encouragement and inspiration to those of us who are finally awakening to the dangers we share. The actions of a small band of courageous passengers and crew onboard United Flight 93 speaks in a powerful way to us all in these troubled times.

Just go with me and consider the following.

We're All Sharing the Same Ride

Are we not all riding together as passengers aboard a common craft called "the United States of America?" Early in our history, as our nation was being initially formed and organized, "We the people" carefully (and prayerfully) chose representatives who crafted the country we now share. They set in the control systems, (the Constitutional separation of powers between the Executive, Legislative, and Judicial Branches). They also wrote a "flight manual" detailing procedures for safe operation, (the Bill of Rights and Amendments). Within these documents, the Founders established the strict qualifications for those who would serve in the cockpit of elected office and operate the craft of State.

As long as these systems and procedures were strictly maintained and followed, no external storm could successfully bring down the craft of State. "We the People" could live out our lives in relative peace and security as passengers aboard our shared craft. We had confidence that our pilots (public servant government employees) could be relied upon to provide skilled and honest leadership for our continued journey toward "life, liberty, and the pursuit of happiness". Because of the wise systems our Founder set in place, "We the people" held the ultimate authority to hire or fire those who serve us, based upon their continued faithful attention to their mandated stewardship.

An air traffic control system (a free and independent press) was encouraged to ensure that the safe and efficient flow of travel was competent and coordinated. Our elected pilots were held accountable for how they operated the aircraft in their trust within established regulations and flight plans. Ground service personnel were trained and set, i.e., our Justice Department, Federal, State, and local law enforcement officers, and military services. Each of these had the responsibility to maintain the craft, service it, and protect it. As long as each person bearing responsibility for the safe and efficient operation of our shared craft remained within their limits of authority and assigned duties, all was well. We in our generations could confidently participate as passengers, secure in the knowledge that we would arrive safely to our various destinations.

In the present crisis, many of us have come to the conclusion that the cockpit (control center) of our country (the White House, Congress, and the Judiciary) has been hijacked. Our shared craft appears to be under the control of unqualified, and even malicious people who are presently flying erratically, far outside established parameters. These hijackers have run our fuel tanks dry with a crushing national debt. To be specific, our national debt far exceeds (as of this date) $123 trillion dollars in unfunded obligations. This burden is a level of debt we can never hope to repay.

In a November 2013 Wall Street Journal article, writers Chris Cox and Bill Archer explain the lack of knowledge about the unfunded liabilities:

> *The actual liabilities of the federal government—including Social Security, Medicare, and federal employees' future retirement benefits—already exceed $86.8 trillion, or 550% of GDP. For the year ending Dec. 31, 2011, the annual accrued expense of Medicare and Social Security was $7 trillion. Nothing like that figure is used in calculating the deficit. In reality, the reported budget deficit is less than one-fifth of the more accurate figure.*
> *Why haven't Americans heard about the titanic $86.8 trillion liability from these programs? One reason: The actual figures do not appear in black and white on any balance sheet.* [2]

Be sure of one thing: debt equals slavery. Apart from a providential miracle, we, along with our children, grandchildren, and great-grandchildren, are facing real slavery born of debt. Many of our cities and states are falling into insolvency due to overwhelming debt, and some are beginning to declare bankruptcy. The latest and most financially devastated city being, Detroit, Michigan. Our inner cities are becoming seedbeds of violence, racial hatred, civil unrest, and moral depravity.

As an interesting historical side-note, the seat of the U.S. government moved from New York City to Philadelphia, Pennsylvania, where it remained until President John Adams ordered the federal government to pack its bags and establish the central offices at the nation's new capital in Washington, D.C.

Congress adjourned its last meeting in Philadelphia on May 15, 1800, and all federal offices were up and running in Washington D.C. by the fifteenth of June. Philadelphia officially ceased serving as our nation's capital as of June 11, 1800.

Upon the opening of the new Washington, D.C. government offices, *there were roughly 125 federal employees.* You read correctly. ONE HUNDRED AND TWENTY FIVE! Since those early years, the federal government has exploded to mind-blowing size.

According to the U.S. Census Bureau, current only through May 2011, the number of Executive Branch employees on the Federal payroll has expanded beyond 2.8 million—with 2.65 million of these paid full time. The sheer size of the federal government makes it impossible to accurately estimate the *actual* number of federal employees. Agencies operate within agencies; therefore, no one in the federal government has a precise inventory of all the multiplied hundreds of sub-agencies now on the public payroll.

Needless to say, the number of federal employees now easily exceeds the population of many small countries. Can anyone say "big government?" The funds that pay the salaries and pensions of these multiplied millions of public employees come almost entirely from "private sector" workers and businesses. As the former British Prime Minister, Margaret Thatcher once said:

> *The problem with socialism*
> *is that you eventually*
> *run out of other people's money.*

We MUST Return to the Original "Flight Plan"

It appears that those who hate our country and all it stands for have illegally broken into the cockpit and control centers of our shared craft with false credentials and taken the controls of our national aircraft. These public employees are blatantly ignoring the original flight plan (the Constitution and Bill of Rights) and taking our country into directions never imagined by our original Founders. We are hurtling toward near-certain destruction, with runaway debt, political corruption, educational malfeasance, aided and abetted by media collusion.

These hijackers have systematically eliminated the original, authorized pilots. They are ignoring repeated calls from ground controllers (We the People) who are *ordering them* to return to the originally filed flight plan (the Constitution and the Bill of Rights). Many of us are beginning to connect the dots. We are awakening to the fact that powerful and ambitious people who hate the original flight plan are zealously laboring to crash our country. They are attempting to impose a foreign Marxist/Socialist system that tramples the Constitution and threatens to enslave our people.

Those of us who are aware of history realize that such people have "crashed" other nations in other times and places with similarly diabolical "flight plans." In each and every instance throughout history where such vicious systems gained power, the result was economic ruin, the deaths of tens of millions of people. Some of us are becoming convinced that unless we confront these hijackers *now* and take back the cockpit, we're doomed as a nation. We MUST place qualified and constitutionally authorized personnel back at the controls.

Those hijackers now occupying the White House have the unmitigated hubris to make arrogant announcements over the only intercom system on board our shared craft (the national stenographer-leftist news media). They lie to us, saying ridiculous things such as: "Everything is going to be fine as long as you cooperate and don't try to resist. If you criticize the pilot or those assisting him you are a racist bigot, Islamophobe, homophobe, you hate women and minorities, and probably want to destroy the earth's climate and kill baby seals. Also, if you *still* believe in the original flight plan (the Constitution and the Bible), then it is YOU, not us, who are the *real* terrorists."

We've obtained intelligence information from sources outside the "official channels," and are now convinced that many of the people now holding the controls have abdicated their lawful authority to operate our national aircraft. By ignoring the supreme legal authority in our nation, our Constitution, the Bill of Rights, *and* their *real* bosses; "We the People," they have lost their legitimacy. The time has come for us to take to heart the bold words of Todd Beamer on board United Flight 93, who led the small band of courageous passengers: "Are you guys ready? Let's roll!"

I was surprised to learn that only three or four of the 37 passengers, and only one flight attendant, actually took any direct action in confronting the terrorists on United 93. Try to imagine the courage and resolve these men and women had to muster while rushing forward to attack the terrorists amid the protests and cries of other terrified passengers, frozen in their seats with fear. The "sheeple" probably wanted to follow the path of complacent appeasement and believed the lies broadcasting from the "official" intercom system. They *must* have thought Beamer and his gang were brash "cowboys" who were going to get them all killed. These responders likely had to ignore the terrified voices of the sheeple passengers as they begged and screamed at them to go back and sit down compliantly like everyone else. Those brave heroes ignored the fearful bleating of these cowards and did their duty.

Is it any different now? Only a relatively small number of the American people stood up against the tyranny of the British in America's first Revolutionary War. The rest were either too fearful or, they were too heavily invested in the status quo to do anything other than to remain Loyalists to the Crown. Many Americans considered Great Britain their "Mother Country" and had friends and relatives in England. It was unconscionable to most of them to imagine going to war against their British kinsmen. Some of these Loyalists even betrayed their fellow Americans who were fighting even for them and their posterity in the Revolutionary War.

To conclude, our shared aircraft has been hijacked. Our enemies are numerous, but they are not invincible. In fact, they *will* ultimately be defeated and brought to justice. However, as I will reveal in the chapter titled: "Our Real Enemies," there are dark forces operating in an unseen realm who are manipulating and directing the groups and individuals assailing our Constitutional and Christian foundations. These invisible minions of darkness are the *true enemies* and they *must and will* bend and submit to the authority we stand in as Christians.

Again, by His grace and mercy God has granted to the United States of America a system of government that stands heads and shoulders above all others in human history. Here, in America, "we the people" are the boss. Public servants are intended to be just that—*servants*. They are our employees, and their legitimacy and authority stem from the people. It is high time we remind them of this fact.

> *The people—the people*
> *are the rightful masters*
> *of both Congresses, and courts*
> *not to overthrow the Constitution,*
> *but to overthrow the men who pervert it.*
> Abraham Lincoln [3]

Our Past Will Guide Us Into Our Future

The next part of our journey is into our nation's past. Perhaps within the history of our founding, we will discover wisdom that will save our shared craft and bring us back the Founder's original "flight plan." I end this chapter with a question to ponder. Suppose you went to a puppet show, and the puppet verbally attacked you with insulting or slandering words, or perhaps, even striking and injuring you? Would you confront the puppet or the puppeteer?

Notes

1. Rogue State: A Guide to the World's Only Superpower, by William Blum, Former U.S. State Department employee Page 37 http://tinyurl.com/otmd9tx

2. As quoted in Redstate.com article http://tiny.cc/ywgj0w

3. From "Abraham Lincoln, [September 16-17, 1859] (Notes for Speech in Kansas and Ohio)," Page 2.

9

We the Sheeple?

*It is the system
of nationalist individualism
that has to go.
We are living in the end
of the sovereign states.
In the great struggle to evoke
a Westernized World Socialism,
contemporary governments may vanish.
Countless people will hate the new world order
and will die protesting against it.*
H.G. Wells, *The New World Order,* 1940

~~~~~~

Who are "sheeple?" Well, you might be a "sheeple" if you follow blindly after whatever popular fad considered "in" by media opinion makers or the latest opinions of Hollywood elites. This dysfunctional mindset applies to political, social, technological, fashion, or religious fads. A sheeple *needs* to feel like they're part of the herd–the "in" crowd. A sheeple seeks to stay within the safe boundaries of "group-think" and use the common buzzwords, slang, or lingo all the other sheeple use. Sheeple laugh at the same jokes and share the same snarky pokes aimed at others who are considered part of the "out" crowd. They tend to dress the same, wear the same slogans on their tee shirts or bumper stickers. To a sheeple, herd approval means *everything*.

The sheeple's *worst* nightmare is to suffer rejection from the "in" crowd and be told they are "politically incorrect." To the sheeple, any accusation of being a "racist," "homophobe," "Islamophobe," "xenophobe" or whatever other epithet that might mark one as "one of *those* people" is the *kiss of death*. Because of this, the sheeple works very hard at conforming, and rarely expresses an opinion that might not agree with what *everyone else* thinks is "cool" or "politically correct." This kind of thought censorship is positively Orwellian and a primary means of mind and behavior control employed by leftist-progressives.

> *The two aims of the Party*
> *are to conquer the whole surface of the earth*
> *and to extinguish once and for all*
> *the possibility of independent thought.*
> *There are therefore two great problems*
> *which the Party is concerned to solve.*
> *One is how to discover against his will*
> *what another human being is thinking*
> *and the other is how to kill*
> *several hundred million people in a few seconds*
> *without giving warning beforehand.*
> — George Orwell, *1984*

In their despair and fear, sheeple often passively shift the responsibility of their lives to someone else (or the government) to "take care" of them just to escape the pressures of life. Sheeple are people who have become helpless sheep and are conditioned to think of themselves as perpetual victims. They are only suitable for shearing or slaughter by those who "take care" of them, and paradoxically, care nothing about them at all. They willingly allow themselves to become helpless, disarmed, and defenseless against the wolves they foolishly deny existence, yet who seek to devour them. One way to identify a "sheeple spirit" in someone is to listen to how they bleat, complain, and whine. They often blame-shift their lack of power onto others—especially venting their frustrations at higher achievers or people more wealthy than they. Their "handlers" (i.e. equally-brainwashed friends, colleagues, relatives, etc.) condition sheeple to fear independent opinions, especially about politics or moral issues, and often feel "victimized" and "offended" by anyone who disagrees with their psychosis.

It is extremely easy to offend sheeple, due to their self-image as an underprivileged, or minority "victim." Sheeple with lighter skin pigmentation often suffer intense feelings of guilt due to the PC views on imagined "white privilege." Everything they read or hear is sifted through a hyper-sensitive "victim" filter. Any comment about their appearance, weight, height, sex, lifestyle, ethnicity, education, politics, or (gasp) their skin color, sets off their "offense" alarms. If you're bold enough to challenge their beliefs, the sheeple will often bleat and whine that you're being sexist, racist, homophobic, xenophobic, Islamophobic, insensitive, intolerant, or committing some other variation of "hate speech." All of this is, of course, is utter nonsense.

Sheeple especially tend to embrace "envy politics" and whine about all the so-called "fat cats" who won't pay their "fair share." Some sheeple even blame God Himself for their imagined problems or failures, often while denying that He even exists. Blame-shifting, however, only leads to the psychosis of liberal-progressive utopian delusions.

Nothing to Live or Die For?

Children are being systematically "whimpified" into "sheeplehood" by an educational system that increasingly promotes the idea that it is *always* wrong to think independently or utilize force in defense of oneself or country. If a school student ever attempts by physical force to defend him or herself (or another classmate) from an aggressive bully, a punishment of the *defender* usually results. Such non-conformists are often suspended or put on psychotropic drugs that potentially trigger psychotic episodes of violence or suicidal ideation. As I've stated repeatedly, guns are nearly *always* typified as *intrinsically evil*. Increasingly, our military servicemen and women are portrayed dishonorably as "warmongers." I can recall even as far back as the early 70s being called a "baby killer" when I came home from military service in Vietnam. I find this supremely ironic now, since many of those same people who made the "baby killer" accusation are now rabidly pro-abortion.

In today's schools, virtually *all* wars are condemned, no matter *what* the provocation, and kids easily slip into the idea that there is nothing worth dying for. It is prevalent in some school districts during choir recitals—once a place where sacred music was welcome—to now sing asinine "peace" songs like "Imagine" by John Lennon. Lennon's song promotes a utopian atheistic worldview that extols a pathetically mindless pacifism.

John Stuart Mill, an English philosopher who lived from 1806 to 1873 said:

> *War is an ugly thing, but not the ugliest of things. The decayed and degraded state of moral and patriotic feeling which thinks that nothing is worth war is much worse. The person who has nothing for which he is willing to fight, nothing which is more important than his own personal safety, is a miserable creature and has no chance of being free unless made and kept so by the exertions of better men than himself.* [1]

78   Destroying the Shadow Agenda

Sir Winston Churchill: NOT a Sheeple

Winston Churchill was not of a "sheeple" spirit. Certainly, he was not a man without his personal sins, and it is important that we keep that in mind, even as we extol what other good virtues he possessed. Often described as the "British Bulldog" Churchill was a tenacious fighter who refused to compromise, no matter how hopeless the situation seemed. During the Battle of Britain in World War II, Winston Churchill led the British people through one of their darkest hours. Hitler's Nazis pounded British cities to rubble from July 10 to October 31st of 1940. During that three-month period, the British people suffered under a near-continual barrage of bombs and rockets. The strain was nearly unbearable, and some of the sheeple "bleated" that it would be better just to surrender to the Nazis rather than risk themselves in defense of their freedom. Churchill rallied not only himself, but also his nation to face the evil confronting them in that dark hour, and in doing so, eventually defeated it and saved Great Britain from Nazi slavery.

Churchill's indomitable "bulldog" spirit inspired courage and resolve in England, and left to history an enduring example of courage under fire for all people who treasure freedom and liberty.

Shortly before the Nazis unleashed the fury of their bombing offensive on Britain, Churchill spoke to the House of Commons on June 18, 1940. In one of the most influential speeches in history, he courageously ripped the "sheeple" spirit out of his countrymen and replaced it with steeled resolve. He inspired them with a vision of national destiny, and this eventually turned the course of the war. Here is an excerpt from that epic speech:

> *I expect that the Battle of Britain is about to begin. Upon this battle depends the survival of Christian civilization. Upon it depends our own British life, and the long continuity of our institutions and our Empire. The whole fury and might of the enemy must very soon be turned on us. Hitler knows that he will have to break us in this island or lose the war. If we can stand up to him, all Europe may be freed and the life of the world may move forward into broad, sunlit uplands. But if we fail, then the whole world, including the United States, including all that we have known and cared for, will sink into the abyss of a new dark age made more sinister, and perhaps more protracted, by the lights of perverted science. Let us therefore brace ourselves to our duties, and so bear ourselves, that if the British Empire and its Commonwealth last for a thousand years, men will still say, that this was their finest hour.* [2]

The Battle of Britain was an unqualified British victory. Under Churchill's leadership, Britain's "sheeple" were transformed and united once again into a courageous nation with steel backbones. It was the first decisive and humiliating defeat for Hitler's Nazi forces. It was a victory achieved, however, at a grievous price.

By December 1940, 23,002 British civilians were dead and an additional 32,138 wounded. [3] To give some perspective, at our present U.S. population of 312 million, an equivalent ratio would mean a toll of over 310,450 American dead and wounded. These numbers demonstrate the measure of resolve the British people expressed in their heroic defense against the evil forces seeking their destruction. A great victory at a terrible price indeed! Another quote from Winston Churchill typifies his basic worldview:

> *A pessimist sees the difficulty*
> *in every opportunity;*
> *an optimist sees the opportunity*
> *in every difficulty.*

We can draw encouragement from the example of Winston Churchill and the British people during their darkest hours in World War II. Their example should be shouted from housetops: courageous people endure, and evil cannot long stand before them.

For some time before the outbreak of World War II, Churchill tried repeatedly to rally the British people to confront the threat of Hitler's rising power in Germany. He was largely ignored and vilified.

Churchill was considered a "prophet of doom" in his time. Only later was he vindicated when his dark visions of the future became everyone's waking nightmare during the Nazi blitz. I'm continually amazed at how quickly fearful sheeple will scoff at, and actively marginalize anyone who warns of the danger, even in our times. "There are no wolves," they will often bleat, or another favorite often heard among sheeple is; "You're just an alarmist!" The British appeasers were eventually discredited by the reality of Nazi bombs raining down on London. Only then did they desperately seek Churchill's leadership. By then it was nearly too late.

> *Last time I saw it all coming and cried aloud to my own fellow-countrymen and to the world, but no one paid any attention. Up till the year 1933 or even 1935, Germany might have been saved from the awful fate which has overtaken her and we might all have been spared the miseries*

> Hitler let loose upon mankind. There never was a war in all history easier to prevent by timely action than the one which has just desolated such great areas of the globe. It could have been prevented in my belief without the firing of a single shot, and Germany might be powerful, prosperous and honored to-day; but no one would listen and one by one we were all sucked into the awful whirlpool. We surely must not let that happen again. [4]

I cannot help but draw an ominous parallel between Churchill's words and our recent situation with President Obama's Iran nuclear arms "deal." How can it be possible that his administration could negotiate in good faith with a regime that regularly signals their firm intention of destroying the United States and Israel? I can almost hear Churchill shouting from the grave those same words; "*There never was a war in all history easier to prevent by timely action than the one which has just desolated such great areas of the globe. It could have been prevented in my belief without the firing of a single shot.*"

Churchill's views regarding Islam are particularly noteworthy. Even in his times, he perceived in Islam a grave threat to Western civilization, and his words now seem prophetic. He delivered a short speech as a young soldier and journalist that uncannily reflects the current situation today. The speech was reproduced in his book *The River War: An Historical Account of the Reconquest of the Soudan*.

> Individual Muslims may show splendid qualities, but the influence of the religion paralyses the social development of those who follow it. No stronger retrograde force exists in the world. Far from being moribund, Mohammedanism is a militant and proselytizing faith. It has already spread throughout Central Africa, raising fearless warriors at every step; and were it not that Christianity is sheltered in the strong arms of science, the science against which it had vainly struggled, the civilization of modern Europe might fall, as fell the civilization of ancient Rome. [5]

In light of these words, it is not surprising that the manifestly Islamic sympathizer, President Barack Hussein Obama, removed the bust of Churchill from the White House and sent it back to England. The bust was a gift from the British people and many viewed this despicable action as the height of hubris. [6]

Courageous People ACT While Sheeple Timidly Bleat

In the wake of 9/11, "we the people" (not, "we the sheeple") must continue to ask hard questions of our elected employees. Nothing should be accepted at face-value, given the obvious and well-documented difficulty they have repeatedly demonstrated with telling the truth to the American people. This seeming inability to tell the truth only gives rise to more questions and undermines our ability to trust our government. This lack of trust is extremely toxic to any republic, and must be addressed with something more than dismissive, snarky comments by officials and especially our Chief Executive. In the absence of clearly presented and logical facts, our people are left to speculate that there might be much more going on than we were being told. This only fuels more conjecture and paranoia about some "insider plot" by a shadowy rogue element operating within the government bureaucracy. Such paranoia may be justified, but even if it weren't, the suspicion is nearly as damaging as the reality.

Our questioning of our elected employees must not be limited to 9/11 however. We must also demand accountability and truthful answers about such contemporary issues as what happened at Benghazi when Islamic jihadists attacked and burned our Consulate, and tortured, sodomized, and murdered our Ambassador, Christopher Stevens. We need to understand why automatic weapons were given to drug cartels in Mexico during the "Fast and Furious" debacle. We need accurate information about why the Obama administration committed these and many other acts that appeased America's enemies and resulted in the deaths of American citizens.

Most ominously, the massive and dramatic increases in all forms of highly sophisticated government surveillance on ordinary Americans since the 9/11 attack must be investigated by Congress. The establishment of new and obtrusive "security" measures are ripping the heart out of our republic and gravely endangering our constitutional rights.

Notes

1. "The Contest in America," Fraser's Magazine (February 1862) http://www.columbia.edu/cu/tat/core/mill.htm

2. http://www.winstonchurchill.org/resources/speeches/1940-the-finest-hour/their-finest-hour

3. The Impact of the Blitz on London http://www.historylearningsite.co.uk/impact_blitz_london.htm

4. Sir Winston Churchill- THE SINEWS OF PEACE Address to the graduating class of Westminster College, Fulton, Missouri, March 5, 1946

5. The River War: An Historical Account of the Reconquest of the Soudan, Winston Churchill, 1899

6. http://www.telegraph.co.uk/news/worldnews/barackobama/9436526/White-House-admits-it-did-return-Winston-Churchill-bust-to-Britain.html

10

America Lobotomized?

> Gandalf:
> *Breathe the free air again, my friend.*
> King Théoden:
> *Dark have been my dreams of late.*
> Gandalf:
> *Your fingers would remember*
> *their old strength better —*
> *if they grasped your sword.*
> J.R.R. Tolkien
> *Lord of the Rings: The Two Towers*

~~~~~~

The United States is in the midst of a severe identity crisis. We simply don't seem to know who or what we are anymore. We have become a nation of divided loyalties, and disparate visions about what it even means to be an "American." Radical leftist-progressives—some of whom are even now serving at the upper echelons of our government—have encouraged aided and abetted our collective amnesia. Our common disability has provided progressive "change" agents nearly unchallenged freedom to promote racial divisions, economic envy, and class warfare among our people. There is little active opposition to them because far too many of us are too distracted to understand what is happening to us. A house divided cannot stand, and unless our people become aware and awakened, and these divisions are healed, our national house stands in grave danger of falling.

Political views always arise out of *someone's* personal convictions about what is right or wrong, good or evil. For the Biblical Christians and orthodox Jews, such opinions are based on the belief that God alone establishes what is good or evil. For professing atheists, such concepts as "right and wrong" or "good or evil" originate from philosophical lumber borrowed (or co-opted) from Biblical principles. While obstinately refusing to acknowledge their Creator, the unregenerate pick and choose (as a matter of their own inventiveness) what virtues or vices may suit them at the moment.

How could it happen that the people of America, who were once so conscious of and grateful for God's blessings, and respectful of His commandments could, within a few generations, so radically forsake their earlier reverential fear and respect for God? We've descended into an abyss of arrogant rebellion and debauchery unmatched in our history.

While some would pin the blame for our moral and ethical decline to immorality in the film and entertainment industry, Rock Music, or atheistic influences in our schools, I would not point to these factors as the *primary* causes of our decline. These, I believe, are *effects*, not causes. The principal *causative* factor that gave rise to the problems we are facing in America is not as obvious but is incredibly profound.

In my view, the principal cause is that a significant number of Christian leaders and churches over the past two centuries neglected to aggressively promote and teach fundamental biblical, theological truth to subsequent generations. This failure opened nearly unchallenged opportunities for the minions of darkness to gradually blind people. They fell into a spiritual slumber and lost the ability to discern and actively resist evil. Even the very *word* "evil"—especially in the context of personal morality—began to be replaced with euphemistic terms like "dysfunctional behaviors" or "unhealthy choices." Liberal theologians increasingly scoffed at the very *idea* of sin or a "real" Devil in favor of the more genteel concepts of "psychological illness" or "emotional deficits." Many seminaries began to come under the influence of theological liberals. Future pastors were indoctrinated to teach their congregants to eschew political involvement and "keep separate" from the world. The importance of teaching historic and orthodox Christian doctrine and theology to their congregations was minimized. The resulting lack of biblically educated Christian participation in these critical areas—particularly in public policy and education—created an ethical and philosophical vacuum that threw open the societal and political gates for wolves to come in among the sheep and devour them at will.

Teaching the full counsel of God is difficult and laborious, and often offends the pride of men. Instead, a more "seeker friendly" social gospel has gained popularity, focusing on people's "felt" needs instead of the critical needs of their souls. Biblical doctrines regarding the sin and depravity of man through Adam's fall, the need for repentance, God's sovereignty, and eternal judgment came to be regarded as divisive and controversial, which of course, it is. The teaching emphasis within many churches shifted toward promoting cordial relationships and making everyone feel "loved and accepted." Perhaps the most damning lie was the idea that "all people are basically good in their own way," and Christians were widely shamed into embracing the false idea that it was always wrong to "judge."

The concept of "Truth" as an absolute—applicable to every person at all times and in all places—was replaced by a vague notion of "many truths." This teaching promotes the idea that everyone's beliefs are equally valid, depending on the circumstances and timing. In this relativistic paradigm, it doesn't matter what one believes as long as they are "sincere." This is nonsense, of course. The most vicious mass murderers and despotic dictators, including the Devil himself, were all "sincere," but their sincerity could never justify their monstrous deeds of evil before God.

In recent times, there is an emerging anti-intellectual attitude arising among many Christians that reject the importance of accurate exegesis, theological education, or the study of church history. Personally-held "revelations," received "directly" from the Holy Spirit are increasingly regarded as superior to historically proven scriptural scholarship. In this mode of thinking, the individual becomes the final arbiter of truth and falsehood according to how they personally sense the "moving of the Holy Spirit" within themselves. Personal revelations (if tested and proven) *can* be extremely edifying. However, they are highly subjective and frequently lead to rather bizarre interpretations of Scripture which are completely unhinged from historical biblical scholarship and proven interpretation.

As a result of this creeping apostasy within Western Christianity, slowly and incrementally, secular historical revisionists and radical leftist Progressives have systematically transformed our schools into secular indoctrination institutions. Atheistic control of the education apparatus progressively filtered out nearly all consciousness of a biblically-based morality and a Christian worldview, unless in the context of mocking derision.

This deconstruction of America's Christian Foundations was no mere accident in my opinion. All evidence indicates it was a deliberate act of national sabotage through misinformation and selective censorship of history. The secularist's goal is to strip American's children—and consequently all future adults—of any real awareness of our nation's rich Christian heritage. This Christian legacy forms the foundation and bedrock of all we hold to be right and good.

As a result, many have lost any real appreciation of our unsurpassed freedoms under our amazing—and unique in all of human history—Constitution and Bill of Rights. We've now come to the point that many school districts are banning the display of the U.S. Flag or Constitutional education in the name of "diversity." This sort of censorship promotes a sense of shame in students about the display of our flag, or open expressions of patriotism. Liberals fear that public displays of love for America might "offend" someone from another country. [1]

Thankfully, some students and communities are beginning to push back against these "politically correct" secular progressive "thought police." [2] They are fighting back and winning reversals on these flag-banning atrocities. [3]

Who Were We in the Past?

Despite decades of our people being systematically dumbed-down by the educational system, there yet remains a flickering memory of a time nearly forgotten when kids could play in their neighborhoods without their parents being overly concerned that they might be abducted or sexually molested by perverts living nearby. In my childhood, people looked out for each other, and police officers were our neighbors and friends, not to be feared, but respected for their service.

It was a time when the entertainment industry honored and promoted ordinary families with mothers and fathers nurturing and training their children to be caring, honest adults. Family traditions like attending church were considered important, never to be mocked or belittled.

Young people were taught in public schools to respect and safely handle firearms, mostly in the context of hunter safety classes, and learned to take serious responsibility for their proper uses. In spite of easy access to firearms by students, either in their homes or vehicles or transported to and from safety classes, I'm unaware of a *single instance* of a student shooting a teacher or classmate.

This begs a question. With all the availability of guns in homes and schools, and the familiarity that students had with firearms even in the earliest grades, why weren't there any school shootings? When I was a boy, it was quite common for my friends to receive their first hunting rifle for a birthday or Christmas gift. What was different then, and how has our society changed?

I believe there are two principal reasons for the increase in firearm violence. The first involves the way people are conditioned to think about firearms. Most people in my childhood regarded guns as a necessary evil for home defense, to be used with care and respect for their deadly potential. Many of us hunted game or belonged to organizations like the Boy Scouts where many young people were taught to respect nature, and take responsibility for the safe use of firearms for hunting. We also had a much stronger sense of community and cared for people around us beyond our immediate family. In recent decades, popular entertainment mostly portrays gun violence without any sense of moral conscience. Gang bangers and the "gansta rap" music idols—as well as the mind-numbing violence of many video games—desensitize young people about the devastating effects of firearm violence without any appeal to conscience or empathy for victims.

The other primary reason (which might surprise some readers) is the exponential increase in the use of psychotropic mind-altering pharmaceuticals upon school children. I deal with this issue elsewhere in this book, but there seems to be a direct correlation between the use of these medications and student suicides and school violence. This cause is largely ignored by the news media, with the primary focus placed upon the types of weapons used in these tragic incidents, particularly when firearms are involved. When knives are used, the media seems to have a serious short-term memory dysfunction.

Many of the favorite TV shows of the 50s and 60s included westerns such as "The Rifleman," "Gunslinger," "Rawhide," "Gunsmoke," "Have Gun – Will Travel," "The Lone Ranger" "Roy and Dale Rogers" and "Bonanza." These productions *prominently* featured people who openly carried firearms in the context of protecting their person, their communities, and families. The stories featured heroic examples of honesty, courage, and personal responsibility. They were mostly morality plays where lawless "bad guys" with guns were kept at bay by "good guys" with guns.

Film and TV actors like John Wayne, Glen Ford, Charlton Heston, James Arness, Chuck Conners, and many others played the roles of heroes and rugged individualists. As a boy, I loved to watch stories of men like Daniel Boone, Wild Bill Hickock, and even a sharp-shooting lady named Annie Oakley. These men packed firearms and were ever-ready to stand up for what was right and defend the weak. The male characters were unashamed to walk tall and talk like a man's man. The roles they played were an inspiration to many little boys who eagerly looked forward to adulthood, and *their* turn to be a man of honor. "Manliness" was understood as providing for and protecting their friends and families, training and disciplining their children, and giving noble, tender devotion to their wives.

John Wayne, who passed away in 1979 at the age of 72, played the part of Col. Davy Crockett in 1960 film, The Alamo, which he produced and directed. Not only was he a talented actor and director, but he was a patriotic American who deeply loved our Republic and our Constitution. In most of his films, he personified the image of a "man's man" who wasn't ashamed of his masculinity and was always ready to stand up for what is right. For those reasons, he is almost universally vilified by radical feminists and leftists who despise the very idea of a strong, independent man of character and integrity. Here is a salient quote from *The Alamo*.

> *I'm gonna tell you something Flaca, and I want you to listen tight. May sound like I'm talkin' about me, but I'm not, I'm talkin' about you—as a matter of fact, I'm talkin' about all people everywhere. When I come down here to Texas I was lookin' for something. I didn't know what. Seems like if you added up my life, I spent it all either stompin' other men, or in some cases, getting' stomped. Had me some money, and had me some medals, but none of it seemed worth the lifetime of pain for the mother that bore me. It was like I was empty.*
>
> *Well, I'm not empty anymore. That's what's important. I feel useful in this old world. To hit a lick against what's wrong or to say a word for what's right, even though you get walloped for sayin' that word. Now, I may sound like a bible-beater yelling up a revival at a river-crossing campmeeting, but that don't change the truth none. There's right, and there's wrong. You gotta do one or the other. You do the one, and you're living. You do the other, and you may be walkin' around, but you're dead as a beaver hat.*

Then, in October 1972, the TV westerns on prime-time underwent a radical transformation with the premiere of a Western-genre program named Kung Fu, featuring a Shaolin monk and Kung Fu expert named Kwai Chang Caine. Actor David Carradine played the part of a contemplative, Eastern mystic who fought without guns against bad guys to protect the helpless and defend the weak. A prominent feature of the program was Caine's hatred of firearms and his peaceful, mystical serenity in the midst of dangerous life or death situations. Following this program, several other similar role-models were produced by Hollywood that seemed to have one very clear message; "Guns are evil." Manliness and masculinity became passe, replaced by a passive-aggressive quasi-religious monk. John Farrier, a writer for Neatorama, succinctly nails the *real* underlying message of Kung Fu in his article, *11 Facts You Might Not Know about Kung Fu*.

> *Kung Fu, which aired from 1972-1975, was an unusual blend of the social questioning of 70s America, an emerging fascination with the martial arts, and the introduction of Eastern thought into American pop culture. It was*

one of the last Westerns of American television and thus straddled a great cultural shift that occurred during that era. [4]

Sometime before the 1960s, radical feminists began openly attacking the very idea of masculinity and traditional (biblically-based) gender role-models as "oppressive" to women. They actively sought to feminize little boys, making them feel ashamed of their male identities.[5]

In recent decades, boys who act like boys in their classrooms, play habits, and personalities, are increasingly "tagged" as ADHD (Attention Deficit Hyperactive Dysfunction). These are often put on psychotropic drugs to suppress naturally aggressive male traits. [6] This, I believe, has been a significant contributing factor in the great harm and damage, inflicted not only upon men but also to women and children. The use of powerful psychotropic medications on school children is becoming increasingly suspect as a contributing factor in the shocking rise of school and workplace violence in recent decades. After being on-scene at several school shootings over the past 16 years, I was shocked to discover that in nearly every case, prescribed psychotropic drug use by the perpetrators was a common factor. In the few instances where a psychiatric drug connection couldn't be verified, the medical records of the offender were sealed. I could say much more about this, but you get my drift. [7]

Our National Frontal Lobotomy
Perhaps you've heard of the term "frontal lobotomy?" It is a surgical, (or sometimes electro-shock or chemical) procedure that damages portions of the frontal lobes of the brain related to higher cognitive and reasoning functions. Those who undergo this barbaric procedure often end up more or less vegetative, with radical personality changes and a marked loss of intelligence and the ability to think clearly. (Come to think of it, this profile seems to match most liberals I've met.) It was often used to treat mental illness until the 1980s in the U.S. [8]

It now appears that an entire generation has been profoundly "dumbed-down," (lobotomized) and rendered ignorant by our pathetic "education" system. Without an accurate historical foundation to work from, how could it be possible for anyone to participate wisely in our republic, vote intelligently, and choose wise leadership? We are dangerously nearing the point of no return when significant numbers of voters are motivated by nothing more than selfish interests and what personal benefits they might obtain from a particular party or candidate.

Our nation's plunge into stupidity was gradual. It required quite some time for the evil brain surgeons of progressivism to dumb down our people from our former state of educated hyper-awareness to where we find ourselves now. I don't believe our present national amnesia is a permanent disability but can be reversed only by massive infusions of "Truth" therapy. Accurate and complete information about our nation's history in our school classrooms is a huge part of the cure. Education has been the problem and education is a significant part of the answer.

William Ross Wallace, (1819-1881) once wrote about the profound influence a mother has on the life of a child in a poem. Here is a verse from it.

> *For the hand that rocks the cradle*
> *Is the hand that rules the world.*

The same principle applies to the force exerted by schools and teachers. For millennia, despots and dictators have known and practiced this principle. If you can successfully indoctrinate even one generation while they're young, you have them for life, as well as their children, and their children's children. Liberal-progressives often howl indignantly about the dangers of "indoctrination" of children by Christians but do not seem to have the slightest problem with it so long as *they* are doing the indoctrination.

Several years ago, I was invited to speak at Punahou School in Hawaii. One of the chaplains at the school engaged me to share some of my experiences at Ground Zero in a week of school assemblies with all grade levels. After two days of meetings and guided tours of the incredibly beautiful campus, as well as meeting many of the teaching staff in their classrooms, I became increasingly alarmed.

Punahou is a private school, founded in the 1800s by Christian missionaries. Sometime in the early 1900s, the school was gradually overtaken by secular progressives. Today, for all I could observe, nearly all of the former Christian influence appears to be reduced to a small chaplain staff representing very liberal denominations. Most of the staff I met openly boasted of their "progressive, enlightened educational philosophy," and proudly proclaimed that their students were being trained to "change the world."

As I read over the extensive list of alumni in their online literature, I was struck by the number of distinguished military, political, educational, diplomatic and civil leaders included in that list. What alarmed me, however, was the fact that nearly every one of them were secular progressives firmly ensconced in the liberal camp. Clearly, Punahou is a school with a vision to raise up liberal leaders to change the world. No one could argue that they are

America Lobotomized? 91

not succeeding in their vision. *Barack Hussein Obama graduated from Punahou in 1979.*

My time at Punahou was abruptly cut short when someone on the staff discovered an article on the internet I had written some years before in which I criticized the cruel violence, sexual perversion, and fundamental intolerance of radical Islam. Mine was decidedly a "politically incorrect" point of view. After a summons by the school's president to his office, I endured a grueling two-hour inquisition, attended by all the various grade school principals. I was berated and castigated for my orthodox Christian and conservative views and my support for the people and the state of Israel. For these politically incorrect "sins," I was summarily dismissed from my speaking contract and banned from further contact with the student body.

This intense judgment was imposed despite the fact that I had followed all pre-agreed contract guidelines to the letter. I carefully avoided saying anything overtly controversial to the students in my assemblies—a fact that they could not deny. I did, however, let it be known in my meetings with the students that I am an unashamed Christian, but only in passing. Evidently, my holding Christian beliefs and political views that did not fit in with their purpose and vision rendered me a "persona non grata," and I was asked to leave the campus.

Although disappointed at the time, I must confess that upon reflection, I regard my banning from Punahou something of a badge of honor. I only hope that my kind and courteous responses to their blistering accusations will in some way be used of God to draw them to the same grace in Christ I have found.

Was This Lobotomy Deliberate?

Just in case anyone is yet unconvinced that Christian values are under assault in America's public (and now in many private) schools, I offer the following quote by John Dewey (1859–1952). Dewey is considered by many to be the "Father" of modern American public education. He was a committed communist/socialist who clearly perceived the need for purging all consciousness of Christianity from educational institutions. His diabolical vision for compulsory public education should alarm every caring parent and grandparent. I quote Dewey from an article by John Dunphy titled, *A Religion for a New Age*, appearing in the January/February 1983 issue of The Humanist Magazine:

> *I am convinced that **the battle for humankind's future must be waged and won in the public school classroom** by teachers that correctly perceive their role as proselytizers of a new faith: a religion of humanity that recognizes and respects the spark of what theologians call divinity in every human*

> being... The classroom must and will become an arena of conflict between the old and new — **the rotting corpse of Christianity, together with all its adjacent evils and misery,** and the new faith of humanism, resplendent with the promise of a world in which the never-realized Christian ideal of 'love thy neighbor' will finally be achieved. (Emphasis added) 9

In an article re-posted on the Marxist.com website, W. F. Warde wrote a piece in the winter of 1960 titled: *John Dewey's Theories of Education.* In it, he sang the praises of Dewey for advancing the cause of international socialism.

Here is one of the most egregious excerpts from Warde's article.

> *This eminent thinker of the Progressive movement was the dominant figure in American education. His most valuable and enduring contribution to our culture came from the ideas and methods he fathered in this field. ...The communist colony in New Harmony, Indiana, founded by Robert Owen in 1826, pioneered a pattern in free, equal, comprehensive and secular education that had yet to be realized throughout this country over a century later.* 10

As Thomas Bailey Aldrich once said, "A man is known by the company his mind keeps."

A one-time close associate with the Communist Robert Owen, (referenced in the above quote) Orestes Augustus Brownson, L.L.D, laid bare the ultimate goal of the socialists of his time in a speech he delivered on June 29th, 1853 titled; *An Oration on Liberal Studies.* Once a "fellow traveler" with those promoting socialism through the manipulation of public education in his time, Dr. Brownson later became a Christian and recanted his former associations with these evil workers. Brownson exposed the insidious agenda envisioned by these early engineers of "progressive" education in the following quote.

> *The great object is to get rid of Christianity, and to convert our churches into halls of science. The plan is not to make open attacks upon religion... but to a system of state schools, from which all religion will be excluded... and to which all parents are to be compelled by law to send their children. [The] complete plan is to take the children from their parents at the age of twelve or eighteen months, and to have them raised, fed, clothed, and trained in these schools at the public expense; but at any rate, [they are] to have godless schools for all the children of the country... the plan has been*

> *successfully pursued . . . and the whole action of the country on the subject has taken the direction we sought to give it. . .* [11]

John Dewey was born six years after this speech was given, but evidently, he later joined ranks with Dr. Brownson's former associates and fellow travelers.

The Dangers of Centralized Education Control

History repeatedly demonstrates that state-controlled education is deadly and dangerous in the hands of totalitarians. Pre-World War II Germany was one of the most educated societies in Europe by the time Adolf Hitler took power. However, by the 1930s, secular progressives and theological liberals in Germany's churches had significantly influenced Germany's school systems, setting the stage for Hitler's despotism.

The notion that man was merely a product of random chance evolution paved the way for the widespread acceptance of the most egregious and monstrous policies of National Socialism in the minds of many of Germany's people. A belief in secular scientific advancements and human evolution provides people and whole societies with moral justification for the false idea that humanity can be self-perfecting and self-actualizing. This is the belief that humans are able, in and of themselves, to reach some imagined pinnacle of human development without the existence or assistance of God.

Hitler drew much practical encouragement from the "pseudo-science" of eugenics, popularized in the United States in the 1920s by secular progressives such as Margaret Sanger. Sanger founded the American Birth Control League (ABCL), which eventually became known as Planned Parenthood. One of Sanger's close associates, Dr. Harry Laughlin, tirelessly promoted policies for the purifying America's human "breeding stock" and purging America's "bad strains." These "strains" included the "shiftless, ignorant, and worthless class of antisocial whites of the South." [12]

Sanger held the same views and promoted the sterilization of black people and those she considered "unfit" to procreate. She also wrote of those who were "irresponsible and reckless," and included those "...whose religious scruples prevent their exercising control over their numbers." She said: "...there is no doubt in the minds of all thinking people that the procreation of this group should be stopped." [13]

> *We should hire three or four colored ministers, preferably with social-service backgrounds, and with engaging personalities. The most successful educational approach to the Negro is through a religious appeal.* **We don't**

want the word to go out that we want to exterminate the Negro population, and the minister is the man who can straighten out that idea if it ever occurs to any of their more rebellious members. [14]

Her unbelievably arrogant words beg a question or two. Why would Sanger encourage the hiring of *"three or four colored ministers, preferably with social-service backgrounds?"* Obviously, because one of the items listed on Sanger's bucket list was the very extermination of "inferior races" and particularly the Negro population. She needed someone who could *"...straighten out"* the *"more rebellious members"* among the ignorant, religious (read; *Christian*) black folk lest they get "that idea." Can anyone say; "**Racist**!"

Can anyone doubt that Sanger's "Frankenstein Monster," (AKA, Planned Parenthood,) yet targets "inferior races?" New research recently released by Protecting Black Life (an outreach of Life Issues Institute) reveals an ominous truth. 79% of Planned Parenthood's surgical abortion facilities are located within walking distance of African-American and Hispanic/Latino communities.

> *"Minority communities are the #1 targets of Planned Parenthood," says Rev. Arnold Culbreath, Director of Protecting Black Life and a founding member of the National Black Pro-Life Coalition. "It's no wonder abortion remains the leading cause of death among African Americans, higher than all other causes combined. Getting this information to as many people as possible is not only critical, it's a matter of life and death for countless babies and oft times even their mothers."* [15]

Standing up against Sanger's madness was a courageous black woman, Dr. Mildred Jefferson (April 4th, 1926 — October 15th, 2010) Dr. Jefferson led a powerful campaign against the monstrous vision of Sanger and other secular racist bigots like her. Dr. Jefferson made history that should never be forgotten. She was the first black woman to graduate from Harvard medical school and dedicated her life to defend the humanity of the pre-born child.

After graduating from Harvard Medical School in 1951, she served as a surgical intern at Boston City Hospital and became the first female doctor at the former Boston University Medical Center. Dr. Jefferson was one of the founders of the Value of Life Committee of Massachusetts, the National Right to Life Committee, Black Americans for Life, and openly spoke up for the pre-born child with other Right to Life organizations. [16]

Dr. Jefferson declared passionately:

> *I became a physician in order to help save lives. I am at once a physician, a citizen, and a woman, and I am not willing to stand aside and allow the concept of expendable human lives to turn this great land of ours into just another exclusive reservation where only the perfect, the privileged, and the planned have the right to live.*

She also said:

> *I became a doctor in the tradition that is represented in the Bible of looking upon medicine as a high calling. I will not stand aside and have this great profession of mine, of the doctor, give the designation of* healer *to become that of the social executioner. The Supreme Court Justices only had to hand down an order. Social workers only have to make arrangements, but it has been given to my profession to destroy the life of the innocent and the helpless.*

Dr. Martin Luther King also lamented the slaughter of black children even back in the 1960s. Alveda C. King, of slain civil-rights leader A.D. King and niece of Martin Luther King, Jr., quotes her uncle often when outlining her opposition of abortion. She writes:

> *[Martin Luther King, Jr.] once said, "The Negro cannot win as long as he is willing to sacrifice the lives of his children for comfort and safety." How can the "Dream" survive if we murder the children? Every aborted baby is like a slave in the womb of his or her mother. The mother decides his or her fate.* [17]

History's Lessons Must Not be Forgotten

> *What did you learn in school today,*
> *dear little boy of mine?*
> *I learned that our government must be strong.*
> *It's always right and never wrong.*
> *That's what I learned in school.*
> Song by Tom Paxton, 1963

Government hegemony over the educational institutions of a nation is deadly serious business. Governments throughout history have long recognized the value and utility of molding the minds and attitudes of their populations toward uniformity and obedience to the perceived interests of the State. Nazi Germany under Adolph Hitler is but one of many governments throughout the millennia who employed the power of the state to accomplish this. Hitler once declared in a speech on November 6, 1933;

> *When an opponent declares, 'I will not come over to your side,' I calmly say, 'Your child belongs to us already. . . . What are you? You will pass on. Your descendants, however, now stand in the new camp. In a short time they will know nothing else but this new community.'* [18]

After coming to power, one of Hitler's first priorities was to take complete control of Germany's educational systems and promote aggressive Nazi indoctrination programs such as the Hitler Youth. [19] Under the Nazis, heavy emphasis was placed on the idea of the "Aryan Supremacy" of the German people and the racial superiority of white, blond-haired, blue-eyed Germans. Extermination programs were implemented to "cleanse" German blood of "defective" genetic material. When the Nazis came to power, mentally challenged people, the insane, and eventually certain people groups such as Gypsies, homosexuals, Christians, and Jews were marked out for elimination.

What resulted from these horrendous ideas entering the educational system in Germany? It was the implementation of extermination policies such as Hitler's "Final Solution" to the "Jewish question."

Are Your Children being Brainwashed?
At the risk of offending some of my friends, I'm compelled to say some hard things here. I'm always amazed to see Christian parents mindlessly sending their children off to public schools and universities where secular Christophobic bigots do their level-best to brainwash their students into humanism and atheism. Later, many of these same parents weep and lament that their precious little Muffy or Buffy came home from High School, college or university *rejecting* Christianity and mocking their parents for being so backward and superstitious. There are, of course, exceptions to this outcome, but they are rare. It just breaks my heart.

According to George Barna, widely regarded as an expert on trends in Christianity, the vast majority of children post-teens, abandon the faith.

> *In fact, the most potent data regarding disengagement is that a majority of twentysomethings – 61% of today's young adults – had been churched at one point during their teen years but they are now spiritually disengaged (i.e., not actively attending church, reading the Bible, or praying). Only*

one-fifth of twentysomethings (20%) have maintained a level of spiritual activity consistent with their high school experiences. [20]

Another Barna analysis shares these alarming thoughts:

84% of Christian 18- to 29-year-olds admit that they have no idea how the Bible applies to their field or professional interests. [21]

As a pastor for nearly 30 years, I can't count the times I've sat with Christian parents as they wept over their children using drugs, engaging in sex outside of marriage, or "coming out" as a homosexual or lesbian. Most of these parents unwisely sent their children to public schools or liberal colleges or universities only to discover the damage later. What could I tell these parents at that point? How could I tell them after the fact that they were foolish for even *darkening the doors* of secular/socialist brainwashing institutions with the bodies and minds of their precious children?

Why is it so *difficult* for people to understand that professors and teachers with liberal/humanist agendas are *not* unbiased, neutral parties? Such people are in rebellion against a God they inwardly *know* exists, but refuse to acknowledge, and they *despise* Him! I stand by this assertion no matter how outwardly "polite" or "spiritual" an unregenerate person may appear outwardly. Like all of us before regeneration in Christ, they have an "inner beast" that cannot be denied. If pressured by the "full moon" of confrontation with the truth-claims of Christ, their "inner beast" will *act out*. I speak from personal experience before God mercifully set me free from slavery to my own "inner beast."

Secular Christophobic bigots project their venom for God by attacking Christian kids, seeking to destroy their innocence and faith. Students are commonly pressured to be "inclusive" and "open-minded" about their sexuality and are encouraged to "explore" their "gender identity." This poison pill is usually coated with pretenses of "compassion" and "tolerance" toward "all people" and their diverse "beliefs." In this vein, young people are told that biblical morality is mean-spirited and "intolerant" hate speech.

If a Christian student ever *dares* to express an opinion that sex outside of marriage or homosexuality is immoral, they can expect to be demonized, mocked, and harangued not only by their teachers but by their fellow students as well. Perhaps the most despised "mother" of all "intolerant" doctrines of biblical Christianity is the core teaching that salvation can be found only in Jesus Christ according to Acts 4:12;

> *Neither is there salvation in any other:*
> *for among men there is given*
> *none other Name under heaven,*
> *whereby we must be saved.*

I'm tired of hearing arguments like; "but *our* public school is *different*, and some of the teachers are even *Christians!*" That may be so, but whatever faith in Christ a teacher (or Principal) may hold, it is hazardous to their continued employment to express their beliefs in the public school setting. Across the country in recent years, Christian teachers have endured reprimands and threats of dismissal for even *displaying* a copy of the Bible in their classroom, or quietly reading it during their break times where others can observe. Christians need to WAKE UP to the culture war raging against their children. We need to stop being naive about this battle and realize that there is no place to hide from it.

I found the following quote from a high school principal who survived a Nazi concentration camp. I cannot give attribution because the author is anonymous. It gives us all a sober warning.

> *Dear teachers,*
> *I am the survivor of a concentration camp.*
> *My eyes saw what no man should witness*
> *—gas chambers built by learned engineers,*
> *children poisoned by educated physicians,*
> *infants killed by trained nurses,*
> *women and babies shot and burned*
> *by high school and college students.*
> *So I am suspicious of education.*
> *My request is; help your students become humane.*
> *Your efforts must never produce learned monsters,*
> *skilled psychopaths, educated Eichmanns.*
> *Reading, writing, arithmetic are important*
> *only if they serve to make our children more humane.*

The process of education is extremely influential in the formation of the values and ethical framework of society. It informs or "forms inwardly" the basic worldview and assumptions regarding the value of life in the minds and hearts of youth. It must be treated with extreme care if it is to "make our children more humane." This is the best argument for the formation of private, Bible-based Christian schools that are independent of outside government or political interference. The exponential increase of private and homeschool education gives evidence to the fact that many Americans are awakening to how far the progressives' "Long March" through our public education systems has come.

We are now confronted with a push by the secular progressives in government to implement the "Common Core" curriculum throughout the education system of America. It should come as no surprise that this represents the most dangerous form of tyranny... the brainwashing of our children into a New World Order and socialist nightmare. [22]

Prepped For Tyranny?

It is comical in a pathetic way to watch recent "man on the street" video polls of college students. Many of them cannot even identify who America fought against in the Revolutionary War, or who the first President of the United States was. The general ignorance is so pervasive that many young adults couldn't even identify who the Vice President is. Many others were willing to sign petitions to put Karl Marx on the next Presidential ballot [23] or repeal the Bill of Rights [24] to help Obama promote his programs for America. Shockingly, a vast majority of people were more than happy to sign-on to such petitions!

Dr. A.A. Hodge, Theologian, and Principle of Princeton Seminary, wrote the following 130 years ago. His words ring as true today as they did then:

> *I am sure as I am of the fact of Christ's reign that a comprehensive and centralized system of national education separated from religion...will prove the most appalling engineery for the propagation of anti-Christian and atheistic unbelief, and of anti-social, nihilistic ethics, individual, social, and political, which this sin-rent world has ever seen.*

Americans living around the late 1700s were far more literate and educated due to the excellent elementary and secondary schools of the time. An "inconvenient truth" for secular Christophobic bigots is the fact that these excellent schools were established primarily by Calvinist and Puritan Christians who valued quality education and regarded the task a holy duty to future generations.

President Abraham Lincoln said it best:

> *I am a firm believer in the people. If given the truth, they can be depended upon to meet any national crisis. The great point is to bring them the real facts.*

Like Lincoln, I'm also convinced that given accurate information, the American people can face and overcome our national problems and re-establish our constitutional foundations. However, unless we are successful in fighting and winning the battle for our nation's schools, all will be lost.

Evil is very real, and it plays hardball. Sometimes it comes in the form of a psychopath attacking children in a school. In its more blatant manifestations, it manifests as abortionists who rip millions of babies to bits and sucks them from their mother's wombs. Recently it came to light that the body parts of these murdered children were being sold to laboratories yielding enormous profits for the abortionists. They get away with this only so long as the general population is ignorant. However, people armed with truthful information will eventually triumph over evil with God's providential help.

The public education system in America does not appear to be focused on equipping students to be great mathematicians, engineers, physicists, philosophers, statesmen, executives, architects, medical healers, or skilled artisans, constructors, or even (gasp) theologians. Instead, they seem to be focused on job security for teachers, the bloated salaries of administrators, and unsurpassed retirement benefits. The other objective is secular social engineering, conforming students to think "correctly" about a plethora of pet progressive-liberal "causes." Their wish-list is long and includes such issues as "global warming," "saving the Earth," and "social justice."

All of this is meant to bring about some form of secular/socialist global "utopia" led by elites who govern pragmatically without any moral or ethical reference other than their imaginations. "Right" and "wrong," "true" or "false" must conform to what is "politically correct" according to these elitists. For this fantasy to work, ordinary people must become ignorant "sheeple." The pathetically inadequate secular education system is cranking out new "sheeple" as quickly as your hard-earned tax dollars can pay for them. Perhaps even more ominously, these progressive "sheeple" are registered to vote, (even after they die.)

Notes

1. Not safe to display American flag in American high school. Washington Post, February 27, 2014 By Eugene Volokh. http://www.washingtonpost.com/news/volokh-conspiracy/wp/2014/02/27/not-safe-to-display-american-flag-in-american-high-school/

2. Supreme Court turns down American flag ban case March 30, 2015, by Scott Bomboy, Constitution Daily, http://blog.constitutioncenter.org/2015/03/will-supreme-court-take-american-flag-ban-case/

3. York school changes American flag policy after demonstration. Student protest prompts flag policy change By Rachel Rollar, WCNC, May 14, 2015 http://www.wcnc.com/story/news/local/2015/05/14/york-teen-told-to-remove-american-flag-from-vehicle-due-to-school-policy/27289405/

4. 11 Facts You Might Not Know about Kung Fu. Neatorama by John Farrier Thursday, August 18, 2011 http://www.neatorama.com/2011/08/18/11-facts-you-might-not-know-about-kung-fu/

5. The War Against Boys: How Misguided Feminism Is Harming Our Young Men By Christina Hoff Sommers, Simon & Schuster. 251 pp. Book Review for the Washington Post, Sunday, July 2, 2000, by E. Anthony Rotundo, author of American Manhood: Transformations in Masculinity from the Revolution to the Modern Era. http://www.washingtonpost.com/wp-srv/style/books/reviews/waragainstboys0703.htm

6. The Drugging of the American Boy, Esquire Magazine, March 27, 2014 http://www.esquire.com/news-politics/a32858/drugging-of-the-american-boy-0414/

7. The Drugging of Our Children In Public Schools http://www.apfn.org/apfn/drugging_children.htm

8. The Surprising History of the Lobotomy, By Margarita Tartakovsky, M.S., World of Psychology http://psychcentral.com/blog/archives/2011/03/21/the-surprising-history-of-the-lobotomy/

9. Secular Humanists Give Dunphy Another Platform http://www.eagleforum.org/educate/1995/nov95/dunphy.html

10. International Socialist Review (Vol. 21, No. 1), Full article available at: https://www.marxists.org/archive/novack/works/1960/x03.htm

11. An Oration on Liberal Studies, By Dr. Orestes Augustus Brownson, L.L.D., delivered before the Philomathian Society of Mount Saint Mary's College, MD, on June 29th, 1853 Ref: http://tinyurl.com/nvm5xja

12. Eugenic Sterilization Laws. Paul Lombardo, University of Virginia http://www.eugenicsarchive.org/html/eugenics/essay8text.html

13. 10-Eye-Opening Quotes From Planned Parenthood Founder Margaret Sanger. Opinion, Lauren Enriquez, March 11, 2013. http://tinyurl.com/b5yu2mw

14. Margaret Sanger's December 19, 1939 letter to Dr. Clarence Gamble, 255 Adams Street, Milton, Massachusetts.

15. http://www.lifenews.com/2012/10/16/79-of-planned-parenthood-abortion-clinics-target-blacks-hispanics/

16. Rebekah Hebbert, "Heroine of human dignity: Mildred Fay Jefferson", Sunday, 12th December 2010 http://bit.ly/i8oP6Z.

17. Alveda King, "How Can the Dream Survive if We Murder Our Children?" http://www.silentnomoreawareness.org/testimonies/alveda-king.html, accessed on January 12, 2011.

18. William Shirer, Rise and Fall of the Third Reich New York: Simon and Schuster, 1960), 249.

19. How did the Nazis control education? From, The Holocaust Explained http://tinyurl.com/k29t6xc

20. Most Twentysomethings Put Christianity on the Shelf Following Spiritually Active Teen Years, September 11, 2006, The Barna Group http://tinyurl.com/nyoxj83

21. Barna Group Research http://tinyurl.com/l73kn5v

22. Common Core Curriculum: A Look Behind the Curtain of Hidden Language, By Rachel Alexander, Christian Post Op-Ed Contributor, March 18, 2013 Full Article at http://tinyurl.com/n5jk4lz

23. Communist Karl Marx Endorsed by Obama as the Next President? [Trolling Obama Supporters] Mark Dice, September 9, 2013, http://tinyurl.com/mnuuyxa

24. Obama Supporters Sign Petition to Repeal the BILL OF RIGHTS to Support the President http://tinyurl.com/pb565za

11

A War on "Terror?"

*War must be while we defend our lives
against a destroyer who would devour all;
but I do not love the bright sword for its sharpness,
nor the arrow for its swiftness, nor the warrior for his glory.
I love only that which they defend.*
J.R.R. Tolkien, The Two Towers
~~~~~~

After the 9/11 attack, we struggled to understand what happened and tried to get a handle on how to respond. In the first weeks, we were mostly focused on immediate response efforts. The entire event shocked and threatened to overwhelm us. It began to dawn on most people that we were at war with someone, but no one seemed to know for sure who we were fighting. We also didn't know where we were supposed to meet the enemy, or even how we might recognize victory.

Because of the growing insanity of "political correctness," most government officials and media pundits could not then, nor can they now, bring themselves to openly admit who or what we are fighting. For some strange reason, no one dared publicly acknowledge that Qu'ran-observant Islam was at fault. Islam clearly enjoys a privileged "protected status" among the media and leftist-progressives on nearly every level. Among them, the tag of "Islamophobe" is almost as dreaded as that of being called a "racist," and people on the left seem to live in terror of being accused of either.

Ironically, there doesn't appear to be the slightest hesitation on the part of liberal progressives to accuse, slander, and even openly attack Jews or Christians. This is partly because they know we will not capture and behead them, or form mobs in the street to burn their businesses or turn over their cars. They *also* know we will not strap on suicide bomb vests and blow them up. However, when a terrorist attack is either attempted or perpetrated by an Allah-praising Islamist, liberals go apoplectic in their efforts to defend the so-called "religion of peace." Never mind that there is little or no evidence that anything *remotely* approximating "peace" is discoverable within this murderous cult. It almost seems as if the subject of Islam is where rationality and common sense go to die.

Intolerant "Tolerance."

Ever since 9/11, we've been fed a steady barrage of "tolerance" exhortations. It is now a virtual "thought-crime" to even *imagine* that members of the "religion of peace" might bear some responsibility for acts of terrorism. It appears the Islamists, who constantly hammer people around the world with horrendous acts of barbaric murder, rape, torture, and beheadings failed to get that "religion of peace" memo. Does anyone else get the feeling that we are all being given the "mushroom treatment?" (If you haven't heard that expression before, it simply means "to be left in the dark, and fed BS.")

Under the Obama Administration, those who sought to expose the true agenda of Qu'ranicly-observant Islam came under threats by the United States Attorney General. Here is a recent quote from Rush Limbaugh.

> *Loretta Lynch…The attorney general promising to prosecute anyone who criticizes Islam. Anybody who criticizes the religion of peace will be called an Islamophobe, and she has threatened prosecution. Can you imagine the attorney general the United States threatening to prosecute anybody for criticizing Christianity, folks?* [1]

In the weeks following 9/11, President Bush wasted no time in making high-profile visits to mosques where he gave tearful impassioned speeches to the American people that Islam is a "religion of peace." One might suppose he was worried that ordinary Americans might angrily take to the streets in vigilante mobs with torches and pitchforks to burn down mosques and the homes of Muslims in acts of xenophobic hatred and rage. This whole idea was ridiculous on its face, for quite the opposite happened. With few and rare exceptions, most Americans reacted with patience, understanding, and even kindness toward their Muslim neighbors and co-workers, and indeed *had* done so long before any politician told them they ought to.By way of contrast, try to imagine what would have happened if a group of Jesus-praising Christians did the same thing in an Islamic country. It's safe to assume that there would be worldwide riots by Islamists and tens of thousands of innocent Christians and Jews around the world would be slaughtered, and their homes and businesses burned to the ground by raging mobs of Islamic zombies. There could be no calculating the widespread, violent riots, murder, and mayhem that would result.

In America, many Muslims nearly died of a "kindness and tolerance" overdose after 9/11. Across the nation, Imams and Islamic spokespersons were invited to large civic and church gatherings where they enjoyed near-rockstar status. There were no anti-Muslim riots or demonstrations in the streets. There were no credible reports of the burning of Muslim homes or businesses by mobs of angry Christians. I heard of only a few acts of violence, but in each and every case, these were done by the KKK, or Nazi white supremacists. No Christian or Jewish groups were *ever* proven to attack Moslems.

As the "Islamo-love-fest" went on, I almost expected some liberal group to issue a letter of apology to the "Islamic Community." I wouldn't have been surprised if they apologized for the way those evil xenophobic, islamophobic Twin Towers maliciously jumped in front of those peacefully hijacked aircraft piloted by pious Muslims who were just seeking to practice their "religion of peace."

In recent times, we have seen the latest roll-out of Islamo-fascism in the form of ISIS brutality. Christian men, women and even little children are being rounded up, sexually abused, tortured, and beheaded by Allah-praising Islamists. Little girls are being kidnaped and either sold into sex slavery or forced into marriages to pedophile Islamo-perverts two or three times their age. Other little girls suffer genital mutilation, and if they try to attend school, in many places throughout the Islamic world, they have acid thrown in their faces. These outrages are all done in full obedience to the teachings and example of their prophet Mohammed, whose teachings condoned their vicious brutality for all the world to see.

Just imagine how Muslims would react if Christians began capturing Muslims, smeared them with pig fat, and beheaded them in the name of Christ! Imagine the Islamic reaction if "infidels" (their word for non-Muslims) began kidnapping little Muslim girls and subjecting them to the same humiliating sexual degradation and horrors as is being done to Christian children by "religion of peace" practitioners.

Obviously, such "tit for tat" is *never* going to happen because Christ commanded *His* followers to "love" their enemies, and do good to those who hate and abuse them. This grace does not imply that Christians must be mindlessly pacifist in the face of evil tyranny, whether religious or secular. There are circumstances when we are to defend the helpless and stand up to the advance of evil. It is supremely ironic that leftist-liberals never miss an opportunity to slander and harshly criticize Christians, and yet turn a blind eye to the vicious crimes committed by Islam without any sense of outrage. I often wonder if liberal progressives could find reality with both hands and a flashlight!

At the same time that he was making excuses for Islam, President Bush was beating the drums of war and mobilizing the country for a "war on terror." Now, for anyone with more than a room-temperature IQ, this seems almost laugh-out-loud funny. For a thinking person, this appears to be an act of political schizophrenia and political correctness unparalleled in American history. Given the asinine pronouncements by many in our present government employ, I sometimes wonder how much male bovine excrement the American people can endure.

A War on "Terror?"

When I first heard President Bush declare a "war on terror," my head almost spun around in disbelief. A *"war on TERROR?"* Try to imagine how Americans might have reacted after the Pearl Harbor attack if President Roosevelt had asked Congress to declare war on "sneak attacks." Americans didn't go to war in 1941 to fight against a tactic of war! We declared war on the nation that utilized that strategy; the Imperial Japanese. The war was against a country and people, not a tactic of war. We knew who we were, and we knew our enemy. It is essential that wars be prosecuted with extreme care and clearly defined goals, achievable objectives, and a laser-like focus on exactly WHO the war is directed against. As the ancient Chinese General Sun Tzu (544 BC to 496 BC) wisely observed in his book, *The Art of War;*

> *If you know the enemy and know yourself,*
> *you need not fear the result of a hundred battles.*
> *If you know yourself but not the enemy,*
> *for every victory gained you will also suffer a defeat.*
> *If you know neither the enemy nor yourself,*
> *you will succumb in every battle.*

The America of the 1940s did not need to fear the result of "a hundred battles," because they knew who they were fighting, and had a clear grasp on their identity. This mindset made the outcome of the war inevitable. The United States was going to win that war, come hell or high water.

War is an ugly, vulgar, unspeakable evil. I know this because I experienced it first-hand during my 18-month tour of duty in Vietnam. Most modern, civilized people—who are at least acquainted with Judeo-Christian concepts of tolerance, mercy, forgiveness, morality, and ethics—*hate* war. We are the least likely people to declare war on others without explicit provocation. The Ten Commandments God delivered to Moses, coupled with the teachings and example of Jesus, are bright beacons of life and truth, serving to suppress the depraved nature of men. Wherever Judeo-Christian ethics and teachings have taken root in nations around the world, their influence has inspired people toward calmer, saner, humane and just societies. I do not say they have *ever* been perfect societies, for such has never existed in all of human history owing to the fact that imperfect humans have an innate talent for screwing things up.

It is also a fact that not all who profess belief in the God of Christianity actually *do* believe the teachings of Scripture and often use religion as a cloak for their evil deeds. (The concept of "wolves in sheep's clothing" comes to mind.) I touched on this in the last chapter, but throughout history, wicked men who falsely claimed faith in Christ have brought significant damage and shame to the reputation of Christianity. I'm going to offend some of my Catholic friends and relatives here, but this cannot be helped. The well-documented history of the Roman Church is a prime example. According to credible sources, upwards of *100 million people* were slaughtered without mercy by the Papacy in over 605 years of persecution during the Inquisition simply for the crime of disagreeing with the Pope. [2]

The vast majority of Rome's victims were Scripture-believing Catholics who sought reforms in their church because of her corruption, immorality, greed, and departure from biblical faith and practice. Regrettably, most non-Christians automatically associate Christianity at large with the egregious atrocities committed by Rome. Of course, no one has *ever* practiced Christ's teachings perfectly, but wherever biblical practices are sincerely and faithfully practiced, their influence tempers the natural tendency of humanity toward brutality and barbarism. As Edmund Burke once opined;

> *There is no safety for honest men*
> *except by believing all possible evil of evil men.*

Fallen humanity naturally gravitates toward the fanciful delusion that "deep down inside," all men are basically good, and only require understanding, persuasion, and inspiration. We tend to project this foolish notion of innate "goodness" upon each other because it's just too painful to imagine that it isn't true of ourselves. The biblical truth, however, is there is *no one* who is "good" except God.

> *Jesus said to him,*
> *Why callest thou me good?*
> *There is none good but one, even God.*
> Mark 10:18

Inside each unregenerate person—thanks to Adam's rebellion—there's an "inner beast" trying to get out. Most people, through childhood training and parental discipline, manage to suppress the worst characteristics of that inner beast, but it's always there. Lurking just beneath the outward "Have a nice day" happy-face smile, the beast within awaits an opportunity to emerge. Our "inner beast" will inevitably appear under the influence of a "full moon" of unsuppressed anger and rage, stressful or painful circumstances or the temptation to lust for power and control. Most people despise this message, for it strips them of the vain facade of "goodness" we all try to project on each other. The unvarnished truth is vile to unregenerate people. The reality of the "inner beast" is the reason we have locks on our doors, bank vaults for our money, and passwords on our accounts. This is why we pay vast sums of money to hire and train police. This is why we tell our children not to talk to strangers, or go anywhere with them. It's why we look over our shoulder while walking darkened streets at night. We *all* know the truth, but we're loath to admit it. There be monsters in our midst, and but for the grace of God, *we ourselves are the monsters we fear.*

This is also why we have a Department of Defense, with guns, bombs, fighter planes, and terrible weapons of mass destruction at ready to pacify and persuade the inner beast in other people living in other nations to behave themselves. History teaches us over and over that displaying weakness and vulnerability before depraved human monsters are an invitation to violence and disaster. Anyone who denies this is living in a make-believe fantasy.

In this present fallen world, wars are sometimes necessary. This is an irrefutable fact of history because there has always been evil, twisted men in the world who care nothing at all for mercy, love, and forgiveness. They will stop at *nothing* to control and dominate others whenever they perceive weakness in their intended victims. Those who naively believe that showing weakness and vulnerability before such monsters will somehow appease and inspire them toward unselfish altruism and goodness are fools or Utopian dreamers. Again, weakness has never, in all of human history, secured peace. It only invites aggression.

Enemies Within the Gates

Within our borders, there are many who hate America and wish to see our republic destroyed. To our credit, Americans tend to be astonishingly tolerant—if not downright naive—about the vitriol and open hatred expressed so freely by hateful racist cretins in our midst. In the minds of many, the "Minister" Louis Farrakhan, who heads the Nation of Islam, stands as a prime example. No other nation in world history would be as tolerant of his raging bigotry. This so-called "minister" once said;

> *God will not give Japan or Europe the honor of bringing down the U.S.; this is an honor God will bestow upon Muslims.*

In a more recent rant, the "minister" made the following seditious statement calling for the slaughter of white people. The following is a quote;

> *I'm looking for 10,000 in the midst of a million. Ten thousand fearless men who say death is sweeter than continued life under tyranny... ...So if the federal government won't intercede in our affairs, then we must rise up and kill those who kill us; stalk them and kill them and let them feel the pain of death that we are feeling!* [3]

This is but one example of this man's outrageous incitements to violence. In recent months we have seen an alarming increase in violence against police officers who were ambushed and murdered by some of Farrakhan's protégés.

Another "minister," Rev. Jeremiah Wright, served as Barack Hussein Obama's pastor for over two decades, performed his marriage ceremony, and baptized his children. Wright ranted freely of his hatred and condemnation of America in a sermon in 2003 in which he said:

> *God DAMN America, that's in the Bible for killing innocent people. God DAMN America for treating our citizens as less than human. God DAMN America for as long as she acts like she is God and she is supreme.* [4]

Arguably, these statements could easily be seen as treason. However, let me be clear, I am not suggesting that these "Ministers" should be arrested, or in any way forcibly constrained to stop expressing their views and opinions. Their right to free speech (which freedom they would foolishly misuse to destroy that very freedom) are a constitutionally protected freedom that all citizens possess equally. However, their freedom to express such vile nonsense does not mean their views should go *unchallenged*. Our free speech rights also allow us the freedom to expose, criticize, discredit, and drown out their hatred and venom in the public marketplace of ideas and dialogue. The deplorable reality, however, is that our brainwashed press and media routinely ignore or excuse such racists because of a twisted concept of "social justice" and a fear of being seen as "politically incorrect" or worse, as racists themselves. Another example of American self-hatred is personified by the Westboro Baptist Church in Kansas. This group pickets the funerals of fallen soldiers and inflict vicious sorrow and pain on grieving military families. Whatever "truth" they might possess is deeply buried under the weight of cruel, mean-spirited insensitivity to people. Our constitution guarantees their right to do what they do, but again, it also guarantees our right to criticize and denounce their activities.

This is the incredible dichotomy of America. We guarantee the right of all our citizens to express their opinions, and we reserve the right to engage the content of their speech and crush it in the court of public opinion without violence through reasoned discourse.

The danger we face, however, is an emerging idea—especially within academia and the media—called, "political correctness." Under this rubric, only "approved" thoughts and ideas are allowed expression. Freedom of speech is increasingly banned and censored if it doesn't fit the "party line." Those on the left have lost all sense of civil discourse and often resort to violent confrontations and vulgar shout-downs and disruptions of speeches by people not toeing the leftist party line.

War IS Declared

For example, it is "politically incorrect" to openly admit that war has been declared upon the United States by Islam. Never mind that Islam is a quasi-religious fascist ideology of aggressive hatred and violence, against women, children, homosexuals, and leftist ideologues. Liberal progressives seem to have a large blind spot regarding Islam. It is a factual reality that in all countries where Islamic influence is strong, and sharia law is established, *every one* of their liberal opinions are banned, and those holding them are imprisoned or killed.

Certainly, it is true, (as it is often said) that "not all Muslims are terrorists." However, it must also be acknowledged that nearly every act of barbarous terrorism in recent decades has been committed by Islamists. One might also argue that not all Germans during World War II were Nazis, but that did not prevent the prosecution of the war against the entire country of Germany while it was in the grips of the Nazis. It is a well-established fact that many German citizens hated Hitler and despised the Nazi Party, and in some cases worked actively in secret to overthrow the evil in their midst.

Islam is an ideology that masquerades as a religion and employs terrorism as a tactic of war. The Islamic nation, (referred to as the "ummah," or "nation of believers" by Islamists) is manifestly NOT (and never has been) a "religion of peace" as progressive political pundits like to chant incessantly.

Any honest person who reads the Qur'an and the teachings of the Hadith will recognize immediately that those who faithfully and diligently follow and obey the teachings MUST become a jihadist. The personal example of their prophet Muhammad only reinforces this truth. Moslems are commanded to conquer the entire Earth and forcefully impose their beliefs and practices on every man, woman, and child. Islam's teachings forbid any "peaceful coexistence" with other belief systems no matter what Islamic apologists try to say. The Qur'an fundamentally rejects any such notion. Under sharia (Islamic) law, you have three choices. You either must convert to Islam, or come under the status of dhimmitude, (conquered state, enslavement, and subjugation) or, refusing these two options, be put to death. The teachings of Islam are very clear on this.

"Smiley Face" Deception

Islamists often smile and tell non-Muslims the above is untrue when confronted. We must recognize that this deception is part of Islamic teaching regarding the permissible practice of lying to non-Muslims called Taqiyya ("al-Taqiyya"). This doctrine, found in Qur'an 3:28 is the Muslims' license to lie to infidels to disguise Islam's holy war strategy (jihad) to conquer the world. The general interpretation of this sura was given by the Islamic scholar, "Al-Bukhari" who opined:

> *We [muslims] smile in the face of some people [non-muslims] although our hearts curse them.*

It's hard to estimate the total number of people killed by Islam, but a rough estimate of 270 million is close. According to a well-footnoted article, written March 3, 2008, by Bill Warner, on his Tears of Jihad blog, this total is comprised of 120 million Africans, 60 million Christians, 80 million Hindus, and 10 million Buddhists. [5]

The Qur'an contains at least 109 verses that call Muslims to war with nonbelievers for the sake of Islam. They include graphic commands to cut off heads and fingers and murder infidels wherever they might be found. Here are just a few examples. (All translations are from the Noble Qur'an)

> Sura (2:191-193) – *And kill them wherever you find them, and turn them out from where they have turned you out. And Al-Fitnah [disbelief or unrest] is worse than killing... but if they desist, then lo! Allah is forgiving and merciful. And fight them until there is no more Fitnah [disbelief and worshiping of others along with Allah] and worship is for Allah alone. But if they cease, let there be no transgression except against Az-Zalimun (the polytheists, and wrong-doers, etc.)*
>
> Sura (4:74) – *Let those fight in the way of Allah who sell the life of this world for the other. Whoso fighteth in the way of Allah, be he slain or be he victorious, on him We shall bestow a vast reward.*

This fallacy is the theological rationale and justification for today's suicide bombers.

> Sura (8:12) – I *will cast terror into the hearts of those who disbelieve. Therefore strike off their heads and strike off every fingertip of them.*

No reasonable person could rationally interpret the above verse to mean only "a spiritual struggle" as some Islamic apologists falsely claim.

> Sura (9:29) – *Fight those who believe not in Allah nor the Last Day, nor hold that forbidden which hath been forbidden by Allah and His Messenger, nor acknowledge the religion of Truth, (even if they are) of the People of the Book, until they pay the Jizya with willing submission, and feel themselves subdued.*
>
> "People of the Book" refers to Christians and Jews.

Any willingness for "peaceful coexistence" exhibited by Islamists as they infiltrate a host nation is a deception and only temporary. Temporary peace is one of a number of tactics employed by Islamists until they gain enough numeric influence through rampant procreation, or political power to overthrow and dominate the countries and societies they infiltrate.

Of course, the objection will immediately arise; "What about all the peaceful Muslims who desire to live in harmony within non-Muslim communities?" To this, I would answer, just as there are Christians and Jews who claim to be followers of their respective faiths, and yet disobey the teachings of Jesus and Moses, so it is with Muslims. Some pick and choose what portions of the Qur'an and Hadith to obey, and are therefore "peaceful" as long as they ignore the clear teachings of Islam to participate in jihad. However, I maintain that a sincere and faithful Islamist, who actually obeys the explicit teachings of Muhammad, MUST become a jihadist warrior against non-Muslims.

So-called "moderate" Muslims within societies often employ a strategy of passive aggression by putting pressure on governments, businesses, and schools to adopt halal Islamic dietary standards. This includes pressure to observe Islamic "Holy Days" and establish mosques within private and public schools to accommodate Muslim students. In the last decade, local communities have received demands that they adopt Islamic Sharia law into our courts and legal systems. It is a creeping strategy to make Western countries more Islamicized.

As John Dawson, a business person and freelance writer from Melbourne Australia said;

> *The indecision and paralysis engendered by moral relativism, coupled with the appeasement and self-sacrifice engendered by altruism, is suicidal. If America does not throw off these moral chains, it will continue to be the prey of the Baby Kims, Ayatollahs, Arafats and bin Ladens of the world. Just as an individual must act unapologetically to preserve his life, so must America.* [6]

We are *indeed* at war against Qur'an-observant Islam. This is because Qur'anically-obedient Muslims are, and have repeatedly declared that they are, at war with us. Qur'anically-obedient Muslims *cannot* faithfully follow the teachings of their "prophet" without imposing by force their beliefs and practices on everyone else. The "peaceful" Moslems we often hear about are hated and resented by their radicalized obedient fellow Muslims as worse than infidels (non-Muslims) and apostates worthy of death. These so-called "moderates" are suffering wholesale slaughter by their more radical brethren all over the Middle East. Unless we admit this reality and confront it appropriately, we will be conquered and enslaved—or dead.

America's First War Against Islam

It is interesting to note that America's first war on foreign soil was fought in 1801 by President Thomas Jefferson against the Barbary Islamist pirates in the Mediterranean. For years, Islamic pirates attacked American merchant ships, taking their crews as ransom captives, forced converts, or slaves. Since 1784, the US Congress had taken the same path of appeasement as most of Europe, paying the demanded ransoms as their ships and crews were increasingly captured and pillaged.

114   Destroying the Shadow Agenda

Two years later in 1786, while serving as an Ambassador for the new United States, Jefferson, accompanied by John Adams, met with Tripoli's Ambassador to Great Britain, Sidi Haji Abdul Rahman Adja. He asked the Ambassador to justify why the Barbary states felt they had the right to kidnap and slaughter the innocent crews of American merchant ships.

> *The Ambassador informed Jefferson that Islam "was founded on the Laws of their Prophet, that it was written in their Qur'an, that all nations who should not have acknowledged their authority were sinners, that it was their right and duty to make war upon them wherever they could be found, and to make slaves of all they could take as prisoners, and that every Musselman [Muslim] who should be slain in battle was sure to go to Paradise."* [7]

Jefferson never forgot Ambassador Adja's shocking statement. He even studied the Qur'an himself, to better understand the enemy his young nation was facing. For the next fifteen years, Congress obediently paid ransoms to these terrorists to free kidnaped American sailors who were undergoing cruel tortures and slavery at the hands of the Islamists. That is until Jefferson became President. The proverbial "straw that broke the camel's back" came when the Pasha of Tripoli sent a demand to President Jefferson for an immediate payment of $225,000. This sum would come to approximately $3,500,000 in today's dollars when adjusted for inflation. The Pasha then arrogantly demanded $25,000 per year after that which would be about $400,000 in today's dollars. Jefferson was outraged and refused to pay. The Pasha then ordered his jihadists to cut down the flagpole of the American consulate and foolishly declared war on the United States. The rest of the surrounding Islamic states then did the same. Does any of this sound familiar?

Unlike the former "occupier" of the White House, Barack Hussien Obama, President Jefferson did not go on an "apology tour," or try to appease the Islamists by sending them money and weapons. Well, I really must qualify that. Jefferson *did* send arms to Tripoli, but those weapons were carried aboard new U.S. naval warships in the capable hands of tough U.S. Marine Corps fighters who possessed a prodigious amount of Marine Corp "attitude." The Marine invasion into Tripoli is in fact where the stanza "...to the shores of Tripoli" originated in the U.S. Marine Corps battle hymn. These Marines were first called "Leathernecks" in this war. This term was due to the thick leather neck protection (body armor) they wore to protect themselves from fanatical Islamic fighters who kept trying to behead them with their scimitars. Again, does anything about this sound familiar?

These Marines majorly kicked Islamo-butt and *took names*. They slapped down and utterly defeated the Barbary pirates, and the piracy problem ended post-haste. American merchant ships could now sail unmolested on the high seas. President Jefferson demonstrated in the clearest way possible how a U.S. president should respond to international extortion and radical Islamic threats.

Hellooo, Hydra!
In Greek mythology, the Lernaean Hydra was a serpent-like water monster with many heads. It was described as having such bad breath (poisonous) that anyone inhaling it would die. Its blood was so diseased that even contact with its footprints was fatal. The big problem for Hercules (who killed the Hydra) was the fact that for each head he managed to hack off, two more would emerge from the stump. According to the myth, the only way Hercules finally defeated the Hydra was to cut off every single one of its heads. Hera, referred to in Greek Mythology as the "Queen of the Goddesses," then placed the Hydra into the heavens, and to this day, stargazers stare up in wonder at the constellation Hydra.

Mythology often serves to reveal insights into more profound truths, and the Hydra myth does this well. According to Scripture, the ultimate defeat of evil will occur only when God in Christ puts all His enemies under his feet. As it is written:

> *But this Man,*
> *after He had offered one sacrifice for sins forever,*
> *sat down at the right hand of God,*
> *from that time waiting*
> *till His enemies are made His footstool.*
> Hebrews 10:12-14 (NKJV) (Emphasis added.)

Until then, there will be evil manifestations of one kind or another. One of the major expressions of evil we are presently forced to deal with is Qur'anically obedient Islam. It is indeed a Hydra monster, for each time a head is cut off, two seem to grow back. The only way to defeat this monstrous cult is to follow the mythical Hercules' example and cut off ALL the heads of the monster. I'm not necessarily speaking in a literal sense, or advocating unprovoked violence against those souls who are presently captives of this evil cult. Armed resistance is appropriate only in the face of armed aggression. I'm speaking of the vicious and hateful Islamic leaders and educators who teach and promote violence and hatred of non-Muslims in the name of their religion. Radical Islam's ability to spread its offensive soul-poison must and eventually *will be* brought to utter ruin. They are on a losing team, and in bondage to a powerful, demonic spiritual deception. Only the power of the gospel and the grace of God moving upon their hearts can break this demonic hold on minds and hearts.

There are encouraging reports coming out of the Middle East recently of Moslems, and even radicalized ISIS fighters receiving dreams and visions of Jesus, and there appears to be a growing Christian underground church in such unlikely places as Iran. I fully expect more such reports in the coming years as the power of Christ sweeps away the darkness before His final appearing.

Notes

1. Obama's Attorney General Vows to Prosecute Anti-Muslim Speech December 04, 2015 http://goo.gl/dMdRqT

2. Estimates of the Number Killed by the Papacy in the Middle Ages and later, David A. Plaisted © 2006 http://www.cs.unc.edu/~plaisted/estimates.doc

3. LOUIS FARRAKHAN CONDEMNS AMERICA AND THE JEWS New York, NY, March 5, 1996 http://archive.adl.org/presrele/natisl_81/2686_81.html and http://www.breitbart.com/video/2015/08/04/farrakhan-we-must-rise-up-and-kill-those-who-kill-us-stalk-them-and-kill-them/

4. https://www.youtube.com/watch?v=Ix-AMYos0Js and http://tinyurl.com/lcucoxj

5. //www.politicalislam.com/tears-of-jihad/

6. Baby Kim's Ace in the Hole: Western Moralists by John Dawson, November 11, 2003 Capitalism Magazine, http://capitalismmagazine.com/2003/10/baby-kims-ace-in-the-hole-western-moralists/

7. America and the Barbary Pirates: An International Battle Against an Unconventional Foe, by Gerard W. Gawalt Library of Congress: http://memory.loc.gov/ammem/collections/jefferson_papers/mtjprece.html

12

A "Crash" Course

> First Officer:
> *What the hell are we into?*
> Captain:
> *We're stuck in it!*
> *Get out of it! Get out of it!*
> (Sound of impact)
> Last words:
> Pilots of AA Flt. 587
> November 12, 2001

~~~~~~

November 12, 2001, will be burned into my memory as long as I shall live. I've often thought back to that fateful day, and for a very long time afterward, my dreams were haunted by the disturbing sounds, smells, and images of what happened. While every day is an opportunity to serve and learn something, on this particular day, I stumbled into the equivalence of a graduate-level "crash course." Even after all these years, I'm still trying to sort it all out.

The previous weeks in New York were a grueling schedule of visits with the friends and families of fallen New York City firefighters, and I was utterly exhausted. It was time to leave, and I was more than ready to get "out of Dodge" and move on. The memories of the faces of the brokenhearted widows and surviving firefighters I'd spoken to filled my mind every waking hour. The stories of these families were nearly all the same. Ordinary lives mostly, of people raising children, pursuing careers, with hopes and dreams for a future; all destroyed on a single morning of unimaginable disaster on 9/11.

After checking in at JFK airport that morning for my flight bound for London, England, I collapsed into a window seat. This small space promised to be my little corner of solitude where I could lean back and catch some much-needed rest. I was looking forward to a busy speaking schedule in Wales and England over the next few weeks. JFK airport was unusually busy that morning with passenger traffic increasing daily following the 9/11 attack exactly two months and one day earlier. On that morning, I had my plans, but it soon became clear that God had more for me to do in New York City. Much, much more.

As our jet taxied out from the gate to Runway 31-Left, I settled back into my seat and tried to relax. The flight attendants prepared the cabin for takeoff with the usual safety announcements regarding emergency exits, flotation devices, and seatbelt demonstrations. Most seasoned travelers ignore these announcements, having heard them so many times. For some reason, I paid more attention than usual. We were, after all, flying over a vast ocean, and somehow the briefing seemed unusually important to me that day. Our aircraft's engines spooled up and down as we taxied forward a short distance, stopped, and waited in the queue for our turn to take to the active runway and depart.

As a pilot since the age of 16, I've always enjoyed watching airplanes. I like to imagine what the pilots are doing up on the flight deck as they maneuver their fantastic flying machines. By virtue of my commercial pilot certificate, I've sometimes enjoyed the privilege of riding the "jump-seat" up in the cockpits of several international flights over the years. This includes those from the Philippines, British, Singapore, and Aeroflot Airlines. I possess a fairly clear image in my mind of cockpit procedures.

From my right-side window, I passively watched a Japan Airlines 747 begin its takeoff roll down the runway with a loud roar. Glancing down at my watch, I noted with amazement that the time was precisely 9:11 A.M. "Weird coincidence," I softly mumbled to myself. "That number sure pops up a lot in my life," and then gave it no more thought.

Looking out of my right-side window just forward of the massive wing, I had a great view and casually watched an American Airlines Airbus A300 just in front of us taxi onto the active runway to takeoff position, and hold. After a few moments, the jet's engines spooled up with a loud rumble I could feel right through our aircraft's skin. The A300 roared down the runway and quickly gathered speed. Finally rotating, it gracefully lifted into the air. *Beautiful takeoff,* I thought to myself, as I watched the craft rise higher and higher into the clear morning sky, gently turn southeast, and fade into the distance. Everything seemed *perfectly* normal.

Our flight was now in number one position, and our aircraft's engines spooled up momentarily as we taxied slowly up to the hold line just short of the active runway. There we waited for the tower controller's clearance to take to the active and depart. Typically, this hold takes only a few minutes. However, we waited and waited longer. Minutes passed, and then more long minutes.

Somewhere in the back of my mind, a faint alarm began sounding. We'd been sitting in the number-one position awaiting takeoff clearance much longer than usual! The preceding flight departed many minutes before. Something started to feel terribly wrong, and my mind became hyper-alert.

Suddenly, the long silence was broken by our pilot's strained voice on the intercom. According to my best recollection, he said:

> *Ladies* and Gentlemen, this is your captain speaking from up on the flight deck.

Sitting up straight, I waited for his next words. I could sense this wasn't just a delayed flight announcement; the hair on the back of my neck bristled. Silence fell over the cabin as all conversations abruptly ceased. Everyone on board listened intently to the captain's next words:

> *Ladies and gentlemen, I'm afraid I have some very bad news. We've just been informed by Air Traffic Control that the aircraft departing just before us has crashed in Queens a few minutes ago.*

A collective gasp of shock and horror went through the cabin like a clap of thunder. Several passengers began sobbing, as others gasped in terror. The captain continued;

> *I regret to inform you that our departure has been canceled, and we are ordered back to the gate. The airspace over New York City has been closed, with all flights canceled until further notice. You will be able to retrieve your baggage inside the terminal and arrange for a later flight. Please feel free to use your cell phones to inform your friends and family.*

I felt as if someone had just punched me in the stomach, and I glanced around at the shocked faces of the other passengers. Everyone was staring at one another. The emotions in the cabin were palpable. I thought to myself, "Could this be another terrorist attack?" My mind was reeling!

The long taxi back to the terminal seemed to take forever as all aircraft on the taxiways, and those just landing had to work their way back to the now overcrowded gates. Finally arriving at the terminal, the doors opened, and we slowly disembarked. One flight attendant stared at the floor weeping as I walked past her toward the aircraft door. Pausing, I asked her if she was okay and patted her shoulder. She looked up with tears streaming down her face, streaking her makeup. "I'm all right I guess, but thanks for asking."

The scene back inside the terminal was chaotic. People were reacting to their flight cancelations in a variety of ways. Some appeared to be in various states of shock; others were venting anger at airline workers as if they were at fault that their flights were canceled. I saw a few people in apparent shock, waving their arms and shouting at no one in particular. Some others clustered in small groups hugging and crying.

A crowd of people was gathered near the south windows of the terminal gate, gazing toward the southwest, where black smoke could be seen rising into the pale blue morning sky across the bay in Rockaway Beach. Like September 11, the day began as a gorgeous, sunlit morning. Now, a feeling of dark foreboding stole away its promise.

Go to the Crash Site!

While taxiing back to the gate, I called my wife back in Colorado. The crash occurred at nearly the same time as my flight's scheduled take off—at the same airport. I feared she might be watching the news, and I wanted her to hear from me right away before learning of the accident on the news. The cell phone system was nearly overwhelmed with the volume of calls being made by people with the same idea, and it took several tries to get through. When we finally got a connection, I reassured her of my safety and told her what had happened. Amazingly, one of the first things she said was; "I believe you are to go to the crash site!"

She knows me so well; I thought she might say that. Her words confirmed what I already knew in my heart; I wanted to help. Although I still had my access credentials from the Office of Emergency Management and FEMA, there was little likelihood that I would be granted access to the site of a plane crash. Even so, I promised her I would make the effort. No doubt, at the site, there be a great need for encouragement and counselors for the rescuers and hopefully, survivors. In my heart, I already knew there would be none.

As soon as I could retrieve my bags and store them, I flagged down the first available taxi and instructed the driver to take me to Rockaway Beach. The cabbie turned and looked at me with astonishment. Incredulously he asked, "Didn't you hear about what just happened over there?" I showed him my FEMA badge. He shrugged, turned on the meter, and went for it.

While weaving through heavy morning traffic past the roadblocks being hastily set up by the police, we were waved through whenever I flashed my credentials. My cell phone rang again. A family friend in California hearing news of the crash in New York was calling to see if I was okay.

I told my friend what happened, and how my plane had taxied out just behind the one that crashed. She immediately said to me, "I believe God placed you there for a reason. I feel you should go to the crash site!" At this point, there seemed to be no use arguing. Besides, I had a certain inner sense that divine destiny had once again placed me in the middle of a situation with hurting people. I felt compelled to at least try to offer whatever assistance I could. Again recalling my old friend Wayne Myers' words; "God uses the available mud, son," and I decided to make my "mud" available once again.

Another Fiery Hell

As we drew nearer to the crash site, traffic became totally gridlocked. An ominous cloud of black smoke rose up from beyond the rows of houses. Cars were streaming out of Rockaway Beach, and police were turning all incoming traffic away except for emergency responders. When we came within about five blocks, the taxi could proceed no further, so I paid the cabbie, climbed out, and ran the rest of the way to the scene.

Putrid smoke assaulted my nostrils. Security was extremely tight, but my credentials got me waved through each checkpoint. A short time later, I found myself standing on the front porch of the house the jetliner fell on. All that remained of the house was the front doorstep, and an immense smoking crater fell away beyond the threshold where the house once stood.

The wreckage was strewn everywhere. Passenger seats—some still occupied by deceased passengers—were scattered throughout the debris. The house and several other adjacent homes were now reduced to a pile of rubble, charred black by fire. Barely anything recognizable remained.

A portion of the tail section of the aircraft lay upside-down across the street. Part of the landing gear was in a twisted pile of metal and burned tires. The smell of jet fuel and smoke mixed with the thick, billowing steam from the fire hoses spraying down the smoldering ruins. By the time I arrived, most of the fires were either extinguished or nearly under control. Hundreds of New York City firefighters were crawling around in the wreckage, desperately searching for any possible survivors. There were none to find on this day.

Strewn throughout the wreckage and up and down the street were hundreds of bodies. Even at the ruins of the World Trade Center, I hadn't seen this much carnage. At Ground Zero, human remains were mostly pulverized into the rubble. One could be walking unaware on bits and pieces of bodies mingled with the mud and debris. This scene, however, was off-scale grisly. Many have been the times I've wished the exposed film of my mind could be erased. I've searched in vain to discover some "reset button" that might somehow erase the images of the horrors I've gazed upon in my lifetime. By God's grace I, and all other responders on that terrible day would have to find a way to live with these memories until God mercifully removes them.

My heart broke for the responders there. Many of them—a few I recognized—had also worked the scene at the World Trade Center. "How much can these guys take?" I asked myself as I looked at their grim faces. It had been just two months and one day since the 9/11 attacks. Now this! These highly-trained responders were professionally doing their jobs, but I knew only too well the nightmares many would endure in the coming weeks, months, and years.

A firefighter stood next to me on the porch, shaking his head as he stared vacantly into the smoking crater in front of us. We both watched in silence as personnel, dressed in biohazard gear, gathered the dead into body bags and placed them on Stokes stretchers to remove them from the wreckage. One can hardly fathom the scars such gruesome duty leaves upon a human soul. I offered him a fresh bottle of water, and he nodded his thanks, screwed off the cap, and took a long swig from it. We wordlessly eyed each other for a few seconds, exchanging a depth of communication only those who have "been there" could ever understand. He looked like a combat veteran. I'd seen that look before on the faces of guys I served with in Vietnam while we huddled in bunkers during rocket and mortar attacks on our base. I could also see the tracks of tears on his gritty, smoke-stained face.

Finally breaking the silence, he waved his water bottle toward the smoking crater and said, "This is a neighborhood where a lot of police and firefighters live." I looked at him and nodded, silently encouraging him to continue. As a crisis counselor, I'd learned long ago that the best way to help a traumatized responder is to get them to talk about what they saw, what they heard, and how they felt. After taking another swig of water, he went on. "Thank God this happened after 9:00 AM. Most of the people living here were either at work or school." I agreed, and for several minutes, he shared his experiences at the scene—some of which were rather grisly—and I will not write of them. It was good for him to vent and process his experiences, though, and this is often just what is needed to help responders not internalize their emotional wounds, but get them out in the open. "Stuffing" emotional trauma can lead to Post Traumatic Stress Syndrome and negatively impact their lives even years later.

I spent most of the day talking one-on-one with many of these people during rotation break times, encouraging and listening to them. I was stealthily "defusing" and drawing out their pain, anger, and the poisonous toxicity of that terrible scene. Sometimes I would offer a prayer but always provided encouragement and solace. I prayed for them—for their families, friends, and for the loved ones of the crash victims. Experience gained before 9/11 and reinforced during my weeks at Ground Zero taught me that during a crisis, the most effective means of helping rescuers and responders is a "ministry of presence." Few words are far better than many (or in some cases, any).

Later I would learn that 260 passengers and crew onboard the airplane perished in the crash, with five people on the ground killed. The small number of casualties on the ground was incredible, considering the destruction caused by the accident.

By late afternoon, it became apparent there was little more I could do, so I began walking away from the crash scene, making my way back toward my hotel near JFK airport. To be honest, I was becoming nauseated and overwhelmed. I desperately needed a break.

The Victim-Family Reception Center
New York City officials set up a large reception room for bereaved family members at a hotel near JFK Airport. Other Chaplains at the crash scene encouraged me to come over to the reception center and assist with the challenging work of ministering to the family members of the crash victims who were being given official death notifications.

Working my way toward the main entrance of the reception center, I came upon a large group of reporters and camera operators assembled outside the door. A circle of men talked to reporters in a press conference. Instantly, I recognized Mayor-elect Mike Bloomberg, Mayor Rudi Giuliani, and Governor Pataki, who were answering reporters' shouted questions and giving statements to the media. I overheard Mayor Giuliani trying to reassure everyone that the crash appeared at first to be an accident—and not terrorism—but a full investigation would follow.

As a side-note, I find it offensive the way the news media often descends like a flock of vultures upon scenes of human suffering following disasters. I've watched this repeatedly happen at school shootings, natural disasters, terrorist attacks, or riots. The news media has an obligation to give the public factual information, but their methods are sometimes crude and insensitive in my opinion. The old saying, "if it bleeds, it leads," is an apt description with the news media. It so often happens that a camera is shoved into the face of some brokenhearted victim of a tragedy, and an eager reporter asks idiotic questions. "How are you feeling right now about the death of your (son, , father, mother, friend, etc.)?" I sometimes think that news reporters ought to be given sensitivity training before being allowed out in public with a camera and microphone.

Another gripe I have about the news media is how their presence can cause more trouble than they came to report. In the case of riots, a news camera often incites violence as people tend to "act out" in a twisted bid to become famous and see themselves on TV. In the case of the summer riots in Ferguson, Missouri and Baltimore, Maryland, some media personnel were arrested because they were inciting people to commit crimes so their news footage would be more cutting-edge and exciting. Again, "if it bleeds, it leads."

Turning away from the press conference, I passed through several checkpoints and entered the building. The families and friends of the dead gathered in the main ballroom. There appeared to be several thousand people there in various states of grief and shock. The sight of so many weeping people was staggering. Parents were holding each other, and children were wailing and crying. The full magnitude of this overwhelming tragedy unfolded in all its horror.

Swallowing hard and praying under my breath, I spotted a pastor friend I'd worked with at Ground Zero. He waved me over to a table where he was ministering to a family. With hardly a word passing between us, we went to our knees and began praying for this broken-hearted family as they screamed and cried.

The situation reminded me once again that in such circumstances, the best thing to practice is the "ministry of presence." In a situation where the shock and grieving are so intense, there is very little one can, or should say.

I heard one young man sobbing out, "My wife, my baby!" I learned that this man's wife was pregnant with their first child. In one stroke, he'd lost his entire family in this tragedy.

Some young children at another table were screaming and crying. They were being held by several people whom I learned later were aunts and uncles. Both of their parents perished in the crash, and the children's entire world was shattered.

Moving from table to table, I sometimes knelt down next to the brokenhearted and offered to pray for them. Never once was I refused. I prayed that God would enfold these mourners in His comforting love and grace, giving them strength to bear their pain and heartbreak. While I'm sure many of them were not Christians, in a moment such as this, nearly everyone appreciates sincere prayers for comfort.

After several hours of ministering to hundreds of people, fatigue began overtaking me. I'd arisen very early that morning in preparation for my intended flight to London, and the intense stress of this traumatic day had taken its toll. It was now far past midnight, and physically, emotionally, and mentally, I was utterly spent. All I'd seen and heard pushed me beyond all limits. I desperately needed to get out of there and rest.

Stumbling out of the family reception center into the cold night air, I took some deep breaths and helpless to stop myself, I began to weep. Weariness and pent-up emotions overwhelmed me. After a long wait for a taxi, I finally arrived at my hotel around 3 AM. Taking a long, hot shower, I tried to wash away the smoke and grit of the day and fell into bed for a few hours of desperately needed sleep.

Early the next morning the airspace reopened and flights resumed. After check-in, I boarded my flight to England with the very same flight time and flight number as the day before. This was a bizarre deja vu experience as our aircraft taxied out for departure to the very same runway as the previous day. After takeoff, we followed the flight path of the doomed airliner the day before out over Jamaica Bay. It seemed incredibly ironic that our jet flew directly over Rockaway Beach and the crash site of American 587. Gazing down at the blackened crash site on the ground below, I marveled at the often weird twists and turns of life in this crazy world. I thought about how so much life-changing activity—so much human suffering, emotion, and pain—could occur in one 24-hour period. There, on the ground, within the confines of what now appeared from my comfortable seat as only a tiny, blackened spot of earth, my life, and the lives of countless other people, changed forever. Leaning back in the seat, I took a deep breath. Mercifully, I quickly fell into a deep, exhausted sleep that lasted nearly the entire flight to England.

Can We Get Out of It?

The haunting, frantic voices on the cockpit flight recorder on board Flight 587 just before it impacted provides a chilling allegory. The voices of the pilots sounded cool, professional, and calm right up to the moment the aircraft suddenly careened out of control and entered a flat spin. The disorientation and confusion expressed by the flight crew are horrifying.

The First Officer's desperate question just seconds before he died jump out at me; "What the hell are we into?" Allegorically, I have to ask, do *we* yet not understand what *we're* "into?" The rapid growth of government efforts to compile detailed data on ordinary Americans in the name of "security" makes the First Officer's question a compelling allegory. Are we even beginning to understand? Perhaps, like me, you're sharing the same thoughts the Captain screamed in the last second before impact;

We're stuck in it! Get out of it! Get out of it!

We'd better hope we can "get out of it" pretty soon because the ground seems to be rushing up at us rapidly. Our nation is at risk. The foundations upon which our Republic was established are systematically being destroyed. Unless we find a way to quickly "get out" of the flat spin our nation is in, we are in grave danger. We could lose our precious freedoms and wake up one day as slaves in a socialist tyranny.

For the crew of American 587, the crisis was far too sudden. There was no time to figure out what was wrong with their airplane or to find a way out of their predicament. According to after-accident reports, over-control of the rudder resulted in the vertical stabilizer failing and separating from the fuselage. Once that critical flight surface broke off, they went into a rapid flat spin that ripped the outboard engines off the wings. With alarms blaring and high "G" forces tossing them violently against their restraining harnesses, the pilots could never overcome their disorientation in time to save their aircraft.

For America, I believe there yet remains a small window of opportunity to find a way to "get out of it." Like the New York firefighter I wrote of earlier, who escaped his entombment under the rubble of the collapsed South Tower by crawling toward a faint light, we must begin feeling our way back toward "the light" that beckons us back to our constitutional foundations.

Remember therefore
from whence thou art fallen,
and repent and do the first works:
or else…
Revelation 2:5

The Chapel of Saint Mary Undercroft

Arriving at London Heathrow Airport, I was met by my old British friend, John Ruffle. Back in the early 70s, we both were a part of a Christian ministry in Eureka, California called, Gospel Outreach. John served as Best Man at my wedding in 1976. In the early 80s, John returned to England and became a leader within London's Christian community.

Through some connections, he secured an invitation for me to participate in a service at the Chapel of Saint Mary Undercroft, located beneath the British Parliament. I was, to say the least, deeply honored.

Within a few hours of my arrival and clearing customs, I found myself seated in an ornately appointed, marble and wood-paneled chapel. I was intrigued to learn later that King Edward I commissioned this chapel in 1297, with final completion by Edward III in 1365. In attendance were several members of Parliament and Christian leaders from the London area.

I remarked to John in a whisper what an irony it was that our two nations, once enemies in war during the American Revolution, now enjoyed the richness of Christian fellowship and sincere friendship. God indeed works miracles. It was awe-inspiring to consider I was sitting in the very place where, just over two centuries before, the Parliament had debated over decisions regarding how to prosecute a war against the rebellious American colonies. I suspect that some of the MPs of that day spent much time in this very chapel agonizing in prayer regarding *that* conflict.

At the proper moment, I was graciously invited by the officiating clergyman to come forward and give some brief remarks. Owing to my state of fatigue and shock from the prior day's events in New York City, I'm certain my comments were profoundly lackluster. Nevertheless, I managed to express my heartfelt gratitude for the support offered by the British people in the wake of 9/11. I also noted that some British citizens also perished in the attack on New York City. I reminded everyone that our unity as Christians and our agreement in prayer must take a position of much greater importance in the coming years. The challenges facing our two nations are far-reaching and must be mutually borne. The meeting ended with sincere and fervent prayers for our leaders, our respective countries, and in particular, for the comfort of all those suffering grief over lost loved ones.

PART III

Truth: Handle with Care

13

Sworn Upon What?

*And some things
that should not have been forgotten
were lost.
History became legend.
Legend became myth*
J.R.R. Tolkien, The Lord of the Rings

~~~~~~

In front of Federal Hall on Wall Street in New York City there stands a large bronze statue of President George Washington, created by sculptor John Quincy Adams Ward in 1882. The statue commemorates the inauguration of Washington as he took the oath of office as the first President of the United States on April 30, 1789. When I first gazed upon this compelling figure during my time of service at Ground Zero I was strongly intrigued, and yet, puzzled.

It struck me as incredibly odd that Washington's right hand is depicted with the palm down, suspended over nothing. I got the sense that something important was missing. At first, I assumed he was gesturing a greeting, but that didn't seem right. It gives the vague impression he is reaching out for something that is no longer there. My reaction sparked an interest in the history of this iconic image. The more I investigated, however, the more this statue became an enigma wrapped in a mystery.

In nearly every other painting, sculpture, or written description of the inaugural ceremony, Washington's right hand is described or shown resting upon a Bible while taking the oath of office. Why is Ward's creation the *only* statue of Washington's inauguration without a Bible under his hand as he took the oath?

Another bronze statue of Washington taking the oath of office—cast by Samuel A. Murray in 1910—stands in front of Independence Hall in Philadelphia, PA. It *clearly* portrays President Washington's right hand resting upon an open Bible. If John Quincy Adams Ward *did* take such artistic license with his New York statue, then why would he depict Washington's hand in such an odd position, suspended over nothing?

So compelling was this mystery, I embarked on a search for every image or written record I could find regarding the Federal Hall statue. To my astonishment, there was little in the historical record to discover. It almost seemed as if a black hole—like the proverbial "tear in the time-space continuum" of a science-fiction story—swallowed up a portion of our nation's history.

After considerable research, I finally discovered a large piece of the puzzle within the pages of an out-of-print book written by Dr. William T. Harris (1835-1909). A preeminent scholar of the time, Dr. Harris served as the U.S. Commissioner of Education. In Volume 4 of his book titled; *The United States of America: A Pictorial History of The American Nation From The Earliest Discoveries and Settlements to the Present Time,* he provided a detailed description of the Washington statue at the moment of its unveiling during the centennial celebration of Evacuation Day. This was a holiday commemorating the withdrawal of British forces from New York City on November 25, 1783 following the United States' victory in the Revolutionary War. From the late eighteenth century onward, Evacuation Day was observed each year with joyous celebrations and fireworks. The *Centennial* Anniversary, held in 1883, was ranked at the time as "one of the great civic events of the nineteenth century in New York City."[1]

According to the New York City Public Library, the Centennial celebrations were monumental.

> *The last spark in Evacuation Day celebrations followed the Civil War, and the holiday's 1883* Centennial *proved to be monumental. Led by the city's military and business leaders, event highlights include a parade of 20,000 marchers (taking over four hours to pass any single location).*
>
> *The centennial was celebrated in true New York fashion. Hundreds of ships flooded the Hudson and East Rivers, thousands feasted at banquets in Madison Square Garden and Delmonico's Restaurant, and fireworks displays took over the city, accompanied by over 500,000 spectators at the day's events.*[2]

Dr. Harris reported that people jammed the chilly, rainy streets of New York City on Monday, November 26, to witness the unveiling of the Washington statue. President Chester Alan Arthur, the 21st President of the United States, with Ulysses S. Grant, our 18th President, officiated. Dr. Harris—an

Sworn Upon What? 133

eyewitness—described the event and the statue as it was unveiled. Pay careful attention to his extremely detailed report: (Emphasis added)

> *By a sharp jerk the governor snapped the slender cord that held the American flags wrapped about the statue, and as the bronze figure burst to view the vast assemblage broke into cheers in which they were quickly joined by the forts whose cannons began thundering the moment the signal was given from the top of the building.*
>
> *Perhaps you have seen this statue in which the sculptor, J. Q. A. Ward, has represented Washington in the act of taking the oath of office as President. The figure is 12 feet 6 inches high and weighs 5,900 pounds. Washington is represented as dressed in the uniform which he bought for the occasion. A military cloak covers the left shoulder, and falls from the right shoulder. There is a short column on which the cloak catches. On this column rests a copy of the Bible, **and the outstretched hand of Washington is supported by it in the act of taking the oath**. The left hand rests on the hilt of a dress-sword. The portrait is from Stuart's celebrated picture and Houdon's bust. The idea of the falling military cloak is to suggest that Washington was leaving the military for the civil life.* [3]

Once again, let me draw your attention to Dr. Harris' very particular choice of words in the prior paragraph.

> *There is a short column on which the cloak catches. On this column rests a copy of the Bible, **and the outstretched hand of Washington is supported by it in the act of taking the oath**.* (Emphasis added)

What Happened to the Bible?

Here is a *great* mystery. There is no longer a column in front of Washington where there *"rests a copy of the Bible"* upon which, *"...the outstretched hand of Washington is supported."* After carefully examining the statue myself while doing research for this book in New York City, I finally did discover the column with a bible on it. However, they are *now* situated *behind* Washington almost entirely hidden underneath Washington's cloak, leaving his oath-taking right hand awkwardly dangling over *thin air*. Dr. Harris' eyewitness testimony of President Washington's hand being *"...supported by it..."* stands in stark contradiction to what the statue now reveals.

Are There Any Photos?

This was *no minor celebration* in our nation's history! However, I cannot discover a *single photograph* of the actual unveiling of the statue! Wouldn't it be reasonable to assume that at least a *few* photographs would be taken at the unveiling, *especially* with a sitting President and former President Grant, and hundreds of thousands of people in attendance? This dedication was a hugely significant news event. However, again, *I cannot discover a single photograph of the event in any archives.* All I could discover was a *sketching* of the unveiled statue on the cover of the December 8, 1883, edition of the Harper's Weekly magazine. The sketch is *reportedly* based on a photograph by the famous New York photographer, George G. Rockwood (1832-1911). The sketch depicts the oath-taking right hand of Washington suspended *over nothing*. My search for the *original* photograph that the Harper's Weekly sketch is supposedly based on has been fruitless. For reasons I'm about to share, I believe there is a plausible case to be made that the Harper's sketch is a fraud.

Photography was a relatively new technology in 1883 but not uncommon. Rockwood reportedly took over 350,000 portraits in his New York City studio during his career. There are many hundreds of photographs in historical archives of the Civil War era taken during the 1860s nearly 20 years before this event. After months of research, combing the newspaper archives of the New York papers, I finally managed to locate a picture of Wall Street taken shortly *before* the Evacuation Day celebration in 1883, showing the front of Federal Hall shortly *before* the placement and unveiling of the statue, judging from the apparent weather in the picture.

The more I tried to find information about this, the eerier the whole thing became. I feel as if I've stepped into some sort of "Twilight Zone" episode. *Where* are the photographic records of the unveiling of this national icon? Why can I only locate a *single sketch*?

The next photograph I could locate of the statue from that immediate time period (which shows it in its present altered state) is *from five years after its unveiling* during the record-breaking blizzard that occurred on March 11, 1888. This storm was called the worst blizzard in American history. [4] The photograph shows the statue covered in snow. As can be seen, it does not depict the column and Bible situated under Washington's hand, as described by Dr. Harris in his detailed account.

Only two explanations seem even remotely plausible. The *first* is that Dr. Harris falsely—or perhaps mistakenly—described the appearance of the statue when initially unveiled. This seems extremely unlikely since he was a preeminent scholar in his day and serving as U.S. Commissioner of Education. His reputation and credibility would be totally destroyed by publishing such a blatantly false account. Tens of thousands of eyewitnesses—present at the unveiling—would denounce his book a fraud as soon as it was published.

The *second* possible explanation is that sometime within the five years preceding the 1888 snowstorm, *unknown persons deliberately altered the statue.* This scenario also seems problematical since the changes would likely be immediately noticed on such a revered public display. Before anyone objects that it would be impossible to make such a significant alteration as moving the column and Bible behind Washington, I would offer the following thoughts. The statue was cast in bronze and most likely created in separate parts, later joined together by welding. Bronze is malleable by heating, and it would be relatively easy to alter the statue into its present form by using welding technology widely available in the 19th century.

According to Wikipedia:

> *Before modern welding techniques, large sculptures were generally cast in one piece with a single pour. Welding allows a large sculpture to be cast in pieces, then joined.* [5]

My Best "Sherlock Holmes" Hypothesis

During the five years following the dedication of the statue, there were likely several reconstructions and repairs of Federal Hall and surrounding buildings. To prevent damage during times of construction work, it would seem reasonable that the statue might be carefully encased in a protective enclosure. It seems unlikely it would be moved to a warehouse during construction work, owing to its immense size and weight. (Over 12 feet tall and weighing nearly 6,000 pounds.) In either case, during the time it was encased (or warehoused) I theorize that someone brought in some welding equipment and deliberately "improved" it by moving the column and Bible *behind* Washington, and very nearly obscuring it with his cloak. Based upon Dr. Harris' detailed report, it seems entirely likely at this point that someone deliberately altered it while it was out of public view. And what of Harper's sketched depiction of the statue without the Bible under Washington's hand? I would answer that "fake news" is not a recent invention in the news media. With the large number of radical Socialists active in the United States in the late 19th century, how could anyone deny that such a coverup is entirely possible? I can think of no other explanation.

The entire scenario is an enigma and begs a question. Why would anyone do that? Perhaps even more ominously, how could it be possible that someone or a small group of persons went to such great pains to eradicate all photos of the original statue from newspaper archives and private photographers? I realize this all sounds crazy, but what other explanation fits the actual forensic data? It's a well-established fact that there are people who desire to promote a secular image of Washington through bogus distortions of the historical record through the news media, entertainment, and education systems.

There were a significant number of committed secular-leftist anarchists operating in the United States around the turn of the 19th century just as there are in our time. In fact, one of the most devastating anarchist terror bombing attacks in the history of the U.S. occurred at 12:01 pm on September 16, 1920, in the Financial District of Manhattan, New York City. Thirty people died immediately, and eight others died later of their wounds. Hundreds of people were seriously injured. Although never solved, authorities believed the Wall Street bombing was carried out by Galleanists (Italian anarchists), responsible for several other bombings the previous year. The attack was related to anti-capitalist agitation in the United States. 6

The anarchist Left and Socialists eventually recognized that terror bombings and murder were not nearly as effective as institutional infiltration. Men like the Socialist educator John Dewey, (detailed later in this book) began seizing control of America's education apparatus in a committed effort to eradicate Christianity from America. Could this be just one component of a much larger deception?

It seems reasonable to imagine that such a powerful icon of America's first president displayed with a Bible under his hand in such a prominent location as Wall Street would quickly become a source of irritation to those hell-bent upon distorting the historical record of America's early Christian/Biblical influences.

Upon What Foundation Do We Stand Now?

Regardless of whether Dr. Harris gave a false report, and J.Q.A. Ward *never* placed the Bible under Washington's hand in the *first* place, or it was *deliberately* repositioned by Christophobic bigots, or the column and Bible *moved themselves* out from under Washington's oathtaking hand, this mystery poses a much more important and compelling metaphor. Upon what foundational values does our Republic *now* stand? In other words, what overarching authority, system of truth, or philosophical principles now guide our nation and people?

Based upon the preponderance of evidence available, I'm willing to boldly declare that America was founded upon the principles of Christianity—and the Judeo-Christian Bible—by our majority Christian Founders. As I will demonstrate in upcoming chapters, the historical record practically shouts out this truth.

The alternative is unthinkable, for without these firm foundations, fallen men are left to make up ethics, truth, and justice on their own, adrift upon the shifting and capricious sands of political pragmatism and the random whims of secular humanism. If right and wrong, or the entire concept of "justice" is merely a matter of emotion-driven preferences or the Darwinian lie of the "survival of the fittest," then we are all reduced to soul-less brute beasts who *create* "truth" according to whoever has the most powerful weapons or the cruelest use of raw force. These issues are incredibly important, and will ultimately direct the course of America into the foreseeable future.

Again, I'm not contemplating the forced imposition of a theocracy or a theonomy in America where everyone is forced to convert and conform. Unlike Mohammed and his cult of Islam, Christ *never* commanded that His gospel be implemented by force or violence. God brings about His kingdom through a work of grace in the heart of people through a purely divinely-initiated New Birth, enabling fallen men to come to Christ by the power of the Spirit of God. While it might be nice if God grabbed everyone in the world and forced them to accept Christ, this is not something taught in Scripture. Nor is it anything we as humans can engineer. Conversion is God's work alone, and Christians are commanded to share the gospel to all indiscriminately. Those who are enabled to hear *will* hear and enter into eternal life. Our responsibility is to pray that people would come to know the peace and forgiveness of Christ just as we have. Our commission is to offer the Gospel freely to all, without consideration as to whether or not they will receive it. Bottom line, however, is that the Bible teaches that one day, all the kingdoms and nations of the Earth will bow their knee to the King of kings, and Lord of lords.

> *That at the Name of Jesus*
> *should every knee bow,*
> *both of things in heaven,*
> *and things in earth,*
> *and things under the earth.*
> *And that every tongue should confess*
> *that Jesus Christ is the Lord,*
> *unto the glory of God the Father.*
> Philippians 2:10-11

In the meantime, we look forward to a day when there will *again* be a time when our oath-taking public employees place their God-fearing hands upon God's Holy Bible and covenant themselves to the faithful execution of their office and keep their oaths. If any secular activists read this, be warned. We're coming for you, but we're not coming with guns and weapons of the flesh. Our arsenal is *far* more powerful. We're coming with the Truth of the gospel of Christ, and with the weapons of prayer and proclamation.

That said, I *do* believe that *any* nation or people would *greatly* benefit in every way from a resurgence of a Christianized worldview in every sphere of life, government, and society. The Christian biblical outlook on life, in general, is far more kind, merciful, compassionate, and ethical than any other in all of human history, bar-none.

In contrast, fallen humanity has repeatedly demonstrated the fruits of their depravity in the holocaust of hundreds of millions of people throughout history in various Marxist, Fascist, or "religious" slaughters. We in America have the blood of 50 million+ murdered unborn children on our hands, and the vulgar sale of their chopped-up body parts for the sake of greed.

When I speak of "religious" slaughters, I'm not speaking of Biblically-based Christianity. Those who are educated in these things realize that there is a vast difference between non-biblical "religionists" and genuine Christians. As for those who can be counted on to raise the standard secular objection regarding the "Crusades" or the "Inquisition," I would remind everyone that the vast majority of these horrendous acts of barbarous violence and cruelty emanated almost exclusively from the Roman distortion of Christ's true church, not Bible-based Protestant Christians. In the case of the Inquisition, *most* of the millions of victims were Protestant Reformed Christians anyway. [7]

If, for no other reason than societal harmony, biblical Christian teachings ought to be regarded as the "gold standard" of harmonious governance. In spite of all objections to the contrary, those societies that embraced the ethics and principles taught by biblical Christianity are, for the most part, happier, more prosperous, just, tolerant, and peaceful. Biblical Christianity never forces anyone to convert, (unlike the historic Roman distortions or the pseudo-religion of Islam) but rather seeks to persuade peacefully with reasoned arguments. Ethics, morality, mercy, the value of human life, and the cherished concepts of tolerance all stem from the Scriptures. A government could operate within the philosophical and ethical framework of a Judeo-Christian foundation without demanding that every citizen become a Christian. This was the de facto order of things in the United States at the founding of our republic *and could be again.*

This was the bedrock upon which our forefathers placed their trust. When

George Washington put his hand on that Bible and took his oath of office for the Presidency, he did so in a pledge of fealty to God, and his country. The wise counsel of Biblical wisdom formed the basis for nearly all of American laws, and during the first decades of our Republic's history, this was almost universally acknowledged. Evidence of this fact is etched in marble throughout our nation's capital upon nearly every monument, pylon, and obelisk. The speeches, correspondence, and the transcribed Congressional Record contain ubiquitous references to Christian/Jewish scripture.

Even upon and within the Supreme Court building in Washington, D.C., there are six depictions of Moses and the Ten Commandments. Predictably, secular revisionists continue to work very hard to deny this truth, or even say that the images depicting the Roman numerals of the Ten Commandments only represent the first ten amendments to the Constitution. This is, of course, unabridged male bovine excrement. [8]

It is not possible for any human government to be completely devoid of a moral and ethical bias as an anchor and reference point. The only question we must consider is, *which* philosophy will be relied upon to inform how we decide the goodness or justice of laws and the basis for our interactions with each other? Concepts like ethics, justice, mercy, truth, duty, honor, goodness, and other virtues do not grow in a vacuum. Ironically, even secular humanists, who claim to hold to such concepts without reference to God's word, dishonestly borrow all their philosophical lumber from Judaism and Christianity, for they can be found nowhere else.

I ask again. Can we hope for a day in which our national foundations are restored? I say *YES*! And with God's help, those foundations eventually *will be* re-established!

Notes

1. http://datab.us/i/Evacuation%20Day%20(New%20York)

2. Evacuation Day: New York's Former November Holiday by Megan Margino, Milstein Division of U.S. History, Local History & Genealogy, Stephen A. Schwarzman Building November 24, 2014 https://goo.gl/1YXuUh

3. The United States of America: A Pictorial History of The American Nation From The Earliest Discoveries and Settlements to the Present Time, Copyright 1906 by William T. Harris, Ph.D., LL.D., U.S. Commissioner of Education. Volume 4, page 119 Published by John, Wilson & Company, 1878 https://archive.org/stream/unitedstatesofam04harr#page/118/mode/2up

4. http://www.history.com/this-day-in-history/great-blizzard-of-88-hits-east-coast

5. http://en.wikipedia.org/wiki/Bronze_sculpture

6. The Wall Street Bombing, Wikipedia. https://goo.gl/686BbP

7. Estimates of the Number Killed by the Papacy in the Middle Ages and later, By Dr. David A. Plaisted http://www.cs.unc.edu/~plaisted/estimates.doc

8. Ten Commandments Stunner: Feds Lying at Supreme Court. By Bob Unruh, Published: 11/14/2006 http://www.wnd.com/2006/11/38823/#y0gJ0BcH49ByAiHb.99

14

Red or Blue Pill?

*When a well-packaged web of lies
has been sold gradually to the masses
over generations,
the truth will seem utterly preposterous
and its speaker a raving lunatic.*
Dresden James [1]

~~~~~~

Much of what we learned in school about America's history simply isn't so. This historical distortion is particularly true regarding America's Christian foundations, and the profound influence God's word had upon our nation's formation in its infancy.

An inaccurate, or at the very least, an incomplete historical record has become embedded in our national psyche. Untruths, and in some cases blatant lies, are now universally accepted almost without question. An oft-repeated saying, widely attributed to Mark Twain has well said:

> *It's easier to fool people
> than to convince them
> they **have** been fooled.*

In most of our public/secular schools, universities, and colleges, the standard assumption is that our nation was primarily founded by secular men. These Founders are assumed to have based their thinking on the ideas of secular "Enlightenment" Humanists such as Kant, Goethe, Voltaire, Rousseau, and Adam Smith. Christian influences upon America's Founding documents are increasingly dismissed, or at the least, minimized. If pressed, secular pundits in our times will sometimes assert that "if" the Founding Fathers were at all religious, they were probably Deists who took little or no interest in religious considerations.

These unfounded allegations fly in the face of overwhelming historical evidences—easily researched but largely ignored—that almost to a man the Founders were Christians. They eloquently and repeatedly acknowledged their Christian faith in their speeches and written correspondences. They also affirmed their belief in God's active participation in America's struggle for freedom and independence. In fact, the very bedrock of our republic's system of government was based upon biblical—and specifically—Christian principles. The evidence is etched upon nearly every monument, statue, and obelisk throughout our nation's capital, and discoverable in nearly every document and correspondence. In spite of this, such factual information has been virtually banned in our government educational system for nearly a century.

We now have a populace who live in virtual ignorance of this reality. Anyone courageous enough to teach American school children about our Christian heritage is sure to be condemned and demonized as a "radical," and "out of step" with "the mainstream." Angry cries about a violation of the "constitutional separation of church and state" myth are sure to be heard. Tragically, most Americans are almost completely brainwashed into believing that the words "separation of church and state" are actually written within our founding documents. In point of fact, these words do not appear anywhere in either the Constitution, Bill of Rights, or Amendments. (We will deal with this issue more thoroughly later.)

This scenario reminds me of something Joseph Goebbels, Propaganda Minister for the Nazi Third Reich, is quoted as saying:

> *If you tell a lie big enough and keep repeating it, people will eventually come to believe it. The lie can be maintained only for such time as the State can shield the people from the political, economic and/or military consequences of the lie. It thus becomes vitally important for the State to use all of its powers to repress dissent, for the truth is the mortal enemy of the lie, and thus by extension,* **the truth is the greatest enemy of the State.**
> 2

Ponder a few moments what Goebbels said. Are we now living in times when we swim in a virtual sewer-pond of lies? Haven't we been lied to even before we were in kindergarten, and in children's television programs? Who can deny that the indoctrination process has continued unabated throughout our education process? We're lied to in our textbooks, entertainment, and in our classrooms. We've even endured lies from the pulpits of many of our liberal churches.

What shall I say of the ludicrous seasonal mythologies dealing with circumstances surrounding the humble birth of Christ, His death on the cross, or His resurrection from the dead? Certainly, I believe these events actually occurred, but why all the add-mixture of paganism? I hate to be the "Grinch who stole Christmas," but what *possible* relevance is there to the birth of Christ and a silly myth about a generous, good-natured, fat old bearded elf in a red suit? This character supposedly lives at the North Pole and flies around the world in a sleigh full of gifts, pulled by magic flying reindeer. (No, I do NOT believe in Santa Claus. Bah! Humbug!)

While I'm at it, what possible relevance do pagan fantasies about colored eggs and bunnies, and Easter ("Ishtar") baskets have with the physical resurrection of our Messiah from the dead? I would answer; *absolutely nothing!* These falsehoods may appear to be harmless "warm fuzzy" traditions to some people, but they are nevertheless lies, and they serve to trivialize the most important events in human history.

These supposedly "harmless" myths also condition children to distrust their parents. Inwardly, children often ask an unspoken question;

> *If mommy and daddy lied to us about **these** things, then what **else** did they lie to us about? How can we believe all the other things they taught us about Jesus? Might not Christianity also be just another religious myth?*

I maintain that these myths cause great damage to the Christian faith and erode confidence in the reliability of the Bible. How? It is precisely *because* they are linked directly to the most significant details regarding Christ's birth, atoning death, and physical resurrection. Have you ever wondered why similar ridiculous myths are rarely associated with other beliefs?

Think about *that* for a moment. Should it surprise anyone that the minions of darkness would target the *real thing*? Jesus told us who the father of lies is, didn't He? The Bible doesn't give us a pass to tell "little white lies" to our children either. In fact, there are no such things as "little white lies." Lies are lies, and no matter how one tries to dress up that pig, it's still a pig. Again, such lies are *especially* damaging to the faith of children when ridiculous myths (no matter how "warm and fuzzy" they may *feel*) are associated with the most significant events in history related to Christ.

Disinformation flows like raw sewage from our radios, our newspapers, magazines, and in most of the books we purchase or check out from our public libraries. How do I know this is so? I give two reasons. First, most people are incredibly gullible. (I used to be an expert in the gullibility department.)

People are conditioned to accept unquestioningly whatever their favorite news anchor says on the evening news, or what they read in their newspapers, tabloids, internet posts, and government press secretaries. Very *few* bother to question *why* they believe *what* they believe. Sadly, I include most Christians in this group. Many of our churches are filled with people who accept whatever they're told from "the pulpit" without carefully consulting and studying their own Bible to "see if these things were so." Remember the example of the noble Bereans, mentioned in the book of Acts, chapter 17.

> *...for they received the word*
> *with great eagerness,*
> *examining the Scriptures daily*
> *to see whether these things were so.*

The second reason should be obvious. There are liars and deceivers in abundance in our world because we are *all* liars to one degree or another. No one had to teach us how to lie. We were all born with that innate ability, (thanks to our first parents, Adam and Eve) and we have to work *very* hard not to do it. Most of the people we talk to every day lie to us. We often lie to them too, and we're so accustomed to lying that we hardly know when we're doing it. For example, have you ever said to someone you dislike, "It's so *nice* to see you" when the truth was, it wasn't "nice" to see them *at all*? Some liars are quite good at it, and they are all around us. Liars come in all ages, shapes, sizes, races, education levels, and professions.

Religious liars are perhaps the *most* dangerous of all, (second only to politicians) evidenced by the historical horrors perpetrated by the well-documented slaughter of millions of people in the name of various political causes or religious beliefs. Human sacrifices to deities have occurred throughout recorded history among pagan cultures. However, pagans weren't the only perpetrators of barbaric cruelty in the name of religion. There is no denying that upwards of a hundred million people were brutally tortured and slaughtered during the Dark Ages by diabolical "Christianists." They cloaked themselves in clerical robes and religious rituals and masqueraded as followers of Christ. I'm bold to state this fact because our secular opponents never miss an opportunity to throw it in the face of real Christians as an argument against Christianity in general. In the darkness of their minds, unregenerate people cannot distinguish between authentic Christianity and a satanic distortion of it. It is all lumped together as the same thing in their mind, quite to the delight of the devil, who created the counterfeit in the first place for that very purpose.

I will deal more with the religious perversion know as Islam elsewhere. But during their entire history, beginning with their founder, their unique brand of torture and slaughter of "infidels" manifests wherever this satanic cult spreads. Suffice to say here that this evil deception now plagues the world with death and destruction wherever it spreads.

Political Liars become extremely dangerous if they worm their way into unaccountable positions of power or policy-forming functions. That is precisely why the Founding Fathers established our republic with "checks and balances" through a power-sharing arrangement between three separate and equal branches. As Christians, the Founders knew all too well how quickly fallen men can and will succumb to the temptations of money, fame, and power.

When deception is institutionalized through corrupt leaders (as illustrated by the Nazi Goebbels's quote earlier) and becomes enforced national policy, it can quickly become a matter of life or death. Ask any survivor of Stalin or Mao's purges, or the Nazi death camps (just to name a few).

Those who deny what I'm saying generally fall into three categories. They are either; 1) promoting a deception, 2) are themselves deceived, or 3) are suffering from what is called "Stockholm Syndrome."

According to Wikipedia:

> *Stockholm syndrome, or capture-bonding, is a psychological phenomenon in which hostages express empathy and sympathy and have positive feelings toward their captors, sometimes to the point of defending and identifying with the captors. These feelings are generally considered irrational in light of the danger or risk endured by the victims, who essentially mistake a lack of abuse from their captors for an act of kindness.*

Where Are All the Lies Originating?

The primary source of lies and deceptions will be found in a personality called "Satan." In biblical theology, the title "Satan" (defined as "accuser") is not his actual name but rather his job description. His primary modus operandi, or "MO," is slander, accusation, and deception. According to orthodox theologians, he was once an indescribably beautiful and powerful Archangel named Lucifer, ("Son of the Morning"). He led the angelic hosts in worship to God. At some time in the unfathomable past—possibly even before the creation of the visible universe—this created being fell from his place of high honor in God's eternal kingdom through pride and rebellion. Because of his corruption, he was cast out of heaven and drew a third of the angels with him in his rebellion.

> *How art thou* fallen *from heaven,*
> *O Lucifer, son of the morning?*
> And *cut down to the ground,*
> *which didst cast lots upon the nations?*
> *Yet thou* saidest *in thine heart,*
> *"I will ascend into heaven,*
> *and exalt my throne above beside the stars of God:*
> *I will sit also upon the mount of the congregation*
> *in the sides of the North.*
> *I will ascend above the height of the clouds,*
> *and I will be like the* most high*."*
> *But thou shalt be brought down to the grave,*
> *to the side of the pit.*
> Isaiah 14:12-15

From that time on, he became "Satan" (the accuser) and his minions employ every strategy to slander God and destroy humanity. According to the Bible, humans were created in God's image and likeness, and this chiefly attracts his vicious hatred. He does this primarily via lies and deceptions, inflaming the baser passions of fallen, depraved men to do his bidding. His motive is to inflict misery and death upon all. When unregenerate religionists sought to murder the Messiah Jesus, He spoke of them in these words, found in John 8:44:

> Ye are of your father the devil,
> and the lusts of your father ye will do:
> he hath been a murderer from the beginning,
> and abode not in the truth,
> because there is no truth in him.
> When he speaketh a lie,
> then speaketh he of his own:
> for he is a liar, *and the father thereof.*

How Did America Get Here?

America's slide into moral and spiritual corruption was gradual and began many, many decades ago. To underscore my previous point many formerly conservative and theologically-sound seminaries became progressively more liberal, and professors began to teach the lie that all politics are "worldly and dirty." A few outstanding examples of this corruption are the venerated Universities of Harvard, Yale, and Princeton.

Harvard University, originally named after a Christian minister, was founded in 1636 with the intention of establishing a school to train Christian ministers. The original Latin motto of the school was; "Veritas Christo Ecclesiae," translated, "Truth for Christ and the Church."

Princeton University was established in 1746 to train ministers also. In fact, the first year of classes was under the tutelage of the Reverend Jonathan Dickinson, a preeminent theologian of his time. Princeton's crest is inscribed with the words, "Dei sub numine viget," which is Latin for "Under God's power she flourishes."

Yale University was founded in 1701 under the motto "Lux et Veritas," Latin for "Light and Truth." If one examines the original seal, at the top, a pair of Hebrew words are written; "אורים ותמים," pronounced "Urim ve-Thummim." There is much mystery surrounding the use of the "Urim and Thummim." According to 1 Samuel 14, the Hebrew priests used them as a means of revealing the will of God. Interestingly, the first Hebrew letters of these words are the "Aleph" and "Tav," which are the first and last letters of the Hebrew alphabet. This is comparable to the "Alpha and Omega," the first and last letters of the Greek alphabet corresponding to the New Testament's revelation of Jesus in Revelation 22:13.

I am Alpha and Omega,
the beginning and the end,
the first and the last.

Yale was originally established to provide academic and theological training for the clergy. Their seal carries the suggestion that knowledge "from A to Z" would be their guiding principle, and would include the revelation of God's limitless wisdom and knowledge through Christ. In fact, most of the colleges and universities originally established in America were profoundly Christian in their emphasis and mission. These institutions have now become bastions of Marxism, Secular Humanism, and Progressive Liberalism. As time went by, many pastoral students in these institutions were taught that Christians should concern themselves only with "spiritual" matters of the heart, and not run for public office or seek to influence public policy. Many seminary professors accepted the "wall of separation" terminology that arose from a 1948 Supreme Court case, McCollum v. Board of Education. The ruling, in part, read; "in the words of Jefferson, the clause against establishment of religion by law was intended to erect 'a wall of separation between church and state.'"

The phrase; "...wall of separation between church and state" was penned by President Jefferson in a letter of personal correspondence between Jefferson and some Baptist ministers in Danbury, Connecticut. The Christians in Danbury wrote to the President on October 7, 1801, with concerns that the government might seek to control or manipulate churches to teach and promote government policies or positions in conflict with their Christian beliefs. The Connecticut Legislature was at that time attempting to infringe upon their religious freedoms. They wanted President Jefferson to offer an opinion on the matter that would; "shine and prevail through all these states and all the world."

In that time of American history, the memory of such government infringements on religious freedoms was fresh in their minds, with the bitter experiences of many centuries of secular/Roman Catholic oppression in England and Europe. Jefferson wrote back to reassure the Christians in Danbury that the U.S. Government has no authority to influence or force churches to adopt or preach things the government may dictate. Jefferson used the metaphor of a "wall" separating church and state to reinforce his point. To quote from his response:

> ...the First Amendment has erected a wall of separation between church and state. That wall must be kept high and impregnable.

For over a century and a half, this "wall of separation" was understood to mean that the secular state has no overriding constitutional authority to dictate to, or *control*, the faith and practices of the Christian religion. Only in extreme cases where such expression might foment violence or endanger public safety could the government justify any interference. Jefferson's words were never meant to exclude Christian influences from society, government, or education systems. Jefferson's original intent in using his "wall of separation" allegory was that a virtual "one-way wall" that must be kept "high and impregnable" to restrain government from controlling Christians in their efforts to preach the gospel and be "salt and light" in the world.

This restraint upon the government extended even to any attempt by politicians to limit Christian influence on public policy through reasoned public discourse and persuasion through a lawful legislature. In 1947 in a Supreme Court case, Everson v. Board of Education, the progressive Justice Hugo Black resurrected Jefferson's 150-year-old letter and imposed a novel interpretation. Justice Black interpreted the First Amendment's establishment clause meant that any government support—or friendly toleration and accommodation—for Christianity would amount to an unconstitutional "establishment of religion."

This dubious decision by Justice Black now forms the bedrock of the secularist's argument against any mention or toleration of Christianity in public forums, legislative processes, or public education.

For those who wish to interpret the First Amendment's "establishment clause" as a ban on all Christian influence from public policy deliberations, I offer the following argument. Just as it would be ludicrous to prohibit any *other* possible bias or opinion on the part of legislators or public officials, so should it be asinine to ban their Christian views. The inner thoughts and religious convictions of any person play a large role in how they form their opinions about everything else. An excellent explanation of Jefferson's original intent in his use of the term "wall of separation of Church and State," is available in a scholarly article, *'A Wall of Separation' FBI Helps Restore Jefferson's Obliterated Draft*. Written by James Hutson and published by the Library of Congress. Hutson was the curator of a major exhibition at the Library dealing with; "Religion and the Founding of the American Republic." The article reveals significant portions of Jefferson's original draft revealing new insights into the President's thoughts as he penned this seminal letter to the Danbury Christians. It provides compelling evidence that Jefferson's views clash starkly with contemporary liberal court interpretations. [3]

For those wishing to study the many overwhelming historical pieces of evidence of America's rich Christian heritage, and the faith in Christ almost universally held by our founding fathers, I highly recommend David Barton's website. (http://www.wallbuilders.com) Barton has done an exceptional service to our Republic by amassing a vast library of the original drafts of our Founder's speeches, correspondence, and historical documents. This evidence has been deliberately suppressed by secular progressives (as I've repeatedly stated throughout this book) and establishes beyond any reasonable doubt that America was indeed founded upon Christian principles by Christians.

The Red Pill, or the Blue Pill?

An allegorical portrayal of the universal web of deception we exist in was cunningly portrayed in the 1999 science fiction movie, The Matrix, written by Andy & Larry Wachowski. In the film, the character Morpheus offers Neo two pills. One pill is blue, and one is red. The "blue pill" would restore the deception and fantasy-world Neo was presently living in as his "normal" reality. The "red pill" promised to tear away the deception and reveal the "real world" beyond anything Neo could have imagined.

In the following chapters, I'm going to offer you a "red pill." Use it cautiously according to recommended dosages. Side effects may include dizziness, temporary disorientation, and shock. These symptoms will wear off with the passage of time. If side effects persist, consult God, the Creator of ultimate reality, according to scriptural prayer protocols.

> *You take the blue pill—the story ends, you wake up in your bed and believe whatever you want to believe. You take the red pill—you stay in Wonderland, and I show you how deep the rabbit hole goes. Remember: all I'm offering is the truth. Nothing more.* [4]

Notes

1. Particulate Matters: "When a well-packaged web of lies has ... (n.d.). Retrieved from http://kosmicdebris.blogspot.com/2013/02/when-well-packaged-web-of-lies-has-been

2. Joseph Goebbels: On the "Big Lie" Jewish Virtual Library https://www.jewishvirtuallibrary.org/jsource/Holocaust/goebbelslie.html

3. Library of Congress. http://www.loc.gov/loc/lcib/9806/danbury.html

4. Scene from The Matrix. https://www.youtube.com/watch?v=zE7PKRjrid4

15

Slavery, Racism, and Natives

> *At some future point,*
> *not distant as measured by centuries,*
> *the civilized races of man*
> *will almost certainly exterminate and replace*
> *the savage races throughout the world.*
> Charles Darwin
> *The Descent of Man,*
> *and Selection in Relation to Sex*
> published 1871, pp. 200–201, Vol. 1

A popular hammer employed by America-haters and secular leftist-progressives to bash the United States is the myth that long before the arrival of so-called "evil white Europeans," native Americans had already been here *forever*, living peacefully in Utopian societies in perfect harmony with nature. Another popular myth is that white Christian Colonists were nearly *all* racists and primarily responsible for slavery and genocide. Indeed, there were human societies living on the continent many years before the arrival of European settlers, but as we will see, the latest scientific data indicates that even the "natives" were, at some time in history, *also* colonists. In this chapter, I intend to shatter some popular liberal historical distortions regarding racism and slavery and unmask the *true* origins of both.

I realize I'm biting off quite a bit here. However, I think it prudent to expose and confront some of the lies and accusations the enemies of liberty typically use as psychological and political weapons to discredit the United States. Our school children are subjected to near-constant brainwashing on these subjects. We must beat back liberal distortions with historical *facts*, and destroy "politically correct" myths if we *ever* hope to refresh the tree of liberty with something *other* than the blood of patriots and tyrants. God help us ALL if it should ever come to *that*.

152   Destroying the Shadow Agenda

Slavery: It's NOT just the "White Man's" Sin

Contrary to the current leftist propaganda narrative that slavery is the European "white man's" sin against "people of color," it would be useful to note that the very first *legal* slave owner in America was a *black man* from Angola named Anthony Johnson. In 1654, fully 34 years after the arrival of the Mayflower Pilgrims in May of 1620, Johnson legally won ownership of another black man, John Castor, and established the *legal* precedent for all subsequent slavery in America. Although human slavery was *practiced* around the world prior to Johnson's case in 1654, it was not *legal* in the American colonies until then. It should also be noted that Mr. Johnson wasn't the *only* black slave owner in the United States. By 1830, there were an estimated 3,775 black families living in the South who owned black slaves. By 1860 in the city of New Orleans *alone*, there were approximately 3,000 slaves owned by black households. [1]

The despicable crime of human slavery was practiced by virtually *all* the ancient civilizations of the world. Uncounted *millions* of people became slaves and the property of others throughout the millennia, often through debt, taken as captives in war, through kidnapping by slave raiders and pirates, or *even* by being sold into slavery by *family members*. A notable biblical example of this was the sale of Joseph into Egyptian slavery by his brothers, recorded in Genesis 37:18-36. In fact, some of the most notorious slavers were, and *are to this very day*, Islamic.[2]

There Were (and still are) White Slaves Too

We should not forget that the victims of human trafficking and slavery were not confined to people "of color." There are ample historical records regarding the capture and enslavement of multiplied thousands of white men, women, and children by Islamic Barbary pirates along the coasts of the Mediterranean from the 1500s to the 1800s, extending even as far north as Iceland. I certainly don't mention this to diminish the crime of slavery against people of color, but *this* history is virtually ignored by modern leftist progressives seem determined to cast all white people as "oppressors" in their imagined "politically correct" universe.

Professor Robert C. Davis, a teacher of Italian social history at Ohio State University, (hardly a bastion of Christian white conservatism) wrote a seminal work titled: Christian Slaves, Muslim Masters: White Slavery in the Mediterranean, the Barbary Coast, and Italy, 1500-1800, Palgrave Macmillan, 2003. Prof. Davis estimated from his research that:

> *Between 1530 and 1780 there were almost certainly a million and quite possibly as many as a million and a quarter white, European Christians enslaved by the Muslims of the Barbary Coast.*

It is important to consider that this number *far*-exceeds the estimated number of 800,000 black Africans who were captured and brought to the North American colonies. Again, this does not diminish the suffering and injustices endured by the ancestors of our fellow black Americans, but it serves to give some needed perspective. Sin is sin, and cruelty is cruelty, no matter what the race of the victims might happen to be. Slavery in all its forms must be resisted and stamped out. For a review of Prof. Davis' book, you may wish to read: The Untold Story of White Slavery by Thomas Jackson, American Renaissance, August 2005 [3]

This subject would not be complete without mentioning the horrendous and nearly pandemic practice of child sex slavery even in our modern times. In nearly every nation including–to our eternal shame–the United States, children are being abducted, abused, used as child sacrifices in satanic rituals, or trafficked as sex slaves by the most despicable and perverted human monsters on the planet. I include young men and women caught up as victims in this nightmare of devastating abuse. I can only imagine that the very hottest places in hell are reserved for those who prey upon the most vulnerable and defenseless among us. Recently discovered evidence shows that a significant number of our political, judicial, and law enforcement officials are participating—actively or passively—in these horrendous crimes. Ultimately, only the power and mercy of God, and the bright sunlight of exposure by uncorrupted leaders will cleanse our nation of this heinous sin.

It's True: Even America's Founders Owned Slaves

It is a historical fact that many of the Founding Fathers, including Thomas Jefferson and George Washington—as well as a significant number of the signers of the Declaration of Independence as well—were slave owners. According to one source, of the 55 delegates to the Constitutional Convention, 49% *owned slaves.* [4]

By the 1770s, the practice of slavery was so ingrained into the culture, it required a divine revelation to awaken people's conscience to grasp the horrendous evil of it. Eventually and inevitably, the words enshrined in the Declaration of Independence; "...all men are created equal..." began to sink in. As we shall see later, many of the Founders changed their views regarding the sin of human slavery and actively sought to abolish it.

Nearly a hundred years after the American Revolutionary War, the powerful idea that "...all men are created equal" became a rally-cry and a major justification for the American Civil War. *That* epic struggle cost the lives of nearly 500,000 Americans, and settled the issue once and for all, abolishing slavery forever in the United States. This important change in our national policy came at a terrible price. For perspective, the total number of dead in the Civil War exceeded America's losses in *every war* from the Revolutionary War to the Afghan-Iraq wars combined.

Why Do People Enslave Others?

For the Islamist, the justification for slavery arose primarily from the teachings of Mohammed himself, as recorded in the Qu'ran and later by the Caliphs in the Hadith. "Infidels" (which included Christians, Jews, and *anyone else* who is not a Muslim) lived under constant threat of the oppression and domination of the "Umah" or Islamic nations. The above-referenced book by Prof. Davis gives much detail to this, and I will not enlarge upon it here.

To understand the underlying reasons why these practices emerged and flourished in Westernized, so-called "Christian" societies," we must grasp the underlying political and humanist presumptions that enabled the entire issue of institutional and legal racism and slavery.

Be They Men, or Be They Monkeys?

One of the most heinous quasi-scientific/ideological factors that threw open the doors of cruelty and human slavery against people of color was the influence of human evolutionary theory. Long before the 1800s, this evil lie was responsible for philosophically justifying countless acts of exploitation and brutality against weaker people all over the world.

Although evolutionary theories of creation and the supposed evolution of humanity from lesser-evolved species were entertained as far back in history as Aristotle and Plato, it was the work of British naturalist, geologist, and biologist, Charles Robert Darwin (1809-1882), that legitimized the concept of evolution in the "modern" scientific mind. His seminal book, *The Origin of Species*, applied evolution to animal *and* human development.

How did Darwin's influence impact relationships between secular Europeans and Native Americans? Thanks to Darwinist philosophy, Native Americans were often regarded as subhuman "savages" by secular explorers. Those who embraced this evil lie regarded darker-skinned natives as lower forms of sub-human "monkeys." Those psychologically poisoned by evolution theory assumed these "lower forms" could be bought and sold, exploited, abused, manipulated, killed, or driven away at will by those of "higher" evolutionary development and superior weapons.

This evil philosophy formed the basis for the entire notion of racism. The twisted concept that certain humans were "farther down" on an imagined evolutionary "scale," and therefore assumed to be "backward" or "behind" higher forms of humans in life's "race" made it seem reasonable to people that it was acceptable to exploit, dominate, abuse, or even kill lesser evolved "proto-humans." Thus, we gained the term "race" in a twisted scientific classification of whole people groups developed according to their skin color or physical characteristics. This evil prejudice made it philosophically easier for evolution-indoctrinated racists to subdue their conscience and "act out" their arrogant cruelty in their quest for some fantasized developmental perfection. Darwin's "Survival of the Fittest" concept, as outlined in his Origin of Species, threw open the evil door of human slavery and—in some cases—mass-murder and genocide upon "inferior races."

For example, untold hundreds of thousands of Native Australian Aboriginals ("Ab-Origines" or "lesser evolved") were often hunted down and slaughtered on sight by white European evolutionists because they considered them sub-human animals. It is impossible to estimate the multiplied millions of people all over the world who suffered abuse and merciless slaughter in the name of "scientific" evolutionary "progress." [5]

Darwin is quoted:

At some future point, not distant as measured by centuries, the civilized races of man will almost certainly exterminate and replace the savage races throughout the world. [6]

Some defenders of Darwin's theories have tried to excuse Charles Darwin's words by asserting that he was personally opposed to human slavery, and would have been appalled to learn that his theories were used to justify racial genocide. He does not get a pass with this writer, however, and any second-guessing about his true motives does nothing to minimize the horrendous impact his ideas had upon the lives of untold millions of people. Emboldened by this monstrous lie, fallen men sought to justify entire political and societal movements to "cleanse the gene pool" of the "lesser races." (E.G., Margaret Sanger's Planned Parenthood and Eugenics efforts, and Hitler's "Final Solution.")

Standing in stark contrast against this repulsive lie is the biblical worldview which teaches us that God:

> *...hath made of one blood all mankind,*
> *to dwell on all the face of the earth,*
> *and hath assigned the seasons*
> *which were ordained before,*
> *and the bounds of their habitation...*
> Acts 17:26 (Emphasis added)

The "Noble Savage" Myth

Leaving the subject of Darwinian human evolution, we will now turn our attention to the subject of how this underlying pseudo-scientific lie influenced the tragic interactions between European expansionists and the "native" populations they encountered.

Another progressive/leftist hammer used to de-legitimatize the United States is the "Noble Savage" myth. The entire construct of this line of argument, based upon the "evolutionary origins of mankind" myth, is the idea that prior "native" populations possess some special standing and moral superiority because they somehow evolved in situ before the "evil white Europeans" arrived and ruined their idyllic paradise.

This hypocritical fantasy represents the other side of the double-edged sword of evolutionary delusions. Simply put, the evolutionist justifies (on the one hand) the exploitation and elimination of lesser-evolved hominids, and then hypocritically seeks to use the *same* logic to lionize and create "innocence martyrs" of native populations in order to bash western civilization.

To cut the legs out from under the "social justice" warriors regarding "evil white colonists" ravaging poor natives, I here state unequivocally that every single person now "occupying" the landmass of North America—or nearly anywhere *else* on the planet—are, in the final analysis, colonists. New and highly credible genetic research points to the fact that all humans began from a single point of origin on Earth—a genetic singularity—and over time spread across the planet. People adaptively diversified according to varying climates and environmental factors into all the varieties and colors of humankind we now observe around the world.

> *The "single origin of humans theory" combines studies of global genetic variations in humans with skull measurements across the world. The research represents a devastating blow for supporters of multiple origins of human evolutionary theory.* [7]

Many evolutionists tout an "Afrocentric" origin of humans, basing their assumption upon a proto-human, ape-like creature discovered in 1974 named "Lucy." Paleontologists working the dig site in Hadar, Ethiopia, where the creature was found, named it after the popular Beatles song: *Lucy in the Sky With Diamonds* because they enjoyed listening to Beatles music while working the excavation. Bone fragments comprising approximately 40% of the creature were discovered and cataloged by paleontologist Donald C. Johanson. [8] Some anthropologists, however, suggest that "Lucy" is nothing more than a previously unknown extinct species of ape, and not in any way human at all.

The Biblical account of the worldwide flood and the repopulation of the earth via the descendants of Noah and his children (described in Genesis chapter six) makes perfect sense. In the biblical model, everyone presently on earth descended from Noah and his immediate family who exited the Ark after it came to rest upon the mountains of Ararat. Naturally, those who reject the biblical narrative out of hand as mere religious mythology *must* come up with an alternative explanation for the scientific fact that humans everywhere share distinct genetic commonalities explicable only via a common ancestor in the past. Adam and Eve works for me.

Recent evidence seems to establish beyond credible dispute that every populated place in the world, including the Americas, is comprised of humans who immigrated from somewhere near modern-day Turkey. Therefore, even "Native Americans" were, at one time, immigrants to this land.

Some anthropologists speculate that the original "Native" Americans first migrated from somewhere in Asia over a once-extant land bridge stretching across the Bering Strait from modern-day Russia into Alaska. Quoting from a Scientific American article:

> *Genetic evidence supports a theory that ancestors of Native Americans lived for 15,000 years on the Bering Land Bridge between Asia and North America until the last ice age ended... A comparison of DNA from 600 modern Native Americans with ancient DNA recovered from a late Stone Age human skeleton from Mal'ta near Lake Baikal in southern Siberia shows that Native Americans diverged genetically from their Asian ancestors around 25,000 years ago, just as the last ice age was reaching its peak.* [9]

From the area of modern Alaska, according to the theory, people eventually migrated to points south and east. As their numbers grew, individual tribes were formed, and eventually, the entire north and south American landmasses were populated. There is a fascinating video which graphically illustrates this global migration of humans across the face of the earth. [10]

While I disagree with the time-stamp assumptions within the above article as well as in the video—which are entirely to be expected from evolution-influenced writers—the basic premise seems sound and is harmonious with the biblical narrative. I am an unapologetic "young Earther," and believe these migrations took *far* less time than estimated by current researchers. Also, as I've mentioned, the Biblical account places the initial point of origin for human populations far more recently upon the mountains of Ararat, where the Ark landed after the global flood.

No matter when or where one thinks humans originated, or how long the migrations took, my *main* point stands. Every people group came to America (and everywhere *else* for that matter) from *someplace* else, migrating across the face of the Earth. Therefore, everyone is ultimately an colonist. I raise this issue only to blunt the arguments of America-hating leftist-progressives who constantly bash the U.S. and regard *anyone* who thinks our national borders should be respected as xenophobic racists. From a purely *evolutionary* perspective, European immigration to colonize America was no more "unjust" or "immoral" as any of the *other* countless immigrations that took place in antiquity. However, the United States has *always* welcomed new immigrants, but national security requires that it be conducted legally, and with due diligence.

Native Americans Didn't Live In "Utopia"

Another lie progressive-leftists promote is the false allegation that before the arrival of so-called "evil white Europeans," Native Americans were enjoying long, healthy, and happy lives in peaceful communities, cohabiting in perfect harmony with nature in a pristine wilderness. This is, of course, a Utopian myth. Prior Americans had their own unique societal problems for many centuries, long, long before white Europeans began to colonize the eastern shores. By the time Christopher Columbus sailed west from Spain in search of new trade routes to Asia in 1492, or the Mayflower pilgrims landed in 1620 at Plymouth Rock 128 years after Columbus' expedition, Native Americans were suffering all the dysfunctions, violence, and greed issues common to all men.

Inter-tribal wars were not uncommon, and Native Americans knew all-too-well how to put on war-paint and mount epic military battles with neighboring tribes before the arrival of the first white Europeans. The very *survival* of a tribe depended upon their ability to learn the art of war and teach their young men to be tough, brave warriors to defend their homes and families. "Homeland Security" was a practical necessity long before it became a bloated bureaucracy.

Native Americans also knew that any display of weakness invited aggression. Many of these tribal people lived with the constant risk of brutal attacks by other tribes. They suffered cruel and violent deaths from wars, diseases, starvation, earthquakes, famines, violent storms, or attacks by wild animals. Despite popular romantic myths about tribal herbal medicine or the esoteric practices of "Medicine Men," people suffered and died from venomous snakebites, falls, and injuries from fighting or hunting. North American life before the arrival of the first European settlers was far from an idyllic paradise—contrary to modern "politically correct" fantasies. Fallen humans, wherever you find them, are evil, no matter how much or little pigmentation exists in their skin or the languages they speak.

The 19th century British Baptist pastor, Charles H. Spurgeon, is aptly quoted as saying:

You cannot slander human nature;
it is worse than words can paint it.

It cannot be denied that many egregious injustices and acts of barbaric violence were committed against these prior inhabitants in the Americas in the subsequent years after European settlers began to arrive and explore westward. A clash of cultures was virtually inevitable, due to the fallen, depraved nature of man, and his constant quest for power, wealth, and lust for blood.

Columbus did NOT "Discover" America

The Italian explorer, Christopher Columbus, has often been falsely credited with "discovering" America, however, as I've demonstrated in previous paragraphs, other explorers "discovered" America long, long before Columbus did. In fact, new evidence indicates that the Phoenicians, Vikings, Chinese, and even Israelis—during the reign of King Solomon—visited the continents of the Americas thousands of years before Columbus. These earlier visitors, however, did not establish permanent colonies until the Puritan Pilgrims established Jamestown in 1607. The Pilgrims later founded Plymouth, Massachusetts in 1620. [11]

Many of the early Puritan colonists were seeking religious freedom, and held to a postmillennial eschatology, believing that the New World would eventually become a bastion of Christian prosperity in order to spread the Christian gospel of Christ to the entire world. The famous 18th-century evangelist, George Whitefield, held this view and often preached about America's place in prophecy and divine destiny. (More about this later.)

Christopher Columbus has become a favorite "whipping boy" for modern leftist progressives, who seize upon him as a quintessential example of the greedy, white, European oppressor. There can be no denying that Columbus was a man with flaws and personal sins, as he himself freely admits in his own writings, however, I do not believe he was the monster that modern leftist progressives paint him as.

A Roman Catholic, Columbus was a man of his times, growing up in a culture where Christianity was primarily understood within the framework of Papal Rome. Born in Genoa in 1451, his life spanned 55 years until his death in Valladolid, Spain on May 20, 1506, nearly 11 years before a Roman Catholic Augustinian monk named Martin Luther nailed his 95 theses to the Wittenburg Castle Church door in 1517, sparking the Protestant Reformation. Roman Catholicism was, for the most part, the *only* expression of Christianity most people of Columbus' time knew. However, there was another side of Columbus' character and personality that is completely ignored in the present atmosphere of "politically correct" brainwashing we are all constantly bombarded with in our schools and universities.

For one thing, Columbus was not, as some foolishly assert, seeking to prove that the Earth was a globe. Even in *his* time, only a very few crackpots seriously thought the Earth was flat. There are a few "flat-earthers" among us even today. In fact, hardly *anyone* in antiquity thought the Earth was flat. Ptolemy in the second century estimated the circumference of the globe to be 180,000 miles, and Aristotle, who lived in the fourth century thought it was 400,000 miles around the equator. Columbus, based on his scientific and scripture studies, was completely convinced that the Earth was a globe, approximately 20,000 miles in circumference. This figure was remarkably close to the actual modern measured distance of 24,901 miles, and *this* was an amazing achievement considering he had no satellite photos, modern technology, etc.

What Motivated Columbus' Voyages?

There remains much controversy regarding Columbus' motives. In 1492, he sailed across the Atlantic in a three-ship flotilla from Spain. He commanded the Santa Maria and was accompanied by the ships Pinta and the Niña. According to his own writings, he was seeking to find a new route to India in order to open up a new trade route to the Far East. The Islamists of his time had virtually shut down the "Silk Road" across the Middle East, and Europe was in desperate need of new trade opportunities. He made a total of four voyages

Slavery, Racism, and Natives 161

to the Caribbean and South America between 1492 and 1504. More than this, however, Columbus held a conviction that his explorations would bring the Christian gospel to the entire world.

To prove this assertion, perhaps it is best to allow him to speak for himself from his only published book, *The Book of Prophesies*. Here are a few excerpts to consider:

> *At a very early age I began to sail upon the ocean. For more than forty years, I have sailed everywhere that people go. I prayed to the most merciful Lord about my heart's great desire, and He gave me the spirit and the intelligence for the task: seafaring, astronomy, geometry, arithmetic, skill in drafting spherical maps and placing correctly the cities, rivers, mountains, and ports. I also studied cosmology, history, chronology, and philosophy.*
>
> *It was the Lord who put into my mind (I could feel His hand upon me) the fact that it would be possible to sail from here to the Indies. All who heard of my project rejected it with laughter, ridiculing me. There is no questions that the inspiration was from the Holy Spirit, because he comforted me with rays of marvelous illumination from the Holy Scriptures, a strong and clear testimony from the 44 books of the Old Testament, from the four Gospels, and from the 23 Epistles of the blessed Apostles, encouraging me continually to press forward; and without ceasing for a moment they now encourage me to make haste.*

As I read Columbus' own words, I was struck by the deep Christian convictions he held. His reverence for Christ and the holy bible are clearly perceived throughout his writings. Again, this is an aspect of his life entirely ignored in modern textbooks. He appears to be extremely well-educated in the scriptures, and if we didn't know he was a Roman Catholic, we'd almost suspect that he was a Reformed Protestant long before the Protestant Reformation swept Europe in the 16th century. Here are a few more excerpts from his book…

> *…I am a most unworthy sinner, but I have cried out to the Lord for grace and mercy, and they have covered me completely. I have found the sweetest consolations since I made it my whole purpose to enjoy His marvelous presence.*
>
> *…Oh what a gracious Lord, who desires that people should perform for Him those things for which He holds Himself responsible! Day and night moment by moment, everyone should express to Him their most devoted*

> *gratitude. I said that some of the prophecies remained yet to be fulfilled. These are great and wonderful things for the earth, and the signs are that the Lord is hastening the end. The fact that the gospel must still be preached to so many lands in such a short time – this is what convinces me.*

Christopher Columbus was unique in several significant ways. He was obviously a highly educated man of keen intellect and an intimate relationship with Christ. This is remarkable in that he lived in a time when very few people had access to the scriptures, and only an educated few could actually read them in Latin. He lived long before the Protestant Reformation took hold across Europe and the scriptures became widely available through the new technology of the printing press.

Postmillennial?

It also appears that Columbus held distinctly Postmillennial eschatological views. For those unfamiliar with that term, Postmillennialism is a belief that Christ's kingdom will increasingly influence and eventually permeate and dominate the entire earth and all nations. He believed, as did many of the early Protestant ministers such as Jonathan Edwards in the English colonies many years later, that the vast American continent was destined to be a springboard for the spread of the gospel of Christ throughout the world.

According to American Reformed theologian, teacher, and author, L. Boettner (1901–1990) Postmillennialism is defined as a period of unknown length prior to the return of Christ in which:

> *…The changed character of individuals will be reflected in an uplifted social, economic, political and cultural life of mankind. The world at large will then enjoy a state of righteousness such as at the present time has been seen only in relatively small and isolated groups, as for example in some family circles, some local church groups and kindred organizations. This does not mean that there ever will be a time on this earth when every person will be a Christian, or that all sin will be abolished. But it does mean that evil in all its many forms eventually will be reduced to negligible proportions, that Christian principles will be the rule, not the exception, and that Christ will return to a truly Christianized world…* [12]

Columbus was not alone in his eschatological views. Following is a *very* partial list of theologians who held to this theological persuasion.

Theodore Beza, John Owen, William Perkins, Samuel Rutherford, Martin

Bucer, Jonathan Edwards, Matthew Henry, John Cotton, John Calvin, George Whitefield, Archibald Alexander, Charles Hodge, A. A. Hodge, Benjamin B. Warfield. If you are unfamiliar with some of these names, you should consider doing a search online, which will provide you with uncountable hours of edifying theological study.

On his first voyage to the Americas in 1492, Columbus brought no priests, for this was purely an exploratory effort. In later voyages, he did bring along Catholic priests. From this writer's point of view, this was regrettable, yet understandable given the times. In subsequent decades, the Jesuits also came. Established by Ignatius Loyola in 1540, the scourge of the Jesuit-inspired Spanish Inquisition brought great suffering and death to the native populations. This is a subject for another book, however. Suffice to say, Columbus was a man who, in spite of his faults and personal sins, was greatly used by God to bring the knowledge of Christ to the New World.

Not All Who Came Had Pure Motives

As I wrote in the previous chapter, many came to these shores with an evolutionary paradigm that the native peoples were uncivilized "savages" ripe for conquering, exploitation, and enslavement. No excuse can ever be made for their cruelty against the native inhabitants they encountered.

These greedy opportunists came seeking gold and land holdings and took advantage of these prior Americans, cheating them in trade, abusing their women and children, and insulting their culture and customs. Native Americans, while less advanced technologically, were far from uncivilized savages. Most tribes lived in highly organized societies with systems of justice, honor, and moral codes that rivaled—in some measure—many of the brutish secular European explorers who came with superior weapons to exploit them. It begs the question as to who the "real" savages were.

To be fair, however, there were also wicked men among the natives. As sons of Adam, they shared the same fallen, depraved nature as every other human being. It is a popular myth in our time to cast all Native Americans as virtuous innocent victims, but this was never the case. Anyone denying this reality is clinging to the "everyone is basically good" myth. There's enough blame to go around on all sides. However, this does not mean that all fallen men "act out" the very worst expressions of their fallen nature. There were also people on both sides who, by the grace of God, were enabled to express a measure of benevolence toward their fellow men.

A Great Native American Leader

One outstanding example was Chief Tecumseh, a great Native American leader. Tecumseh sought to unite the scattered tribes of eastern North America to negotiate better with the expanding empire of the United States. Chief Tecumseh's wisdom was profound and reflects a keen intellect. His wisdom continues to speak to us.

> *So live your life that the fear of death can never enter your heart. Trouble no one about his religion; respect yours. Love your life, perfect your life, beautify all things in your life. Seek to make your life long and of service to your people. Prepare a noble death song for the day when you go over the Great Divide.*
>
> *Always give a word or sign of salute when meeting or passing a friend, or even a stranger, if in a lonely place. Show respect to all people, but grovel to none. When you arise in the morning, give thanks for the light, for your life and strength. Give thanks for your food and for the joy of living. If you see no reason for giving thanks, the fault lies in yourself.*
>
> *Touch not the poisonous firewater that makes wise ones into fools and robs the spirit of its vision. When your time comes to die be not like those whose hearts are filled with the fear of death, so that when their time comes they weep and pray for a little more time to live their lives over again in a different way.*
>
> *Live your life so that when you sing your death song, you will die like a hero who is going home with no shame to meet the Creator and your family.* April 9, 1809

As far as we know, Tecumseh was not a Christian, but a strong case could be made that much of what he thought and believed was built from lumber he borrowed from a Jewish carpenter in Israel.

Among the European immigrants were many Christian men and women who were fleeing centuries-long oppressions by cruel, despotic religionists and the governments controlled by them.

Unfortunately, it was nearly inevitable that some of their oppressors would also make their way to the "New World" as well, and continue their sinister mischief. Fallen and evil men can always be counted upon to express the lowest forms of barbarity, as repeatedly shown by history, no matter what their skin color or country of origin.

Slavery, Racism, and Natives 165

The Influence of Christianity on Early American History
The Founding Fathers of America were powerfully inspired by a radical concept, based on the Bible. That concept was first penned (as far as I can determine) by a British Christian writer named John Dryden (1631-1700). I shared this quote on the first page of his book:

> *God has endowed man with inalienable rights, among which are self-government, reason, and conscience. Man is properly self-governed only when he is guided rightly and governed by his Maker, divine Truth, and Love.*

I believe it is entirely possible that Dryden's words—borrowed obviously from biblical texts—were an influence upon the sermons of Calvinist itinerant preachers such as George Whitefield, Jonathan Edwards, and Samuel Davies during the 1700s in the early-American colonies. These men of God echoed and amplified the *biblical* idea that "inalienable rights" were a gift from God and not merely the capricious toleration of earthly rulers. This idea stirred up a hurricane-force wind of controversy in the face of European royal elitists who formerly claimed a "divine right" of kings to absolutely rule over other men.

There can be no doubt that the Founders were powerfully influenced by this Biblical view of man. Thomas Jefferson clearly borrowed philosophical lumber from Dryden when he penned the immortal words at the beginning of the Declaration of Independence, 76 years after Dryden's death;

> *...all men are created equal and endowed by their Creator with certain unalienable rights.*

I must point out that Jefferson *added* the words; "...all men are created equal," which likely sprang from his manifestly humanistic training. Dryden *never* penned the words, "...all men are created equal," because this is not supported by the Bible. All persons are created with lesser or greater portions of gifts and abilities according to the predeterminate purposes of God for *each* of His creatures. Jefferson championed the concept of "self" government in a humanistic political sense, but, as Dryden aptly penned, *"Man is properly self-governed only when he is guided rightly and governed by his Maker."*

However, the power of this idea moved a generation of Colonial Americans to establish a new nation. The very idea that the Creator *Himself* is the one who bestows upon men "...certain inalienable rights..." was a radical and revolutionary concept in the 1700s. It threatened to strip kings, dictators, governments, or earthly potentates of any authority to "grant" rights. God alone possesses such power. The full implications of those words took some time to take hold of the minds and consciences of men, but eventually, it did.

Dangerous Thinking

The idea all men are "created equal" (at least in the sense that all humans were created in the image and likeness of God and deserving of respect in political matters) shook the very foundations of old European royalty and aristocracy to its core. Despotic governments and power-addicted men despise the very idea of human political equality, for it wrests from their grasping hands the control they crave over other men. This foundational concept eventually gave rise to the American Revolutionary War. The Founders well understood that certain individual freedoms granted to all men—such as life, liberty, and the pursuit of happiness—came directly from the hand of God alone.

In my view, the arrival of Reformed Christians to the shores of America was also God's benevolent gift of His grace to this land. These believers sought freedom from the widespread political and religious oppression of Old Europe, and their Bible-based theology guided their interactions with Native Americans. In most cases, these Reformed Christians, or "Puritans" as they were so called, enjoyed peaceful relationships with their native neighbors. They understood the Bible teaches that all men are created in the image and likeness of God and, therefore, each person should be treated with kindness and respect out of honor to their Creator. Native Americans, like most people everywhere, mostly respond positively and peacefully when they were shown genuine love and respect.

With the conclusion of the Revolutionary War and America's separation from England, a Constitutional Republic was established, based upon biblical principles. This resulted in unparalleled strides forward in science, medicine, social, and economic development. It was not without struggle—fallen human nature being what it is—for abuses of power and selfish exploitation were inevitable. However, the means required to correct such evils were embodied in the founding documents, and as the rule of law became established, many wrongs were corrected, eventually including the scandal of human slavery. Fallen humanity requires an appropriate government to suppress the natural tendency toward acts of selfish evil. The wisely-crafted Founding Documents established the means and the ability to govern and establish justice.

Destroying the Lie of Racism

Nearly 98 years after the final battle of the Civil War at the Battle of Palmito Ranch in May of 1865, true racial equality was yet but a dream unrealized in America. Old prejudices and attitudes often die slow deaths. Nearly 100 years after the Civil War, racial segregation was still a painful reality for many people of color. However, the dream of true equality under the law for all citizens, no matter what the quantity of melanin in their skin, inspired by our Constitution and Bill of Rights, burned brightly in the hearts of many people, particularly Christians. The struggle came to a major high point during a massive civil rights rally in our nation's capital in 1963. I was only a boy of 13 at the time, but remember watching the rally and speeches on our family's black and white TV in Missouri. My mother carefully taught me as a child that all people, no matter what the color of their skin, were to be honored and respected because humans are created in the image and likeness of God. I never forgot my mother's wisdom.

I would be remiss if I neglected to give due recognition to the American Christian leader, Dr. Martin Luther King, Jr.. Dr. King courageously took up the torch of racial equality and appealed to the conscience of his fellow Americans to do something about the plight of men and women yet suffering under the cruel yoke of racial segregation and hatred. Dr. King was not content to merely react with anger and rage at racial injustice, nor did he cower in fear. Unlike many modern race-baiting shake-down artists who masquerade as "civil rights activists" in order to personally profit through perpetually stirring up racial hatred and divisions, Dr. King stood up for truth within a truly Christian framework. He appealed to the higher aspirations of all men of every color. When he raised his voice on the steps of the Lincoln Memorial in Washington D.C. on August 28, 1963, and delivered his now-famous "I have a dream" oration, an entire nation was impacted. His words ring as true today as they did then:

> ...let us not wallow in the valley of despair, I say to you today, my friends. And so even though we face the difficulties of today and tomorrow, I still have a dream. It is a dream deeply rooted in the American dream. I have a dream that one day this nation will rise up and live out the true meaning of its creed: "We hold these truths to be self-evident, that all men are created equal.
>
> I have a dream that one day on the red hills of Georgia, the sons of former slaves and the sons of former slave owners will be able to sit down together at the table of brotherhood. I have a dream that one day even the

state of Mississippi, a state sweltering with the heat of injustice, sweltering with the heat of oppression, will be transformed into an oasis of freedom and justice.

I have a dream that my four little children will one day live in a nation where they will not be judged by the color of their skin but by the content of their character.

I have a dream today! [13]

Surely Dr. King was not a perfect man, for he was a fallen son of Adam just as are we all. His moral failures and personal sins are a matter of public record. However, who among us could make any claim of sinless perfection and cast the first stone of condemnation upon him? We have all, without a single exception, committed sin and stand condemned before a Holy God. But for the grace and mercy of Christ, and the forgiveness of sin through His sacrifice, we would all justly end up in hell. We cannot judge Dr. King's spiritual status—for only God knows this—but it cannot be denied that he influenced an entire generation, giving them a higher vision of life. This was the legacy he left for posterity. He was a fearless leader who stood up against the tyranny of injustice and racial hatred leaving an enduring example of perseverance, courage, and compassion that would inspire generations.

Notes

1. America's first slave owner was a black man. http://tinyurl.com/mhtet52

2. ISLAM AND SLAVERY, First published by the Barnabas Fund in Barnabas Aid, April-May 2007 ©2007 http://www.answering-islam.org/Green/slavery.htm

3. https://tinyurl.com/yd8efqyq

4. https://tinyurl.com/ju3h3cn

5. Genocide in Australia - EXPOSED Australian Aborigines Genocide https://www.youtube.com/watch?v=myGZL9r6LQc

6. The Descent of Man, and Selection in Relation to Sex, by Charles Darwin, published 1871, pp. 200–201, Vol. 1:

7. New Research Proves Single Origin Of Humans In Africa, Date: July 19, 2007, Source: Biotechnology and Biological Sciences Research Council https://tinyurl.com/2v3bzp

8. What Was "Lucy"? Fast Facts on an Early Human Ancestor, National Geographic News, September 20, 2006, https://tinyurl.com/by2qee

9. First Americans Lived on Bering Land Bridge for Thousands of Years, by Scott Armstrong Elias, March 4, 2014 https://tinyurl.com/kvs5vsd

10. Charting Prehistoric Human Migration. Alex Kuzoian and the Geographic Project, National Geographic https://tinyurl.com/ycewz2cd

11. Did King Solomon's Navy Discover America? Tamar Yonah, 02/11/07 Israel National News https://tinyurl.com/y8vz9f8e

12. L. Boettner, The Millennium, p. 14

13. I Have a Dream speech by Dr. Martin Luther King. http://www.americanrhetoric.com/speeches/mlkihaveadream.htm

16

No Borders=No Nation

*Please think about national security.
People are coming across our borders
to do very bad things to us.*
Tom Tancredo
Former U.S. Congressman

~~~~~~

The subject of illegal immigration and border security is currently a "hot button" issue and cause célèbre among progressive leftists in the United States. All efforts to enforce immigration law to stem the flow of millions of illegal aliens into the United States across our vast and marginally enforced southern border is almost always met with passionate opposition by those who regard any such efforts as acts of oppression against poor and disadvantaged people of color. President Trump's policies to limit the influx of people from rogue Islamic nation-states have faced stiff opposition from leftist judges and courts, in spite of all evidence that it is nearly impossible to credibly vet potential immigrants from certain areas because these failed nation-states are controlled by radical Islamic jihadists.

Liberal-leftists find it easy to turn a blind eye to the real and present danger that millions of undocumented people—among whom are those with violent political or religious agendas—now crashing our borders represent. There are two identifiable groups who resist and rebel against the enforcement of U.S. Immigration laws. The one group is made up of liberal-progressives and certain liberal Christian denominations who are motivated (often sincerely) by stereotypical and intensely emotional images of poor, disenfranchised, and oppressed refugees of color. These are primarily "social justice" advocates, and regard U.S. Immigration laws as oppressive and unfair to the poor. The *very idea* of a desperate refugee pulls sharply at their heartstrings.

A second group operates under a far more sinister flag. These are the Socialist/Communists who see open borders as a means of "crashing" the U.S. economy and overwhelming the welfare system with the aim of fomenting civil unrest and the eventual overthrow of the United States and the Constitution. Those within these ranks often disguise their true agenda by working within the system as educators, politicians, and judges within the court system. These comprise what has been called the "shadow government," worming their way into positions of influence *within* the system in order to *destroy* it. One well-known advocate of this strategy in recent decades—among many others—was the American Communist, Saul Alinsky, who published his widely-read book; "Rules for Radicals" in 1971. Alinski's *Rules* had two well-documented fans in recent decades who admired and utilized his strategies: Barrack Hussein Obama, and Hillary Clinton. *Much* more could be written about these radicals, but I will leave this for others to explicate.

Under the above situation, *anyone* who *dares* call for secure borders or reasonable restrictions on immigrants—*even upon those coming in from radical Islamic rogue states*—is immediately targeted and slandered as a hateful bigot or selfish "white separatist" racist who cares *nothing* for the disadvantaged. Such vicious slander is calculated to intimidate and silence those who call "BS" on the insanity of open border social-justice warriors. If *anyone* becomes too credible in exposing and identifying this sinister agenda, there is *no limit* to the degree of slander, character assassination, or accusations that the leftist-controlled media will employ. Some whistleblowers who dared expose the "shadow agenda" in recent years have turned up quite dead under highly suspicious circumstances. It is entirely in God's hands as far as my own life is concerned, for I'm fully convinced that no one can harm me unless God permits it for His own purposes and glory.

Immigration Policies: NOT About Emotions
Thinking people realize there are other serious considerations than emotions that cannot be ignored regarding illegal immigration. Employment opportunities for U.S. citizens are being lost because illegals are flooding the labor markets with cheap labor. Our towns and cities are spending scarce tax revenues to deal with the added strain upon our social and law enforcement systems. Liberals wink at these growing problems because many entertain an assumption that wealthy North Americans somehow "owe" poorer people of color "social justice" as some sort of "payback." This worldview makes the entire border enforcement situation an emotional and highly-politicized issue.

As mentioned above, liberal progressives seize upon these objections, accusing people who place a high priority on national security as "xenophobes" and/or "racists." They tend to stereotype *all* people of color as victims, and conversely, all white people are—you guessed it—racist oppressors. This narrative is heralded in college and university classrooms as the raison d'être for leftist policies now being promoted by haters of the United States. A commonly employed psyop-strategy used by the progressive left is the concept of "Social Justice," and nowhere is that strategy more in play than in our nation's border enforcement policies.

For decades, under successive Presidential Administrations, tens of millions of undocumented illegal immigrants flooded across our porous southern border, with border enforcement efforts consistently hamstrung by Presidential Executive Orders that penalize Officers who too-zealously try to enforce existing immigration laws. Hopefully, under the new Trump Administration, we will see a reversal of this trend, and effective enforcement of existing immigration laws, while fair immigration reforms are crafted.

According to a recent New York Times article, approximately 12 million illegal immigrants are living in the United States. [1] Other sources, such as the Colorado Alliance for Immigration Reform (CAIRCO.org), scoff at this estimate, and put the actual numbers much, much higher.

> *There are currently 15 to 20 million illegal aliens in this country by many estimates, but the real numbers could be much higher and the numbers increase every day because our borders are not secure (no matter what the politicians tell you—don't believe them for a second).* [2]

According to another article by By Fred Elbel, copyright 2004-2014

> *...Under the Obama administration, the Border Patrol has been essentially incapacitated. Obama's DACA amnesty has been issued, the child illegal alien invasion has occurred, and deportation numbers have been fudged. It would be reasonable to project that if 20 million illegal aliens were present in 2005, 38 to 40 million illegal aliens could certainly reside in the United States in 2014.* Emphasis added [3]

Not All Illegals "Hate" the U.S.

There is no doubt that the *vast* majority of people trying to enter the United States are desperately seeking a better life for themselves and their children. Who can blame them? The grinding poverty, political corruption, disease, crime, and despotic governments of many Central American countries make life there nearly unbearable. I speak from personal experience, having traveled numerous times to Central and South America over the years as a Christian worker. The vast majority of people I met there are suffering terribly, and yearn for the freedoms and economic opportunities that are available in the United States.

However, we cannot simply ignore the fact that *not all* who are sneaking across our borders have the best intentions. Ensconced among the poor immigrants are narco-gangsters, violent criminals, sexual predators, and Islamic Jihadists on errands of evil, masquerading as poor oppressed immigrants. In addition, some of these border crashers are carrying untreated virulent diseases. Without effective border screening and vetting, it is impossible to tell who is who, or what their health status is, or the quality of their intentions. This represents a clear and present danger to the citizens of the U.S.

Citizenship: A Right or a Privilege?

America's earlier immigrants, who entered our nation legally through Ellis Island's doors or other border crossing facilities during the 1800s and early 1900s, eagerly embraced—for the most part—America's founding principles, culture, language, and laws. Most of these new immigrants loved the very idea of America and hoped and prayed for the day that they could stand tall and unashamed as proud American citizens.

Sadly, this is often no longer the case. Increasingly, people entering our country illegally are showing little or no interest in assimilating into "norte americano" culture or language. Incredibly, some illegals even express outrage and resentment when U.S. Citizens show their patriotism or display the United States flag. There is no shortage of liberal-progressives who fall all over themselves to accommodate this nonsense by incessant efforts to ban the U.S. flag from schools or on clothing by American citizens in order to not "offend" anyone. The intense gravity generated by the "black hole" of political correctness and the emotional siren-call of "social justice" is hard for emotionally-driven "sheeple" to resist.

I expect it is inevitable that I will be accused of being xenophobic, anti-immigrant, racist, or worse, for even raising this issue. As I said before, such lies and accusations are the standard psyop "weapon of choice" for leftist-progressives seeking to shout down and intimidate anyone who dares to challenge their Marxist agendas. The fact that my family is multi-racial means nothing to leftist ideologues and their mindless "social justice" agenda.

As far as I'm concerned, the *real* racists are liberal progressives. They obsess over people's skin color and categorize people according to their race—giving greater consideration to those with the "correct" skin color—while denying those same benefits to others with less melanin in their skin. This is utter insanity! When I receive surveys or forms from the government or other organizations asking questions about my race or ethnicity, I REFUSE to answer them. It shouldn't matter *one damn bit* what my skin color is, and I object to such racist questions on principle.

Progressive-liberals, Communists, and the Democrat party—but I'm repeating myself—also entertain the hope that tens of millions of illegal "benefit immigrants" will become a massive potential Democrat voting block that could potentially guarantee Democrat/Progressive victories in all future elections. Progressives are well aware that humans are basically selfish and highly likely to vote for those who promise the most benefits. Politicians know well how to exploit this human weakness for political advantage. No one could have said it better than Rush Limbaugh in his reliably astute commentary after the astonishing re-election of Barack Hussein Obama in November 2012.

> *Conservatism, in my humble opinion, did not lose last night. It's just very difficult to beat Santa Claus. It is practically impossible to beat Santa Claus. People are not going to vote against Santa Claus, especially if the alternative is being your own Santa Claus* [4]

A hopeful footnote is required here. An unexpected turn of events that Progressives could never foresee is the *very real possibility* that God might move by His Spirit upon the hearts and minds of the millions of immigrants already in the country. Many of these people are culturally oriented toward Christianity. Many highly value family, hard work, and are genuinely seeking a better life for themselves and their children.

They are also not stupid. If enough of them ever "catch on" to how they are being "played" as fools by liberals, and that the benefit promises that liberal politicians toss out like candy during their campaigns for office to patronize them are unaffordable lies calculated to bankrupt America, they may turn en-mass against the Democrat agenda and vote for conservatives. When they realize that it is in their best interest and the interests of their children (whom they love more than their own lives) to vote to preserve, protect, and defend the Constitution and the Bill of Rights, it will be "game over" for the progressive agenda.

No Borders = No Nation

Returning to our consideration of illegal immigration, the inescapable fact of our time is that the United States can only hope to endure as a nation if our borders are defended and secured. This is not to say that we should selfishly seal our borders in such a way that we do not welcome people who desire to come here and legitimately share the dream and vision of America. To do so would be equivalent to changing the torch of freedom, held high by the Statue of Liberty, into a fisted hand with the middle index finger extended. No, we are a *nation of immigrants*, and our borders should ever welcome sincere men and women who share a love for our Constitution, our Bill of Rights, and our country, and wish to join us legally.

If we fail to control our borders and diligently vet those entering to determine their *true* intentions, we imperil the safety and security of our nation and people. In my opinion, national security—one of only a few of our federal governments' constitutionally mandated responsibilities—is the essential priority. In fulfillment of this responsibility, our borders MUST be secured. Then, and *only* then, should we establish immigration policies that would make it reasonably possible for honest people to enter legitimately.

As stated before, our southern border is so porous, and enforcement of existing immigration laws so ineffective, we've virtually *no idea* how many people are pouring in, who they are, or the quality of their intentions. Irrefutable evidence reveals that mingled among those who are seeking a better life in a nation they might otherwise admire and love, are violent gang members, drug smugglers, rapists, murderers, and Islamic Jihadists seeking our destruction. The FBI's 2012 National Gang Report, details the peril America faces from criminal elements streaming across our porous borders.[5]

According to a recent article in World Net Daily by Aaron Klein:

> One section of the 79-page report details "Gangs and the U.S. Border." It documents gangs, "especially national-level Hispanic gangs, such as MS-13, the Eme, Sureños, and TB, continue to pose a significant threat to the Southwest border region. The report reveals that "in many cases, gang members who commit criminal activity in the region are not U.S. citizens nor lawful permanent residents." [6]

Open Borders = Clear and Present Danger

A far more ominous threat, which is only rarely discussed by the so-called "mainstream" media, is the threat of terrorism. The recent spate of school shootings over the past two decades may very well be a mere dress rehearsal of carnage to come. I was intensely involved in the response to the Columbine High School massacre in 1999. (See my previous book, *The Martyrs' Torch*) Since that tragedy, I personally responded to numerous school shootings in

America and abroad. Student-on-student violence is horrible, and it is maddening to witness progressives and leftists mindlessly blame the weapons used in these sad events instead of dealing with the underlying societal and mental health issues—as well as the glaring failures of law enforcement agencies to lawfully prevent the violence before it happened—that gave rise to the carnage. I will not get into a debate on the nonsense of "gun free" zones—read; "target-rich kill zones"—at this point, but there is a *much greater threat* our nation's schools are facing, having the potential to cause inestimable psychological damage to our people. I speak of *militarized terror attacks* on our schools.

On September 1, 2004, Islamic Jihadist terrorists in Russia attacked Beslan School Number 1, murdering hundreds of children, teachers, and parents on their first day of the new school year. Unofficial reports set the death toll at over 400. However, numerous eyewitnesses I personally spoke to in Beslan placed the number much higher.

I led a small response team to Beslan a few days after this attack. We visited hospitals full of wounded children, whose eyes stared vacantly in pain and shock. We brought stuffed toys and colorful letters from children at Front Range Christian School in Colorado where my wife and daughter taught and rallied their students to help these grieving young Russians. We also brought financial support for some of the families who lost children or adult family members, to help them get back on their feet after suffering so much physical and emotional trauma.

As a side note, I need to mention something very important. During the weeks I spent in Beslan, few other nations sent delegations to this scene of inhuman outrage. One prominent exception, however, shines out, yet, as far I am aware no Western media outlet reported it. The State of Israel delivered many, many thousands of flowers and letters of condolence encased in clear plastic bags, and placed them every few feet *all around* the Beslan school ruins and atop each and every fresh grave of the victims outside of town. Despite the rabid hatred and anti-Semitic vitriol regularly spewed upon the State of Israel, I have personally witnessed occasions around the world—from Russia to Sri Lanka, including the United States after hurricanes—many acts of kindness and compassion at the scenes of tragedy by the Israeli people. I boldly declare that Jew-hatred and anti-Israel sentiments are moronic at least, and demonic at worst.

Congressman Tom Tancredo of Colorado and his wife Jackie came to Russia in response to this attack. Tom visited Beslan at the same time we were there and also witnessed the heartbreaking carnage first-hand. He was one of a handful of American officials who traveled to Beslan to express America's sorrow and condolences at this despicable act of Islamic terrorism. At great personal risk because of his high-profile diplomatic status, Tom went to the Beslan school ruins under a UN security detail in armored vehicles and placed a large banner of condolence signed by teachers and students from Columbine High School in Littleton, Colorado, the site of our own school tragedy in 1999. Our losses at Columbine paled in comparison to the mass-slaughter of so many hundreds of children in Beslan. My heart swelled and my eyes filled with tears when I first looked at that Columbine banner hanging on the bloodied, smoke-stained wall in the school building's burned-out gymnasium where so many were viciously tortured and slaughtered by Chechen Muslims.

Shortly after my return to the United States following several weeks of ministry in Beslan and Vladikavkaz, Tom and his wife Jackie invited my family and me to his home for some personal time. We traded stories, recalling all we'd both seen and experienced in Russia during the previous weeks.

As we were visiting, I mentioned my deep concern that America might *also* one-day fall victim to such an attack by an organized Islamic terror organization against our school children. Tom shuffled an unclassified congressional report across the table for me to read, and asked if I'd seen this information since returning from Russia. I had not.

The contents were truly chilling. The pages contained a recent intelligence report that there had been an infiltration across our southern border by a group of Islamic radicals from Chechnya, the same country where the Beslan terrorists came from. The report was made public just over a year later in a Washington Times article. Tom cited this report in his book In Mortal Danger: The Battle for America's Border and Security. Here is an excerpt from his book:

> *As if to underscore the horror I had witnessed in Beslan, a news story a few weeks after I returned to the States reported that twenty-five suspected Chechen terrorists had entered the country from Mexico. American intelligence officials said that they believed the Chechens had ties to Islamic militants in their home country—just like the thugs who slaughtered scores of men, women, and children in Beslan.* [7] [8]

Now, over a decade later, it has become clear America's virtually unguarded and open borders could now be used by enemies determined to take our nation down. Islamic jihadist fighters would be *fools* if they didn't try to exploit this weakness in our national security. We will be even *greater fools* if we don't close this vulnerability down before these enemies strike.

Our Daily Dread

I live with a daily sense of dreaded anticipation that the *next* target for a terrorist attack will be against our children in *our* schools. As horrible it is to see a few scores of students killed or wounded in recent student-on-student attacks, try to imagine the crushing psychological blow it would be to the United States if Islamic jihadists staged a Beslan-style attack against several elementary schools on a single day and slaughtered *hundreds* of school students. For those wishing to explore this almost unthinkable scenario, I highly recommend Dr. William R. Forstchen's recent book; *Day of Wrath*. [9]

Many of these fanatics are well-trained assassins, very familiar with the power of psychological warfare. It is likely they would attempt to broadcast their rampage over social media to maximize the psychological impact. How would Americans react if they witnessed school children having their heads sawed off by Allah-praising fanatics over the internet just as they do in the Middle-East? It is almost too horrible to contemplate, but what I saw them do to those little children in Beslan, Russia, should be enough to convince even the most skeptical person that these monsters would do the same on our own soil if given opportunity.

Liberal leftists often express outrage when the subject of arming teachers and school administrators comes up. Their insane fixation on guns being "the problem," and their moronic "gun free zone" signs, displayed prominently at the entrances of schools, merely serve to paint a giant "bullseye" on those buildings. Such well-meaning—yet foolish—policies are a *recipe for disaster*. "Gun free zone" signs only serve to notify violent lawbreakers that they are entering a virtually defenseless, target-rich environment.

Some sheeple will bleat, "but we have a 'resource officer' at *our* school, to guard the children." Think that through for just a moment. What could one or two uniformed (and easily identified) police officers, armed only with small-caliber sidearms, do against a group of highly-trained terrorists armed with military-grade weapons and tactics? The "resource" officers would be the *first* persons the terrorists would locate and murder; thereby rendering the entire school defenseless. The first 911 call would require *at least* 5 to 10 minutes for other responding officers (good guys with guns) to arrive and try to stop the bad guys from capturing hostages, setting up explosives, establishing defensible positions, and slaughtering their young victims within the first few minutes. In the most recent school shooting in Florida, we are faced with the fact that armed officers took cover *outside the school* as they listened to gunfire *inside* the school! Outrageous.

I admit the above scenario is nearly unthinkable to the average American, but that is what makes it such an attractive strategy for terrorists. I've seen the effects of terrorist attacks up close in the U.S., Israel, and Russia, and even made a documentary film about it. I've walked upon the blood of murdered men, women, and children, and met with their broken-hearted families in their homes and hospitals. Without effective border screening, vigilant (and well-trained intelligence services that focus on *real* threats) and even well-armed and trained civilians at points of greatest vulnerability, we're nothing more than naive sitting ducks.

I KNOW there are Islamic terrorists constantly seeking ways to strike us here in the U.S. HOW do I know this? I am aware of how they think. I've lived in Israel and have visited several Islamic countries over the years. I've read some of their literature online and in print. This tragedy can be prevented, but only if our government employees get busy and DO THEIR JOBS according to their Constitutionally-mandated job descriptions. They *must* close the borders and aggressively identify, pursue, and apprehend members of Islamic terror cells *before* they strike.

Since the 9/11 attacks, I've often wondered if our world-envied freedoms—purchased by the blood, sweat, and tears of our honored forefathers and military veterans—might now be sacrificed upon a moronic altar of "Political Correctness." At this time, trends would seem to indicate so, but I remain hopeful. America, not unlike the character Lemuel Gulliver in Johnathan Smith's famous tome, *Gulliver's Travels*, has been tied down by Lilliputian, politically-correct liberal midgets *for far too long*. However, the American people *appear* to be awakening and struggling to throw off the bonds of their oppressors.

With the election of President Trump, there appears to be a major shift toward political sanity once again as a Constitutional Republic. I don't imagine President Trump as some sort of "messiah" for America. That job is already taken by one infinitely more qualified and worthy: the Lord Jesus. I do believe, however, that because the Bible teaches that God rules in the affairs of men, that Donald Trump is *where* he is because *God wanted* him there for a time such as this. He needs our prayers, for he is a human being, subject to all the temptations of fallen mankind. May God use him as He pleases, and bring America back to greatness as a fountainhead of gospel proclamation.

Notes

1. New York Times by Julia Preston, September 23, 2013, http://tinyurl.com/q2qlq2b

2. [footnote]Colorado Alliance for Immigration Reform, http://tinyurl.com/mnnrdld quoting the U.S. Border Patrol Local 2544 (covering most of Arizona) from their website at www.local2544.org Footnote # 36, July 2005

3. How many illegal aliens reside in the United States? A methodology using Border Patrol "got away" statistics, By Fred Elbel, copyright 2004-2014 http://tinyurl.com/mnnrdld

4. http://www.rushlimbaugh.com/daily/2012/11/07/in_a_nation_of_children_santa_claus_wins

5. https://tinyurl.com/pdg694w

6. FBI DATA BACKS UP TRUMP CLAIMS ON ILLEGALS AND CRIME 'American people are sick of watching our glorious nation be destroyed' by Aaron Klein. http://tinyurl.com/ofkozbh

7. In Mortal Danger, By Congressman Tom Tancredo, Cumberland House Publishing, 2006, p. 97

8. Bill Gertz, Chechen Terrorists Probed, Washington Times, October 13, 2005

9. Day of Wrath, a Novella by Dr. William R. Forstchen https://tinyurl.com/ycwmkhlr

17

Our Real Enemy

Please allow me to introduce myself
I'm a man of wealth and taste
I've been around for a long, long year
Stole many a man's soul and faith.
And I was 'round when Jesus Christ
Had his moment of doubt and pain
Made damn sure that Pilate
Washed his hands and sealed his fate.
Pleased to meet you
Hope you guess my name
But what's puzzling you
Is the nature of my game
"Sympathy for the Devil"
Lyrics by Mick Jagger, Keith Richards
Essex Music Int. Ltd.

~~~~~~

Hell is empty, and all the devils are here.
William Shakespeare, The Tempest

~~~~~~

We will face many opponents in our efforts to re-establish our Constitution and Bill of Rights to their rightful place of prominence and honor. However, we must keep in mind that our *real* enemies are not human beings, even if *they* think they are. Ultimately, our real enemies are in the unseen realm where malevolent spirit beings seek to blind humans to truth and inflame the baser passions of fallen humanity to do evil. They operate behind the facade of the tangible, visible world around us, and they profoundly affect how people think and behave. Admittedly, this is a metaphysical outlook, but I assure you, it is very real.

Conspiracies (meaning; "to breath together") have always existed. Some conspiracies are benign and even useful, like when your friends conspire together to throw a surprise birthday party for you. However, there are also some exceedingly evil conspiracies afoot, which seek to bring slavery, misery, and the destruction of humankind. My emphasis here is that conspiracies are not confined exclusively to the physical realm of men.

We are dealing here with an ancient evil spiritual conspiracy, predating perhaps, even the creation of the material universe. This conspiracy is the "mother" of *all* evil and seeks to slander God in a realm we can scarcely imagine. God granted us glimpses of this realm in the Bible and revealed some of the principal actors. All of mankind are born into an ages-long war between light and darkness, good and evil. However, unlike merely human conflicts, where battles rage exclusively between physical combatants on an earthly battlefield with material weapons, *this* clash is also fought in a spiritual realm unseen by physical eyes. It often manifests in physical wars and violence, but the source is spiritual. I'm not just dealing with "religious" things here, although it may seem so to some.

In this chapter, I will attempt to shed some light on this age-old conflict, and how it relates to our present experience. This is a complex theological issue, and I'll try to deal with it in simple, rather than technical theological terms. I will share some chapter and verse proof texts for what follows, but I urge the inquisitive reader to research what I'm sharing in the spirit of the Bereans described in the book of Acts;

These were also more noble men…
which received the word with all readiness,
and searched the Scriptures daily,
whether those things were so.
Acts 17:11

Theology 101

To understand the complex issue of evil, I think it will be helpful to review a few fundamental things we understand from the scriptures about God Himself. I didn't intend this book to be a theological work, but it is impossible to grapple with the subject of good and evil without some foundation to start from. Some will disagree with me on several of these points, but I offer them to bring clarity to the subject.

The study of God is technically known as "theology," –a term derived from two Greek words; "theo" (God) and "logy" (knowledge) or, "God knowledge."

Actually, *everyone* is a theologian to one degree or another. Even a professing atheist holds some opinion about God, or at least the *concept* of God even while denying God exists, and therefore is a theologian.

To begin with, God's name is not "God." The widely-used term "God" is a *descriptive* title only, because His *revealed* name is *Yahweh*, often defined as; "the self-existing One, who reveals Himself." His actual name was considered too holy by ancient and modern Hebrew theologians to be uttered by human lips. Therefore, we often find His name replaced in translations of the scriptures as "Lord" or "God" out of traditional respect. Among the Jewish Orthodox, even the *title* "God" is written as "G-d" or "L-rd" out of respect for the holiness of God. It would take volumes to do such a profound subject justice, but this will do for now.

> *In the beginning,*
> *God created the heaven and the earth.*
> Genesis 1:1

Yahweh is the creator of all things both visible and invisible. His creation encompasses the material universe, as well as humans, vegetable, and animal life, and includes angelic (spirit) beings. The material universe was made "Ex nihilo," a Latin term for; "from nothing."

> *Through faith we understand*
> *that the world was ordained by the word of God,*
> *so that the things which we see,*
> *are not made of things which did appear.*
> Hebrews 11:3

God's power is described by theologians as "omnipotent," or all-powerful. There is no other in all the universe more powerful than He. Also, all things that exist are His creations, for nothing came forth by or of itself.

> *By the word of the Lord*
> *were the heavens made,*
> *and all the host of them*
> *by the breath of his mouth.*
> Psalm 33:6

The Bible also reveals that God is "omniscient" and knows all things in their tiniest details from endless eternity past to endless eternity future. This concept is difficult to describe for we humans exist "in" time and cannot comprehend the realm of timeless eternity where God dwells.

> *Remember the former things of old:*
> *for I am God, and there is none other God,*
> *and there is nothing like me,*
> *which declare the last thing from the beginning,*
> *and from of old: the things that were not done,*
> *saying, My counsel shall stand,*
> *and I will do whatsoever I will.*
> Isaiah 46:9-10

God is also described in scripture as simultaneously present in all places ("omnipresent," or everywhere present) throughout the entire universe. This attribute includes His omnipresence in time itself. From God's infinite perspective in eternity, the past, present, and future are all one simultaneous experience. Therefore, God exists as the eternal "I Am."

> *Thy knowledge is too wonderful for me:*
> *it is so high that I cannot attain unto it.*
> *Whither shall I go from thy Spirit?*
> *or whither shall I flee from thy presence?*
> *If I ascend into heaven, thou art there:*
> *if I lie down in hell, thou art there.*
> *Let me take the wings of the morning,*
> *and dwell in the uttermost parts of the sea:*
> *Yet thither shall thine hand lead me,*
> *and thy right hand hold me.*
> Psalm 139:6-10

Yahweh never learns anything new or experiences surprises or emergencies, for all things are ultimately unfolding according to His predetermined purpose and foreknowledge. All things (including those things that are visible and invisible) throughout the entire universe operate and exist eternally under His unblinking gaze. Unlike humans, God will never be heard saying, "I didn't know they were going to do *THAT*! Whatever am I going to do *now*?" Even those times in the Bible where God is asking questions and demanding answers, He is already well-aware of the answers and seems to be engaging in a "teachable moment" dialog. This teaching method is sometimes called the "Socratic" or "elenctic" method, where the instructor poses questions the teacher already knows. This technique stimulates critical thinking in students. For example, in Genesis 3 Yahweh asks several such questions E.G.; vs. 9 *"...But the Lord God called to the man, and said unto him, Where art thou?"* Also, in vs. 11 *"...Who told thee that thou wast naked? Hast thou eaten of the tree whereof I commanded thee that thou shouldest not eat?"* And in vs. 13, *"...Why hast thou done this?"*

In this, and every other Biblical example, God *already knew* in precise detail the answers to His questions. These "Q and A" exchanges throughout the Bible *always* serve to illustrate a point He wishes to make. In theological studies, there is a rule of interpretation (or "hermeneutic") which deals with verses that are "explicit" and others that are "implicit." Without question, there *are* certain scriptures that appear contradictory on the surface. A skilled interpreter will employ this hermeneutic by asking a question; "Does the "implied" meaning of this verse *contradict* another verse that reveals an "explicit" interpretation?" "Explicit" *always* trumps "implicit" interpretations.

To illustrate this principle in Genesis 3, God's questions to Adam and Eve "imply" that He didn't know the information He was seeking. However, we must interpret this verse in the light of the *explicit* meaning of Isaiah 46:9-10 (quoted above) which reveals God's omniscience and knowledge of all things from all eternity.

To elaborate further, all that is discoverable about anything that exists, or *ever did* exist in all times and places, is known to Him already. He is all-powerful (omnipotent) and exercises total and complete control of all things down to the tiniest details. There's nothing out of Him that should be in Him. There's nothing in Him that should be out of Him. The entire universe's existence is held together by His infinite power, down to and beyond the sub-atomic particles of every atom.

It is not possible for us as finite beings to comprehend more than a tiny fraction of His infinite mind, let alone the reasons *why* He does what He does, or the *way* He does it. However, He has granted to His people, according to the measure of His grace, a small portion of insight into His ways. To summarize, He is the *most wonderous of all that is*, excelling in power, wisdom, intelligence, and *thankfully*, He has revealed Himself as ultimate Love.

> *O the deepness of the riches,*
> *both of the wisdom, and knowledge of God!*
> *how unsearchable are his judgments,*
> *and his ways past finding out!*

188   Destroying the Shadow Agenda

For who hath known the mind of the Lord?
or who was his counselor?
Romans 11:33-35
For who hath known the mind of the Lord,
that he might instruct him?
But we have the mind of Christ.
1 Corinthians 2:16

From our limited perspective, we cannot comprehend God's ultimate purposes, and we struggle with questions about why so much suffering occurs, or why evil even exists in the first place. Obviously, if God created everything, and knows all things past, present, and future, and is all powerful so that nothing can occur outside His ability to intervene and impose His perfect will in every situation, then it begs a question. If God is "good" and "love," then why is He permitting evil to exist? The existence of evil is a profound mystery, and a question humankind has struggled with ever since Adam and Eve sinned and did the "perp-walk of shame" out of the Garden of Eden with dead animals draped over their nakedness to hide their shame. With paradise fading away behind them in the rear-view mirror of memory, their inner natures and minds were darkened by the spiritual death God told them they would suffer "on the day" they ate of the forbidden fruit of the knowledge of good and evil. Perhaps they realized they had just "blown" an exceptional situation. However, God did not leave them (or us) without hope, for even their fall into spiritual death was part of a much larger and grander plan. He promised a Redeemer, who would one day crush Satan's head and restore all things to perfection and beauty.

Then the Lord God said to the serpent,
(allegorical for the Devil)
Because thou hast done this,
thou art cursed above all cattle,
and above every beast of the field:
upon thy belly shalt thou go,
and dust shalt thou eat all the days of thy life.
I will also put enmity between thee and the woman,
and between thy seed (Satan and his demonic minions)
and her seed (The Messiah who would eventually come).
He shall break thine head,
and thou shalt bruise his heel.

(Emphasis added)
Genesis 3:14-16

For myself, I'm comfortable with Scripture's frequent assertion that God is love and as merciful as He is just. I'm also comfortable with the idea that God's understanding of ultimate "good" is *infinitely higher than mine.* My personal concept of goodness orbits tightly around the planet "ME," and corresponds mostly to what looks, sounds, tastes, smells or feels "good" to me. Armed with the awareness that *my* standards of "goodness" are rather personal and selfish, it seems a bit presumptuous to sit in judgment on God as to what *He* thinks is best. Those of us who are graced with the ability to "walk by faith and not by sight" are comforted even in times of pain, suffering, and tragedy. The Scriptures constantly remind us that a greater good is being worked out in the larger purposes of God, beyond anything we could ever imagine. This higher perspective is hard to see when we're hurting, but the Spirit of God assures us in those dark times to trust God unwaveringly.

> *For I count that the afflictions*
> *of this present time*
> *are not worthy of the glory,*
> *which shall be showed unto us.*
> Romans 8:18
> *But as it is written,*
> *The things which eye hath not seen,*
> *neither ear hath heard,*
> *neither came into man's heart, are,*
> *which God hath prepared for them that love him.*
> *But God hath revealed them unto us by his Spirit:*
> *for the Spirit searcheth all things,*
> *yea, the deep things of God.*
> 1 Corinthians 2:9-10

I must confess that there have been times when I was sorely tempted to judge God and be angry with Him. (Yes, I still battle my carnal mind.) In 2004, I responded to Beslan, Russia, after the massacre of nearly 600 children by Islamic terrorists. I walked through the ruins of that burned-out and bloodstained school for days, and often, all I could do was weep and sob. It deeply wounded my soul to see small handprints in blood around broken windows or the blown up remains of little kids splattered across walls and ceilings. "Why Lord?" I heard myself mumble over and over, as I stumbled through the ruins and beheld the cruel slaughter of the innocents. For several months after I returned home, I struggled to accept what happened as even *remotely* an expression of God's love or predestined purposes. I battled depression and the temptation to *hate* the Islamists, or, be angry at God. Deep down inside, I *knew* that *HE knew* what was happening to those children in Beslan, even as it was happening, but for reasons known best only to Him, didn't stop it. I spent many nights out under the stars crying out for answers and healing for my broken heart. There finally came a point of surrender by the grace of God, even in the face of the unexplainable horror. The hermeneutic I shared above preserved my soul. Using it, I was able to grasp that although the natural evidence "implied" that God was cruel and uncaring for all those hundreds of tortured and slain children, I also knew "explicitly" that He is infinitely wise and good. He sees the larger picture in a depth of love and grace far beyond my mind's ability to understand. God mercifully healed my broken heart, and in ways that I still can't make sense of, He gave me a supernatural confidence that His judgments are righteous and good. This trust is far beyond anything I could self-generate by some force of personal "free will." I can honestly say today that I accept the will of God in this, in spite of my total inability to understand *why* it happened, confident that a time will come when all things will become clear.

The Goodness and Severity of God

The mystery of good and evil has gripped the imaginations of theologians for millennia. The obvious question is: If God created all things, including the devil and the fallen angels, why did He do it? He *knew* from the beginning the outcomes that would result from that creation. This reality often prompts the accusation that God is the ultimate author of evil! This question has puzzled reasonable men for thousands of years and remains a significant stumbling block to thinking people.

For the reasons I've given above, the only way I can personally reconcile the "allowed" existence of evil in the world is to rely utterly on trust and faith in God's purposes. An ultimate "goodness" will someday manifest far above our present capacity to understand. Not all men, however, possess this grace of faith. The apparent contradiction of God's "goodness and love" mirrored by the nearly pandemic horrors of violence, disease, pain, and death occurring all around us is impossible to reconcile. Impossible that is, *by mere human logic*.

Satanists hate and condemn God as the ultimate evil player in the universe. They zealously raise this accusation at every opportunity. Ironically, the malevolent spirit that animates their hatred drives them to elevate Lucifer as the *real* hero in this unfolding drama.

What does all this have to do with our present struggle to save America? It has everything to do with it! For purposes known only to Him, God has allowed wicked (twisted) men and women into positions of power and influence who are leading our country into misery, poverty, chaos, and ruin. They are acting in concert with evil spirits in the unseen realm who despise humans and wish to destroy us. Some of the "puppets of evil" are entirely unaware of these dark influences, and vainly imagine they are truly doing good. Great political and religious movements in history were fostered by such "puppets," and brought incalculable destruction and misery to the world.

By and through the grace of God, we perceive reality in a *much broader context* than the merely sensible, material, and the visible world around us. The Apostle Paul spoke plainly of this truth.

> *For we wrestle not against flesh and blood,*
> *but against principalities, against powers,*
> *and against the worldly governors,*
> *the princes of the darkness of this world,*
> *against spiritual wickedness,*
> *which are in the high places.*
> Ephesians 6:12

Here's the same verse from the New Living Translation.

> *For we are not fighting*
> *against flesh-and-blood enemies,*
> *but against evil rulers and authorities*
> *of the unseen world,*
> *against mighty powers*
> *in this dark world,*
> *and against evil spirits*
> *in the heavenly places.*

Professing atheists boldly (and foolishly) declare that "There are no gods or spirits!" They defend that belief by citing the lack of "tangible physical evidence" for their existence. However, no truly rational person could assume with absolute certainty that anything does not exist somewhere just because it isn't manifesting to their five physical senses. How can I say this with such conviction?

Consider the existence of thoughts. I imagine you are having some right now, but can the existence of your thoughts be proven physically, perhaps in a laboratory? There are no tangible, physical "proofs" that anyone "thinks" or possesses ideas. How does one measure a thought? Thoughts cannot be seen, smelled, tasted, touched, or heard. We can only *assume* that they exist because of outward expressions of their *effects*. If thoughts lead to some outward expression or action, then we can assume that an idea existed and motivated an action. For example, if I have a thought such as "I'm going to write a book, and it will say this, this, and this." Until my thoughts find expression in a readable form, no one could ever physically prove such a book existed, except in my fertile imagination.

Everyone assumes that thoughts exist, and hopefully, most of us have them now and then, but no one could ever *prove* conclusively by tangible, physical tests that they exist. My point here is, there are many "real" things extant in the universe that we cannot detect physically, and their existence can only find confirmation by their effects.

So it is with the unseen spiritual forces that influence and motivate human behaviors and activities. We observe effects, but we cannot always perceive the cause of these effects operating behind the scenes in the invisible realm. The next time an atheist friend tells you with certainty that God does not exist, ask this question. "Are you present everywhere in the universe and simultaneously able to see inside, behind, under, over, and through everything that exists, and knows everything there is to know about everything that is? If you cannot, then how can you say for certain God doesn't exist *somewhere* you don't know about or can't see?"

To illustrate my point, I will share a brief profile of three of the most prominent leaders who ever lived, and how manifestly sinister forces influenced their thinking and actions. I chose these three (out of many other similar candidates far too numerous to mention here) due to their writings and activities. These human monsters collectively accomplished the slaughter of hundreds of millions of people. Their influence is still causing untold human misery in our times.

Karl Marx

In his youth, Karl Marx, author of the *Communist Manifesto* (with F. Engels) and *Das Kapital*, considered to be the foundational documents of world communism, was once a "confessing" Christian. In his youth, Marx wrote beautiful things about the glory of Christ and his love for Him. For example, his first written work is titled *The Union of the Faithful with Christ*.

> *Through love of* Christ *we turn our hearts at the same time toward our brethren who are inwardly bound to us and for whom He gave Himself in sacrifice.*
> *...Union with Christ could give an inner elevation, comfort in sorrow, calm trust, and a heart susceptible to human love, to everything* novel *and great, not for the sake of ambition and glory, but for the sake of Christ.* [1]

However, when he entered University, he came under the influence of a professor, Bruno Bauer. According to Wikipedia, "...Bauer was a German philosopher and historian. As a student of G. W. F. Hegel, Bauer was a radical Rationalist in philosophy, politics, and Biblical criticism." Many believe that Bauer was also a Satanist, who attacked and destroyed Marx's earlier Christian convictions with "that question" about of the ultimate source of evil–the accusation being–God Himself. There can be no doubt that a radical change came over Marx during these university years. He began to write horrendous works that could just as easily give voice to Lucifer himself. For example, in his poem "*Invocation of One in Despair*":

> *So a god has snatched from me my all,*
> *In the curse and rack of destiny.*
> *All his worlds are gone beyond recall.*
> *Nothing but revenge is left to me.*
> *I shall build my throne high overhead,*
> *Cold, tremendous shall its summit be,*
> *For its bulwark–superstitious dread.*
> *For its marshal–blackest agony.*
> *Who looks on it with a healthy eye,*
> *Shall turn back, deathly pale and dumb,*
> *Clutched by the blind and chilly mortality,*
> *May his happiness prepare its tomb.*
> [2]

Marx was apparently initiated into Satanism and passed through the Satanic ritual of receiving an "enchanted" sword that supposedly grants success to the candidate. The candidate purchases the sword with his blood and enters a covenant to belong to Satan when he or she dies. Marx made a chilling confession in the following poem called "The Player."

> *The hellish vapors rise and fill the brain,*
> *Till I go mad and my heart is utterly changed.*
> *See this sword?*
> *The prince of darkness sold it to me.*
> *For me he beats the time and gives the signs.*
> *Ever more boldly I play the dance of death.*
> 3

Adolph Hitler

One of the best examples of evil spiritual influence upon a human being is Adolph Hitler. I once met an elderly woman in Germany who, as a young girl, personally met Hitler. She told me that the most striking thing about him was the power of his presence. She said Hitler's gaze was terrifying and intimidated everyone around him.

In the Hofburg Library in Vienna, Austria there was an ancient spear that, as the legend goes, was the spear that pierced the side of Christ at His crucifixion. Hitler believed the spear, known as "The Spear of Destiny" possessed potent occult powers. Hitler was known to stand and stare at the spear for extended periods of time, apparently inviting the demonic powers supposedly resident in the spear into himself.

An eye-witness, Dr. Walter Stein, once stood next to Hitler during one of these vigils, and relates;

> *Adolph Hitler stood…like a man in a trance, a man over whom some dreadful magic spell had been cast…He was swaying on his feet as though caught up in some totally inexplicable euphoria…His whole [facial appearance] physiognomy and stance appeared transformed as if some mighty Spirit now inhabited his very soul, creating within and around him a kind of evil transformation of its own nature and power."* 4

One of Hitler's childhood friends, August Kubizek wrote about their friendship in his book *The Young Hitler I knew*. (1955) Kubizek wrote that when Hitler was only 17 years old he spoke of "returning Germany to its former glory." August recalled that when Hitler said those words,

> *It was as if another being spoke out of his body, and moved him as much as it did me.* 5

When Hitler eventually went to Munich, he joined others who sought occult powers. Many people are unaware that most of the original members of the National Socialist Party (Nazis) were committed Satanists. Hitler dove into this cult with both feet and sought complete dominion over it. A practitioner of black magic, Dietrich Eckart, gloated to some friends about his influence upon Hitler just before he died.

> *I have initiated him (Hitler) into the 'Secret Doctrine,' opened his centers in vision and given him the means of communication with the Powers…I shall have influenced history more than any other German.* [6]

There is little doubt that Hitler was demon possessed, and many biographers who had direct contact with him corroborate this fact. At the very least, the fruits of his life certainly prove it.

Abū al-Qāsim (Muhammad, The Prophet of Islam)

I have so much to say about Islam, yet I hardly know where to begin. I've touched this subject already, but a few words about the founder of Islam should suffice to make my point about how malevolent spiritual influences impact humans.

Muhammad is believed by Muslims to be a prophet. He is also assumed by Muslims to be the *last* prophet sent by God to humankind. Undoubtedly a powerful and highly influential man, I will deal here with the question regarding from where he received his powers. To answer this, we must consider *how* the original revelations came to him, and how they affected him.

One highly sympathetic writer about Islam and Muhammad, Karen Armstrong, wrote of what happened at Muhammad's first "close encounter" with what Muslims believe was Gabriel (Jibril) the "angel" in the cave of Hira:

> *Muhammad was torn from his sleep in his mountain cave and felt himself overwhelmed by a devastating divine presence. Later he explained this ineffable experience by saying that an angel had enveloped him in a terrifying embrace so that it felt as though the breath was being forced from his body. The angel gave him the curt command: 'iqra!' 'Recite!' Muhammad protested that he could not recite; he was not a* kahin, *one of the ecstatic prophets of Arabia. But, he said, the angel simply embraced him again until, just as he thought he had reached the end of his endurance, he found the divinely inspired words of a new scripture pouring forth from his mouth.* [7]

196   Destroying the Shadow Agenda

This account of Muhammad's encounter with a supposed angelic being contrasts starkly with the description of angelic interactions in the Judeo/Christian scriptures. In nearly every close encounter in the Bible, the angel says something like, "Be not afraid." In no instance does an angel in the Bible attempt to strangle and make violent demands. The only possible exceptions that come to mind are Jacob's wrestling with an angel in Genesis 32:24, and Balaam's encounter with an armed angel in Numbers 22:34. In later instances of his life, at times when he supposedly received visions and revelations of the Quran, Mohammad would fall into seizures. There is evidence that he may have suffered an affliction known to medical science as Temporal Lobe Epilepsy (TLE). A partial list of the Temporal Lobe Seizure Symptoms & Signs as defined in health.allrefer.com include;

- Hallucinations or illusions such as hearing voices when no one has spoken, seeing patterns, lights, beings or objects that aren't there.
- Rhythmic muscle contraction Muscle cramps are involuntary and often painful contractions of the muscles which produce a hard, bulging muscle.
- Abdominal pain or discomfort.
- Sudden, intense emotion such as fear.
- Muscle twitching (fasciculation) is the result of spontaneous local muscle contractions that are involuntary and typically only affect individual muscle groups. This twitching does not cause pain.
- Abnormal mouth behaviors.
- Abnormal head movements.
- Sweating.
- Flushed face.
- Rapid heart rate/pulse.
- Changes in vision, speech, thought, awareness, personality.
- Loss of memory (amnesia) regarding events around the seizure (partial complex seizure). [8]

According to eyewitness accounts, Mohammed demonstrated all the above symptoms when he had these fits. For example, the following is a quote from one witness in the Islamic writing, Bukhari.

> *He fell to the ground like one intoxicated or overcome by sleep, and in the coldest day his forehead would be bedewed with large drops of perspiration. Inspiration descended unexpectedly, and without any previous warning.* [9]

At the risk of offending medical professionals (along with the billion Muslims

I've *already* offended), I need to say something about seizures. The Bible speaks of them often as caused by demonic spirits. I realize that there are medical circumstances also, as in the case of closed head blunt-force injuries involving neurological damage. Not *all* seizures are caused by evil spirits. However, this does not mean that *none of them* is caused by spirits, for some of them are.

In the gospel of Mark, we read one of the several instances where Jesus cast out spirits (demons) who were afflicting people with seizures.

> ...Master,
> I have brought my son unto thee,
> which hath a dumb spirit:
> And wheresoever he taketh him,
> he teareth him, and he foameth,
> and gnasheth his teeth, and pineth away:
> and I spake to thy disciples,
> that they should cast him out,
> and they could not.
> Mark 9:17-18

To summarize, it seems manifestly clear that the spirit motivating and energizing Islam, from its founder right through to the individual Islamist, is Satanic. If we only examined the historical evidence, there is no possible way we could reconcile the vicious barbarity, slaughter, sexual perversions, and violence committed by the followers of Islam as having any commonality with Jesus or the God of the Bible. Critics of Christianity often try to point to the "Christian" Crusades as a ploy to establish a "moral equivalency" argument against Christianity, but it won't work. The Crusades were decidedly *not* "Christian" in any biblical sense. They ought to be called what they were; "*Roman Catholic*" Crusades. But I digress. All three examples I've given should establish to any reasonable person that dark spiritual forces have, and continue to play, a large role in the miseries we witness throughout history by demonized tyrants. Puppets all, and we must constantly keep in mind that these "puppets" are not our *real* enemies. The spirits that drive them in their murderous rampages *are*. I believe our once great Republic is under attack by unseen, malevolent, spiritual forces that have captured the hearts and imaginations of far too many of our people. Incrementally, America has fallen under massive spiritual deception. Our present problems are not merely of human manufacture. Allow me to share an experience that amplifies this point.

My Vietnam Vision

In 1970, while serving in the Air Force at Bien Hoa Air Force Base in South Vietnam, I had a waking vision that would change the entire course of my life. It was so overwhelming and compelling that it set me on a quest for truth. This search eventually took me through Thailand, India, Pakistan, Lebanon, Turkey, Germany, Switzerland, and finally to Rome, Italy. My hunger for truth stretched my mind and heart to the limits of sanity. It became an obsession. I *had* to make sense of the vision I'd seen.

The vision came one evening while I sat with some Security Police buddies on perimeter guard duty upon a tall water tower overlooking the countryside outside our base. Our voices were hushed as we watched an incredibly beautiful sunset over the rice paddies and tropical landscape all around us.

All of us scanned the deepening gloom for the telltale flashes of 55-mm rockets launched at our base. The Viet-Cong often launched these missiles toward our base at night. When these weapons fired off, they looked almost like 4th of July fireworks, arching up into the sky before falling behind our perimeter, raining down on our living quarters.

When these vicious weapons launched, we only had mere seconds to sound the alert sirens. Our guys would dive into bunkers for protection from the shrapnel these missiles spewed out in all directions upon impact, ripping flesh and bone. The Vietcong used delayed launch fuses, so by the time they fired off, there was usually no one "out there" to fight back. That was the most frustrating thing about these weapons. We rarely had the satisfaction of "payback" against our elusive enemies.

As gloom and darkness of night deepened, I watched the stars begin to twinkle overhead. My mind drifted, and a question that continually nagged me in previous months resurfaced: "Who are these guys out there trying to kill us?"

They were our enemies. The *bad* guys. At that time, I only knew them as the "Cong" or "commies." Some of the guys derisively called them "gooks" to dehumanize them. That night, I couldn't help thinking about them as human beings. I wondered who they were.

On a battlefield, such thoughts can be dangerous. Empathizing with the enemy may cause a soldier to hesitate at a critical moment, costing not only *his* life but also the lives of others who are counting on his vigilance. At that time, I had only a vague understanding of the political issues of this conflict. But I couldn't help wondering; "Why are we all fighting?" I knew the importance of obeying orders and doing one's duty, but I felt no hatred for these adversaries out there in the darkness. I realized they were probably just as young and dumb as we were, and just trying to do *their* duty and follow the orders of their superiors.

As I pondered these thoughts, a flash in the sky drew my attention upward. One of our troops fired off a phosphorous night flare, sending it out over the barbed wire, minefield, and concertina wire that formed our perimeter. Suspended by a small parachute, the intensely bright light of the hissing flare illuminated the entire countryside in an eerie, phosphorescent glow, casting moving shadows on the ground as it descended.

At that very moment, as I gazed out across this ethereal landscape, a flash of understanding suddenly came over me. It's hard to tell of it even now. It shook my very foundations.

Glancing back up to the sky, I had a vision of several ethereal, twisted, demonic beings. It was the stuff of nightmares—only I wasn't sleeping!

These creatures were flying through the air, back and forth, making sounds like snarling, cackling laughter. They seemed to be pulling strings of some sort that connected to unseen people on the ground below. These lines extended downward on both sides of the perimeter, both our side and the enemy side as well.

A flash of understanding revealed that these demonic beings were controlling people on the earth! Like evil puppeteers, these horrendous creatures were manipulating people on the ground in ways that suited and delighted them. One thing that impressed me was that the strings the demons were pulling were just as much on "our" side of the perimeter as they were on the "enemy" side. We were *all* being "played!"

This revelation was the first time I'd ever considered the idea of "spiritual warfare." Before that moment, I would have laughed at anyone who even suggested that people might be operating "under the influence" of evil beings. So compelling was this vision I nearly lost awareness of my surroundings.

Then, a second revelation came: I knew in my heart that God was calling me to be a warrior. The battleground upon which I would stand, however, would not be like Vietnam, a place where men fought natural battles with physical weapons of war. God was calling me to be a warrior on a much larger and more profound battlefield—in the spiritual realm.

In the years that followed, I've come to realize that the greater battleground lies in the hearts and minds of people. I realized that humans were often used as "puppets of evil," bringing death, misery, and slavery upon humanity.

All We Are Fallen

I'm convinced that fallen, unregenerate humans are *well capable* of committing unspeakable evil, even *without* a demonic component. However, these sinister demonic influences intensify fallen humanity's natural tendency toward evil. Who could deny this in the face of well-documented human history?

The good news is; Christ utterly defeated these evil forces. Colossians 2:15 declares:

> *And hath spoiled*
> *the Principalities, and Powers,*
> *and hath made a show of them openly,*
> *and hath triumphed over them in the same cross.*

In Christ, we are already victorious over all the evil forces that assail us. The problem is one of enforcement. Most Christians struggle with temptations to sin, fear, doubt, and lack of courage because they do not enforce the victory already won by Christ's victory on the cross. Too many of Christians have bought into the lie that everything is *supposed* to go from "bad to worse" before Jesus can return. They see each disaster, earthquake, or court decision against Christians (just to name a few) as some requisite problem so Jesus can "come back." This kind of thinking, in my view, is bad theology on parade. Again, our actual enemies are not evil humans. We contend on a much higher battlefield against those beings whose sole power is their ability to deceive and obscure truth. Their influences emanate from a malevolent realm fueled by fear, hate, envy, and lust for power and control. We, however, possess the weapons of heavenly love, wisdom, divine authority, and the infinitely powerful Word of God. Ponder for a few moments the following.

> *Nevertheless, though we walk in the flesh,*
> *yet we do not war after the flesh.*
> *For the weapons of our warfare are not carnal,*
> *but mighty through God, to cast down holds.*
> *Casting down the imaginations,*
> *and every high thing that is exalted*
> *against the knowledge of God,*
> *and bringing into captivity every thought*
> *to the obedience of Christ...*
> 2 Corinthians 10:3-51

Reclaiming our Constitution and our nation is *not* our *ultimate* goal. It is only a means to an end. (More on this point later.) The Constitution and the Bill of Rights are neither perfect nor biblical. Men with their sins and failures penned them. However, these documents do reveal, as well as any earthly human government ever has or ever could, a code of relationships that enable flawed humans to live together in reasonable harmony. Our efforts to preserve and protect the Constitution of the United States has a higher purpose. It is to safeguard and secure those freedoms and rights among fallen men. Also, we seek domestic tranquility so that the gospel might spread unhindered. We want to live quiet and peaceful lives free from want, cruelty, violence, and tyranny. In a letter to his son in the faith, Timothy, the Apostle Paul sets forth the strategy:

> *I exhort therefore,*
> *that first of all supplications, prayers,*
> *intercessions, and giving of thanks*
> *be made for all men,*
> *for Kings, and for all that are in authority,*
> *that we may lead a quiet and a peaceable life,*
> *in all godliness, and honesty.*
> *For this is good and acceptable*
> *in the sight of God our Savior.*
> *1 Timothy 2:1-3*

We do not pray for "kings and authorities" because we happen to like them or agree with all their actions or policies. Quite the contrary, we pray for them so that malevolent unseen forces of darkness will not overly influence their decisions and move them to evil mischief. In fact, *the more diabolical they act, the more we must pray for them.* We do this so that we may "lead a quiet and peaceable life in all godliness and reverence."

For untold thousands of years, humanity has yearned for an eventual triumph of good over evil, love over hatred, truth over lies. This struggle is the great theme of all epic literature, and the core reality of our world's present conflict.

There yet remains much beauty in the world in spite of the many ugly things fallen men have done to one another throughout history. The Bible promises one day there will be a time when all of Christ's enemies will become His footstool, and the nations of the earth will come under His absolute rulership in peace and righteousness. I'm looking for an *ultimate* and inevitable redemption that will establish justice and truth throughout the land. However, from the looks of things, we may have to wait *a while longer.* Until then, we need to get busy with our "salt and light" agenda and obey God.

Notes

1. Karl Marx, The Union of the Faithful with Christ, (Works) (MEW), Supplement, I, P. 600

2. Karl Marx, "Invocation of One in Despair", p.30

3. Karl Marx, "Spielmann" (The Player"), op. cit., Deutsche Tagespost, pp. 57, 58

4. The Spear of Destiny Ravenscroft, Trevor Published by G.P. Putnam's Sons, New York, 1973

5. August Kubizek, The Young Hitler I knew. (1955) p 51

6. ibid, Ravenscroft, p.91

7. Karen Armstrong, Muhammad: A Biography of the Prophet (Harper Collins Books, 1993), 46

8. Muhammad and Temporal Lobe Epilepsy (TLE), http://www.faithfreedom.org/Articles/sina41204.htm (accessed September 14, 2015).

9. Bukhari 7, 71, 660)

PART IV

Who Might We Become?

18

National Destiny?

The General hopes and trusts
that every officer and man
will endeavor to live and act
as becomes a Christian soldier
defending the dearest rights
and liberties of his country.
Order to the Troops,
General George Washington
Orderly Book, July 9, 1776

~~~~~

The term "destiny" is often-used in our time, but I suspect it is only vaguely understood. Therefore, when I write concerning America's national destiny, I wish to be precise about my meaning.

According to the Merriam-Webster Dictionary, destiny is defined as;
1: something to which a person or thing is destined
2: a predetermined course of events often held to be an irresistible power or agency

According to Dictionary.com, Destiny is described as; "A noun meaning fate, destiny is synonymous with other nouns like divine decree, fortune, and serendipity."

To the secularist, the entire concept of "destiny" is a pure absurdity. In a universe that is assumed to be a mere conglomeration of infinite chance-random occurrences, the *very idea* of a "divine decree" or "a predetermined course of events often held to be an irresistible power or agency" attracts derision and contempt. Therefore, modern secular humanists tend to view all of history as a chain of accidental happenstance, with no overarching guidance beyond human influences. To such a person, any notion of "National Destiny" must be reduced to the "invisible hand" of enlightened human self-interest. The "invisible hand" concept was coined by the Humanist Adam Smith in his 1759 book; *The Theory of Moral Sentiments.*

I for one, however, have become convinced that America was founded through the agency of the "invisible hand" of God, in accordance with His *own* purposes and destiny, *far beyond* the grasping fingers and feeble intellect of mere humans in their futile efforts to seize control of their *own* destinies.

> *Many are the plans in the mind of a man,*
> *but it is the purpose of the LORD that will stand.*
> Proverbs 19:21 ESV

One evening, after a long and exhausting day of work at the Pile, I walked over to Saint Paul's Chapel. Completed in 1766, the building is over 250 years old, and is the oldest structure still in use in Lower Manhattan. Located just adjacent to the World Trade Complex and Ground Zero on a small plot of tree-covered land, amazingly, not a *single window* of the church was broken when the World Trade towers came down with a hurricane-force blast-wave. Massive amounts of rubble fell all around the chapel, severely damaging nearby buildings. An ancient sycamore tree, situated at the back of the chapel facing the collapsing towers, took the brunt of the falling debris and was broken in two. Many regarded the survival of the chapel as nothing short of a miracle. Considering the significant damage I observed to buildings all around the chapel, the word "miraculous" did seem appropriate.

I'd heard from other responders that food and refreshments were being shared over there, and I was curious to see this unique undamaged edifice. Wandering into the church, I found that the entire sanctuary was set up to serve workers at the site. Food tables and various medical care stations were available, with cots provided in darkened areas for those who needed some rest, or a short nap.

As I strolled around, a nurse in scrubs came over and asked if I'd like a free podiatrist exam and a foot rub. A little embarrassed at first, I sheepishly followed her to a small boxed-in area and sat down on an obviously very old wooden bench that creaked under my weight. The nurse removed my boots and socks, and gently washed and disinfected my feet. I felt embarrassed about how dirty my feet were, for they must have smelled terrible after days of trudging around on the rubble pile. She made no complaint as she wordlessly dedicated herself to the unsavory task. Finally, a Podiatrist came over and made his examination, declaring my feet healthy except for some minor bruises and blisters. This was a relief considering all the abuse my feet endured over the past week. As the doctor went on to the next patient, the nurse offered to give me a foot massage. Reluctantly, I agreed, and I must admit it was one of the most soothing, relaxing massages I've ever experienced.

As the nurse gently worked on my tired and bruised feet, she looked up, and with a smile, asked; "Do you know where you're sitting?" I stared blankly at her, clueless. She looked back down to my feet and continued to massage them. "You're seated in President George Washington's prayer booth where he prayed after his inauguration as the nation's first President!"

I was stunned.

A powerful sense of connection with history swept over me, and my goosebumps grew goosebumps. Suddenly, it seemed as if a bright light blinked on in some dark recess of my mind. When I'd first stepped into the building, a peculiar feeling swept over me that I couldn't describe. There seemed to be an extraordinary presence and sense of significance about this place. The sudden realization that I was sitting in the very spot where George Washington, our nation's first President, had come to pray and seek God immediately after his Presidential inauguration sent chills up and down my spine. I felt I was on hallowed ground, and somehow, it seemed entirely appropriate that I didn't have my boots on! It reminded me of God's command to Moses to

> ...put thy shoes off thy feet:
> for the place whereon thou standest
> is holy ground.
> Exodus 3:5

Please understand, I'm not seeking to exalt George Washington beyond the respect he deserves as an elected leader. He was, just as you and I, a flawed, fallen human being, desperately in need of God's grace and mercy. From my study of his writings and the biographical records, I am certain that he *well* recognized his personal need for Christ. Without question, he was *also* a gifted leader and possessed—by the grace of God—an excellent spirit and temper of character. This is well-evidenced by the fact that he humbled himself before God and prayed for wisdom and guidance for our infant nation on the very day of his inauguration as our nation's first President. What occurred in that particular place of prayer was, in my estimation, an act of holy consecration. The place is hallowed and unique because it represents the place and point in time when God and our nation's first president met in holy communion and covenant.

I suspect President Washington might have appreciated the irony of modern "bootless men" getting foot rubs in his prayer booth. I awkwardly mumbled something to the nurse about how Washington might feel if he knew that someone was sitting in his prayer-booth getting a foot massage. The nurse giggled and said, "Yeah, we get that a lot!"

Finishing my massage, she helped me put on my socks and boots. I thanked her profusely for her kindness and the great foot-rub. She brushed my thanks aside with a wave of her hand, but I could tell that it brought her some satisfaction to employ her skills in "helping the helpers." These volunteers gave a large chunk of their personal time to come to this chapel and bless those of us working out on the rubble pile. It was easy to see that theirs was a labor of love. It reminded me once again of how the response to 9/11 truly was a team effort.

As much as I appreciated that soothing foot rub, something about sitting in President Washington's prayer-booth troubled me. That small wooden prayer booth represents something profoundly significant to our nation's founding and spiritual heritage. Using it to give foot massages seemed beneath the dignity and importance that special place deserved.

Clinging to Hope—The Crucible of Faith

Later, as I reflected on my bootless experience in Washington's prayer-booth in Saint Paul's, I realized that bootless men were not an unusual sight for President Washington during the Revolutionary War. In the bitter winter of 1777-78, morale fell to its lowest point at Valley Forge. Rag-tag bands of American Patriots of the fledgling Continental American Army were bivouacked outdoors in forest camps while desperately fighting against the well-trained, equipped, and provisioned British forces. Many of those desperate patriots suffered severe frostbite without shoes or boots to ward off the bitter cold. According to climate records, the world at that time was experiencing a "mini" ice age with unusually cold global temperatures.

General Washington was no stranger to such adversity in those difficult years. He endured times of extreme anxiety over the lack of equipment and provisions for his troops, and the seeming impossibility of the military situation. As some have written of him, and his letters reveal, when strength and courage failed, it was only during times of desperate prayer to God that he found solace. In its tender infancy, America's future seemed to hang by a thread during the great War of Independence with England.

Throughout his life, Washington clearly demonstrated a profound reverence for God's word and a deep faith in Christ. That faith was sorely tested during the war. The American Patriots experienced repeated defeats as the troops suffered hunger and exposure to the elements with only the barest of necessities. There is no known record of the exact prayers General Washington addressed to God in those desperate hours when he cried out for His aid and assistance. However, the following prayer, penned by George Washington sometime later in his prayer journal, gives some insight into the temper of his devotion to Christ.

> *O' eternal and everlasting God, I presume to present myself this morning before thy Divine majesty, beseeching thee to accept of my humble and hearty thanks, that it hath pleased thy great goodness to keep and preserve me... Increase my faith in the sweet promises of the gospel; give me repentance from dead works; pardon my wanderings, and direct my thoughts unto thyself, the God of my salvation; teach me how to live in thy fear, labor in thy service, and ever to run in the ways of thy commandments; make me always watchful over my heart, that neither the terrors of conscience, the loathing of holy duties, the love of sin, nor an unwillingness to depart this life, may cast me into a spiritual slumber, but daily frame me more and more into the likeness of thy son Jesus Christ, that living in thy fear, and dying in thy favor, I may in thy appointed time attain the resurrection of the just unto eternal life...* [1]

The great modern painter Arnold Friberg—who passed away on July 1, 2010, at the age of 96—is perhaps best known for his epic portrait of George Washington kneeling in desperate prayer next to his horse in the frigid woods near Valley Forge, Pa. Some secular historians have tried to dismiss this portrayal of Washington's prayer as the product of Friberg's religious imagination. Thankfully, however, the story is not without historical basis.

The following eyewitness account originates from Isaac Potts, a resident of Valley Forge in 1777. He shared the following with Rev. Nathaniel Randolph Snowden who recorded it in his personal journal. Rev. Snowden's writings span a period from his youth up to 1846. In these records may be found Dr. Snowden's observations in own handwriting: [2]

> *I knew personally the celebrated Quaker (Isaac) Potts who saw Gen'l Washington alone in the woods at prayer. I got it from himself, myself. Weems [author Mason Weems 1918] mentioned it in his history of Washington, but I got it from the man myself, as follows:*
>
> *"I was riding with him (Mr. Potts) in Montgomery County, Pennsylvania, near to the Valley Forge, where the army lay during the war of the Revolution. Mr. Potts was a Senator in our State & a Whig. I told him I was agreeably surprised to find him a friend to his country as the Quakers were mostly Tories. He said, 'It was so and I was a rank*

> *Tory once, for I never believed that America could proceed against Great Britain whose fleets and armies covered the land and ocean, but something very extraordinary converted me to the Good Faith!" "What was that," I inquired? "Do you see that woods, & that plain?" It was about a quarter of a mile off from the place we were riding, as it happened.' "There," said he, "laid the army of Washington. It was a most distressing time of the war, and all were for giving up the Ship, but that great and good man. In that woods," pointing to a close in view, "I heard a plaintive sound as of a man at prayer. I tied my horse to a sapling & went quietly into the woods & to my astonishment I saw the great George Washington on his knees alone, with his sword on one side and his cocked hat on the other. He was at Prayer to the God of the Armies, beseeching to interpose with his Divine aid, as (if) it was the Crisis, & the cause of the country, of humanity & of the world."*
>
> *"Such a prayer I never heard from the lips of man. I left him alone praying. I went home & told my wife. 'I saw a sight and heard today what I never saw or heard before,' and just related to her what I had seen & heard & observed. We never thought a man could be a soldier and a Christian, but if there is one in the world, it is Washington. She also was astonished. We thought it was the cause of God, & America could prevail."*
>
> *"He (Mr. Potts) then to me, put out his right hand & said, 'I turned right about and became a Whig.'"*

The war against England did indeed seem utterly hopeless at times, yet General Washington continued to seek humbly God's Providence for strength and endurance. It was during these dark times of the nation's early struggle for liberty that Thomas Paine penned a series of articles titled "The Crisis." The most memorable part is contained in the first paragraph of the first article, written on December 23, 1776:

> *These are the times that try men's souls. The summer soldier and the sunshine patriot will, with this crisis, shrink from the service of their country; but he that stands by it now, deserves the love and thanks of man and woman. Tyranny, like hell, is not easily conquered; yet we have this consolation with us, that the harder the conflict, the more glorious the triumph.* [3]

My experience at Saint Paul's Chapel, where Washington came to pray after his inauguration inspired a near-obsession in me to search out what I sensed is a profound connection between his time and ours. As a General, Washington and other intrepid patriots bravely confronted the mighty British—perhaps the greatest military force in the world at that time—and against overwhelming odds, decisively defeated them. Washington clearly recognized his utter dependency upon God, and by the assisting hand of Providence, received the strength to persevere in the struggle until the forces of tyranny were defeated.

Those of us who *now* struggle to preserve our constitutionally-guaranteed freedoms face a conflict no less formidable. At this point, we may feel tempted—as Washington must have felt at times—that the outcome is doubtful. However, President Washington left us a powerful example of faith and courage. His secret to remaining steadfast to the cause was a divinely-inspired and unbending trust and reliance upon God's divine providence, all by the grace of God.

> *Unless the Lord builds the house,*
> *those who build it labor in vain.*
> *Unless the Lord watches over the city,*
> *the watchman stays awake in vain.*
> Psalm 127:1-2 (ESV)

In our present exertions to preserve, protect, and defend our Constitutional Republic, all will hinge on the aid and assistance of God, and how diligently we seek it. Our failure in this battle will be in direct proportion to our succumbing to the sin of self-reliance and arrogant pride. It will also depend in great measure on how successful we are at educating our fellow Americans about our Christian heritage, how fervently we proclaim the gospel of Christ, *and* how quickly we can do it. Like Paul Revere, who rode with his brave companions through the dark of night to alert his fellow Americans to the imminent peril about to befall them, we are raising the alarm among modern fellow patriots, awakening them to God's greater calling and destiny.

Tyrannical forces are now manipulating our government and surveillance agencies. Measures are underway to limit our ability to communicate freely with one another through unconstitutional Presidential Executive Orders (EOs) which could shut down the internet during a "declared emergency."[4]

Be sure of this, evil players are trying very hard to seize control of all electronic and data communications. These cretins intend to monitor, identify, and—if they think it in their interests—eliminate those who pose a threat to their sinister plans. We yet have a small window of opportunity to stop them, but that window appears to be closing. We must move quickly before it will become too dangerous to communicate about anything more important than the weather, or who the sheeple think will win the next entertainment award, Oscar nomination, or sporting event. Most sheeple blithely dismiss the real danger, and refuse to believe this could *ever* happen here in America, but so did people in scores of other now-enslaved countries down through history. Modern examples of this include North Korea, China, Iran, Cuba, Venezuela, and the list is growing. Historically, when basic freedoms are suspended, dissidents are identified and often disappear in the night, never to be heard from again. [5]

In spite of all we face, I remain confident that we shall eventually triumph—perhaps through peaceful resolution—but that possibility yet exists only if we will seize it *now*. America's early Patriots were providentially blessed with victory in the War for Independence in the ceaseless struggle for freedom and liberty. That struggle continues to this day. Perhaps we in our times will also enjoy the favor of heaven just as our forefathers did.

What Drove Those Early Patriots to Sacrifice So Much?

The issues and political currents of the American Revolutionary War were complex. Some of the revolutionaries were indeed driven by greed. England's taxes and laws were hindering economic opportunity. We must remember, however, that the power to tax is the authority to enslave. The lust for wealth and power has *always* been in play among fallen men. However, I believe we must also rediscover a deeper, more powerful driving force that will carry us beyond mere human aspirations.

The Christian Faith had taken deep root down into the American soul, particularly after the First Great Awakening in the 1740s. Many people came under the conviction that God was bringing about a new nation, and they understood that freedom from oppressive government control was essential to all other freedoms. They wished to worship God according to their conscience and convictions, without a state-mandated national religion. This required the right to freedom of speech, the press, and the right to keep and bear arms for their defense. In the following chapters, we will try to catch a glimpse into the minds and hearts of our Founding Fathers. Perhaps we will discover that they weren't all that different from us after all. More importantly, we may be able to light our torches of inspiration from their campfires and see our way forward more clearly. Let's walk with them a bit.

Notes

1. George Washington: Excerpt from A Prayer for Guidance. From Washington's prayer journal, Mount Vernon http://www.beliefnet.com/Faiths/Faith-Tools/Meditation/2005/01/Prayers-Of-The-Presidents.aspx

2. Rev. Dr. Nathaniel R. Snowden, Princeton Grad, Doctorate, Co-Founder Presbyterian Church in USA, Verifies Valley Forge Prayer http://goo.gl/BrZ8B5

3. Thomas Paine, "The Crisis," December 23, 1776. Full article at http://www.ushistory.org/paine/crisis/c-01.htm

4. https://www.whitehouse.gov/the-press-office/2012/07/06/executive-order-assignment-national-security-and-emergency-preparedness-#.T_sYsRJrreM.twitter

5. https://www.rt.com/usa/obama-president-order-communications-770

19

Faith of Our Fathers

The general principles
on which the fathers achieved independence
were the general principles of Christianity.
John Adams
Second President of the United States

~~~~~~

Unto Him who is the Author and Giver of all good,
I render sincere and humble thanks
for His manifold and unmerited blessings,
and especially for our redemption
and salvation by His beloved son.
Last Will and Testament
Chief Justice John Jay
First Chief Justice of the US Supreme Court

~~~~~~

My exposure to early American history in public school was superficial at best, and profoundly boring at worst. Perhaps I wasn't paying attention, but about all I could recall from my history classes consisted of a few seemingly unimportant dates, names of battles, and a few anecdotal stories about principle characters of the times. For example, George Washington was called the "Father" of our country: "First in war, first in peace, first in the hearts of his countrymen." I recall a story—which I later discovered to be fictional, yet reflective of his renowned excellent character—telling how he reportedly chopped down one of his father's cherry trees. When called upon to give account for the crime, young Washington virtuously told his father the truth by saying something like; "I cannot tell a lie."

I also recall reading that Benjamin Franklin was something of an eccentric who once flew a kite with a key attached to the string so he could catch a lightning bolt in a jar. I couldn't fathom at the time why anyone would do such a crazy thing. Only much later did I learn that Franklin was a very serious scientist who made important electrical discoveries, and he really did—*in a virtual sense*— capture lightning in a Leden jar, an early capacitor. For those who would like to read more of Dr. Franklin's electrical experiments, please refer to the footnote for an interesting article titled; *Ben Franklin as my Lab Partner* detailing the construction of a capacitor and electrostatic motors written by Robert Morse, published by the Wright Center for Science Education at Tufts University. [1] I also learned after reading Franklin's autobiography that he was a hard-working publisher of a newspaper and published the first Poor Richard's Almanack on December 28, 1732, and was a writer of wise and pithy sayings. I recall some of them, such as: "A penny saved is a penny earned," or, "Early to bed, early to rise, makes a man healthy, wealthy, and wise."

Regarding Dr. Franklin's Christian beliefs—or lack thereof—there is much controversy. Some historians regard him as a Deist, while others saw him as a practical atheist. As we shall see in the following chapters, Franklin, as well as most of the Founders, have become the objects of slander, historical distortion, and even ridicule.

Sadly, my public school experiences with early American history left me only with one-dimensional black and white caricatures of these famous—and amazing—historical personalities. Given what I was taught, it was hard to imagine them as real people who laughed, loved, made mistakes, or even cried. The full depth and color of these people escaped me.

Only much later in life, after I took the time to read Benjamin Franklin's autobiography and the other historical accounts and documents of our nation's founding fathers, did I begin to appreciate them. Not only was I astounded at their brilliant intellects and depth of wisdom, but was amazed to discover that nearly *all* of them were *Christians*. Perhaps most shocking of all, I discovered the nearly overwhelming volume of Christian references and biblical verses quoted by these Founders in their speeches and correspondence.

As a student in the 1950s and 60s, I honestly cannot recall a single mention of President Washington's Christian beliefs, or those of any of the other Founders for that matter. Their faith in Christ is almost entirely ignored in our modern history textbooks. The only reference to their religious beliefs I could recall in public school was the oft-repeated assertion that Benjamin Franklin and most of the other Founding Fathers were "Deists." The clear implication—pounded into the minds of our nation's children for decades by our secular-humanist schools—is that the Founders didn't take Christianity or biblical principles into consideration while crafting America's founding documents, and *especially* within their official deliberations. America's Founders are primarily portrayed as worldly-wise and sincere secular statesmen who relied on their wits and humanist assumptions to form our government.

In recent times, emboldened under the rubric of "political correctness," progressive-leftist critics of the Founders have become shrill and vicious in their denunciations of these honorable men, holding them up to open mockery and demonization. Portrayed as greedy, slave-owning, white European profiteers, they stand charged with "human rights" abuses, and the criminal disenfranchisement of the peaceful natives, along with the systematic enslavement of darker-skinned "people of color."

America's Founders and the Sin of Slavery

The circumstances of America's early history are far more complicated than such simplistic tripe now crammed down the throats of our nation's children. The Founders were men of their times. And while it is true many of the Founders were slave owners, these were mostly inherited circumstances, and in the end, many of them made efforts to free their slaves with careful consideration to their welfare. Also, I think it is important to remember that the heinous sin of human slavery did not originate with white Europeans. The sin of slavery was a common practice by darker-skinned persons in the ancient world for thousands of years.

Following are but a few quotes from the Founding Fathers on the subject of abolishing slavery.

Patrick Henry is quoted:

> *I believe a time will come when an opportunity will be offered to abolish this lamentable evil. Everything we do is to improve it, if it happens in our day; if not, let us transmit to our descendants, together with our slaves, a pity for their unhappy lot and an abhorrence of slavery.*[2]

President George Washington, in a letter to Marquis de Lafayette, 10 May 1786, echoed Henry's sentiments:

> *[Y]our late purchase of an estate in the colony of Cayenne, with a view to emancipating the slaves on it, is a generous and noble proof of your humanity. Would to God a like spirit would diffuse itself generally into the minds of the people of this country; but I despair of seeing it.* [<footnote]Reference: Washington's Maxims, 159. http://tinyurl.com/naxk44c [/footnote]

218 Destroying the Shadow Agenda

Washington, in a letter to Robert Morris, 12 April 1786, continues this thought.

> *[T]here is not a man living who wishes more sincerely than I do, to see a plan adopted for the abolition of [slavery].*[3]

In the Draft of Washington's first Inaugural Address, delivered in New York City Federal Hall in 1789, we find the words;

> *I rejoice in a belief that intellectual light will spring up in the dark corners of the earth; that freedom of enquiry will produce liberality of conduct; that mankind will reverse the absurd position that the many were, made for the few; and that they will not continue slaves in one part of the globe, when they can become freemen in another.*

Dr. Benjamin Franklin was the first president of the first anti-slavery society in the United States. On February 3, 1790, Dr. Franklin's last act in public service was to petition Congress to abolish the scourge of human slavery and exhorted the delegates to;

> *...devise means for removing the inconsistency from the character of the American People and to promote mercy and justice toward this distressed Race.*

John Quincy Adams, in a letter penned 8 June 1819, said;

> *Every measure of prudence, therefore, ought to be assumed for the eventual total extirpation of slavery from the United States....I have, throughout my whole life, held the practice of slavery in...abhorrence.*[4]

Thomas Jefferson called slavery;

> *...a moral depravity*[5] *and a "hideous blot..."*[6]

Jefferson was prolific in his condemnation of human slavery, which he described as a *"great political and moral evil."*

> *In the very first session held under the republican government, the assembly passed a law for the perpetual prohibition of the importation of slaves. This will in some measure stop the increase of this great political and*

moral evil, while the minds of our citizens may be ripening for a complete emancipation of human nature.[7]

With rare exceptions, the Founders were men of deep religious convictions firmly rooted in the Scriptures and Christianity strongly influenced by Calvinist and Puritan doctrines. This does not mean that they were "perfect" or had no personal faults or failures that fell short of their highest ideals and biblical aspirations. No true Christian would ever claim sinless perfection just because they trust in Jesus Christ for the forgiveness of their sins. This is an oft-repeated accusation by leftist progressives and atheists, who despise a God they claim doesn't exist. These never miss an opportunity to throw the "hypocrisy flag" against anyone who admits their desperate need for a Savior. God worked *through* the Founders, in spite of their personal faults and failures. These flawed vessels were well-aware of the fallen depravity of man, and deliberately crafted a system of government equipped with abuse-of-power circuit breakers designed to limit government so that no one person or single political party could possess too much power. They also wrote in legislative mechanisms to allow for improvement without the need for repeated revolutions.

A Former Slave Defends the Founders
Frederick Douglass, a brilliant black man, and former slave escaped to the North in the 1800s and gained his freedom. Douglas used his freedom to educate himself historically and came to appreciate deeply the genius of the Founders and the constitutional republic they established. Douglas campaigned tirelessly against human slavery and became a personal friend of President Abraham Lincoln.

In a speech delivered in 1852 entitled "What to the slave is the 4th?" Douglass spoke admirably of the observance of Independence Day on the Fourth of July.

> *On that day in American history, our Founders boldly declared in the Declaration of Independence that "all men are created equal, and endowed by their Creator with certain unalienable rights."*

Secular-liberals often try to twist Douglass' words to *slander* the Founders and the Republic, but any honest reader of his speech would come to an entirely different conclusion. Here are several quotes from Douglass' famous speech:

> *Fellow citizens, I am not wanting in respect for the Fathers of this Republic. The signers of the Declaration of Independence were brave men. They*

> *were great men too – great enough to give name to a great age. It does not often happen to a nation to raise, at one time, such a number of truly great men. . . I cannot contemplate their great deeds with less than admiration. They were statesman, patriots, and heroes, and for the good they did, and the principles they contended for, I will unite with you to honor their memory. . . With them, nothing was "settled" that was not right. With them, justice, liberty and humanity were "final," not slavery and oppression. . . Their solid manhood stands out the more as we contrast it with these degenerate times. . . .Their statesmanship looked beyond the passing moment, and stretched away in strength into the distant future. They seized upon eternal principles, and set a glorious example in their defense. Mark them!* (Emphasis added) [8]

Joshua Charles, the author of the newly published book: Liberty's Secrets: The Lost Wisdom of America's Founders, wrote the following in an article in World Net Daily in which he said:

> *Imagine: Douglass, a former slave, heaping praises upon the Founders. How could he do this? In short, because Douglass was historically literate. He knew that though they had done it imperfectly, the Founders had advanced the ball down the field significantly, to use a modern sports metaphor.* [9]

In stark contrast to modern critics of the Founders and the Constitution, Frederick Douglass *praised* the Founding Fathers. He also expressed profound gratitude for their strenuous efforts to give America a system of government which made it possible for freedom to flourish. Here is another quote from his epic speech:

> *But I differ from those who charge this baseness on the framers of the Constitution of the United States. It is a slander upon their memory, at least, so I believe-interpreted as it ought to be interpreted, the Constitution is a GLORIOUS LIBERTY DOCUMENT.*
>
> *Read its preamble, consider its purposes. Is slavery among them? Is it at the gateway? Or is it in the temple? It is neither. . . [I]f it be not somewhat singular that, if the Constitution were intended to be, by its framers and adopters, a slave-holding instrument, why neither slavery, slaveholding, nor slave can anywhere be found in it. . . Now, take the Constitution according to its plain reading, and I defy the presentation of a single pro-slavery*

clause in it. On the other hand it will be found to contain principles and purposes entirely hostile to the existence of slavery. [10]

Secular revisionists, however, never miss an opportunity to distort the historical record and minimize the profound influence of Christianity upon the founding of our republic. The historical record clearly reveals this influence—for those willing to see—and all arguments to the contrary are utter nonsense.

The simple truth is, we have been deliberately "dumbed down" as a society and nation by a sinister secular-humanist educational oligarchy. Their spiritual and political agenda is the establishment of a secular-socialist "Utopia," extant nowhere on earth in all of history except in their vain imaginations. Our modern history textbooks reflect this socialist propaganda—and if we ever hope to rescue and protect our Constitutional Republic—we *must* put a stop to this gross indoctrination of our youth.

James W. Loewen, in his remarkable book, *Lies My Teacher Told Me*, laments the fact that school textbooks in America contain many dangerous distortions, exaggerations, and exclusions of factual information. In the interest of full disclosure, Loewen's book is what lawyers refer to as a "hostile witness" to my entire thesis. He is a progressive liberal who is primarily focused on the premise that there isn't *enough* criticism of the Founders and their personal failings. However, he makes an undeniable point. Our schools are not telling us the *real* story of history, and as a result, most of our people are woefully ignorant of America's history. Personally, I think we should fully embrace the facts of our history: the good, the bad, and the ugly. Only *then* can we appreciate not only the depravity of fallen man but also the good things God can accomplish through such broken instruments when it pleases Him.

The following is a salient quote from Loewen's book that sums up, I believe, something we can all agree on:

> *Thomas Jefferson surely had it right when he urged the teaching of political history so that Americans might learn "how to judge for themselves what will secure or endanger their freedom." Citizens who are their own historians, willing to identify lies and distortions and able to use sources to determine what really went on in the past, become a formidable force for democracy.* [11]

To enlarge upon Loewen's quote of Jefferson, I share part of the *original* letter from Jefferson to Thaddeus Kosciusko in 1810 quoted by Loewen:

> *I have indeed two great measures at heart, without which no republic can*

maintain its strength. 1. That of general education, to enable every man to judge for himself what will secure or endanger his freedom. 2. To divide every county into hundreds, of such size that all the children of each will be in reach of a central school in it.[12] (Emphasis added)

Some progressives argue that Jefferson was championing the establishment of *secular* Public Education. I think it is safe to assume, however, that what *he* had in mind is a *far cry* from the woefully inadequate and socialist-oriented nightmare secularists eventually established.

Were Those Founders Really Christians?

To answer this question, I will share two separate accounts detailing the fact that nearly every one of the Founding Fathers was profoundly influenced by the teachings of the Bible via one denomination or another. I'm giving two separate accounts by two different historians to head off any objections that a single report might attract. The testimony of two witnesses should settle the matter for any intellectually *honest* person.

The representatives of the individual states came together on May 25th, 1787 to hammer out a mutually-binding Constitution that would govern the infant Republic going forward.

According to political historian M. E. Bradford, *nearly every one* of the 55 delegates to the convention maintained membership in Christian denominations. Fully 27 of them held degrees from seminaries. Many of them were church elders and officers. [13] According to Bradford's account, the delegates were comprised of:

- Twenty-Nine Episcopalians
- Nine Presbyterians
- Seven Congregationalists
- Two Lutherans
- Two Dutch-Reformed
- Two Methodists
- Two Catholics
- One lapsed Quaker and sometimes Anglican
- One Unitarian

The second witness I wish to call to the stand is Robert G. Ferris, editor of *Signers of the Constitution: Historic Places Commemorating the Signing of the Constitution*:

There were 55 delegates to the Constitutional Convention of 1787 at which the U.S. Constitution was drafted and signed. All participated in the proceedings which resulted in the Constitution, but only 39 of these delegates were actually signers of the document. [14]

Ferris then lists the religious affiliations of the delegates, which differs only slightly from Bradford's, but my point is nevertheless well-established.

- Twenty-Nine Episcopalians
- Nine Presbyterians
- Seven Congregationalists
- Two Lutherans
- Two Dutch-Reformed
- Two Methodists
- Two Catholics
- Two Quakers

I would add for emphasis that *none* of them identified as Deists, Atheists, Islamists, Buddhists, Hindus, Shintoists, etc., etc. The "politically correct" diversity nonsense of our times—implemented by progressive-secularists as a weapon against biblical Christianity—would not blossom until the 1960s. As an important side-note, "political correctness" flourished during Josef Stalin's Marxist dictatorship in Russia to denote one who heels to the Communist Party line. The term was originally minted by a Marxist Party hack named Leon Trotsky to refer to the "useful idiots" who mindlessly conformed to the Bolshevik Party line. This rotting corpse was revived in the 1960s by Marxist University professors. Indoctrinated graduates of these schools became the New Progressives and "community organizers" who fancied themselves as intrepid, above-average intellectuals and revolutionaries following in the steps of dictators and genocidal maniacs like Ernesto "Che" Guevara, Fidel Castro, and "Chairman" Mao (to name just a few). Under Josef Stalin's brutal regime, *anyone* who dared express an opinion differing from the "Party," or Comrade Stalin personally, could expect an unpleasant experience before a firing squad, or permanent—and short-lived—exile to the coal and uranium mines of Siberia.

How could *any* rational person say with a straight face that the Christian faith was a minor, or at best, insignificant influence in the lives and deliberations of our nation's Founders? Such a position is at best, disingenuous, and at worst, insane. Of course, no matter how much evidence is presented, many will continue to deny America's rich Christian foundations simply because of an

224 Destroying the Shadow Agenda

irrational indoctrinated secular bias. John Heywood is credited with coining the saying in 1546:

> *There are none so blind*
> *as those who will not see.*

In *A History of the American People*, eminent historian Paul Johnson stated:

> *The American Revolution in its origins, was a religious event, whereas the French Revolution was an anti-religious event. That fact was to shape... the nature of the independent state it brought into being."* Johnson continued; *"The Declaration of Independence was, to those who signed it, a religious as well as a secular act, and the Revolutionary War has the approbation of divine providence.* [15]

A Nation Saved by a Prayer?

The pre-convention debates during the months leading up to the Constitutional Convention in Philadelphia were difficult, even rancorous at times, for there was considerable tension between the anti-Federalists and those who saw the need for a stronger central government. For example, the great patriot and orator, Patrick Henry, was personally opposed to the ratification of the Constitution. As you will recall, Henry is famous for his "Give me liberty, or give me death" speech to the Virginia Convention in 1775, at St. John's Church in Richmond, Virginia. He fanned the flames of patriotism leading up to the American Revolution, but was deeply suspicious of any centralized government, and foresaw the great danger it might pose to individual states rights. Interestingly, this debate continues to this very day as Americans struggle to come to grips with the grave dangers of a too-powerful central government and the rights of individuals and States.

The convention in Philadelphia was a pivotal point in America's history, and there was real danger that the delegates might never find a way to come into agreement over the final wording of the Constitution. Without a national consensus, our nation might have torn itself apart before it even began.

At one critical point in the debates, amid the angry shouts of the deeply divided delegates, Dr. Benjamin Franklin—then 81 years old and the eldest attending delegate—slowly rose from his seat. Franklin was a well-respected elder member of the assembly, and no-doubt the angry exchanges in echoing in Constitution Hall quickly died down into deferential silence as this venerable aged statesman stood and respectfully sought recognition from the Chair to

Faith of Our Fathers 225

speak to the assembly. Given the floor, he presented an address to the deeply-divided assembly that may *very well* have saved the Republic.

His words in the now-silent hall penetrated the hearts and minds of the delegates and stunned them as they listened respectfully. Franklin's remarks set in motion a proposal that would steer the course of future deliberations even to *this very day*. The following is an excerpt from Dr. Franklin's speech:

> *In this situation of this Assembly, groping as it were in the dark to find political truth, and scarce able to distinguish it when presented to us, how has it happened, Sir, that we have not hitherto once thought of humbly applying to the Father of lights to illuminate our understandings?*
>
> *In the beginning of the Contest with Great Britain, when we were sensible of danger we had daily prayer in this room for the Divine protection. Our prayers, Sir, were heard, and they were graciously answered.*
>
> *All of us who were engaged in the struggle must have observed frequent instances of Superintending Providence in our favor. To that kind Providence we owe this happy opportunity of consulting in peace on the means of establishing our future national felicity. And have we now forgotten that powerful friend?*
>
> *I have lived, Sir, a long time, and the longer I live, the more convincing proofs I see of this truth-that God governs in the affairs of men. And if a sparrow cannot fall to the ground without His notice, is it probable that an empire can rise without His aid?*
>
> *We have been assured, Sir, in the sacred writings, that "except the Lord build the House they labor in vain that build it." I firmly believe this; and I also believe that without His concurring aid we shall succeed in this political building no better than the builders of Babel...I therefore beg leave to move, that henceforth prayers imploring the assistance of Heaven, and its blessings on our deliberations, be held in this Assembly every morning before we proceed to business, and that one or more of the Clergy of the city be requested to officiate in that service.* [16] [17]

As Dr. Franklin slowly retook his seat at the conclusion of his speech, the assembly sat for some time in thunderstruck silence. One of the delegates, General Jonathan Dayton, a delegate to the Convention was quoted by another representative, William Steele, in a letter to his son written in September 1825. This account also found its way into at least one national periodical, the

National Intelligencer, and other sources as well. According to Steele, Dayton offered the following account of Franklin's words:

> *The doctor sat down, and never did I [General Dayton] behold a countenance at once so dignified and delighted as was that of Washington, at the close of the address! Nor were the members of the Convention, generally less affected. The words of the venerable Franklin fell upon our ears with a weight and authority, even greater than we may suppose an oracle to have had in a Roman Senate! A silent admiration superseded, for a moment, the expression of that assent and approbation which was strongly marked on almost every countenance.* [18]

Upon Franklin's suggestion, the convention adjourned for three days of prayer and seeking God's wisdom. During that time, many of the delegates gathered at the Calvinist Reformed Church in Philadelphia, where according to a 1787 newspaper, the Rev. William Rogers prayed a very special prayer over the Constitutional Convention. After three days, the Convention came back into session and made surprisingly significant progress. They finished the U. S. Constitution ten weeks later, and many of the Founders later acknowledged the profound influence of God upon their deliberations.

Alexander Hamilton enthusiastically declared:

> *For my own part, I sincerely esteem it a system which without the finger of God never could have been suggested and agreed upon by such a diversity of interests.* [19]

James Madison also said:

> *It is impossible for the man of pious reflection not to perceive in it the finger of that Almighty Hand, which has been so frequently and signally extended to our relief in the critical stages of the Revolution.* [20]

Most of the delegates became convinced that God's Divine power had guided their writing of the Constitution. Benjamin Franklin concurred, explaining:

> *I beg I may not be understood to infer that our general Convention was Divinely inspired when it formed the new federal Constitution . . . yet I can hardly conceive a transaction of such momentous importance to the welfare of millions now existing (and to exist in the posterity of a great nation) should be suffered to pass without being in some degree influenced,*

guided, and governed by that omnipotent, omnipresent, and beneficent Ruler in Whom all inferior spirits "live and move and have their being" [Acts 17:28]. [21]

Are These The Thoughts of a Deist?

In light of this well-documented speech by Dr. Franklin, how is it possible that secular historical revisionists could dare declare that Franklin was an atheist—or perhaps even worse—a "Deist"? By definition, a Deist is one who believes that after God created the universe, He adopted a "hands-off" wait and see policy. Some have described Deism as the belief that God wound up the universe like a big clock, stepped back, and is now allowing it to run down on its own without further divine intervention. Under this paradigm, men are left almost entirely in control to make their libertarian "free will" decisions and determine their personal destinies while God impartially observes events as they unfold according to man's decisions.

Dr. Franklin's appeal for prayer seeking God's "concurring aid" in their deliberations would seem to render ludicrous any argument that Franklin was a Deist. A true Deist would *never* appeal for God's active participation in their activities as Franklin clearly did.

Patrick Henry is also often "tagged" as a Deist by secular revisionists, even during his own lifetime. Here is a direct quote by Henry on this subject:

> *The rising greatness of our country…is greatly tarnished by the general prevalence of Deism, which, with me, is but another name for vice and depravity….I hear it is said by the Deists that I am one of their number; and indeed that some good people think I am no Christian. This thought gives me much more pain than the appellation of Tory (being called a traitor), because I think religion of infinitely higher importance than politics…Being a Christian…is a character which I prize far above all this world has or can boast. (Emphasis added)* [22]

Again, due to our deeply dysfunctional and currently secularized public education system, nearly all memory of America's Christian roots are suppressed and have nearly passed out of memory. Intensely determined secularists are laboring tirelessly to expunge Christianity from our nation's schools and textbooks. This is no mere accident or oversight. It is, I'm convinced, a deliberate, painstaking effort to scrub *all traces* of Christianity out of American history and memory and promote a secular-humanist worldview upon all future generations.

228   Destroying the Shadow Agenda

God: Guest of Honor at the First Inauguration

No single event in America's historical record better illustrates the significant influence of Christianity in American society and politics than the inauguration of George Washington as our first President. On April 30, 1789, a standing-room-only crowd of cheering people filled the street before the old City Hall, located just down the street from Saint Paul's Chapel in the modern district of Lower Manhattan in New York City. The City Hall was later rebuilt and named Federal Hall and served as the seat of the Federal government until the U.S. Capitol moved to Philadelphia in 1790. There it remained for ten years until the final move to Washington, D.C. in 1800.

Benson J. Lossing wrote a series of articles chronicling the American Revolution from 1760 until the early days of independence around 1800 in his *Household History for All Readers.* Lossing related the following highly significant events surrounding President Washington's inauguration. Here are a few quotes from Lossing's work:

> *On the 30th of April Washington was inaugurated President of the republic. The ceremony took place in the open gallery of the old City Hall (afterward called Federal Hall), on the site of the present Custom-House, in the presence of a vast multitude... The oath of office was administered by Robert R. Livingston, then chancellor of the State of New York. The open Bible (then and now the property of St. John's Lodge of Freemasons of the City of New York), on which the President laid his right hand, was held on a rich crimson velvet cushion by Mr. Otis, Secretary of the Senate...*
>
> *After taking the oath and kissing the sacred book reverently, Washington closed his eyes, and in an attitude of devotion said; "So help me God!" The Chancellor exclaimed, "It is done!" and then turning to the people he shouted, "Long live George Washington, the first President of the United States." That shout was echoed and re-echoed by the multitude, when the President and the members of Congress retired to the Senate Chamber, where Washington pronounced a most impressive inaugural address.*

Lossing continues; (Emphasis added)

> *At the conclusion, (of the inaugural address) he, and the members went in procession to Saint Paul's Church (which, with the other churches, had been opened for prayers at nine o'clock that morning),* **and there they invoked the blessing of Almighty God upon the new government.** [23]

Another historian, Dr. William T. Harris, also wrote a *slightly* different account of the inauguration—which differs in no significant way—in his seminal work; *The United States of America: A Pictorial History of The American Nation From The Earliest Discoveries and Settlements to the Present Time.* Here is an excerpt from Dr. Harris's book:

> *A profound stillness fell on the populace, when, rising, Washington again advanced, supported on the right by John Adams, and on the left by Chancellor Livingston, while just behind were a number of his old friends and comrades in arms. Mr. Otis, Secretary of the Senate, held the crimson cushion with the Bible on top, while the Chancellor, in a distinct voice, read the oath in these words; "I do solemnly swear that I will faithfully execute the office of the President of the United States and will to the best of my ability, preserve, protect, and defend the Constitution of the United States..."*
>
> *While the Chancellor was repeating the words, Washington stood with his hand resting on the open Bible, and his eyes fixed on the face of the Chancellor. At the conclusion of the oath, the President said in a clear voice, "I swear–so help me God!"*
>
> *Before Mr. Otis could raise the Bible, Washington leaned over and reverently kissed it. The Chancellor turned his face toward the crowd, and taking one step forward, shouted; "long live George Washington, President of the United States!*

Dr. Harris continues:

> *The assemblage now walked to Saint Paul's Church, where prayers were read by Bishop Provost, who had been appointed by the Senate (as) one of the Chaplains of Congress. The city was illuminated and fire-works set off in the evening.* [24]

Dr. Harris' account of Washington's "prayer walk" after his inauguration closely mirrors Dr. Lossing's account.

The First "Executive Order."
Please ponder the importance of the previous paragraphs for a moment. President Washington's *first official act* as President of the United States—indeed the very *first order of business* for his administration—was to set himself publicly

to *prayer*. His purpose was clearly to invoke the blessings of Almighty God upon the new nation.

Immediately following his Inaugural Address, the President led the Congress of the United States out of Federal Hall in a solemn procession to pray at nearby Saint Paul's Chapel. A short walk, the chapel is situated only three-tenths of a mile away. *The entire government of the United States gathered for a CHRISTIAN prayer meeting!* Also, it is noteworthy to mention that it wasn't to a mosque or a Hindu or a Buddhist temple they marched. They went to a *Christian church*! No one even *considered* the possibility that anyone might be offended, nor did they give the slightest thought to our modern obsession over "separation of Church and State" or "cultural diversity."

Imagine how modern secular watchdogs and today's liberal press would react if any President *dared* to do the same today? The howls and screeches of apoplectic atheists and Marxist law professors would likely be heard across the country (thanks largely to our modern leftist news media). Threats of legal action in the name of the false and oft-used mantra: "constitutional separation of church and state" would soon follow.

I'm unaware of any written record regarding what Washington prayed during his time in that booth at Saint Paul's (where I was privileged to sit 212 years later). I can only imagine that he, like King Solomon of Israel's antiquity, must have sought God's aid and wisdom. No human could hope to lead the infant nation in pathways that would bring forth God's plan and purposes without God's help and active assistance. Washington was clearly a man of deep faith in Christ, and it is beyond question that his Christian faith heavily influenced his leadership and temper of spirit.

Based on the sheer volume of Christian references in their speeches and correspondence, it should be crystal-clear to any honest person that the vast majority of the Founding Fathers were men of deep devotion and faith in God. They also held the Holy Bible in profound reverence and respect. Therefore, it would also seem reasonable that the Founders would regard the events surrounding the establishment of a new nation as a sovereign act of God. Considering the seeming impossibility at the onset of the Revolutionary War that military victory against Great Britain could *ever* happen in a *hundred years*, that eventual American victory must have seemed tantamount to a miracle on par with the parting of the Red Sea by Moses. Moved by this frame of mind, it would only be logical to assume that as representatives of this infant republic, their first order of business would be to dedicate it to God in humble obedience.

Just prior to this time of prayer at Saint Paul's Chapel, President Washington's first inaugural address to Congress was *filled* with his humble acknowledgments of God's Providence. He spoke of God's guiding protection for our nation during the difficult and seemingly unwinnable war with the British.

Here are just a few excerpts of his moving words that clearly reveal his Christian convictions in his inaugural address on April 30, 1789;

> ...it would be peculiarly improper to omit in this first official act, my fervent supplications to that Almighty Being who rules over the universe, who presides in the councils of nations, and whose providential aids can supply every human defect, that His benediction may consecrate to the liberties and happiness of the people of the United States...
>
> ...In tendering this homage to the Great Author of every public and private good, I assure myself that it expresses your sentiments not less than my own, nor those of my fellow-citizens at large less than either.
>
> No people can be bound to acknowledge and adore the Invisible Hand which conducts the affairs of men more than those of the United States. Every step by which they have advanced to the character of an independent nation seems to have been distinguished by some token of Providential agency...
>
> ...We ought to be no less persuaded that the propitious smiles of Heaven can never be expected on a nation that disregards the eternal rules of order and right which Heaven itself has ordained...
>
> ...I shall take my present leave; but not without resorting once more to the Benign Parent of the Human Race, in humble supplication that, since He has been pleased to favor the American people with opportunities for deliberating in perfect tranquility, and dispositions for deciding with unparalleled unanimity on a form of government for the security of their union and the advancement of their happiness, so His divine blessings may be equally conspicuous in the enlarged views, the temperate consultations and the wise measures on which the success of this Government must depend. [25]

It must be pointed out that although Washington did not directly reference the name of Jesus Christ in this speech, we must keep in mind the protocols of formality in his day. Speakers often omitted any direct reference in public discourse to the name of Jesus out of reverential respect. There can be no doubt everyone in his audience would have clearly understood precisely whom Washington was referencing as he used words like "Providence" or "He" and "His." This substitution of God's holy name is still commonly practiced to this

232 Destroying the Shadow Agenda

day among Orthodox Jewish people. They consider the Name of God so holy that the mere utterance of the Name on unholy lips could be disrespectful and possibly blasphemous. They address God as "L-rd" or even "G-d."

One portion of Washington's address bears repeating. It should stand as a warning to us all in our present times.

> ...*We ought to be no less persuaded that the propitious smiles of Heaven can never be expected on a nation that disregards the eternal rules of order and right which Heaven itself has ordained...*

I could argue that the societal and economic woes we are presently experiencing in our day stem directly from our national sin of disregarding... "the eternal rules of order and right which Heaven itself has ordained..."Is it any wonder that most Americans are nearly *completely unaware* of what our first president said in our nation's first presidential inauguration? Washington's complete speech has been deleted from public school classrooms and history textbooks. This censorship resulted from an unwitting collusion of militant secular educators *and* passively-*ignorant* church leaders who held their silence and *allowed* it to happen. As a result, our people are almost entirely unaware of the significant contents of this speech, and especially its religious content.

Imagine for a moment what would happen if any brave public school history teacher in our time required their students to study, memorize, or (gasp) *recite* Washington's inaugural address in their Public School classroom? What do you think would result if a school Principal *dared* to read the entire text of Washington's inaugural speech in a school assembly, or allowed a character actor to recite it? Quite likely, such a brave soul would be severely censured or fired in our present atmosphere of militant secularism and "political correctness."The *manifestly* "religious speech" contained in Washington's speech would no doubt trigger lawsuits by secularly-brainwashed parents or indignant Christophobic bigots. All this in *spite* of the *irrefutable* historical record that these are actually Washington's words, and a matter of public record. How have we come to a place when our own first President's words are banned and censored from Public Education? Whether anyone agrees with him or not, shouldn't our first President's words be heard by our nation's students?As an aside, does anyone else find it odd that Islamic prayers and practices are now finding a warm welcome within public schools in the name of "religious and cultural diversity?" All expressions of Judaism or Christianity are censored or banned altogether while the religion of Islam is given favored status. Is this not the *height* of hypocrisy and intellectual dishonesty? [26]

Notes

1. Part four of the Ben Franklin as my Lab Partner materials, including the construc[tion] of a capacitor and electrostatic motors. https://goo.gl/7xmVtk

2. (letter to Robert Pleasants, 18 January 1773) Reference: The Spirit of 'Seventy-Six, Henry Commager and Richard Morris, p. 402.

3. Washington's Maxims, 157.

4. Vindicating the Founders, West (5); original Selected Writings of John and John Quincy Adams, Koch and Peden p. 209

5. Jefferson to Thomas Cooper, September 10, 1814, in PTJ:RS, 7:651-52. Transcription available at Founders Online.

6. Jefferson to William Short, September 8, 1823, Papers of Thomas Jefferson, College of William and Mary, https://goo.gl/kzH68oull

7. "Notes On Virginia," Query No. VIII: the Number of Its Inhabitants, 1781; "The Works of Thomas Jefferson," Federal Edition, Editor: Paul Leicester Ford, (New York and London, G.P. Putnam's Sons, 1904-5) Vol. 3

8. What to the Slave is the Fourth of July? JULY 5, 1852 FREDERICK DOUGLASS http://tinyurl.com/ohzfvu2

9. EX-SLAVE PRAISES ... THE FOUNDERS! By Joshua Charles for WND.com. http://tinyurl.com/ptetnfn

10. Ibid

11. *Lies My Teachers Told Me; Everything Your American History Textbook Got Wrong*, by James W. Loewen, Simon & Schuster, pg 362

12. Andrew Lipscomb and Albert Bergh, editors, The Writings of Thomas Jefferson, 20 Volumes, (Washington, D.C.: 1903-1904), 12:369

13. M.E. Bradford. A Worthy Company: Brief Lives of the Framers of the United States Constitution (Marlborough, NH: Plymouth Rock Foundation, 1982), pp 81-87.

14. Signers of the Constitution: Historic Places Commemorating the Signing of the Constitution, published by the United States Department of the Interior, National Park Service: Washington, D.C. (revised edition 1976), page 138:

15. A History of the American People By Paul Johnson, Harper Perennial Publishers, Page 84

16. Franklin's Appeal for Prayer at the Constitutional Convention http://tinyurl.com/k2y932f

17. Memoirs of the Life and Writings of Benjamin Franklin, LL.D. (London: Printed for Henry Colburn, Brithish and Foreign Public Library, Conduit Streetl 1818. p. 388 http://tinyurl.com/o9xwc2q

18. Ibid

19. https://www.thefederalistpapers.org/founders/alexander-hamilton

20. http://foundersquotes.com/founding-fathers-quote/it-is-impossible-for-the-man-of-pious-reflection-not-to-perceive-in-it/

21. Memoirs of the Life and Writings of Benjamin Franklin, LL.D. (London: Printed for Henry Colburn, Brithish and Foreign Public Library, Conduit Streetl 1818. p. 395 http://tinyurl.com/o9xwc2q

y; Life, Correspondence and Speeches, Volume 2 By William Wirt
vurl.com/ne2tsfq

ory of the United States from The Aboriginal Times to The Present
, LL.D. 1895 Chapter 87, p. 1124

tes of America: A pictorial History of The American Nation From
id Settlements to the Present Time, Copyright 1906, by William T.
Commissioner of Education. Volume 3, pp 202-203 Published by
.npany, 1878

25. U.S. National Archives and Records Administration; Washington's Inaugural Address of 1789, A Transcription http://www.archives.gov/exhibits/american_originals/inaugtxt.html

26. American Thinker Magazine, Public School Teaches the Shahada, the Islamic prayer for Conversions By Carol Brown http://tinyurl.com/pljbb7o

20

America in Covenant?

God, who gave us life,
gave us liberty.
And can the liberties of a nation
be thought secure
when we have removed their only firm basis;
[that being] a conviction in the minds of the people
that these liberties are of the Gift of God?
That [our liberties] are not to be violated
but with His wrath?
Indeed, I tremble for my country
when I reflect that God is just;
that His justice cannot sleep forever;
That a revolution of the wheel of fortune,
a change of situation is among possible events;
that it may become probable
by [evil] Supernatural influence!
The Almighty has no attribute
which can take side with us in that event.
President Thomas Jefferson,
Notes on the State of Virginia,
Query XVIII, p. 237

~~~~~~

At the time of Washington's inauguration, the land to the west of St. Paul's Chapel belonged to the church and was considered hallowed church grounds. In later years, parcels were sold to subsequent owners and eventually became part of the New York City metroplex and the site of the World Trade Center complex.

The history and potential prophetic significance of this tract of land are compelling. At the very least, it is ironic that the very place where President

George Washington prayed and dedicated America to God following his inauguration also happens to be the same site where, 212 years, four months, and twelve days later, Islamic terrorists plunged a dagger of vicious hatred deep into our nation's heart.

From the first day of America's founding, we have seen our nation alternately fall into tragedies only to rise again to new triumphs. It's been quite a ride spanning these past 226 years, yet I believe God's hand has never strayed from the controls. This thought begs the question. Is it *possible* that the attacks of 9/11, and the painful and heartbreaking destruction of the World Trade Center was part of a larger unfolding master plan? And is it also possible (as some say) that 9/11 was a divine chastisement upon our country because of our arrogant departure from a solemn covenant Washington made with God on this *very site*?

I realize that such conjecture may be offensive to some, due to the present-day presumption that God "all loving" and kind, and would *never* inflict judgment upon "good" people. This would be especially true for those who lost loved ones in the attack or suffered significant financial losses. However, I think we should be very cautious about dismissing such ideas out of hand. The Holy Bible records numerous occurrences of Gods' chastisement upon nations and peoples. Added to this, the record of history gives ample evidence that our Founders may have entered into a holy covenant with God at our nation's establishment, and we ought to take these things seriously. As President Jefferson—a *most* unlikely source to many—said in the opening quote;

> *And can the liberties of a nation*
> *be thought secure*
> *when we have removed their only firm basis;*
> *[that being] a conviction in the minds of the people*
> *that these liberties are of the Gift of God?*
> *That [our liberties] are not to be violated*
> *but with His wrath?*

Could it be that we are a nation "set apart" for a particular, and perhaps, even a holy purpose? If so, I think it is logical to assume that the misuses of sacred things—even whole nations dedicated and set apart unto the Lord—is *serious business* and could result in grave consequences if continued.

What might happen if the United States, founded upon God's righteous principles and dedicated by solemn prayer by our nation's leaders, should ever turn away from God as a matter of *public policy*? President Jefferson was *deeply* concerned about this very thing. He foresaw the very *real possibility* that our people and nation might one day abandon God's gracious gift of liberty, and arrogantly forsake His holy commands.

It looks as if what Jefferson feared has already begun to happen, and is increasing at an alarming rate. Each news cycle brings ever-worsening reports of ethical and moral failures among our national leaders. Increasingly bold efforts are being made by arrogant, militant atheists to obliterate all expressions of the Christian faith from our schools, government institutions, and the public square.

At present, our school children are progressively subjected to shrill denunciations of Christianity at all grade levels, with any notions of biblical morality and modesty commonly mocked. Christianity is viciously attacked and falsely accused of being "repressive" to women's "rights," homosexual "rights," minorities' "rights." Racial and ethnic violence is rapidly increasing in our cities as people—who believe that every "want" or perceived "need" is somehow a "basic human right" that someone *else* owes them—demand that the government force "rich people" to give them whatever they want.

In the meantime, the corporate murder-machine of Planned Parenthood and the abortion industry rolls on unabated, leaving a bloody trail of the shredded bodies of babies. In light of this and much more, can we reasonably expect that God's wrath will be long silent in the face of such wickedness? I have no doubt that some will call me a "religious fanatic" for even suggesting such things as God's wrath, but I'm in good company. Again, Thomas Jefferson's ominous words of warning ring in the ears of those who have ears to hear;

> *... Indeed, I tremble for my country*
> *when I reflect that God is just;*
> *that His justice cannot sleep forever;*

Jefferson—and most of his fellow Founders—were *well aware* of the tendency of depraved, wicked men to subvert godliness, even in the earliest years of our nation's history. Almost prophetically, he seemed to foresee a future apostasy, driven by evil supernatural influence. He knew his Bible well enough to "tremble" for his country in the light of God's justice. Should not we *also* tremble?

Too many of our politicians have become corrupt and increasingly drunk with power, prestige, money, and moral compromise. We have allowed unprincipled and unscrupulous men and women into positions of political leadership and traded our birthright for a few crumbs of materialistic bread.

At the risk of angering my fellow Christians, I must say something that will be difficult to accept. The *one group* that carries the lion's share of blame for this sad state of affairs in the United States is, in my view, Christian ministers. They didn't *create* the problems facing us, but they *allowed* them to happen. Christian leaders in previous generations who *knew* the truth stood by and did nothing. Complacency by leaders in the face of evil carries ominous implications. Such leadership failure eventually lulls people to sleep and indifference toward evil. Edmund Burke, a British parliamentarian, philosopher, and politician, summed up the problem in a single sentence.

> *All that is necessary*
> *for the triumph of evil*
> *is that good men do nothing.*

Amplifying this thought, the British philosopher and political theorist, John Stuart Mill, delivered the following words in an inaugural address in 1867 at the University of St. Andrews. His words echo Burke.

> *Let not any one pacify his conscience by the delusion that he can do no harm if he takes no part, and forms no opinion. Bad men need nothing more to compass their ends than that good men should* **look on and do nothing**. (Emphasis added) [1]

I *must* use a graphic example here to underscore my point. It is as if Lady Liberty is being assaulted in broad daylight in the middle of the street by a mob of ignorant, brutish thugs. This crime is occurring right before our eyes while most of us are standing around merely watching it happen. We can hear her cries for help, but are *afraid* to intervene and put a stop to it. It's all too easy to close our eyes and turn away, comforting ourselves vainly that "someone else" will step forward with courage and rescue her. Too many of us are just too busy and fearful about what might happen to *us* if we get "too involved."

I cling to the hope that God—who founded this great nation in the first place—yet has a plan for the United States. As it pleases Him, He is entirely able to reach into the heart and mind of the most depraved human being who has ever lived and transform their heart to love and obey Him. I also believe God sovereignly chooses ordinary people like you and me to effect His purposes. I'm certain if God should favor us, we will find our way back to our firm foundations, and the Rock supporting them. The Rock I speak of is, of course, the Lord Jesus Christ.

Are there "Special" Nations or People?

The Bible contains numerous references to certain people, nations, and objects as "holy unto the Lord." The very *idea* of "American exceptionalism" is vile to modern Progressive Liberals and humanistically indoctrinated people who are conditioned to regard such concepts as "racist," "unfair," or "discriminatory." However, Scripture teaches us through the example of His people Israel that the entire nation of Israelites were chosen as a "holy nation."

> *Now therefore if ye will hear my voice indeed,*
> *and keep my covenant,*
> *then ye shall be my chief treasure above all people,*
> *though all the earth be mine.*
> *Ye shall be unto me also a kingdom of Priests,*
> *and a holy nation.*
> *These are the words which thou shalt speak*
> *unto the children of Israel.*
> Exodus 19:5-6

Although the Israelis were chosen and highly honored, the depraved nature of fallen man made it inevitable that they would eventually fall short of their high calling and break God's covenant. God foresaw this even from the beginning, and He warned the Israelites of the consequences of their eventual rebellion. The ominous warning of Moses to the Israelites just before his death is clear on this point:

> *For I know that after my death*
> *ye will utterly corrupt [yourselves],*
> *and turn aside from the way*
> *which I have commanded you;*
> *and evil will befall you in the latter days;*
> *because ye will do evil in the sight of the LORD,*
> *to provoke him to anger*
> *through the work of your hands.*
> *By idolatry, and worshiping images,*
> *which are the work of your hands.*
> Deuteronomy 31:29

God repeated this warning by the voices of His prophets throughout the Tanakh, popularly referred to as the Old Testament.

> *If you forsake Yahweh,*
> *and serve foreign gods,*
> *then He will turn and do you evil,*
> *and consume you,*
> *after He has done you good.*
> Joshua 24:20

When President Washington and our nation's leaders prayed upon the occasion of the first Presidential Inauguration, did they, in fact, place America into a "holy" (set apart for God's purposes) covenant? And if so, are we now being held to a higher standard before God, and liable to His chastisements and judgments if we set aside that covenant and defile ourselves? Reluctantly, I've come to believe this is so, and strongly suspect that the attacks of 9/11 may have only been the first volley in a series of coming chastisements.

Divine Judgment: A "Teachable Moment?"

The nation of Israel stands for all time as a prime example of the consequences of persistent rebellion and disregard for God's commandments and covenants. After repeated warnings by God's prophets, judgment came upon Israel several times, with destruction and exile into slavery from their promised land. The most horrendous divine judgment occurred in 70 A.D. and was so terrible; the mind recoils at the horrors that took place. According to the Jewish historian, Flavius Josephus, in his book, *The Wars of the Jews or History of the Destruction of Jerusalem.*, well over 1.1 million people died within the walls of Jerusalem of starvation, disease, murder, and at the hands of the Romans. This number is disputed by some historians, but the siege began around Passover, and people flooded the city each year from all around the region for this Holy Day. Josephus also reported that 97,000 surviving Jews were captured and enslaved. This event is commemorated upon the Titus Arch in Rome. Blood ran in the streets like streams.

Josephus described the circumstances after the enraged Roman army finally breached the city's walls.

> *"...everywhere was slaughter and flight. Most of the victims were peaceful citizens, weak and unarmed, butchered wherever they were caught. Round the Altar, the heaps of corpses grew higher and higher, while down the*

Sanctuary steps poured a river of blood and the bodies of those killed at the top slithered to the bottom."

The Roman General Titus ordered the utter destruction of the Holy City and Herod's magnificent temple and leveled the entire city to the ground. The Romans then cut down every tree, threw stones into the fields, and salted the earth so nothing could grow there.

Approximately 40 years before Jesus accurately predicted the destruction of Jerusalem. His words came to pass in 70 AD in precise detail.

> *And Jesus went out,*
> *and departed from the Temple,*
> *and his disciples came to him,*
> *to show him the building of the Temple.*
> *And Jesus said unto them,*
> *See ye not all these things?*
> *Verily I say unto you,*
> *there shall not be here left*
> *a stone upon a stone,*
> *that shall not be cast down.*
> Matthew 24:1-2:

Ironically, General Titus refused to accept a wreath of victory upon his victorious return to Rome, declaring that the victory did not come through his own efforts, but that he had merely served as an instrument of God's wrath.

Another "Teachable Moment" in the Book of Daniel

One of the clearest illustrations of the grave consequences of misusing holy things comes from the ancient Babylonian Empire, as recorded in the book of Daniel, chapter five. In this account, King Belshazzar of Babylon presented a feast one day:

> *And Belshazzar*
> *while he tasted the wine,*
> *commanded to bring him*
> *the golden and silver vessels,*
> *which his father Nebuchadnezzar*
> *had brought from the Temple in Jerusalem,*

that the king and his princes,
his wives, and his concubines
might drink therein.
Daniel 5:2

Belshazzar's father, King Nebuchadnezzar, took these holy objects from the temple in Jerusalem after conquering the city in 599 BC. These gold and silver vessels were exclusively set apart (sanctified) for the worship of God. Belshazzar deliberately defiled and dishonored these holy instruments by using them for a drunken orgy. He then compounded his sin by arrogantly inviting his guests to revel in their drunkenness and mock the God of Israel, insulting His Majesty by worshipping idols with these holy vessels:

They drank wine,
and praised the gods of gold,
and of silver, of brass, of iron,
of wood, and of stone.
Daniel 5:4

Belshazzar's insolence exceeded the limits of God's patience. Within the hour, the Lord sent a personal memo to Belshazzar via an ethereal, disembodied hand, which *terrified* the king and everyone present. Ironically, this story is still imprinted upon the collective consciousness of people worldwide. 2,500 years after it occurred, we still often hear people speak of a solemn warning as "The handwriting is on the wall."

None of the king's wise men could read the message, so Belshazzar sent for the Hebrew Daniel, who was renowned as an interpreter of visions and dreams. Daniel's testimony to Belshazzar might just as easily be applied today to the United States:

O king, hear thou,
The most high God gave unto
Nebuchadnezzar thy father a kingdom,
and majesty, and honor, and glory.
And for the majesty that he gave him,
all people, nations, and languages trembled,
and feared before him:
he put to death whom he would:
he smote whom he would:

> *whom he would he set up,*
> *and whom he would he put down.*
> *But when his heart was puffed up,*
> *and his mind hardened in pride,*
> *he was deposed from his kingly throne,*
> *and they took his honor from him.*
> *And he was driven from the sons of men,*
> *and his heart was made like the beasts,*
> *and his dwelling was with the wild asses:*
> *they fed him with grass like oxen,*
> *and his body was wet with the dew of the heaven,*
> *till he knew that the most high God*
> *bare rule over the kingdom of men,*
> *and that he appointeth over it,*
> *whomsoever He pleaseth.*
> Daniel 5:18-21 (Emphasis added)

Pay particular attention to Daniel's words regarding God's sovereign rule over nations. For clarity, I will quote it from the New International Version:

> *...the Most High God*
> *is sovereign over all kingdoms on earth*
> *and sets over them anyone he wishes.*

These passages raise an issue that may be difficult for some to accept. Daniel makes clear in this verse that God sets "anyone He wishes" over the kingdoms of the earth. He didn't say; "except in modern nations that hold free and fair elections." No country is excluded from this reality. God appoints leaders according to His sovereign choice. Think carefully about this.

As much as we might wish it otherwise, according to this, we would be wise to remember the lesson contained in the above scripture verse. Barack Hussein Obama would not have held the highest office of our country if God had not wanted him there. This underscores a point that not every leader God appoints will be godly or "good" as men estimate goodness. King Nebuchadnezzar (in the example above) was put in his position by God, even though he was a violent, brutal man. For those who can hear and accept it, the same is true of President Trump. Personally, I regard a Trump Presidency as a "divine reprieve" granting us the opportunity to mend our ways.

God's plans and purposes are infinitely higher than our minds can comprehend. His will is immutable, and not subject to the counsels of men. "But," someone will object, "If this is true, why bother with praying, voting in elections, or campaigning for leaders?" I would answer, we do all those things because God *requires* it of us. We do not obey God for the sake of results. We obey for the sake of obedience. Autonomous, humanistic persons, will reliably take offense at this statement, for the fallen nature of man ever seeks to exercise control over all things.

We bear a responsibility to participate in the process God establishes. I realize this can quickly become complicated. Someone might ask, "If God sets up kings and rulers, then what justification did the American Revolutionaries have in resisting King George?" I would answer that God raised up ministers in the early to mid-1700s who cried out that religious freedom, and its natural byproduct, political liberty, was a God-given right. A long process of pious and learned men deliberated long and prayed diligently over what they sensed was God's will for the former British colonies. America's separation from England as an independent sovereign nation was not the rash actions of a few radical patriot hotheads. As I've established, the American patriots frequently acknowledged the active hand of God in their efforts.

We now enjoy the fruits of their sacrifices and efforts, and we, by God's grace, possess God-given rights to vote, speak out on issues, and to choose righteous leaders. I believe that, in a very real sense, if we fail to give our participation and exercise our rights, we are dishonoring God and His grace toward us. To quote Jefferson again,

> *...these liberties are of the Gift of God...*
> *they are not to be violated **but with His wrath**...*

Things are occurring behind the scenes far beyond our ability to understand. We must each stand before His judgment seat to answer for our personal obedience. We are called to do what good may be done, as much as we can, for as long as we can, wherever we can, and seek to obey God even in the act of voting. At the end of the day, all outcomes are directed by God, and His purposes will be established. Proverbs 19:21 says:

> *Many devices are in a man's heart:*
> *but the counsel of the Lord shall stand.*

The actions of President Obama, in my estimation, lead America down a pathway to tyranny and economic ruin. In light of the above point, is it possible that Barrack Hussein Obama was an instrument of God's judgment upon our nation? And will a Trump Presidency be a signal of God's merciful favor as many hope? Only time will tell, but I cannot deny that very real possibility in light of what we see unfolding. We can be completely confident of one thing, however. God will reliably and inexorably move all things toward some greater good that we cannot presently discern from our limited perspective. Daniel in the above story is a great example. He served God within the sphere of the circumstances God placed him in, and God's purposes were advanced by his obedience.

As the Scriptures teach, the Lord God and Creator of the universe is truly sovereign over all nations, circumstances, and people. By God's grace, we are given to know that God is "Sovereign" over all His creation down to, and far beyond, the very sub-atomic particles that make up what we call "matter." We do not call Him "Lord of All" or "the Sovereign One" merely as a title of honor or an expression of worship. God's Sovereignty and Lordship is a fact. Jesus clearly taught us that not even a sparrow could fall to the ground apart from our Father's knowledge and consent. The implications of this truth are staggering. If this is the case, then we're forced to accept that even the heartbreaking tragedy of 9/11 had to be part of a much larger plan. Perhaps it was an act of warning—against imminent and even worse judgments coming upon America. If that's true, wouldn't we be wise to consider carefully how we should conduct ourselves in the light of events unfolding in our times?

Whether or not this makes sense to us is immaterial. This truth also does not negate our responsibility to hold this (or any other) president accountable to faithfully execute the office of President according to the oath made.

I do solemnly swear (or affirm) that I will faithfully execute the office of President of the United States, and will to the best of my ability, preserve, protect, and defend the Constitution of the United States.

We do *no dishonor* to the Office of the President by challenging policies and decisions that run contrary to constitutional boundaries, sound wisdom, and biblical commandments, no matter who might presently occupy that office. Remember Jefferson's warning. If we are blessed by God with the freedom to speak the truth, we will dishonor God's gift if we fail to exercise that freedom. Again, if "We the People" fail to hold our leaders accountable, we are committing an act of dishonor toward the God-given office they hold, and to ourselves.

All Public officials in the United States serve—in point of fact— as the servants of God and are employees of "We the People" under our Constitution and Bill of Rights. Now and then, we must remind our public employees of this fact. However, we must remember that God holds the final vote, and it is manifestly true that the inclinations of leaders are often moved in directions beyond our understanding.

Does God Use Tyrants for His Eternal Purposes?

The very idea God would "allow" an evil leader to come to power is repugnant to most people. Everyone carries around an inner mental "template" of who God is, and how He ought to "act." The prevailing model is that God's "goodness" means that when God is actively involved in something, then only "good" things will occur. The problem is, our concept of "good" is narrowly defined as that which *we* deem as safe, comfortable, convenient, joyful, prosperous, or easy, according to human standards. How often have we heard someone joyfully declare when things were going their way, "God is good!" Seldom, if ever, will we hear someone in the middle of a painful, difficult, or heartbreaking circumstance say with equal enthusiasm, "God is good!" I've had the privilege of meeting a few who can and have, and I always feel like I should lower my eyes in the presence of someone who walks in such depth of spiritual maturity and faith.

The scriptures contain numerous examples of God's goodness expressed in the midst of intense personal or national suffering. We would be wise to remember that God is not "sovereign" because we in any way "allow" Him be so. He is Sovereign over all things because He IS the Sovereign God. In fact, if God is not Sovereign over His creation at all times, in all places, with infinite power, wisdom, and knowledge, then He is not God at all. In that case, He would be nothing more than just another (albeit formidable) player in the collective drama of unfolding existence.

Throughout history, God placed leaders in power, often as unwitting agents of His divine purposes or judgments, even for the purpose of chastising nations to bring about His greater purposes. At the same time, He commands His people to maintain their integrity and interact appropriately toward those leaders.

What do I mean by "appropriately?" I certainly do not mean groveling before them in unquestioning obedience. Scripture instructs us to honor authorities and obey their *lawful* commands. This mandate is balanced by Scripture's superseding order that we honor and obey God *first and foremost*, and His commandments *supremely*. God's commandments are binding upon all men, including rulers and public servants, without a single exception.

If leaders violate God's higher laws and commandments and do evil, they disobey and dishonor Him, and we are *required to resist them*, albeit, lawfully. If necessary, such leaders must be removed from power by every lawful means. While this may seem enigmatic, throughout biblical and human history, this has been played out. Be forewarned. Your obedience to God may require significant sacrifices, including your freedom, and possibly your life.

Notice Daniel's bold message of rebuke to King Belshazzar, and consider how appropriate such a message might be to leaders today:

> *But you his son, Belshazzar,*
> *have not humbled your heart,*
> *although you knew all this.*
> *And you have lifted yourself up*
> *against the Lord of heaven.*
> *They have brought the vessels*
> *of His house before you,*
> *and you and your lords,*
> *your wives and your concubines,*
> *have drunk wine from them.*
> *And you have praised*
> *the gods of silver and gold,*
> *bronze and iron, wood and stone,*
> *which do not see or hear or know;*
> *and the God*
> *who holds your breath in His hand*
> *and owns all your ways,*
> *you have not glorified.*
> *Then the fingers of the hand*
> *were sent from Him,*
> *and this writing was written.*
> *And this is the inscription that was written:*
> *MENE, MENE, TEKEL, UPHARSIN.*
> *This is the interpretation of each word.*
> *MENE:*
> *God has numbered your kingdom,*
> *and finished it;*
> *TEKEL:*

> *You have been weighed in the balances,*
> *and found wanting;*
> PERES:
> *Your kingdom has been divided,*
> *and given to the Medes and Persians.*
> Daniel 5:21-28

Following this ominous warning by Daniel, Belshazzar died *that very night*. The Babylonian kingdom soon fell to the Medo-Persian Empire, and Darius the Mede became ruler in Belshazzar's place.

The Egyptians Received the Same Memo
Another notable example would be Pharaoh Rameses of Egypt and his dealings with Moses and the liberation of the Jewish people from slavery. Rameses was God's appointed leader who played a significant role in the Exodus drama.

> *And indeed, for this cause*
> *have I appointed thee,*
> *to show my power in thee,*
> *and to declare my name*
> *throughout all the world.*
> Exodus 9:16

Paul referred to this verse again in Romans:

> *For the Scripture saith unto Pharaoh,*
> *For this same purpose*
> *have I stirred thee up,*
> *that I might show my power in thee,*
> *and that my Name might be declared*
> *throughout all the earth.*
> Romans 9:17

Note carefully the words: "I raised (or stirred) you up for this very purpose…" God declared it was HE who raised up Rameses and used him as a key player in Exodus. The Israelites suffered terribly under Rameses. Many died excruciating deaths under the cruel lash of Egyptian whips. Children and the elderly perished. We are told unequivocally God raised Rameses up "for this very purpose." Even further, there are clear scriptural references that reveal that at the same time God was directing Moses to demand the liberation of the people, God was not allowing Rameses to let them go even when he wanted to do so. Carefully consider the following references from the books of Exodus and Joshua:

And the Lord said unto Moses,
When thou art entered
and come into Egypt again,
see that thou do all the wonders before Pharaoh,
which I have put in thine hand:
but I will harden his heart,
and he shall not let the people go.
Exodus 4:21 (Emphasis added)
Again the Lord said unto Moses,
Go to Pharaoh,
for I have hardened his heart,
and the heart of his servants,
that I might work these my miracles
in the midst of his realm,
Exodus 10:1 (Emphasis added)
But the Lord hardened Pharaoh's heart,
and he did not let the children of Israel go.
Exodus 10:20 (Emphasis added)
So Moses and Aaron
did all these wonders before Pharaoh:
but the Lord hardened Pharaoh's heart,
and he suffered not the children of Israel
to go out of his land.
Exodus 11:10 (Emphasis added)
And he made ready his chariots,
and took his people with him,
and took six hundred chosen chariots,
and all the chariots of Egypt,
and captains over every one of them.
(For the Lord had hardened
the heart of Pharaoh king of Egypt,
and he followed after the children of Israel:
but the children of Israel went out

> *with an high hand.)*
> Exodus 14:6-8 (Emphasis added)

To be sure, many struggle mightily with the entire concept of God deliberately "hardening" the heart of someone (Pharaoh) so that they will inflict pain and harm upon God's people. And then, hold the one "hardened" accountable for their actions. (E.G. the judgment upon Egypt and the destruction of Pharaoh's entire army in the Red Sea.) I can't help you very much here. Human intellect cannot fathom the mind and purposes of God. All we can know is what is revealed by scripture. However we may "feel" about it, God's ways are infinitely higher than ours.

The Divine Memo Also Came to the Canaanites

This truth is further demonstrated in the book of Joshua, related to the Israelite conquest of Canaan.

> *For it came of the Lord,*
> ***to harden their hearts***
> *that they should come against Israel in battle,*
> *to the intent that they (the Israelites)*
> *should destroy them utterly,*
> *and show them no mercy,*
> *but that they should bring them to naught,*
> *as the Lord had commanded Moses.*
> Joshua 11:20 (Emphasis added)

Lest anyone attempt to say that this "hardening" activity by God was exclusively an "Old Testament" way that God dealt with the world before the coming of the Messiah, I offer the following verses from the New Testament.

> *And though He had done*
> *so many miracles before them,*
> *yet believed they not on Him,*
> *that the saying of Isaiah the Prophet might be fulfilled,*
> *that he said, Lord, who believed our report?*
> *and to whom is the arm of the Lord revealed?*
> ***Therefore could they not believe,***
> *because that Isaiah saith again,*
> ***He hath blinded their eyes,***

> *and hardened their heart,*
> *that they should not see with their eyes,*
> *nor understand with their heart,*
> *and should be converted,*
> *and I should heal them.*
> John 12:40 9 (Emphasis added)
> *Therefore He hath mercy*
> *on whom He will,*
> *and **whom He will He hardeneth**.*
> Romans 9:18 (Emphasis added)

Romans chapter 9 is quite possibly the most controversial chapter in the entire Bible. I suspect this is because what Romans 9 teaches *directly contradicts* fallen human nature, and our inclination to be independent, self-determining, and prideful. Paul sets forth in Romans 9 the inconvenient truth that it is God, *not you—not me*—who possesses ultimate control. The humanistic person *hates* the very idea of external control. In fact, Romans 9 declares God's total control is unlimited, and His sovereignty is such that He can and does show mercy to some people *while hardening the hearts of others*. It also declares that He is perfectly just in doing so with no obligation to explain Himself to anyone.

The way people react to Romans 9 can often reveals the *true state* of their heart and submission to Christ. Humanly speaking, people require God to "be fair" and "non-discriminatory" according to *their* standards, understandings, and approval. It pushes some people's buttons when they are told that God isn't all that terribly interested in their opinions as to how He runs His universe. And while I'm on the subject of "fairness," let me add the following. The greatest act of "unfairness" in all of time and eternity occurred on a cross of torturous execution at Golgotha around 33 A.D. The innocent, sinless, righteous, and holy Son of God, Jesus Christ, took upon Himself the entire brunt of just punishment for His people's sin, rebellion, and depravity and fully satisfied the demands for justice and wrath. In fact, it is unfair in the *extreme* that *anyone* finds mercy and salvation, and that should make us profoundly thankful upon whom this mercy has come.

To return to my original question: "Does God Use Tyrants...?" I would say without hesitation... Yes, *He certainly does.*

> *As many as I love,*
> *I rebuke and chasten:*

> *be zealous therefore and amend.*
> Revelation 3:18

To Whom Much is Given, Much is Required

Is America a "holy" nation? I can almost hear the snickers, but before anyone dismisses the idea out of hand, please allow me to unpack this. First of all, most people tend to assume that "holy" just means "a state of perfection, purity, or sinlessness." However, I would like to point out that according to the Merriam-Webster Dictionary, "holy" can also be defined as "Set apart to the service or worship of God; hallowed, sacred, reserved from profane or common use... devoted entirely to the deity or the work of the deity... having a divine quality."

It would be irrational to declare that the United States is a "holy" nation under a narrow definition of "perfection or sinlessness." Our history proves this point amply. Individually and as a nation, we stand guilty of falling far, far short of anything *nearing* perfection. Our national and personal sins, moral and political corruption, greed, pride, and arrogance clearly disqualify us all from the "perfect" moniker. Our many blessings are purely the result of God's grace, and NOT because we *earned* them. This statement may anger and annoy some people, who prefer to think of America and our people as being "good." However, consider Romans 3:10-12 (Emphasis added):

> *As it is written,*
> *There is **none righteous**,*
> *no not one.*
> *There is **none that understandeth**:*
> *there is **none that seeketh God**.*
> *They have all gone out of the way:*
> *they have been made altogether unprofitable:*
> *there is **none that doeth good**,*
> ***no not one.***

Note the repetition of the word "none" in the passage. There is no exception but Jesus of course, who was born without Adam's fallen nature, and, therefore, was without sin.

To recap:

— **NONE righteous**
— **NONE who understand**

— NONE seeking God
— NONE doing good
"...no, not ONE."

There are no unregenerate "good people" according to God's word. *No exceptions.* Whatever "good" has ever been accomplished in this world has been granted by God's grace and mercy and He alone deserves the praise and glory for it. Certainly, unregenerate people are capable of showing kindness, compassion, mercy, and perform "good" works (at least in the eyes of other men). No one can deny this. And it is true God has *often* used fallen humans at times to accomplish His purposes. However, fallen humanity will reliably seek to twist truth and circumstances for personal glory or advantage. Again, this statement may annoy some people, for human pride is rather touchy on this subject. In fact, this truth is one of the primary reasons unregenerate people hate God and reject Jesus and the Bible. Jesus is where all human arrogance and pride go to die.

However, this does not negate in the slightest the historical reality of America being "set apart" or "devoted entirely to the deity or the work of God." In fact, if this is true then we are operating under an even stricter standard of judgment.

Did the Founders Make a Covenant with God?

It is ironic that modern Israelis refer to America as "Artzot haBrit," [ארצות הברית] translated: "the lands of the covenant." From the historical record of America's founding, I'm convinced America was "set apart, devoted, or reserved from everyday use." When President Washington and Congress dedicated our nation to God by solemn oath and affirmation, we became a holy nation in covenant with God, and set apart for God's purposes, in *spite* of ourselves. This will be difficult for some people to accept, given the incessant secular indoctrination in our schools and universities for the past two hundred years. Again, I must reiterate I'm not defining holiness as sinless perfection, nor am I saying that America is a "perfect" nation. It most certainly is not.

America is holy because our Founding Fathers (imperfect as *they* were) made a deeply reverential solemn oath of dedication. We can infer from the Founder's writings that in all likelihood, they gave a promise of obedience to God's Holy Word in that prayer service at Saint Paul's Chapel following President Washington's inauguration on April 30, 1789.

God's invisible guiding hand was manifestly active in the formation of our Republic, as well as in the ongoing deliberations that followed. It is my conviction that God took those early oaths seriously and established our nation for His greater purposes.

So what now? Are we divinely warned of impending judgment? Is our nation now receiving similar messages and warnings as King Belshazzar did? Can we now perceive some "writing on the wall" directed to our times? Is there a parallel application to our republic, dedicated to God from its birth? Are we not uniquely blessed as no other nation in history has been, save that of Israel? Is America holy, set apart, and dedicated to God?

If this is so, then our nation and people are treading on *extremely thin ice*. We as a people have fallen into corruption and debauchery undreamt-of by our Founding Fathers. We collectively stand guilty of profaning and setting to "common" uses, our higher calling, either by active participation or passive acquiescence. Think carefully upon this, for the evidence is compelling. The knowledge of this ought to drive every Biblical Christian to our knees in fervent prayer for God's mercy upon our people.

I consider it crass and hateful that God's people should ever entertain the hope—as the Prophet Jonah did toward the evil Ninevites—that God's wrath and judgment would fall upon the United States. We certainly ALL deserve God's condemnation, but we who have received mercy ought to pray that everyone *else* might *also* be shown the same undeserved grace and kindness. We're assured from Scripture that not all will be redeemed, but we should labor and pray and love people as if everyone *might* be.

Was 9/11 an Act of God's Judgment?

By the early spring of 2010, despite my inner resistance, an undeniable message of divine judgment upon America seemed to be breaking through my previous assumptions. There appear to be striking parallels between the historical behavior of the ancient chosen people of Israel and that of modern-day America. Mockers usually try to conjure up an image of a disheveled, crazed-looking whacko who is in desperate need of a bath walking the streets with a big sandwich board sign declaring "The End is Near" to discredit anyone who believes God judges people and nations. *Nothing new there.* However, the growing evidence of God's chastisement upon America now seems too compelling to ignore.

For example, Israel, like America, enjoyed the blessings of God until moral and political corruption gutted the righteous foundations upon which their nation was built. Israel's eventual moral corruption and rejection of their mandate––their covenant foundations––resulted in God's removal of blessing and divine protection from their enemies, just as their prophets foretold.

I now believe the attacks of September 11, 2001, carried an unmistakable prophetic significance. Far beyond mere acts of human terrorism perpetrated by a group of America-hating Islamic Jihadists—and enabled perhaps by *equally* evil America-hating corporate elitists—I believe this was one of our "handwriting on the wall" moments. We'd better decipher the message quickly because the clock is ticking.

No matter *how* you might think these attacks were planned and carried out, there is a larger game afoot. Some people suspect the attacks were planned and carried out by a "shadow government." This is a possibility, for governments throughout history were often compromised by clandestine agents who sought to maneuver within the "halls of power" for nefarious purposes. Nothing new there. In the end, *it doesn't make any difference.* These attacks seemed to convey a message that our national divine blessings are not without limits or responsibility.

Obviously, my research for this book kept bringing me back to the theological issue of God's sovereignty in His dealings with nations and peoples throughout history. My studies also forced me to reexamine some of my former theological and historical presuppositions. Sometimes I feel God has dragged me—kicking and screaming at times—into a depth of surrender to His total Lordship *far* outside my previous comfort zones. I often hear people say that we *ought* to "make Jesus the Lord of our lives." I have a memo for those who say this. We cannot "make" Jesus Lord. His Lordship is *already a fact* whether we realize it or not. If He is our Lord and Saviour, it is because *He* made it so, and transformed our hearts and wills to joyfully surrender to Him. Bottom line: We don't "allow" God to be God. He *is* the great "I AM," *not* the great "I wannabe if you'll only allow me according to *your* will."

> *For it is God which worketh in you,*
> *both the will*
> *and the deed,*
> *even of his good pleasure.*
> Philippians 2:13

Without the grace of God, it is impossible for us to release our desperate grip on the imaginary steering wheel of control and simply trust God. If what I think will happen in the near-future happens, we're *all* going to have to learn to rely on God more than *ever* before.

Our Ultimate Source of Courage

Sometimes people ask me if I've ever been afraid in some of the dangerous situations I've been in over the years in various places of the world. Truth be told, I've been tempted to be fearful now and then, but I've always received comfort from the sure knowledge that God already knows the full number of my days, and is guiding my steps according to a much larger master plan. Until my time to die comes, I believe I'm bullet-proof. When my time does come, nothing I could ever do will prevent it.

There is a story told of the famous Confederate Civil War General, Thomas "Stonewall" Jackson, that illustrates this principle well. General Jackson was a devout Reformed Christian, who walked through this life with grace and serenity. He was nicknamed "Stonewall" by his men because he seemed entirely serene and calm in the chaos of mortal combat, even as bullets and bombs came so near him. According to the story, Captain John D. Imboden once asked the General how it was that he could remain so calm in the thick of battle, and General Jackson's response is illuminating:

> *Captain, my religious belief teaches me to feel as safe in battle as in bed. God has fixed the time for my death. I do not concern myself about that, but to be always ready, no matter when it may overtake me. Captain, that is the way all men should live, and then all would be equally brave.* [2]

Let me remind you *again* that God chastises those whom He loves!

> *For whom the Lord loveth,*
> *he chasteneth:*
> *and he scourgeth*
> *every son that he receiveth.*
> Hebrews 12:6

In the interest of accuracy and sound interpretation, or exegesis, this verse is speaking on an individual basis and directed to "the one He loves" and "every son He accepts." However, we must remember God's chastisements and judgments have often applied to nations as well as individuals. My point here is that divine punishments do not originate from God's hatred, or a sadistic desire to destroy people. This assumption is an oft-used false accusation against God, and just another excuse employed by fallen men to reject and hate Him. As we will see, God may yet provide a way of escape, and the grace to follow it, according to His glorious plans. We should take great comfort and encouragement in this thought. President Jefferson's sober warning in the opening of this chapter should motivate us rather than foster fear.

Notes

1. https://en.wikiquote.org/wiki/John_Stuart_Mill
2. Stonewall Jackson as Military Commander (2000) by John Selby, p. 25

21

Dreams From My Founders

*Evil is powerless
when the good are unafraid.*
Ronald Reagan, 1981

~~~~~

In the days following 9/11, a tourist yacht named Spirit was moored at the North Cove Marina near Battery Park just west of the World Finance Buildings. Quickly reconfigured as a rest station for workers at the pile, the Spirit offered cots on the upper decks where we could get a bit of rest, refreshment, and even a back massage. The galley below decks served hot meals continuously. It was a peaceful haven to relax and decompress.

Several times late in the evening, I'd walk over to the Spirit for a hot meal and to rest for a little while. On this floating island of relative tranquility, I met quite a few fellow responders from all over the country. We would sit around the dining table in the galley drinking coffee and trading stories about where we came from, our hometowns and departments we served with. We shared about how we came to be there at this scene, passed around family pictures, told some jokes, and sharing some laughs. Our unspoken mutual grief over the loss of so many fellow firefighters and police officers bonded us as we laughed and cried together. It was therapeutic for us all on board this peaceful haven in the midst of hell.

One particularly clear night, I sat alone in the darkness of the upper deck gazing out over the shimmering waters of the Hudson River. Moored in the westernmost part of the marina, Spirit offered an excellent view of the relative peace and tranquility out on the water. Off in the distance, I could clearly make out Liberty Island and the beautiful illuminated Statue of Liberty.

The soft light of her torch––held perpetually high––could be seen faintly glowing across the harbor through the late-summer haze. Seeing proud Lady Liberty out there standing tall, a silent witness to our fresh national wound, made me misty-eyed. Seemingly in defiance of all the horror and destruction just across the Hudson, she still held her torch of freedom high for the entire world to see.

I thought about the newly arriving immigrants who came to America in earlier years. Hundreds of thousands of sea-weary immigrants rejoiced at the sight of Lady Liberty's welcoming torch as they sailed into the harbor of their new nation. Steaming toward Ellis Island's Customs and Immigration office, they must have gazed up in wonder at her beacon of liberty, and many of these new Americans wept tears of joy. Hopeful men, women, and children—fleeing Old Europe's oppressive, authoritarian governments and the long history of slaughter and repression of fundamental freedoms—yearned for America's promise of liberty and opportunity.

I've often contemplated the words engraved on the bronze plaque displayed just inside the statue since 1903. Composed by Emma Lazarus in 1883, the poem is titled "The New Colossus."

> *Not like the brazen giant of Greek fame,*
> *with conquering limbs*
> *astride from land to land;*
> *Here at our sea-washed sunset gates*
> *shall stand a mighty woman with a torch,*
> *whose flame is the imprisoned lightning,*
> *and her name; Mother of Exiles.*
> *From her beacon-hand glows,*
> *world-wide welcome;*
> *her mild eyes command the air-bridged harbor*
> *that twin cities frame.*
> *"Keep, ancient lands, your storied pomp!"*
> *cries she with silent lips.*
> *"Give me your tired, your poor,*
> *your huddled masses, yearning to breathe free,*
> *the wretched refuse of your teeming shore.*
> *Send these, the homeless, tempest-tossed to me.*
> *I lift my lamp beside the golden door!"*

Embracing the Dream

The famous filmmaker, Frank Capra, who immigrated to America from Bisacquino, Sicily with his parents and six siblings, arrived aboard the ship Germania at Ellis Island in New York on May 10, 1903. Only six years old,

Capra remembered how his father, Turiddu, brought him up on deck and showed him the Statue of Liberty as the ship steamed into New York harbor. "Cicco look!" his illiterate peasant father said with tearful excitement. "Look at that! That's the greatest light since the star of Bethlehem! That's the light of freedom! Remember that. Freedom!" (Ref: Remarks by Dr. John Marini, professor of political science at the University of Nevada, as noted in Imprimis, a publication of Hillsdale College.)

Capra never forgot what his father said that day, and fully immersed himself in his new country's language and culture, eventually becoming one of America's greatest filmmakers. His love of America and the greatness of our Constitutional Republic were a favorite theme of most of his films. He epitomized his affection for the United States in his immortal movie; *Mr. Smith Goes to Washington*, and the classic favorite, *It's a Wonderful Life*, both featuring the iconic actor, Jimmy Stewart. A major theme of these films—and the thing I love about both of them—is that an average, ordinary person *can* and *ought* to make a powerful, positive impact on the world.

Like Capra and his family, most immigrants came here to be *Americans*—to reside and assimilate into what people called "The New World." They came to embrace freedom's promise, principles, and opportunities. Many came seeking freedom to believe in and worship God (or *not* believe) according to the dictates of their consciences, far from the reach of bloody and oppressive religious and political tyranny. They rejoiced to be *able* to speak their minds freely in American English, without the constant fear that someone might overhear and report them to the authorities. They wanted to live in peace without the dread someone might break down their door in the middle of the night and drag them out to murder or imprison them. They celebrated their Constitutional rights to associate with whom they pleased, choose their representatives in free and honest elections and even challenge and overthrow corrupt and despotic leaders through the ballot box without fear of retaliation. In short, they were drawn onward by the beckoning warmth of freedoms' fire and emboldened by the truth that their rights were God-given and not the capricious tolerations of a king or dictator. Long-held dreams could now blossom into fruitful vines from which the nectar of prosperity, happiness, and success might spill over into the lives of their children and their children's children.

Most of them came at a high personal cost, arriving on American shores with little more than a few meager coins in their pockets. Many left behind businesses, friends, families, and their native language and culture. To be sure, they preserved a special love and appreciation for the land of their nativity, but they understood—for the most part—that beyond their skin color, ethnicity, or land of origin, they were first and foremost *Americans*. Many of them held deep faith as Christians that God was leading them onward toward a greater destiny.

What fueled their patriotic zeal? I suspect that most of these people knew WELL what they were fleeing FROM. Their appreciation and love of freedom was forged in the hellish furnaces of the Dark Ages when the Papal Inquisition brutally tortured and murdered well over 50 million people across Old Europe during more than 605 years of terror. They remembered all too well the long history of rape, mutilation, confiscation of property, and burnings inflicted without mercy upon people of every age and sex. They retained memories of the helplessness they and their ancestors endured under despotic popes, kings, and princes who arbitrarily ruled their subjects without conscience or restraint.

Sadly in modern times, America's people have almost *entirely* forgotten the *value* of freedom or the uniqueness of our Constitutional Republic. They've never suffered under the cruel boot of oppression. I have often encountered new immigrants from places like Vietnam, Cambodia, certain Middle Eastern countries, Central and South America, and Africa who fled tyranny to live free in America. They often tell me how horrified they are when they witness people burning the American flag or disrespecting the Constitution.

And what of those who riot and rage against "American Imperialism" and incessantly tear down our country, charging America with slavery, racism, and oppression? No one can deny that injustices have been committed in America's history. However, as I've tried to say elsewhere, our *system* of Constitutional government has a built-in capacity written into the nation's genetic code to right wrongs, heal wounds, and yet remain free. It is not a perfect system, but I believe it is as close to perfection as fallen humans will experience in this present world. We must count our blessings. No living black American has experienced the sting of the cruel whip of government-sanctioned slavery upon their back. The heartbreaking stories of the dehumanizing and humiliating chains of slavery should *never* be forgotten, but they are now only dim memories passed down from grandparents. The sacrifices of our great-great-grandparents who fought a bloody civil war to abolish slavery should remind us all of how precious liberty and freedom are, and the diabolical results that will occur if those freedoms should ever perish.

Too many people take for granted that the evils of the past could never occur again in our "modern" times. Those who warn that such dark times could *indeed* happen again usually find themselves regarded as "kooks and conspiracy theorists." However, human nature has not changed one iota over the past few thousand years. As President Ronald Reagan once said in an address to the annual meeting of the Phoenix Chamber of Commerce on March 30, 1961:

> *...freedom is always just one generation away from extinction. We don't pass it to our children in the bloodstream; we have to fight for it and protect it, and then hand it to them so that they shall do the same, or we're going to find ourselves spending our sunset years telling our children and our children's children about a time in America, back in the day, when men and women were free.* [1]

Reagan used a variant of these original words in another speech given six years later. I think it is even more on-point.

> *Freedom is a fragile thing and is never more than one generation away from extinction. It is not ours by inheritance; it must be fought for and defended constantly by each generation, for it comes only once to a people. Those who have known freedom and then lost it have never known it again.* (Emphasis added) [2]

George Washington had been president of the United States for less than a year when he gave his first annual speech to Congress on January 8, 1790. Seemingly, overwhelming challenges were facing our infant republic, and despite the strong temptation to despair, Washington remained firm in his belief in God's overriding hand of guidance. In his address, he included the following salient remark:

> *...the blessings which a gracious Providence has placed within our reach...*

I find Washington's reference to "the blessings" which God's "gracious Providence has placed within our reach" interesting. It implies that the grace of God already gives everything needed for the benefit of our nation. I would contend that the provision Washington referred to is God's word, for within its pages contain all the wisdom and guidance needed for our national blessing. I would further say this provision is indeed "just within our reach" because most Americans have multiple copies of God's word easily within arms-reach in most our, or readily available on the internet. It is no coincidence that within many oppressed nations of the world, the Bible is banned by law.

Firm Reliance Upon Government, or God?
It appears the further our people move away from a "firm reliance upon Divine Providence"—repeatedly enshrined in our founding documents—the more they become dependent upon and are controlled by the government. History

repeatedly demonstrates that human government—untethered to the higher wisdom and counsel of God's word—is not only incredibly inefficient but will inevitably become extremely dangerous.

Thomas Jefferson famously said:

> *The course of history shows that as a government grows, liberty decreases.*

President Reagan echoed Jefferson's words in his farewell speech on Jun 6, 2004:

> *There's a clear cause and effect here that is as neat and predictable as a law of physics: As government expands, liberty contracts.*

I love the United States of America as originally conceived by our Founding Fathers and consider myself a patriot. That's not to say I don't see the nation's flaws nor, by any stretch of the imagination, believe she is perfect. In all of history, no earthly nation or kingdom governed by humans could ever make such a claim. Even the fabled kingdom of Camelot was not without its evil Prince Maleagant or the intrigues and betrayals of Lancelot and Guinevere.

America is a unique and *exceptional* nation. Within her heart and soul lays a spark of divinely inspired genius. Founded as a Republic, she bears a Constitution and Bill of Rights superior to any other form of government yet conceived in the entire world's history. May Almighty God grant America compassion, moving upon the hearts of our people to seek and return to Him.

Utopian Fantasies?

Those who seek an earthly utopia, regretfully, will not find it anywhere. In fact, the very *word* "Utopia" was coined in 1516 by Sir Thomas Moore in his book written under the same title. A compound of the Greek syllable ou-, meaning "no," and topos, meaning "place," the word utopia *literally* means "nowhere" or "no place." *Utopia* was, in fact, a sardonic expression of Moore's contempt for the very *idea* of human-engineered perfectionism. Moore recognized no such perfect society exists anywhere in this world, nor shall it *ever* unless and until God Himself makes it so.

The laws and political institutions of the United States, as originally conceived by our Founding Fathers, remain well worth defending. As it stands today, America has become a mere shadow of her former self. However, the mechanisms of our Constitutional government will work if we will but apply and allow them, for woven into the fabric of our founding documents is a self-healing thread of genius.

If enough of us awaken in time and re-embrace all that is good and right in our Founder's wise leadership, and return to a humble regard for God's word, our present crisis may resolve. As President Washington exhorted, "the propitious smiles of Heaven can never be expected on a nation that disregards the eternal rules of order and right." I believe it is possible that America could rise once more like that ancient, mythic Phoenix, and shine as a bright beacon of liberty for the entire world.

Duty requires that we not stand idly by in frustration, merely complaining. Our government employees' current unconstitutional overreach in the name of "safety and security" is alarming. At present, those of us who are seeking to return our nation to its Constitutional roots are now called "radicals" by *real* radicals—Progressive/Socialists—operating right in the midst of our government. We are in good company, however, for many Americans in the late 1700s thought our nation's Founding Fathers were radicals as well.

We would do well to follow our Founder's example, and learn from the wisdom of the ancients, such as the Athenian politician, Solon, (638-558 BC). considered by Plutarch one of Greek antiquities' ten wisest men, *Solon declared it a crime for any citizen to shrink from controversy.*

We who are deeply concerned with the direction the country is moving have a sacred duty give voice to those concerns––controversial or not. I, like many, now greatly fear that the freedom and prosperity our republic has enjoyed for these nearly 225 years now stands in mortal danger.

As a people, we're deeply divided regarding how to address our national problems. Unethical politicians, working in an unholy partnership with certain multinational corporate, media, and banking interests, exploit our lack of unity and consensus. If they can keep us divided and distracted by other "shiny things" such as racial, ethnic, or religious differences, we will be easily conquered.

The questions are these: What is the pathway back? How do we recapture the ethical, moral, and spiritual strengths that once made us renowned as a kind and generous people? How can balance be found between legitimate security obligations *and* freedom's open heart? What will it take for our nation to return to fiscal discipline and political restraint, and thereby restore our nation as a land of opportunity?

Some may resist the very thought of "going back." We've been conditioned by the Progressive-Leftists in our schools and news media to think that things in our society were *much* worse in the past, but that isn't entirely accurate. We've *always* had our problems, but individual liberty, lower taxes, and economic opportunity weren't among them. If we're serious about recapturing the essence of our national optimism and rebuilding our spiritual strength, then we need to go "*back* to the future" instead of stumbling carelessly forward into a dark night of despotic socialist "progressivism."

Is it possible to rediscover the pathway back to national and societal greatness—along with moral and fiscal sanity? Again, our answers will be found in both the Holy Scriptures and the Founding Documents so wisely crafted by our national Fathers under that inspiration. For the most part, the mechanisms of our constitutional system functioned as designed to help the country "right" itself (no pun intended). We've seen many of our national sins corrected, and if we continue in the wisdom of the Founders and the Constitution, even more can be done.

However, no other nation on earth throughout all of human history achieved such progress, righted more wrongs, or provided a better environment for personal freedom and economic opportunity than the United States. These things were accomplished through people living free, not by central planning elites.

Our Founding Fathers shared one essential commonality that we would be wise to embrace as well. They were *extremely wary* of government. They knew all too well the perils of government tyranny, and they maintained a deep distrust of government and its potential abuses of power.

A quote some have attributed to George Washington declares:

> *Government is not reason; it is not eloquent—it is force. Like fire, it is a dangerous servant and a fearful master. Never for a moment should it be left to irresponsible action.*

This is why the Framers established the republic upon the principle of "checks and balances." Within the very framework of our three-branched system are built-in "circuit breakers" that make it nearly impossible for one party or individual ever to dominate and rule over the people. As originally established, our form of government is unique in human history in that "We the People" rule over the state!

Our government is to be the *servant* of the people–never our *master*. It is accountable to and under the authority of the people as set forth by the Constitution and the Bill of Rights. Sadly, this entire concept is now nearly forgotten by our people, owing in no small part to a socialist-oriented public education system.

Well, Doctor, What Have We Got?

Due to a near-constant barrage of disinformation, most Americans erroneously believe the United States is a democracy. However, facts are stubborn things, and it is a fact that America *is not*, and *never was meant to be* a democracy by the Founders. Rather, our form of government was deliberately and painstakingly crafted as a *Constitutional Republic*. Our Founders wisely recognized the *vast* difference between a republic and a democracy. Sadly, this is not the case in our times.

One of my favorite quotes is found in the 1960 film, *The Alamo*. John Wayne, who produced and directed this epic film, shared one of the best lines that summarize the gist of what a Republic means to the common man in his character as Davy Crockett.

> *Republic. I like the sound of the word.*
>
> *It means people can live free, talk free, go or come, buy or sell, be drunk or sober, however they choose. Some words give you a feeling. Republic is one of those words that makes me tight in the throat. The same tightness a man gets when his baby takes his first step, or his first baby shaves, and makes his first sound like a man. Some words can give you a feeling that makes your heart warm. Republic is one of those words.*

After Congress ratified the new Constitution at Independence Hall in Philadelphia in 1787, large crowds eagerly stood outside desiring to see what their delegates had accomplished. James McHenry, a signatory to the U.S. Constitution, documented in his personal diary an exchange between Dr. Benjamin Franklin and a Mrs. Powell of Philadelphia. This account was later reproduced in the 1906 edition of the American Historical Review. McHenry recorded that as Dr. Franklin departed Independence Hall, Mrs. Powell approached him and asked a question:

> *"Well, Doctor, what have we got, a republic or a monarchy?"*
>
> *Without hesitation, Franklin replied, "A republic, if you can keep it."*

The question Mrs. Powell asked Dr. Franklin yet challenges us today. Can we keep our republic? More importantly, are we *willing* to keep it? Are there yet enough brave patriots in our time who possess that same faith in God, temper of will, fortitude, and courage to pledge—as did our Founding Fathers in their day— "Our lives, our fortunes, and our sacred honor" in order that we too might "keep" our republic? I would submit that unless our people are educated quickly enough to realize the difference between a democracy (or, as some call it, "mob-oc-racy") and a republic we cannot guarantee our long-term

268 Destroying the Shadow Agenda

freedoms. Even more importantly, we need to grasp an underlying principle that makes liberty something worth living and *dying* for.

In fact, almost to a man, the Founders considered pure democracy the very *worst* possible form of government. Here are just a few quotes from some of them to prove this.

–Thomas Jefferson said:

> *A democracy is nothing more than mob rule, where fifty-one percent of the people may take away the rights of the other forty-nine.*

–John Adams agreed:

> *Remember, democracy never lasts long. It soon wastes, exhausts, and murders itself. There never was a democracy yet that did not commit suicide.*

–Dr. Benjamin Rush, MD, stated:

> *A simple democracy … is one of the greatest of evils.*

–Noah Webster wrote:

> *In a democracy, there are commonly tumults and disorders. …Therefore, a pure democracy is generally a very bad government. It is often the most tyrannical government on earth.*

–John Witherspoon wrote:

> *Pure democracy cannot subsist long nor be carried far into the departments of state; it is very subject to caprice and the madness of popular rage.*

–James Madison wrote in Federalist #10

> *Democracy is the most vile form of government … democracies have ever been spectacles of turbulence and contention: have ever been found incompatible with personal security or the rights of property: and have in general been as short in their lives as they have been violent in their deaths.*

Madison further expands his reasoning that a Constitutional Republic is far superior to a democracy in Federalist #15:

In a single republic, all the power surrendered by the people is submitted to the administration of a single government; and the usurpations are guarded against by a division of the government into distinct and separate departments. In the compound republic of America, the power surrendered by the people is first divided between two distinct governments, and then the portion allotted to each subdivided among distinct and separate departments. Hence a double security arises to the rights of the people. The different governments will control each other, at the same time that each will be controlled by itself. (Emphasis added)

Another quote—widely attributed to Benjamin Franklin—was more likely coined by the modern personality, Gary Strand, in a Usenet group sci posting on April 23, 1990. No matter *who* said it, the words sum up the danger of pure democracies:

Democracy is not freedom. Democracy is two wolves and a lamb voting on what to eat for lunch. Freedom comes from the recognition of certain rights which may not be taken, not even by a 99% vote.

Pay careful attention to the phrase; "…Recognition of certain rights which may not be taken, not even by a 99% vote."

Modern Americans have no idea what it was like to live under the tyranny of dictatorial kings throughout the Middle Ages. We cannot easily understand the fear and anguish our ancestors endured. Those were times when a King or his favored agents could break into homes at will, sexually assault wives and daughters, or kidnap and rape brides on their wedding night. Their husbands and fathers could do nothing about it because no one was allowed to possess weapons except the King's men.

The grinding poverty and servitude of the masses under the cruel whims of the elite class was a living nightmare, and no document, law, or counter-force could stop it. It would be good for all mature school students to be required to watch films like Rob Roy or Braveheart and do history lessons on the reality of life under the cruel boot of capricious royalty.

A great cultural and political battle is now raging in our times between two opposing and irreconcilable worldviews. On the one side are those who embrace the idea of an all-powerful centralized government that rules *over* the people. Standing in resistance are those of us who embrace the principles enshrined in our Constitution and Bill of Rights. A Constitutional Republican government—established by and for the people—is precisely what the Framers had in mind. Eventually, one ideology will emerge the victor. Between these clashing worldviews, there can be no lasting compromise.

In his famous "Gettysburg Address," Abraham Lincoln eloquently stated:

> *It is rather for us to be here dedicated to the great task remaining before us—that from these honored dead we take increased devotion to that cause for which they gave the last full measure of devotion—that we here highly resolve that these dead shall not have died in vain—that this nation, under God, shall have a new birth of freedom—and that government of the people, by the people, for the people, shall not perish from the earth.*

It is my belief that "We the People" *can and will* eventually emerge victorious in this epic struggle. There is hope for a brighter future yet burning in the hearts of millions of Americans. Be sure of this: We who love the Constitution and Bill of Rights ARE presently the majority. If we awaken our fellow Americans to the wonder and beauty of our Founder's wisdom, our lives, liberties, and honor *will* be preserved. By God's grace, we must conduct our lives in peace and optimism––infused with hope and enduring for the blessings of successive generations.

If we should fail, however, as Winston Churchill declared in his epic "Battle of Great Britain" speech:

> *…then the whole world, including the United States, including all that we have known and cared for, will sink into the abyss of a new dark age made more sinister, and perhaps more protracted, by the lights of perverted science.* **Let us therefore brace ourselves to our duties.**

Freedom's Struggle Continues

Although the United States won the War of Independence and signed the Treaty of Paris with Great Britain in September 1783, she remained for many years a nation deeply divided politically. Many Americans remained loyal to the British Monarchy. In fact, over 100,000 American Loyalists to the British Crown fled to Canada. Many of them felt that the Patriots were nothing more than rebellious traitors to the Crown. In most respects, those wounds eventually healed, with the passage of time.

One example of this early turmoil is notable. A few years after the seat of the Federal Government moved from New York City to Philadelphia, the newly established Republic was nearly overthrown by a large mob seeking to abolish the central government.

In a letter written by John Adams to Thomas Jefferson on June 30, 1813, Adams recollected that during the summer of 1793:

> ...*ten thousand people in the streets of Philadelphia ... threatened to drag Washington out of his house, and effect a Revolution in Government.*

Adams wrote only an outbreak of yellow fever dispersed the mob and saved the national government.

The internal divisions within the new republic were not the only challenges they faced. There were external forces yet to be dealt with. Less than 20 years after the 1793 insurrection in Philadelphia, the British *once again* invaded America's shores in 1812, and this renewed war threatened our national destruction. On August 24, 1814, the British army burned the White House and the Capitol building, along with most of the other government buildings and numerous homes throughout Washington, D.C. One member of the British forces, George Gleig, was an eyewitness to these events and recorded the scene:

> ...*the blazing of houses, ships, and stores, the report of exploding magazines, and the crash of falling roofs informed them, (the British forces) as they proceeded, of what was going forward. You can conceive nothing finer than the sight which met them as they drew near to the town. The sky was brilliantly illuminated by the different conflagrations, and a dark red light was thrown upon the road, sufficient to permit each man to view distinctly his comrade's face ...Of the Senate house, the President's palace, the barracks, the dockyard, etc., nothing could be seen except heaps of smoking ruins.* [3]

This assault on our nation's capital city reduced it to scorched rubble.

The British Attack on Ft. McHenry

On September 13, just one month after the burning of Washington, D.C., British naval gunships attacked Fort McHenry, bombarding the fort throughout the night. Shortly before the attack began, Francis Scott Key—as part of a small delegation of American attorneys seeking to arrange a prisoner release—boarded a British frigate under a flag of truce. During the negotiations, the British navy suddenly opened fire on Fort McHenry with all their cannons blasting from their warships anchored in the harbor.

A story is told that the British aimed the brunt of their cannon fire at the large flagpole mounted on the fort displaying the stars and stripes of the flag of the United States. They thought that by knocking down this flag, the Americans could be demoralized into surrendering the fort. All through the night, hundreds of shells exploded over the fort and around the flagpole. As the story goes, several times the United States flag appeared to be falling over in the light of exploding shells as the British sailors cheered. Then, to their utter astonishment, the British commanders were enraged to witness through their spyglasses the flag rising again.

As the gloom and darkness of the night began to fade into a new dawn, Francis Scott Key beheld—through the smoke and mist of early dawn—the scorched and shrapnel-torn American flag yet flying proudly over the fort. So inspired was Francis Key at the sight of that flag, he immediately scribbled on a scrap of paper the now-famous poem: "The Star-Spangled Banner." Later set to an English drinking song, Key's poem became our country's national anthem on March 13, 1931.

Key's poem describes the scene he observed all through the night as he earnestly strained to see his nation's flag over the fort:

> O say can you see,
> by the dawn's early light,
> What so proudly we hail'd
> at the twilight's last gleaming,
> Whose broad stripes and bright stars
> through the perilous fight
> O'er the ramparts we watch'd
> were so gallantly streaming?
> And the rocket's red glare,
> the bombs bursting in air,
> Gave proof through the night
> that our flag was still there,
> O say,
> does that star-spangled banner yet wave
> O'er the land of the free
> and the home of the brave?

According to the legend, the American defenders inside the fort also understood the importance of the fort's flag remaining up and determined that it would not, under *any* circumstances, fall to the ground in defeat and disgrace. As the story goes, a British shell nearly scored a direct hit on the flagpole, and the flag began to fall. American defenders inside the fort rallied to the pole, exposing their bodies to the incessant blasts and vicious shrapnel to physically hold the flag up with their bare hands. As they tired or were wounded, others abandoned shelters and took their place in harm's way, making certain the flag remained up and flying. Although I cannot find the source of this story, it seems entirely plausible considering how important this symbol of our Republic was to *both* the British and the Americans. Certainly the British understood this, and this is further proven by the fact tht Francis Scott Key based the *entire theme* of his famous poem upon this very point.

Most Americans are familiar only with the first stanza of the anthem, but in my opinion, the last may be the most powerful:

> *O thus be it ever*
> *when freemen shall stand*
> *Between their lov'd home*
> *and the war's desolation!*
> *Blest with* vict'ry *and peace,*
> *may the* heav'n *rescued* land
> *Praise the Power that hath made*
> *and preserv'd us a nation!*
> *Then conquer we must,*
> *when our cause it is just,*
> *And this* be *our motto –*
> *"In God is our trust,"*
> *And the star-spangled banner*
> *in triumph shall wave*
> *O'er the land of the free*
> *and the home of the brave.*

Once again, Americans rose up and defeated the British at the high cost of life and treasure. After the war, they returned to Washington, D.C. to rebuild the White House, completing it in 1817, just in time for the inauguration of President James Monroe. Our nation's freedom came at a terrible price. From the outbreak of hostilities at Lexington and Concord in 1775, until British and American forces fired the last shots of war in 1815, the number of American dead is estimated at nearly 70,000. These perished in battle, and from disease and starvation. Such a precious thing freedom is—yet *how little-valued it is in our times*. It appears to me that modern Americans know the prices of everything, but the value of *nothing*.

As I sat there musing in the shadows aboard the Spirit, Lady Liberty held my gaze out across the Hudson. I couldn't help wondering if our cherished freedoms and liberties, symbolized by that icon might someday slip through our fingers. Would Lady Liberty, and the freedom she represents, one day end up as one of the casualties of the 9/11 attacks, tossed upon the scrap heap of discarded ideas? In an allegorical sense, her bright torch of freedom seems dimmer of late.

A sacred duty remains for us in our generation to continually re-enflame Liberty's torch with the "imprisoned lightning" of patriotic love. May her beacon of freedom continue to shine brightly across lands and oceans, inspiring the minds and hearts of men and women everywhere and for all time.

> *There's a peace that may be found*
> *only on the other side of war.*
> *If that battle must come, I will fight it!*
> King Arthur of Camelot,
> from the film, First Knight

Notes

1. Address to the annual meeting of the Phoenix Chamber of Commerce. Ronald Reagan, March 30, 1961

2. California Gubernatorial Inauguration Speech. Ronald Reagan, January 5, 1967

3. The British Burn Washington, D.C., 1814. Eyewitness account of British soldier, George Gleig http://tinyurl.com/yejt9c

PART V

The Way Forward

22

The Price of Mercy

*The Lord's mercy
often rides to the door of our heart
upon the black horse of affliction.*
Charles H. Spurgeon

~~~~~~

Will the people of the United States find the grace to repent and grope our way back to our previous constitutional foundations? The dangers we face are serious, but the solution cannot be found solely in the political realm. The political views of men merely reflect the underlying worldview or convictions of the heart. All politics are the means of implementing binding policies of law according to the inner convictions people hold as to what is right or wrong, true or false. The record of history repeatedly demonstrates that when those convictions are formed according to the baser passions of pride, arrogance, avarice, lust for power or fame, or the pursuit of physical pleasures; the nation becomes corrupt, impoverished, and eventually unlivable. However, when God's word is held in honor by a people, and His wisdom and precepts are implemented into binding political policies, the nation prospers, violence diminishes, and happiness is possible. According to Proverbs 29:2:

*When the righteous are in authority,
the people rejoice:
but when the wicked beareth rule,
the people sigh.*
(1599 Geneva Bible)

America cannot and *will not* continue as a Constitutional Republic if God's grace is withheld. However, if His grace is shed upon us once again, we will find transformation and days of refreshing in His gracious favor. Our cities and towns will undergo renewal, and people will reflect goodness and biblical ethics in all areas of their lives and interactions with one another. Our priority as

Christians is to step up and take our civic and prayer responsibilities seriously. We must proclaim via every means possible the gospel of Christ to all who can hear it. By God's grace, we will do so, with fearless boldness.

Those who reject God's counsels, and entertain fantasies about transforming America into a secular-socialist/Marxist country will ultimately suffer a humiliating defeat. All their plans and plots will come to naught and will end in bitter disappointment and frustration as Christ infiltrates every nook and cranny of this present world with His sweet and irresistible presence and dominion. As it is written in Psalms 2:1-4:

> *Why do the heathen rage,*
> *and the people murmur in vain?*
> *The kings of the earth band themselves,*
> *and the Princes are assembled together*
> *against the Lord, and against his Christ.*
> *"Let us break their bands,*
> *and cast their cords from us."*
> *But He that dwelleth in the heaven shall laugh:*
> *the Lord shall have them in derision.*

Some might argue that based upon the outward appearance of things, the forces of darkness are winning. However, at any given moment, God in His might and fury will bring to nothing all the plans of the wicked. Christ's victory over all the kingdoms of this world is a "fait accompli." For those unfamiliar with that French expression, it is defined as;

> *a thing that has already happened or been decided before those affected* hear *about it, leaving them with no option but to accept.*
> – Oxford Dictionary

However, we must not underestimate the determination of fallen, rebellious men—and the minions of darkness in the unseen realm who control them—to mount a determined resistance to the plans and purposes of God right to the bitter end. Dedicated secularists will *never* content themselves with merely tweaking a few economic policies, or healthcare programs, or controlling the education systems to brainwash future generations. They *cannot* tolerate biblically-based standards, and will not rest until *every vestige* of Christian thought or expression is obliterated and forgotten. We are locked in a spiritual battle and culture war that will not end until either one side or the other achieves complete victory and totally dominates the other.

We who are privileged to number ourselves among God's elect have no reason to fear the outcome of this epic battle. According to 1 John 3:8-b (ESV)

> *The reason the Son of God appeared*
> *was to destroy the works of the devil.*

Unregenerate humans are in an unwinnable war against God. As stated above, Christ's total victory is a "fait accompli." Any talk of "coexistence" or "tolerance" is a fantasy. The word "coexistence" is often heard or read on pious-sounding bumper stickers by those seeking to signal their moral superiority and tolerance. However, just beneath that thin veneer of feigned civility there seethes a hatred and resentment within the heart of the unregenerate borne of their spiritual father, Lucifer. "Tolerance" is a one-way street in the little dominion of "Rebellionville." Secular bigots (or false religionists like those entrapped in Islam) *cannot* merely "put up" with Biblical Christians. If they ever achieved the political control they lust for, *everyone* would be required under duress to give *whole-hearted* acceptance, agreement *and affirmation* for whatever immoral, hedonistic, or narcissistic "lifestyle" they favor. Any demonstration of tolerance by Christians toward those caught up in darkness is often met with indignation or rage. The very *act* of extending mercy to an unregenerate person is often offensive, for it *implies* their guilt before God, and that they are actually in *need* of mercy.

Secular-progressives continually harp—either subtly or openly—that people who still "cling" to Biblical or Constitutional standards are hopelessly out of step with the times. They often complain that America "isn't working" anymore. These are lies, of course, meant to demoralize and silence those of us who still hold to the dream of a Christianized America as originally founded.

The Price of Faithfulness

Regrettably, far too many Christians in our time have been seduced by the siren-call of a distorted theology of personal peace, security, and well-being during their earthly sojourn. Many falsely believe that their relationship with God somehow guarantees their prosperity and success in every area of their lives. The most popular books and preachers of our times appeal to the near-universal desire of humans to relate to God as a kindly, grandfatherly, all-loving and all-accepting being who eagerly yearns to give them whatever their hearts desire. The God of the Bible—the one who will judge sin and rebellion with wrath and eternal punishment—is almost universally scorned and rejected.

It's important to count the cost when we dare to stand "Contra-Mundum" (against the world) and share the full counsel of God. Trust me, those who rise against you will be legion, even from among your family and Christian brethren. Beyond what you can expect to suffer from those *within* the "household of faith" there will be *many* unregenerate foes who will hate and persecute you. The Apostle Paul was no stranger to this reality. In 2 Corinthians 11:26 he wrote:

> *In journeying I was often in perils of waters,*
> *in perils of robbers, in perils of mine own nation,*
> *in perils among the Gentiles, in perils in the city,*
> *in perils in wilderness, in perils in the sea,*
> *in perils among false brethren...*

If we dare to step up and confront those who are laboring to transform our country into a socialist-atheist amoral nightmare, we may be required to pay a heavy price. The struggle for Christ's eventual victory over all His enemies will require our blood and tears—all to the glory of God. The spirits that are driving progressive leftists and socialists (or their unwitting bedfellows, the Islamists) are irrational, hateful, violent, and viciously unmerciful. History repeatedly demonstrates that there are *no limits* to the degree of slander, violence, subterfuge, and blatant brutality these enemies of freedom will stoop to in promoting their agendas. The proof of this can be found in the killing fields of Cambodia, the mass-graves in China or the Soviet Union, the dead and starving people of North Korea, and the Rwandan slaughters in Africa.

Biblical Christians must seek Providence to stand in the storm, lest we are silenced by fear and intimidation. Prepare to be called cruel and even vulgar names. Prepare yourself to be lied about and slandered. Lower your expectations of unregenerate men, for they will "act out" the will of their defeated spiritual father, Lucifer. Here are a few words of encouragement in Luke 6:22 from our Lord and King, who suffered *far more* than any of us *ever* will.

> *Yea, ye shall be betrayed also*
> *of your parents and of your brethren,*
> *and kinsmen, and friends,*
> *and some of you shall they put to death.*

And ye shall be hated of all men for my Name's sake.
Yet there shall not one hair of your heads perish.

And again in Luke 21:16-18

Blessed are ye when men hate you,
and when they separate you,
and revile you, and put out your name as evil,
for the Son of man's sake.

We must remember the faithful testimony of those who went before us and draw strength from their examples. I realize I'm potentially alienating a large part of my readers by hammering this point so much, but this issue can't be ignored or sugarcoated. Paul's admonition to his son in the faith, Timothy, summarizes well in 2 Timothy 3:12:

Yea, and all that will live godly in Christ Jesus,
shall suffer persecution.

The above quote begs the question. If we are *not* experiencing some level of persecution, could that mean we're not living "godly?" And, does "living godly" concern itself only with our private inner "spiritual" life of love and devotion to God, or could it possibly *also* mean living out our convictions in every area of life out in the open view of the world?

"Keep Your Religion to Yourself!"
Secularists are often heard to say; "You Christians should keep your religion to yourselves! Don't impose *your* beliefs and values on "our"… (politics, education, business, ethics, legislation, morality, entertainment, etc., etc.)" Well, I have a memo for the minions of darkness and the secular-progressive puppets you control. Can the sun fail to shine? Can the winds cease their blowing? Neither can we cease from speaking the truth of God's word nor fail to give faithful witness concerning Christ! You may rage against us, and even torture and murder some of our numbers, but our blood will cry out from the earth to the throne of heaven. The full manifestation of your defeat is as certain as the dawn in the strength of our King. *Resistance is futile.*

Here's a comforting thought for Biblical Christians. Remember it well. Nothing can come to you, or happen to you *unless* it first passes through the loving hands of your Father in heaven. If you are honored to suffer shame and abuse for the name of Jesus, you're *blessed*! If you experience the rare privilege of suffering martyrdom for the sake of Christ, you must receive it with joy and thanksgiving. When Jesus stood before Pontius Pilate before His crucifixion, Pilate asked Him an important question. Jesus' answer from John 19:10-11 in the English Standard Version should encourage us all;

> *So Pilate said to him,*
> *"You will not speak to me?*
> *Do you not know that I have authority*
> *to release you and authority to crucify you?"*
> *Jesus answered him,*
> *"You would have no authority over me at all*
> *unless it had been given you from above."*
> *...the blood of the martyrs*
> *is the seed of the Church*
> (Quintus Tertullian, Apologeticus, Chapter 50)

There are some who sincerely—yet erroneously—declare that Christians who suffered persecution or died in the service of Christ were somehow walking in unbelief, or failed to grasp scriptural "principles" relating to "victory" in this present world. If this is the case, then we would have to conclude that virtually *every* Christian in the early Church, including *all* the apostles, failed to appropriate the promises of God and walk in "victorious faith." Such an assumption is a bit arrogant, I think.

All the early apostles suffered for Christ. They were called upon to write the testimony of their faith in Jesus with their blood. According to church tradition, the following were their fates:

- **Matthew** suffered martyrdom by being slain with a sword at a distant city of Ethiopia.
- **Mark** died at Alexandria after being brutally dragged till through the streets of the city.
- **Luke** was hanged upon an olive tree in Greece.
- **John** was put in a caldron of boiling oil, but he miraculously escaped death and was afterward banished to the island of Patmos to starve.
- **Peter** was crucified at Rome.
- **James the Greater** was beheaded at Jerusalem.
- **James the Less** was thrown from a high pinnacle of the temple and then beaten to death with a fuller's club.
- **Bartholomew** was skinned alive.

- **Andrew** was bound to a cross, from which he preached to his persecutors until he died.
- **Thomas** was run through the body with a lance at Coromandel in the East Indies.
- **Jude** was shot to death with arrows.
- **Matthias** was first stoned and then beheaded.
- **Barnabas** of the Gentiles was stoned to death at Salonica.
- **Paul**, after various tortures and persecutions, was finally beheaded at Rome by Emperor Nero.

As established in the previous chapter, nations rise and fall unfailingly according to the immutable plans and purposes of God. God is the one who sovereignly sets rulers in positions of authority as it pleases Him, *and He may remove them at any time*. Again, this does not exempt us who love and serve Christ to petition and pray, making our requests (*not demands*) to Him as our loving, merciful Father in Heaven. Prayer is our duty, not to manipulate God to do *our will* but to petition Him and commune with Him as children.

The most desirable outcome I can imagine is that God—mercifully responding to the prayers of His people—would send a spirit of repentance upon our nation and call many to Himself. In that case, those who are now enemies and hostile to God would miraculously become our brethren and fellow-workers. We should always remember the apostle Paul (or Rabbi Shaul) before his regeneration. Paul began his "ministry" (if you could call it thus) as a hateful and vicious persecutor of Christ's followers. God violently interrupted his murderous rampage and transformed him into one of His "chosen" vessels to bring the gospel to the non-Jewish peoples. As we will see later in this chapter, God's mercy also sometimes extends to entire nations.

Do Nations Ever Repent?
People often dislike the word "repent" for one very simple reason. It sounds religious, and because of unflattering stereotypes in movies, it is associated with fire-breathing, pulpit-pounding, wide-eyed, foaming-at-the-mouth bible-thumping preachers yelling up a revival at frightened congregations. (To be fair, some "preachers" have unfortunately reinforced these stereotypes in their manner of preaching.) Also, as a general rule, people instinctively dislike being told that what they're thinking, believing, or doing is wrong. However, the word "repent" simply means "to change your mind or turn around."

There is a major fly in this ointment, however. I don't believe people *can* willingly repent without God's *initiating* grace. Please note my deliberate use of the word "can." Indeed, anyone *may* turn to God if they choose to do so, for no one is preventing them. But based on my study of history and the scriptures, and the incalculable depth of man's fall in Adam, unregenerate persons have *no ability or desire to do so*, and *never would*. Contrary to the ancient heresy of Pelagianism, all men have inherited the fallen nature of Adam, and *by nature*, are rebels and in the darkness of their minds, *unable* to repent. *Unless*, as Jesus taught in John 6:65:

> *And he said, Therefore said I unto you,*
> *that no man can come unto me,*
> *except it be given unto him of my Father.*

Spiritually dead people are *incapable* of resurrecting themselves from among the spiritually dead. But for God's mercy and grace, all of us would be doomed. It will be an unspeakably horrifying experience for unregenerate people when they stand judgment before the Holy, Sovereign God.

In recent decades, America has descended into a depth of moral depravity, violence, greed, sexual debauchery, and spiritual corruption unequaled in our history. There is an unspeakably evil sex-slave trade operating right within our own borders, preying upon even the youngest children, and well over 50 **million** people have been slaughtered in abortions since 1973. The "normalization" of these atrocities through incessant brainwashing via the media and entertainment industry has seared the conscience of many of our people, who are no longer shocked by it, and ignore the cries of the victims. Some people express their moral corruption with breathtaking arrogance in public displays of their debauchery in parades and "pride" days as they rage impudently against God and anyone who dares to disagree with them. We *desperately* need an awakening.

We who have been regenerated are commanded to pray for all people. Our "prime directive" in prayer is that God would mercifully soften hearts and grant people the same mercy we have received to love and desire God. He may yet grant those prayers, according to His will. When He purposes to bring anyone into the kingdom of His love, the regenerated person is set free from their former darkness and inability to love and respond to God. Paul again exhorts believers to remember God's mercy to them in Colossians 3:6-7

> *On account of these*
> *the wrath of God is coming.*

> *In these you too once walked,*
> *when you were living in them.*

Lest anyone take an uncharitable "holier than thou" attitude toward the wicked of this world, we should always remind ourselves that we too were once numbered among them. None of us can claim any individual merit or exceptional gift of faith that made us acceptable to God. Salvation is *all* of God, and not of us, so we cannot boast except in God's mercy. Paul reminded the Christians at Ephesus of this truth in
Ephesians 2:3-5 (ESV);

> *...among whom we all once lived*
> *in the passions of our flesh,*
> *carrying out the desires of the body and the mind,*
> *and were by nature children of wrath,*
> *like the rest of mankind.*
> *But God, being rich in mercy,*
> *because of the great love with which he loved us,*
> *even when we were dead in our trespasses,*
> *made us alive together with Christ*
> *—by grace you have been saved—*

But what of America? Are we to assume that all that is in store for our nation and people is God's wrath and judgment, ending in destruction? I believe there is yet hope.

The Example of Jonah

Jonah was a Hebrew prophet who God called to a seeming "Mission Impossible."

> *The word of the Lord came also*
> *unto Jonah the son of Amittai, saying,*
> *Arise, and go to Nineveh, that great city,*
> *and cry against it:*
> *for their wickedness is come up before me.*
> Jonah 1:1-2

Some critics mock and dismiss the entire story of Jonah because of the astonishing part about his being swallowed up by a "great fish." His survival in the belly of a sea creature for three days and nights seems—on the face of it—ludicrous. Before anyone dismisses out of hand the possibility that a man could be swallowed up whole by a sea creature, I would encourage further study of the subject in a scholarly article titled; *Did Jonah Really Get Swallowed by a Whale?* Authored by Dr. John Morris, Ph.D. [1]

No matter how incredible one thinks this part of the story is, try to keep in view the larger message of the book of Jonah. Nineveh and the people dwelling there were in imminent danger of well-deserved judgment and destruction because of their great wickedness. God commanded Jonah to go and proclaim a coming judgment that would destroy the Ninevites. Jonah's response? He tried to run away!

Why did Jonah attempt to dodge this assignment and flee? The Ninevites, according to all historical accounts, were a cruel, evil, and vicious people, famous for their many acts of abuse against the Israelites. In a sense, they were the "Mad Max" crazies of their time, *on steroids*. Jonah knew this well, and we might assume he might take a certain amount of satisfaction in pronouncing God's wrath upon Nineveh as punishment for all their crimes against his people. We might even imagine Jonah saying something like; "I'm your *man* Lord! Send *me!* I'll tell those stinking Ninevites you're going to kick their evil butts! I can't *wait* to see *this*!"

However, something much larger was in play. Jonah realized that if God was bothering to *warn* these evil brutes instead of just destroying them outright, there must remain a *possibility* the Ninevites might heed Jonah's warning and repent. The truth is, Jonah didn't *want* them to repent. He wanted them all *DEAD*. He understood something of God's tendency to show mercy, and he had no desire to give the Ninevites even the *slightest* chance at forgiveness. He *hated* these people so much, all he wanted was for God to destroy *every last one of them*.

This is the reason he attempted to escape! He quickly booked passage on a boat going the *opposite direction* from Nineveh. He wanted to get as far away as possible from that evil kingdom. In the end, his worst fears were realized. After the drama on the high seas with the great storm that the Lord sent to "communicate" with Jonah, the sailors (at the command of Jonah) threw him overboard. He was then taken aboard a divinely-provided submarine in the form of a "great fish." Following divinely-provided navigation, the beast vomited him up on the beach near the *one place* he was trying to avoid. Jonah finally showed up and delivered God's message. By the grace and mercy of God, the king of Nineveh believed Jonah and repented, and led his people, from the

The Price of Mercy

least to the greatest of them, to do the same. In the book of Jonah 3:5-10 we pick up the story.

> *So the people of Nineveh believed God, and proclaimed a fast, and put on sackcloth, from the greatest of them, even to the least of them. For word came unto the king of Nineveh, and he rose from his throne, and he laid his robe from him, and covered him with sackcloth, and sat in ashes. And he proclaimed and said through Nineveh, (by the counsel of the king and his nobles) saying, Let neither man, nor beast, bullock nor sheep taste anything, neither feed nor drink water. But let man and beast put on sackcloth, and cry mightily unto God: yea, let every man turn from his evil way, and from the wickedness that is in their hands. Who can tell if God will turn, and repent and turn away from his fierce wrath, that we perish not?*
>
> *And God saw their works that they turned from their evil ways: and God repented of the evil that he had said that he would do unto them, and he did it not.*

Jonah was *outraged!* In Jonah 4:1-3 we see why.

> *Therefore it displeased Jonah exceedingly, and he was angry. And he prayed unto the Lord, and said, pray thee, O Lord, was not this my saying, when I was yet in my country? Therefore I prevented it to flee unto Tarshish: for I knew, that thou art a gracious God, and merciful, slow to anger, and of great kindness, and repentest thee of the evil. Therefore now, O Lord, take, I beseech thee, my life from me: for it is better for me to die than to live.*

Jonah was so offended he wanted to die. God's mercy to the Ninevites seemed unfair and unjust. Jonah took the attitude that many hold today when they first hear of the doctrines of grace. "That's not *fair!*" The Ninevites were *guilty*, and Jonah wanted them all dead and their city destroyed. However, God made it crystal clear He reserves the right to forgive anyone He chooses, without any regard for their merits *or lack of them*. By sovereign decree, God showed grace toward the Ninevites in spite of their great wickedness. God's answer to Jonah in verse eleven is instructive.

> *And should not I spare Nineveh that great city, wherein are six-score thousand persons, that cannot discern between their right hand and their left hand, and also much cattle?*

Consider this carefully. If God would show such unmerited mercy toward Nineveh, and its exceedingly wicked inhabitants, might it be a possibility that He may *also* show mercy toward America? We certainly do not deserve His mercy, but I think *it is entirely possible*! The recent election of Donald Trump as President may signal a favorable change in the political winds in America. However, if it is God's determinate counsel to humble us through the refining fires of affliction, we must also accept this.

At this point, some will arrogantly scoff at the *very idea* that America or her people might even *need* God's mercy and forgiveness. Arrogance and narcissism are the earmarks of modern man. Many people of this generation are full of themselves, puffed up with an arrogant pride that blinds them to the actual condition of their soul.

Many vainly imagine that technology will save and even somehow perfect them, and have grown utterly dependent upon it for the very necessities of life. This generation is accustomed to living in comforts never before experienced in human history. However, most people are blithely unaware that our much-vaunted technology could all go away in a moment of time. It would only take one well-placed solar flare—like the 1859 "Carrington Event" X-class solar flare, or a deliberate EMP (Electro-Magnetic Pulse) attack via a small-yield nuclear detonation high over the United States—and most of our electronic technology and electrical power systems would be severely damaged or totally destroyed. This would very likely plunge us all into a pre-industrialized age where hardly anyone remembers how to survive. Perhaps we are ripe for such a major humbling. I'm praying that God may yet show mercy, regenerate people's hearts and minds, and turn us back from our present path of imminent destruction for His honor and glory.

2 Chronicles 7:14 (ESV) gives us hope. It reveals God's promise and should give us hope.

> *If my people*
> *who are called by my name*
> *humble themselves, and pray and seek my face*
> *and turn from their wicked ways,*
> *then I will hear from heaven*
> *and will forgive their sin*
> *and heal their land.*

Note the words, "If *my* people will humble themselves and pray…" This scripture applies *exclusively* to God's elect people. It has nothing whatsoever to do with the salvation of His people. That is already an established fact. However, this promise pertains to a powerful tool God has given to His people to influence the world. Those who are captives and slaves of darkness could *never* humble themselves, seek God's face, and turn from their wicked ways. They *WILL* not because they *cannot*. The responsibility is on *His* people to intercede for them. Let's be diligent to cooperate with the Spirit of Grace for the sake of those yet to come into Christ's fold, and see God's favor upon our nation to heal our land.

Notes

1. Did Jonah Really Get Swallowed by a Whale? by John D. Morris, Ph.D. http://www.icr.org/article/did-jonah-really-get-swallowed-by-whale/

23

God's Invaders

*Be very careful, then,
how you live—
not as unwise
but as wise,
making the most
of every opportunity,
because the days are evil.*
Ephesians 5:15-16

~~~~~

Some argue that God is only interested in affecting the "inner world" of men's religious beliefs. They imply by this that Christians should stay out of politics or governance and leave it to secular "experts." To such nonsense, I offer the following remarks.

Far too many Christians have "bought in" to this silly notion, and the results are disastrous. God's people have a moral duty to wisely guide the policy-making apparatus of our republic. When Christians took their hands off the steering wheel of national leadership near the end of the 19th century, things began to fall apart dramatically. Crime and dysfunctional families increased and divorce skyrocketed. Greed and corruption filled the halls of power. One major tragic result is that we now have the blood of over 50 million people on our hands–slaughtered without mercy in their mother's wombs.

A Loving Exhortation to Christian Leaders
Regrettably, relatively few ministers in our times are willing to wade into political—or any other controversies for that matter—fearing divisions within their congregations. Many Pastors serve in churches with long-standing traditions and policies that prohibit the preaching of controversial sermons that might "upset the apple-cart."

Because many Pastors and church governing boards tend to value large, homogenous congregations, modern churches are often made up of a wide diversity of political, theological, and social viewpoints, and ministers must tread *very* carefully upon certain subjects that may offend any particular "camp" within their church. As a result, the proclamation and teaching of historically orthodox Christian theology is too-often downplayed in favor of less-controversial "seeker friendly" sermons that emphasize personal success, happiness, prosperity, health, and emotionally pleasing "stories." Sadly, many ministers are *themselves* morally and theologically compromised to one degree or another and fear speaking out boldly under the threat of exposure of their failures. This fear, of course, renders many churches ineffective in their influence upon the morals, ethics, and conscience within the larger community surrounding them. Evil men and demons *love* this situation, for it gives them free reign to destroy people's lives right under the noses of Christians virtually unopposed.

The Dark Side of Influence

America was once profoundly influenced by biblical Christianity and a Biblical worldview. Secular progressives (and the wicked spirits that drive them) realize that it took them over two hundred years of hard and painstaking work to subvert America down to its present state of spiritual blindness and moral corruption. They're not likely to give up those gains without a fight.

Progressives *greatly* fear the cultural and societal resurgence of Christian influence in America. They are in the minority and know that an enormous sleeping giant could easily crush their evil agendas if ever awakened and mobilized to action. They also realize that once a biblical worldview becomes ensconced into the collective consciousness of a culture, it is nearly impossible to isolate and suppress it. This fear of a resurging Christian influence is the reason Marxists and secular progressives historically resorted to rounding up and "re-educating" all those believed to be infected with the former "pollutions" of "politically incorrect thinking." If re-education fails, they have and *will* resort to mass-murder if given opportunity. This horrible scenario has been played out repeatedly in the last hundred years of world history in Russia, China, Cambodia, North Korea, and many other places around the world where militant secularism and the insanity of Marxism came to power.

The enemies of freedom and Christian conservatism understand well how important the strategic cultural and societal penetrations of their ideas are. This is precisely why they have worked so diligently to seize and monopolize their control of the organs of education and the entertainment culture.

Rudi Dutschke, a German Communist student movement leader in 1967, reformulated the philosophy of the Italian Communist, Antonio Gramsci, who called for a gradual and strategic domination and cultural hegemony of all institutions with Marxism. Dutschke coined the phrase: "Der lange Marsch durch die Institutionen" (Translated: The Long March through the Institutions). This is a cultural war strategy utilized for the past century in America calculated to gradually dull people to deadly dangers of Marxism. [1] [2]

Most Neo-Marxists and Socialists—throughout Europe, Russia, South and North America—embraced the concept of "The Long March through the Institutions" with great success. Indeed, there remain some Marxists who prefer more violent and "direct action" to forcibly overthrow societies, especially in Central and South America and the Philippines, but there they have had limited success. In fact, their vicious cruelty and violence often backfire as PR disasters and only strengthen the determination of non-Communist populations to resist their so-called "liberation" movements.

The "Long March" strategy—on the other hand—has been *very* effective in the United States, rendering most people unalarmed or even completely *unaware* that their schools, libraries, churches, news media, entertainment, movies, and political institutions have been taken over. Socialist/Marxist agents of "change" subtly and progressively promote Marxist ideology through these institutions. In fact, America has been in a 'soft' revolution for decades. Fortunately, people are beginning to wake up. I believe it's not too late.

During his presidency, Barack Hussein Obama once contemptuously referred to "small town" people as "religion clingers." [3] Mr. Obama, if you're referring to our belief in the Bible, Jesus, and the faith of our Fathers, you *nailed* it! If you're talking about our "clinging" to the dream of liberty and freedom guaranteed by the Bill of Rights and Constitution (which *you* swore a solemn oath to defend), then I would say heartily, "Guilty as charged!"

I'm one of those "clingers," and even more so now than *ever* before, thanks to your less than sterling leadership. I offer this insight into the hearts and minds of those "small-town clingers" you spoke of, Mr. Obama. The harder you pound on a nail, the deeper it penetrates the wood. You and those who work with you cannot discourage us. We're going deeper into the grain of America.

How DARE Christians Influence Public Policy?

Conservative Patriots and Christians must *also* employ the same "Long March" strategy the enemies of freedom have used to such evil effect. Our *greatest* weakness is the delusion that significant shifts in the culture and the national mindset will come through a "quick-fix" of some kind. Many seem to imagine our social and political future only as far ahead as the next election cycle. We *must* take a longer view. We must *change our strategy* and learn to appreciate the power of a "Long March" through the institutions that will influence the *long-term* values of our nation.

In spite of the progressives' diligent efforts, there yet remains a vast majority of American "religion clingers" who still possess the glowing embers of the Founders' Fire burning within their hearts. This stubborn tenacity causes considerable frustration to progressive liberals. I believe the Founders' Fire is poised to re-ignite into a mighty, all-consuming wildfire that promises to incinerate the progressive "house of cards." With God's help, we *will* reawaken our people and nation, and fan the flames of God's agenda and purpose to *white-hot intensity*.

Christ expects His church to aggressively imprint *His* values upon the world. The ludicrous idea that people should "check" their Christian values at the door of policy-forming deliberations did not originate in the counsels of our earliest Founders *or* Heaven. While we are forbidden (and unable) to *force* anyone to convert to Christianity, we are nevertheless compelled to follow the Apostle Paul's example who never missed a chance to bring the *influence* of Christ upon every culture and person he met. Paul exhorted in 2 Timothy 4:1-5 The Message (MSG) (Emphasis Added)

> *I can't impress this on you too strongly.*
> *God is looking over your shoulder.*
> *Christ himself is the Judge,*
> *with the final say on everyone, living and dead.*
> **He is about to break into the open with his rule,**
> *so* **proclaim the Message with intensity;**
> *keep on your watch*
> Challenge, *warn, and urge your people.*
> *Don't ever quit.*
> *Just keep it simple.*

Conversion is *God's* work, not *ours*. We are only mandated to "preach" (i.e. proclaim, publish, promote, broadcast, and teach) the gospel to all men, leaving the work of converting people to God alone. We are also commanded to influence our society with biblically-based principles such as ethics, honor, respect for life, property stewardship, mercy, forgiveness, and love. Christ meant *exactly* what He said when He taught in Matthew 5:13-15 (NKJV):

> *You are the salt of the earth;*
> *but if the salt loses its flavor,*
> *how shall it be seasoned?*
> *It is then good for nothing*
> *but to be thrown out*
> *and trampled underfoot by men.*
> *You are the light of the world.*
> *A city that is set on a hill cannot be hidden.*
> *Nor do they light a lamp*
> *and put it under a basket,*
> *but on a lampstand,*
> *and it gives light*
> *to all who are in the house.*

The importance of obedient Christian leadership within the ranks of every human endeavor cannot be over-emphasized. We are called to be a salt and light influence on the world.

Theology Determines Methodology

A more recent outstanding example of involved Christian leadership in our nation was the late Dr. D. James Kennedy, who passed away in 2007. Dr. Kennedy was intensely involved in public discourse over subjects and social issues impacting our nation. His ministry produced many films and books supporting the fact of America's Christian heritage. In his "God and Country" sermon, he boldly declared:

> *We hear today that this is a pluralistic nation and that it is not a Christian nation. But Christianity itself, general Christianity, was conceived as the support of all our government... Indeed, this is a nation that was founded by men and women who were Christian. Some were not. But even those who were not believers embraced the Christian world and life view that was almost universally prevalent at the time and according to the dictates of the Word of God.*

Due to the pervasive anti-Christian brainwashing in our educational and entertainment sectors, many people react negatively when they hear words like "Christian ethics," "fundamentalism," or even the word "pulpit." They're conditioned to associate such words with "intolerance," "hate-speech," "bigotry," and "religious oppression." In the early days of our nation, the Christian pulpit was the prime fountainhead of public discourse. It was, in a very real sense, the "Internet" of the times, with many of the sermons transcribed and printed, or published in newspapers for people to read far and wide. In fact, many of these sermons were highly influential upon the thinking of America's early Patriots and the Founding Fathers.

Christian ministers—particularly after the "Great Awakening" that occurred in the years following 1740 under the influence of such great Calvinist preachers and theologians as George Whitefield and Jonathan Edwards—were not merely men who sermonized and harangued people about immorality with "fire and brimstone" warnings. The pulpit was also the primary means of communication that the most highly educated men, and foremost scholars—as these ministers most often were—on nearly *every* subject. They carried on an ongoing dialogue with their communities regarding biblical matters *and* contemporary subjects, providing commentary and editorial reviews on topics ranging from the weather, earthquakes, local events, and even political matters—all within a biblical framework. In a very literal sense, these men of God were the "News Media" of their day, and any "fake news" was immediately condemned by a Biblically literate and educated populace.

This entire scenario is nearly a foreign concept in our times, mainly because—again—people have been conditioned to compartmentalize "spiritual" truths—and especially Christian ones—as unreal, personal, and "private." People now mostly regard materialism and "scientific" issues as "real" (and superior) under the rubric of a Gnostic-like duality. Post-modern secularly brainwashed people regard biblical truth as foolish sentimentality and unscientific emotional nonsense related only to imaginary fantasies about a hoped-for future in an assumed afterlife ruled by a non-existent grandfatherly "God."

We *will* eventually gain the upper hand in the current culture war—and any others that may pop up—but it is crucial that Christians become *educated apologists* for the "faith once delivered unto the saints." I say this because in times past so much of our witness to the unregenerate world has been boring, inaccurate, emotional, and in some cases, manifestly silly. All one needs to do to prove this is tune into some of the current "Christian" radio and television broadcasts. There you will find what the unregenerate (legitimately) regard as charlatans and sideshow barkers who display their ignorance and lack of solid theological training for all the world to see. Think I'm being too harsh? Just ask your non-Christian co-workers, neighbors, or fellow students what they *honestly* think of "televangelists" or most "radio preachers."

> *Beloved, when I gave all diligence*
> *to write unto you of the common salvation,*
> *it was needful for me to write unto you,*
> *to exhort you, that ye should earnestly contend*
> *for the maintenance of the faith,*
> *which was once given unto the Saints.*
> Jude 3

In spite of all, I believe we Christians should stop feeling ashamed about our faith in Jesus, or allow unbelievers to intimidate and make us afraid to mention Christ in mixed company. Where is it written we mustn't make anyone feel "uncomfortable" or "offended" when we speak up for Truth? It's high time we recognized that those voices who demand we confine our beliefs strictly within the four walls of church buildings are speaking the counsels of *hell*. The minions of darkness want us to *sit down, shut up, and keep our views to ourselves*. Darkness increases when institutions and our culture are bereft of the moral voice of fearless and uncompromised Christians. Blessings follow when believers make it their business to bring the counsel of Heaven to bear upon *every* sector of society. When we fail to shine the light of Christ's gospel, darkness will spread like cancer and dominate. Darkness *cannot* resist light. Those who walk in darkness will *always* hate the light—even violently—when their tactics of intimidation fail to silence us.

The Early Church implemented the strategy of the "Long March," and the permeation of kingdom-yeast eventually swept throughout the entire pagan Roman Empire. Should we not in these modern times *also* dedicate ourselves to be a "city on a hill" in every stratum of society? And can we not expect that the light of Christ would dispel the darkness in our times as well?

Quintus Septimius Florens Tertullianus, (Tertullian) was an early Christian theologian who lived from 160–225 AD. Commenting on the spread of Christianity throughout the known world in his times, he wrote:

> *We are but of yesterday, and yet we have filled all the places that belong to you; cities, islands, forts, towns, exchanges; the military camps themselves, tribes, town councils, the palace, the Senate, the market-place; we have left you nothing but your temples.*

Getting "Attitude"

Serving at Ground Zero—as well as many other disasters around the country and the world—awakened and gave me "attitude." By this, I mean these experiences didn't match up with my former theological frames of reference. I was forced to re-examine some of my previously-held theological assumptions about God's person and sovereignty, and what He was doing in the unfolding drama we share in this present world. This catharsis drove me to a much deeper study of the Scriptures. In the end, these studies radically changed my worldview.

At first, I felt disoriented and confused. I wasn't much fun to be around for a while. (Some would say I'm *still* not all that much fun to hang out with, but I digress.) After responding to various scenes of disaster around the world, I'd come home drained and wounded emotionally. My former theological beliefs no longer matched the world I was encountering, and I spent many late nights out under the stars crying out to God for answers and healing for my mind and soul.

Proverbs 27:5-6 (ESV) speaks deeply to me now.

> *Better is open rebuke*
> *than hidden love.*
> *Faithful are the wounds of a friend;*
> *profuse are the kisses of an enemy.*

The world no longer made sense to me within my old frames of reference, but the wildest thing of all was a growing conviction that it was God *Himself* working in my heart—*even wounding me*—to draw me closer to Him and into a new and more accurate understanding of His being and ways. This thought flew in the face of my former paradigm of God's goodness and mercy. Like many, I always automatically assumed that God was only involved when "good" things happened, and when "bad" things happened, it was always the devil doing it. God's overarching sovereignty and Lordship over all things seemed a foreign concept. In the end, by God's grace, I found peace and a greater ability to trust God and His word. Also, my reverence for God and my love and admiration of Christ for all He did for me deepened immeasurably.

As a Christian minister for decades, I preached and taught the Bible sincerely as best I understood it. I chose my topics primarily around subjects that seemed relevant to the "felt needs" of my congregations. Most of those "felt needs" related to issues that were personal and immediate to people. These included subjects such as healing, deliverance, financial prosperity, and how to be a better and more "successful" Christian in this or that.

American Christians are very attracted to messages that help them in some practical way and move them emotionally. This isn't necessarily wrong, but looking back I can now see how my ministry was becoming too anthropocentric (man-centered) instead of Christ-centered. I was too focused on the "benefits package" of being a Christian in order to attract more people to the church. Now and then I'd stray over into teachings on eschatology or "end times" subjects. The main focus of *these* messages centered on the rescue of Christians through what I now see as a "rapture ejection system" that would snatch all true believers off of the earth just before the appearance of a "big bad" Antichrist. (If you're in the Premillennial/Dispensational camp, that previous sentence may have wounded you a bit. Bear with me; my wounds are those of a friend, not the deceitful kisses of an enemy.)

As the world seemed to grow darker and more dangerous, we took it all as a prophetic "sign" that Jesus would come back soon and rescue us. As you will discover, I *now* view the challenges of this present darkness as a *great opportunity* to shine the brilliant light of the gospel of Christ and assault the gates of hell which Jesus told us *could not* prevail against His church. I'm now certain that *nothing* in the universe happens accidentally, for *all things*—even the painful, heartbreaking stuff—has a glorious purpose toward a greater and irresistible consummation in God's magnificent purposes.

Proactive or Reactive?

As I've said repeatedly, Christianity played an *enormous* role in the formation and early foundations of the United States. Christians actively participated in every nook and cranny of America's political institutions, deliberating bodies, and schools. After the Great Awakening in the 1740s, America's pulpits were ablaze with the gospel and was a powerful influence upon the minds and hearts of early Americans. This conviction of the heart translated into *action* as people stepped up as leaders or voted into office representatives who reflected Christian morals and values. America became the envy of the nations, with freedoms and opportunities that surpassed all the other countries of the earth.

The formerly profound influence of Christianity has waned dramatically during the past century. We've come to the point that not only are Christian opinions and influence nearly absent, but any effort to revive this former influence is met with public outrage, derision, and censure. This is *especially* so because Biblical Christian morality directly contradicts "politicly correct" progressive leftist agendas. Also, due to the high-profile failures of marginally "Christianized" preachers, there is plenty of "accusation ammo" in the hands of those actively seeking to discredit and marginalize Christianity. In most cases, the full sum of most Christian congregations' influence on their surrounding communities consists only of banal "pithy" sayings displayed on their billboards in front of their buildings. This to our shame, but it doesn't change the truth of God's eternal decree according to His word.

American Christianity has become almost exclusively "reactionary." By this, I mean that we "react" every time some new immoral outrage is reported by the media, or some atheist group succeeds in banning the public display of another religious icon from schools, courthouses, or public places. Christians then tepidly react and complain on Facebook or Twitter. We whine among our friends at church. We may even write a letter to the editor or call into a local talk show and gripe. We react and grumble for a while, and then, far too often, go back to whatever we were doing before, distracted by the next "shiny thing." When the *next* moral or ethical outrage comes at us in the form of a new attack on our religious liberties the cycle repeats. Same actions. The result is nothing significant changes. Until recently, relatively few churches or Christian organizations pursued an aggressive strategy of infiltration and influence on society. Thankfully, there are signs of late that this is beginning to change in a BIG way.

In the past, we Christians have been like a fire department that arrives on-scene only *after* everything has burned to the ground. There are evil pyromaniacs running around and working as fast as they can to destroy everything that even *remotely* reminds them of their Creator. They're like fire-breathing dragons that swoop down on us with a "scorched earth" policy, intent on devastating all we hold dear and precious. The "dragon" image might be on-point since Satan is often depicted as a dragon in the Bible. As I see this *now*, I believe God is allowing these things *for now*, but I suspect that His greater glory will be revealed as He raises up His elect to confront the darkness and proclaim His word with boldness.

Here's a radical idea to consider. How about we begin actively *stalking* the dragons, laying traps for them, and expose them for who and what they are? How about we start arresting (through prayer, public exposure, and even legal actions) secular dragons before they have a chance to blow up or set fire to everything we love and cherish? In a word, why not become PRO-*active dragon-hunters* instead of just reactive *"crispy critters"*?

"Oh!" some sheeple will say..."THAT wouldn't be very 'Christian' of us, would it? Aren't we supposed to 'turn the other cheek,' and *love* our enemies?

After all, we wouldn't want people to think we're "mean-spirited" or anything, right?"

We are indeed commanded to love our enemies, but as any parent knows, sometimes *genuine* "love" is more effectively expressed in harsher and more painful ways. (Like the well-substantiated practice of applying the "board of education" to the "seat of understanding.")

I wonder if anyone would accuse Jesus of being "un-Christlike" when He went outraged into the temple, pulled out a whip, (a "scourge of cords") and began whacking people and kicking over the tables of the money-changers? *Seriously*, could anyone "out-Christian" Jesus Himself? He didn't seem the slightest bit concerned about hurting anyone's "feelings," or offending "politically correct" fools. He was only interested in doing the will of His Father in heaven. On *that* particular day, the will of His Father was to "love" the money changers by kicking some "money-changer booty" and taking names. He *also* didn't apologize for losing His sinless temper. Just try and imagine Jesus coming back to the temple the *next* day and holding a press conference for the Jerusalem Post, saying something like;

> *"I'm...I'm just so **sorry**! I just don't know what came over me! I acted without any sensitivity toward those who were expressing their religious "diversity" in the temple. I mean, that was just so totally not like me!"*

Now, I'm *not* suggesting that Christians start beating up modern money-changers or kick over their tables. *That* kind of missionary activity requires a personal memo *direct* from the desk of God with Him showing at least two forms of picture-verified ID and an authenticating code. Being obnoxious and angrily "acting out" only gives our adversaries extra ammunition to slander us more than they *already* do. There are many effective ways to wisely engage the wicked of our times and expose their unfruitful works of darkness. Wisdom *always* wins the day. Acting stupid: *not so much*.

Join the March!

Christians have a Christ-mandated duty to take their place in the "Long March" through the institutions of society to infiltrate and boldly seek to influence *everyone* toward a biblically-based worldview. We must expect fierce opposition, including perhaps some violence, for the minions of darkness will throw *everything* they have at us to discourage and silence us. This is an act of desperation because deep down inside; they know that rebellion against God is a fool's errand doomed to failure. We do not need to fear. By God's grace, we're convinced of the biblical assurance that Christ has conquered death, and are no longer controlled by the fear of it. Hebrews 2:14-15 illuminates this point perfectly.

> *Since the children have flesh and blood, He too shared in their humanity so that by his death He might break the power of him who holds the power of death—that is, the devil— and free those who all their lives were held in slavery by their fear of death.*

God calls His people to live in hope, and speak the Truth in love, without intimidation or the fear of man, resisting the temptation to be angry or vindictive toward people. We direct our anger toward the devil and his demons, yet even in this, we walk in the peace of Christ. Our highest priority is to please God and thereby enjoy *His* honor and approval. All who are called into this grace hope to appear one day unashamed among those men and women who—down through the centuries—stood boldly for Truth. Let us follow the example of those who laid down their lives when necessary for the cause of freedom and Christ's gospel.

Living Infectiously

Carefully consider what Jesus taught His disciples in Matthew 13:33, (NIV):

> *The kingdom of heaven is like yeast that a woman took and mixed into about sixty pounds of flour until it worked all through the dough.*

Jesus described the kingdom of heaven as a "yeast" that slowly permeates the entire lump of dough. The dough is understood as the world as a whole, as well as those elect individuals who become "impregnated" with the "yeast" of the kingdom. It is interesting that Jesus spoke of "sixty pounds of flour" in his parable. The biblical number of man is six. As time goes on, the yeast of Truth slowly and surely permeates (leavens) a nation or an entire person. When God calls someone into the grace of Christ, he or she is "leavened" with a small foretaste of the kingdom yeast of God. Even the tiniest portion will do for a start and is *more than enough* to eventually transform those granted this gift of grace into a child of God–a new creation in Christ.

As the yeast of God's word spreads into the mind and soul, it begins to profoundly transform the entire life. All the thoughts, motives, attitudes, worldviews, priorities, behaviors, decisions, ethics, traditions, family life, child-rearing efforts, politics, and business practices of the person change. In other words, *every aspect of life* is now lived increasingly "under the influence" of the kingdom yeast. This *increasing* influence defines a *real* Christian, not just someone who "decided for Jesus" during an emotional "altar call" in a religious service but now lives as a functional atheist in their daily life. An emotional response to an invitation to respond to Christ *might* be a good *starting point*, but it is *only* a start. A *born-again person* is one who grows in the grace and knowledge of Christ and increasingly hungers and thirsts for His word. The fruits of the Spirit becomes more evident, these being "love, joy, peace, patience, kindness, goodness, meekness, and self-control. Increasing in the knowledge of God becomes a lifelong quest for a Biblical Christian.

Is a Mission Field Coming to Us?
During his Presidential term, Barrack Hussein Obama opened the floodgates to Muslim "refugees" and without public comment, dropped them into American communities across the country. At this point, it's hard to believe that he was unaware of the age-old Islamic strategy of "Al-Hijrah," or "immigration jihad." This tactic is *well-known* in the Islamic world and is calculated to overwhelm recipient countries with Muslims and eventually force the implementation of Islamic rule through shariah law over the whole world. 4

This cynical move by the Obama Administration is causing a growing public uproar because of the obvious danger to our national security. It is a well-known fact that there are over 20 Islamic "compounds" scattered across the country in secluded places that serve as jihadist paramilitary training bases. Recent FBI raids revealed huge arsenals of military-grade weapons and explosives on these "compounds." Many of these "refugees" are young Islamic men of military age who have no interest in assimilating into American culture for reasons noted above.

We can whine and complain about this, but the fact is that hundreds of thousands of these "refugees" are already here, and more are coming. Thankfully, the Trump administration is attempting to stem the flow of Muslims into our country from failed nation-states where no credible vetting is possible. Progressive liberal judges in our courts consistently throw impediments in front of the President in his efforts to protect our people. So, what are *we* to do?

May I suggest that we aggressively "infect" these immigrants with the leaven of Christ's gospel? This "infection" would, of course, take the form of acts of charity, compassion, and love. However, the bold proclamation of the gospel of

Christ is, and always *has* been, the "means of choice" for God's faithful servants. However, if all we do is "make nice" with them, we could end up defrauding them of the truth-claims of Christ, and God's command that all men repent and trust in His Messiah for salvation.

For many years, Christian missionaries have sought to take the gospel to Muslims in their native countries. This noble endeavor has proven extremely difficult and expensive. Such "missionary" activity is extremely difficult in that Christians from Western nations stand out like a sore thumb in the Islamic communities of the Middle East. The workers are easily targeted for kidnapping or assassination. Not only this, but *any Muslim* who becomes a Christian as a result of these outreach activities suffers violent persecution and even death at the hands of the Muslim community at large.

However, when Islamic people come *here*, they are on *our* turf where *our* laws and societal norms *greatly* restrain the more radical among them to commit acts of violence. Also, Muslims who come to Christ in America have *much greater freedom* and support from the Christian community than they would have in their home nations. They have much greater opportunities to attend seminaries and training centers to prepare them for ministry to their own people. God could and would raise up powerful evangelists and Christian apologists to reach out to their communities here in America and perhaps later, in their countries of origin.

Could it be that God is somehow sovereignly bringing these people to *us* so that we might more easily reach them for Christ? If any Muslim happens to be reading this, be sure of one thing. We're coming for *you* with *our* gospel. *We're the Christians Mohammed warned you about*, and we're going to "get" you with Christ's mercy and forgiveness, and offer you the gift of eternal life in Him. Again, all the Earth will eventually come under the dominion of Christ's kingdom, either willingly or otherwise. Let us be wise enough to seize the opportunities right in front of us.

Throwing Fuel on the Fire

The pulpits of America's churches once burned intensely with a holy flame in the early to mid-1700s under the powerful ministry of Calvinist preachers like George Whitefield and Jonathan Edwards. Their passion enflamed the hearts of our people *and* the framers of our republic. I like to call it the "Founders' Fire." Should the grace and providence of God rekindle that same passion afresh in the hearts and minds of our children and fellow citizens, America may yet see a rebirth of freedom under the blessing of God. All things are possible with Him!

A sure signal that this new awakening is starting is when we begin to see men and women showing greater concern for their *own* sin and hunger for God's grace and forgiveness. I think we will also see a renewed interest in learning about our Christian foundations. Our people have largely forgotten our heritage and therefore, have forsaken God. We have lost sight of His plans and purposes. Providentially, voices are beginning to rise to remind us of God's historical favor, and why we came into existence as a nation.

Another sign that God is sparing our republic will be when we begin to see men and women in positions of leadership genuinely showing more concern for the security and welfare of our citizens than for their own political careers. Also, when we see public servants coming to Christ in bold and public ways, this will indicate God's blessing on our nation. This is *especially* true when we see conversions among those who once stood in the enemy's camp of darkness and enmity and perhaps persecuted Christians and Jews. We must always remember that God has the ultimate veto power over the plans of the wicked.

Perhaps most importantly, we must always view unbelievers—even the most outwardly hateful and vicious—as potentially "unawakened brethren" who may yet hear God's call to righteousness just as we did. In the book of Acts chapter 9, Saul of Tarsus' conversion stands as an outstanding example of God's unmerited grace. Saul zealously began his "ministry" to Christ's church as a cruel, vicious, hateful persecutor. Even as he journeyed to Damascus to destroy Christians, Saul spat out threats about what he planned to do to Christ's people when he got his hands on them. Quite contrary to his "free will," Paul was miraculously transformed by the grace of God into one of Christ's chosen servants. His conversion was so dramatic that Saul changed his name to Paul, signifying his rebirth into an entirely new life. He eventually *did* get his hands on the Christians, but it wasn't in the way he imagined.

Excuse Me, But May We Keep our Republic?

Mrs. Powell's question to Benjamin Franklin after the Constitutional Convention remains valid today. May we keep our Republic? I believe God still has an extraordinary destiny for the United States of America to fulfill. He indeed favored our nation in the past and shed His grace upon us in spite of our many personal failures and national sins.

By His grace we must, as did those early Americans, answer the call of duty. May we declare as they did: "…with a firm reliance on the protection of divine Providence, we mutually pledge to each other our Lives, our Fortunes, and our sacred Honor." We must seek the "ancient paths" that served our forefathers so well. We must rebuild the foundations of the greatest nation ever extant in all of human history. As the ancient Jewish scholar Hillel is often quoted as saying; "If not now, when? If not you, who?"

If our nation endures, it will do so only if God's hand extends to us in mercy and forgiveness. If godly men and women pray and stand up fearlessly to proclaim the gospel, even in the face of death or incarceration, America may yet survive and prosper. May we serve as a "city on a hill" giving the light of God's good news to the world. As President Lincoln once expressed:

> *Having chosen our course,*
> *without guile and with pure purpose,*
> *let us renew our trust in God,*
> *and go forward without fear*
> *and with manly hearts.*
> Abraham Lincoln

Duty, Honor, Country

General Douglas MacArthur gave a solemn warning to us all in his immortal speech at West Point on May 12, 1962. With eloquence, he warned that if future generations should fail in the faithful execution of our duties to preserve our liberty:

> *...a million ghosts in olive drab, in brown khaki, in blue and gray, would rise from their white crosses, thundering those magic words: Duty, honor, country!*

At the conclusion of the war against Japan on September 2, 1945, General MacArthur spoke important words of warning in his worldwide radio address broadcast from the U.S.S. Missouri following the ceremony of Japan's surrender. His words apply to us now as much as they did then. Here are a few salient excerpts from that speech:

> *...I thank a merciful God that he has given us the faith, the courage and the power from which to mold victory... The destructiveness of the war potential, through progressive advances in scientific discovery, has in fact now reached a point which revises the traditional concepts of war... We have had our last chance. If we do not now devise some greater and more equitable system, Armageddon will be at our door.* **The problem basically is theological and involves a spiritual recrudescence and improvement of**

human character that will synchronize with our almost matchless advances in science, art, literature and all material and cultural development of the past two thousand years. It must be of the spirit if we are to save the flesh.
5 Emphasis added

I draw particular attention to Gen. MacArthur's words: "The problem basically is theological..." Here I believe Gen. MacArthur struck upon the core issue in the struggle against evil. Perhaps without realizing it, he laid the ax of truth to the root of humanity's core problem. Our problems are *spiritual*, and we cannot hope for victory over our miseries without a "spiritual recrudescence" (defined as *breaking out afresh or into renewed activity; revival or reappearance in active existence*) "and improvement of human character..." These words bring to mind what Jesus said to Nicodemus in John 3:3:

> *Jesus answered him, "Truly, truly, I say to you, unless one is born again he cannot see the kingdom of God."*

With the aid and blessings of Providence, another Great Awakening in America may flourish, for without such an awakening, our situation is hopeless, and we are doomed. A God-orchestrated chorus of voices is beginning to emerge in the present crisis who are hungering and thirsting for His eternal purposes and praying for His mighty hand to move to our deliverance. We must not allow time and opportunity to slip through our fingers through neglect of duty. By the grace of God, we may yet see a new and brighter day.

SAM:
This shadow, even darkness must pass.
A new day will come, and when the sun shines
it will shine out the clearer.
Those are the stories that stay with you,
that meant something,
even if you were too small to understand why.
I think Mr. Frodo, I do understand...I know now...
folk in those stories had lots of chances of turning back,
only they didn't. They kept goin'
because they were holdin' onto something.
FRODO:
What are we holding onto Sam?

SAM:
That there's some good in this world Mr. Frodo,
and it's worth fighting for.
J.R.R. Tolkien, *The Two Towers*

Notes

1. Rudi Dutschke and the German student movement in 1968 International Socialism Journal http://socialistworker.co.uk/art/14460/Rudi+Dutschke+and+the+German+student+movement+in+1968

2. An Introduction to Gramsci's Life and Thought, By Frank Rosengarten https://www.marxists.org/archive/gramsci/intro.htm

3. Barack Obama's small-town guns and religion comments (Recording) https://www.youtube.com/watch?v=DTxXUufl3jA

4. http://pamelageller.com/2015/01/obama-imported-300000-muslims-into-the-us-in-2013.html/#sthash.Ndw53IbL.dpuf

5. General Douglas MacArthur: "Today the Guns are Silent" Aboard the U.S.S. Missouri, Tokyo Bay, September 2, 1945 http://tinyurl.com/kcpcas3

24

Our Bucket List

> *It is the common fate*
> *of the indolent*
> *to see their rights*
> *become a prey to the active.*
> *The condition upon which God*
> *hath given liberty to man*
> *is eternal vigilance;*
> *which condition if he break,*
> *servitude is at once*
> *the consequence of his crime*
> *and the punishment of his guilt.*
> John Philpot Curran
> Speech upon the Right of Election, 1790
> 1

~~~~~~

As most people know, a "bucket list" is a list of things we hope to accomplish before we "kick the bucket" and die. Let's face it. We're *all* going to die someday. As I see it, a question that should guide our brief time in this world is some variation of the following; "Did my life harmonize with God's purposes and leave the world a happier, saner, and more blessed place than when I entered it?" My guiding principle is; "Did my life and death honor and glorify God?"

I'm convinced that the founding of America was for the specific purpose of facilitating the light and glory of God in Christ throughout the world. Our Founding Documents, and indeed, the Founders *themselves*—although imperfectly—reflect this truth. The freedoms we enjoy were not meant to give us a comfortable life or license to live merely for pleasure. Our prosperity, liberty, and abundance are a *means* to an *end*. I believe that when we began to lose that vision, we dishonored God. I also believe that God can and *will* reawaken us to our higher calling and purposes, albeit perhaps, through some pain and suffering. In that awakening, we will find strength and resolve to preserve, protect, and defend our God-given liberty and our Constitution and Bill of Rights. Through those instruments, we are enabled to fulfill our national destiny. If we should fail to do this, slavery and misery will inevitably befall us.

It's Time to Make Some Noise!

In the early stages of the War of Independence, Paul Revere's famous ride of April 18, 1775, was a wake-up call to a slumbering citizenry. On that particular night, the British military stealthily marched toward Lexington and Concord to arrest Samual Adams and John Hancock. They also intended to impose "gun control" and confiscate all gunpowder and firearms from the citizens to render them defenseless.

Henry Wadsworth Longfellow later immortalized Paul Revere in his famous poem, *Paul Revere's Ride.* Here is the last stanza:

> *So through the night rode Paul Revere;*
> *And so through the night went his cry of alarm*
> *To every Middlesex village and farm,—*
> *A cry of defiance, and not of fear,*
> *A voice in the darkness, a knock at the door,*
> *And a word that shall echo for evermore!*
> *For, borne on the night-wind of the Past,*
> *Through all our history, to the last,*
> *In the hour of darkness and peril and need,*
> *The people will waken and listen to hear*
> *The hurrying hoof-beats of that steed,*
> *And the midnight message of Paul Revere.*

Paul Revere wasn't the *only* person riding that night to warn of the British advance. Several other brave souls did the same or more. Two other Patriot riders, William Dawes and Samuel Prescott, also rode at great personal risk along the dark roads that were patrolled by British soldiers. Five days prior to Revere's ride, Israel Bissell, began the longest ride on April 13, to warn the colonists of the British advance. He rode hard for four days and six hours, racking up 345 miles. According to the story, *he* was the one who shouted along the way "To arms, to arms, the war has begun."

One other alarm rider deserves recognition. A young girl named Sybil

Ludington—the sixteen-year-old daughter of Colonel Henry Ludington—made her night ride on April 26, 1777, to warn the colonists at Danbury Connecticut of the approaching British. This incredibly brave young woman rode *twice* the distance of Paul Revere (over 40 miles). President George Washington later gave her a commendation for her heroism and patriotic service to her country. In Carmel, New York, a statue honoring Sybil was erected along her route. 2

These riders were "disturbers of the peace." Without any doubt, there were also highly annoyed British Loyalists along their routes who were enraged at the sound of their cries of alarm. The riders probably heard some flowery language and threats as they rode past some Tory houses. However, these Patriots weren't seeking to comfort people in their slumber or sing lullabies. They certainly *didn't* ride madly through the night shouting at the top of their lungs things like:

> *To sleep! To sleep!*
> *No cause for alarm;*
> *For the British are coming*
> *and will do you no harm.*
> *They march to protect you*
> *from bad men with guns*
> *by taking them away*
> *from your fathers and sons.*
> *To sleep! To sleep!*
> *There's nothing to see.*
> *Only invaders in red coats*
> *to ensure your slavery!*

They sounded a dire warning of an approaching enemy. According to historians, Revere, and his fellow riders raised the alarm at each house throughout the countryside, awakening the people to the danger coming toward them in the darkness. According to one story, at about midnight Revere galloped up to the house at Lexington where Adams and Hancock were sleeping and made a loud ruckus. A night guard indignantly told him not to make so much noise. "Noise!" Revere cried, "You'll have *noise enough* before long! The [British] regulars are coming out!"

The tragic events surrounding the 9/11 Islamic terrorist attack, and the rise of violent anarchist leftist fascism, and the fomenting of racial divisions by leftist politicos in recent years *should* have awakened us. Instead, most people yawn, roll over in their beds of complacency, hide under a blanket of politically-correct silence, and hit the "snooze" button. Evil is *very real* and is now boldly marching upon our land. We *need more* Paul Reveres, William Dawes, Samuel Prescotts, and yes, even young girls like Sybil Ludington to sound the alarm and call our people to action.

Take up the Torch: Rekindle the Founders' Fire

What must we do now? What *practical* steps can be taken to revive the Founders' Fire and raise up again the bright torch of liberty? First of all, we must realize that *each of us has a part to play*. Each of us has a gift to bring. The ongoing battle for Freedom is not a spectator sport. It is not just the "mighty deeds" of so-called "great" men and women that will win the day. It is rather the countless small acts of ordinary people (the "hobbits" of our world, to borrow from J.R. Tolkien) that eventually overcome and conquer evil. Remember, God has graciously given each of His people a "little broom" to help clean up the mess.

There are some who yearn for excuses to violently attack and crush Christians as well as defenders of the Constitution. They'll seize upon *any* statement that they can twist into a weapon of anti-Christian propaganda. They *despise* our Constitutional Republic (in spite of any "tolerant" rhetoric to the contrary) because they *hate* the underlying spiritual foundations that brought it into existence. Ultimately, it is *God* they hate and wish to erase *all* memory or mention of Him from history.

To head off potential accusations by those who would seek to cast me—and those who agree with me—under the rubric of "dangerous radicals," I must make the following disclaimer. We have *no* plans to overthrow the government by violent means. I want that to be crystal clear. Our quarrel is not with our great Constitutional Republic or our legally-established government so long as it is *restrained and controlled* by that Constitution. We must keep in mind that the *vast* majority of violent attacks against government officials or institutions over the past 100 years have come at the hands of progressive leftists and anarchists. This well-established fact is routinely ignored by our left-leaning news media, who consistently look to far-left organizations like the SPLA (Southern Poverty Law Center) for *their* "spin" on so-called conservative "hate" groups.

Our *primary* battle—as I stated previously in my chapter titled; *Our Real Enemies* is against the forces of evil *spiritual* powers and demonic spirits *in the unseen realm*. These dark spiritual influences are *the* prime motivators of those who are presently seeking to destroy our country. We *will* win this war, but our victory will come primarily on prayerful knees through the supernatural weapons we receive from God's armory. The sharp two-edged sword of the invincible word of God comes forth from our mouths when we proclaim the gospel and the truth. No earthly weapons can long stand against these.

There are some hopeful signs as of this writing. Encouraging things are beginning to happen, but unless we get our news from somewhere other than corporate leftist sources, we probably would never hear about it. To entirely infiltrate America and the world, we need to "slug it out" in the trenches of Christian apologetics on the campuses with the power of persuasive argument, well-written literature, and prayer. Success will likely take some time—perhaps even several generations, and most likely, blood will be shed. (Not by us, but by those on the left and secular progressives who seek to silence our voices through violence and intimidation.) I once mocked the idea of a Christian transformation of society by foolishly tossing out the expression; "that's just polishing the brass on the Titanic." Further study of scripture and church history have convinced me otherwise.

Here are some suggestions for you to occupy your time while waiting for the final return of Christ (*however* you may *think* that will occur). Keep in mind; His glorious appearing might take *a bit longer* than you hoped. You certainly won't waste the time you're given if you continue in faithful obedience and good works. You may add to the following list as you wish. Greater minds than mine will think of even more effective strategies. However, keep in mind as you read it that it represents *nothing less than a Declaration of TOTAL WAR* against secular bigotry.

Category One: Education Reforms

- We must *take control* of the education of our nation's youth and stop relying on a centralized secular government bureaucracy to handle this crucial task. Secular educational agendas have decimated our republic by brainwashing generations of our young with "approved" worldviews that are antithetical to Biblical truth—and as a consequence—our freedoms, prosperity, and happiness. Be sure of one thing; Unless these secular indoctrination institutions undergo a reformation, ALL ELSE WE DO will be in *vain*. Today's students are tomorrow's voters! Someone once wisely said; "The hand that rocks the cradle, will one day rule the world."

Reversing this will be an *uphill battle*, for liberal progressives now enjoy virtually unchallenged dominance in nearly all public education. They will *not* passively give up their monopoly without a furious fight. Leftist/secular progressives have a clear vision of *total* dominance over *all* education and are constantly seeking legislation to force *every child* into government-controlled public schools. They would joyfully deprive Christian parents any opportunity to raise their children according to Biblical moral, spiritual, and civic standards. For those who are still skeptical that this could happen here in America, consider the fact that in many countries, it is *illegal* for Christians to home-school their children, punishable by fines, prison, and loss of custody.

- Parents and grandparents must attend school board meetings, get involved, and seek election to local school boards and committees of policy influence, *particularly* concerning curriculum development and textbook selection. Again, expect *vicious opposition* by leftist groups like the NEA and liberal teacher's unions.
- Christian conservatives who are unashamed of America's Christian heritage and conservative founding must infiltrate public schools and secular universities and colleges acting as agents of influence in those venues.
- Gifted Christian Scholars should be encouraged and supported to gain professorships and teaching positions in colleges and universities, especially in the science, history, and humanities departments.
- New private schools should be established and supported as well as quality home education, and school voucher initiatives to give parents a greater choice. Liberals often *howl* over this because it represents a direct threat to their monopoly over government education funds.
- We must gradually dismantle the unconstitutional Department of Education. This goal, of course, will require a long-term strategy, for this massive bureaucracy employs millions of people, including many Christians. It will take some time and wise planning to transition those many dedicated and honorable teachers into new and more efficient systems where they as well as their students can flourish. All the above steps would gradually make the present inefficient and bloated "public education" monopoly irrelevant and unattractive to teachers *and* parents. Lobbying initiatives and pressure must be directed at politicians on the local and national level to dismantle this disastrous failure. At the same time, legislative protections must be maintained for home and private education.

Category Two: Political Activism

- We must encourage and train those who are gifted and qualified (possibly YOU?) to run for public office at the city, county, state, and federal level. After they are in office, we must hold them accountable to maintain their integrity and uncompromising faithfulness to the Constitution and Bill of Rights.
- We must identify every politician who violates their Oath of Office —*no matter what their party affiliation*—and pursue litigation to impeach and put them *out* of office. Recall elections must be both initiated and supported where possible.
- Conservatives must be encouraged to *cease* the practice of political factionalism—forming small separate single-issue parties—and bring their influence and agendas to bear on one united party. While this is extremely difficult in practice, we must remind each other that a "house divided cannot stand."
- Every lover of America and the Constitution should exercise their God-given privilege and responsibility as a citizen *to vote*. It is disheartening to hear of recent polls that show millions of eligible Christian and conservative voters *refusing to vote* because their "favorite" candidate or particular social or moral issue was underrepresented by an otherwise conservative candidate. Politics is an *inexact science*, and no one *ever* gets to vote for a "perfect" candidate because none has ever existed. There *is (and always has been)* a lesser of two evils. Our founders fought for the right for the people's voices to be heard; we should honor their efforts and exercise our rights.
- Publicly available educational initiatives should be established to inform and educate people in our communities concerning our nation's history, heritage, and national destiny. An excellent conservative free course on subjects covering the U.S. Constitution, American History, Economics, Great Books, K-12 Education to name a few, is available on-line from Hillsdale College. [3]

Category Three: Legal Activism

- Christian law associations and individual attorneys must be supported and encouraged to wage this battle in our nation's courtrooms, utilizing every legal recourse within our power to prevent and overthrow damaging litigation. A few of them would be the Christian Law Association [4] and the American Center for Law and Justice (ACLJ) [5]

Category Four: Cultural Activism

- Christian and conservative writers, film producers, musicians, and artists must pull out "all the stops" to promote America's heritage and Christian history to stand up for Truth. This would include Christian playwrights and composers.
- Christian radio and television stations should promote and set up venues for debates with progressive secularists engaged by qualified Christian apologists.
- Christian podcasters and writers must crank up their efforts to inform, inspire, and motivate people to community action and awareness through books, articles, and podcasts.

Category Five: Clergy Activism and Prayer

- Christian pastors and teachers should be encouraged to boldly raise their voices against evil and take courageous stands on moral issues. Pastors and qualified guest "activists" should be regularly scheduled to teach their congregations about their civic responsibilities. Churches could sponsor their pastor and elders to attend Christian Conservative and Political Action conferences to raise awareness and help them develop their own strategies and activist efforts in their local communities.
- Prayer:
  I wanted to list this as the very **FIRST** priority, because, without *lots of it*, nothing else will succeed. I only list it last because I know most people skim-read, and their eyes will likely fall on this point with the most lasting impact.

Allow me to expand this thought, for I believe that prayer is the equivalence of a "*nuclear weapon*" in our struggle with the present darkness. Although prayer is our most potent weapon, it is often the least-used. I'm as guilty as anyone in this regard, for I am a man of action, and (full disclosure) spending time on my knees seeking God sometimes seems like a waste of valuable time. This is a lie of course. History and the Bible teach us over and over that every great movement of God was accompanied by much fervent prayer.

> *Prayer plumes the wings of God's young eaglets so that they may learn to mount above the clouds. Prayer brings inner strength to God's warriors and sends them forth to spiritual battle with their muscles firm and their armor*

in place.
– Charles H. Spurgeon

Are We "Fed Up" Yet?

We are seeing an increasing number of brave pastors and Bible teachers who are fed up with the "politically correct" nonsense and moral compromises assailing their congregations and our nation at large. They see evil devouring families and marriages, destroying young children and teens with drug use and sexual confusion. We must pray for and encourage the Shepherds of God's people, for it takes great courage and personal sacrifice to stand up against spiritual darkness and endure the inevitable backlash that comes when Christian leaders challenge the status quo with a biblical perspective. One prominent example of this sort of moral courage was the recent release of *The Nashville Statement* by CBMW.org: *A coalition for biblical sexuality.* [6]

This documents affirms the biblical and orthodox view of human sexuality and marriage. Those who are seeking to "normalize" aberrant sexual behaviors are enraged by such proclamations, and *will actively seek* to destroy anyone and any institution that opposes their radical agendas.

The very real temptation leaders face is to take the path of least resistance, preach sermons that are uncontroversial and make people feel warm and fuzzy, and collect their salaries and pensions. I'm sorry for speaking so harshly about this, but as the Shepherds of God's flock, we are *required* to lay down our lives for God's flock, *no matter what the cost.* I predict that God is now "winnowing the chaff" within His church, and separating the sheep from the goats.

The Clergy's Finest Hour

The bright torches of liberty in America were *originally* kindled upon the pulpits of America's churches. It was brave men of God like the itinerant Calvinist evangelists, George Whitefield and Jonathan Edwards, who raised up that torch of freedom before the people in the early 1700s. Courageous pastors refused to be intimidated by threats from the Crown of England or discouraged by the fearful bleating of the sheeple of their time.

> [T]*he first movement toward democracy in America was inaugurated in the house of God and with the blessing of the minister of God.* [7]

Clergy involvement in politics and public policy are nothing new in our nation. During America's Revolutionary War, many courageous ministers took a stand in favor of separation from England, leading prayer, preaching sermons related to freedom and liberty, and condemning tyranny. Some of them rode with the Continental Army as Chaplains, giving spiritual counsel and comfort to our Patriots. The British referred to them derisively as the "Black Robe Regiment," referencing the black clerical robes the ministers often wore over their Continental Army uniforms. The following quotes are illuminating:

> *As a body of men, the clergy were pre-eminent in their attachment to liberty. The pulpits of the land rang with the notes of freedom.*
> –The American Quarterly Register, 1833 [8]

The involvement of Christian ministers in the Revolutionary War was *well-known* to the British.

> *If Christian ministers had not preached and prayed, there might have been no revolution as yet – or had it broken out, it might have been crushed.*
> –Bibliotheca Sacra, (A British Periodical) 1856 [9]

Also,

> *The ministers of the Revolution were, like their Puritan predecessors, bold and fearless in the cause of their country. No class of men contributed more to carry forward the Revolution and to achieve our independence than did the ministers. . . . [B]y their prayers, patriotic sermons, and services [they] rendered the highest assistance to the civil government, the army, and the country.* [10]
> B. F. Morris, Historian, 1864

And,

> *The learned clergy… had great influence in founding the first genuine republican government ever formed and which, with all the faults and defects of the men and their laws, were the best republican governments on earth. At this moment, the people of this country are indebted chiefly to their institutions for the rights and privileges which are enjoyed.*
> –Letters of Noah Webster [11]

Concerning the role of Christian leaders in the present struggle for our constitutional republic:

- Congregations should provide support to pastor's families should they (or *any* faithful Christian) be arrested or persecuted for standing boldly for biblical truth.
- Pastors must also openly urge their congregations to vote for godly candidates who share our moral and ethical values even if they are from a different Christian tradition. Remember the example of Rahab the harlot, who stood with the people of God at Jericho. Although she was a pagan harlot and a liar, she became a heroine of faith when she stood with the God of Israel. More than this, according to Matthew 1:5, she received the high honor of being a mother in the genealogy of Christ.
- Christian evangelists and apologists must be encouraged, trained, and supported. Public debates with progressives, atheists, and evolutionists must be encouraged and promoted, laying bare the lies and deceptions of these false cults of pseudo-intellectualism. In this context, every effort should be made to make the gospel of Christ known to all men.
- *Every* Christian should set aside extra time to study and pray. In our age, distractions of all kinds are always pulling our attention away from what is important toward the next new "shiny thing." As Charles H. Spurgeon once wrote:

We are quite persuaded that the very best way for you to be spending your leisure time is to be either reading or praying. You may get much instruction from books that afterwards you may use as a true weapon in your Lord and Master's service. Paul cries, "Bring the books" — join in the cry.

This call to study is not just the duty of the "Clergy." Christians, in general, must throw off any excuse of theological ignorance and stop depending upon the "Clergy" to do *everything*. It is true that Christ appointed certain "offices" of the church in the form of Apostles, Prophets, Evangelists, Pastors, and Teachers. However, these gifts were never given to do *all* the work of ministry. According to Ephesians 4:10-12, their primary responsibility is to *equip the saints* for the work of the ministry.

He that descended, is even the same that ascended, far above all heavens, that he might fill all things. He therefore gave some to be Apostles, and some Prophets, and some Evangelists, and some Pastors, and Teachers for the repairing of the Saints, for the work of the ministry, and for the edification of the body of Christ...

We live in a time when virtually unlimited access is available via the internet to biblical educational resources *undreamed of* in previous eras. We are entirely without excuse to remain in ignorance. Each believer must make it his or her goal to become a walking library of knowledge and wisdom. Certainly, some are more gifted than others in this regard, according to God's grace. However, each follower of Christ should be able to "give an answer" to every person regarding the hope that is within them by sharing *what* they believe, and *why* they believe it. If we are effective, we *will be* attacked and criticized by those wishing to silence us. If we're *not* experiencing criticism, we're probably not saying or doing anything of importance.

Most important of all, (to repeat myself) Christians must purposefully lay aside time each and every day to pray for the nation and leaders. This mandate *especially* applies concerning prayer for those leaders who fight against us. Our Father in Heaven is *well-able* to jerk *anyone's* chain, no matter how outwardly evil they may be at present. God may show mercy to them—and by extension—to us, by opening their blinded eyes and breaking their proud, hardened hearts.

Can anyone imagine what might happen if even *ten percent* of our elected government employees had a massive, industrial-strength encounter with the Living Christ? Remember the lesson of Saul of Tarsus, who later became the Apostle Paul.

Hold On! Help Is On The Way!

Most Christians have at least heard of times in America's history when great revivals or Christian "Awakenings" occurred. The first "Great Awakening" came at a time when Americans had virtually lost all interest in Christianity, and the nation was sliding into corruption, immorality, and spiritual decay. According to Martin Kelly, American History Expert:

> *The Great Awakening was a period of great revivalism that spread throughout the colonies in the 1730s and 1740s. It de-emphasized the importance of church doctrine and instead put a greater importance on the individual and their spiritual experience.* [12]

According to Wikipedia:

> *Historians and theologians identify three or four waves of increased religious enthusiasm occurring between the early 18th century and the late 19th century. Each of these "Great Awakenings" was characterized by*

widespread revivals led by evangelical Protestant ministers, a sharp increase of interest in religion, a profound sense of conviction and redemption on the part of those affected, an increase in evangelical church membership, and the formation of new religious movements and denominations. [13]

I will not go into great detail regarding these Awakenings in this book. Much has been written on the subject by authors and scholars far more qualified than I. For anyone interested in further study of this important topic, I highly recommend an excellent free audio series by Dr. J. Edward Orr titled, *Great Awakenings in American History.* [14]

However, I *would* like to comment on the subject in a general way, and particularly regarding what has been called the "First Great Awakening" during the period of the 1730s until around 1743. Some have postulated that the First Great Awakening was a major factor and philosophical and spiritual catalyst that shaped the world-view of people in that period. This eventually led to the American Revolution in the late 1700s. John Adams wrote of this time of awakening;

> *The Revolution was effected before the War commenced. The Revolution was in the mind and hearts of the people: and change in their religious sentiments of their duties and obligations.*

Adams nails his point that the Revolution and the resulting freedoms won, occurred primarily because the "pulpits thundered!" Again quoting historian Paul Johnson in *A History of the American People:*

> *The Great Awakening was thus the proto-revolutionary event, the formative moment in American history, preceding the political drive for independence and making it possible.* [15]

The term "Great Awakening" was actually coined by Rev. Joseph Tracy in a powerful book first published in 1867 titled: *The Great Awakening.* Tracy observed that the Awakening came at a time in America's history when most people had become more or less indifferent to Christ and the state of their immortal souls. The Awakening not only swept multitudes of people into the Christian faith by the sovereign power of God, but also brought a dramatic transformation in society as people sought to follow and trust God in every area of their lives. Rev. Tracey quotes Jonathan Edwards, the great Calvinist revivalist. Not only were the pious alarmed, but, Edwards informs us:

"Many, who looked on themselves as in a Christless condition, seemed to be awakened by it, with fear that God was about to withdraw from the land, and that we should be given up to heterodoxy and corrupt principles; and that then their opportunity for obtaining salvation would be past; and many, who were brought a little to doubt about the truth of the doctrines they had hitherto been taught, seemed to have a kind of a trembling fear with the doubts, lest they should be led into the by-paths, to their eternal undoing; and they seemed with much concern and engagedness to inquire, what was indeed the way in which they must come to be accepted of God." 16

God mercifully initiated a stirring in the hearts of people who were not seeking Him, and by His own power and will, sparked a deep hunger for salvation, and profound remorse and loathing for their sin. Edwards, Whitefield, and other evangelists like them expressed amazement at the way God would call out for Himself men and women from the midst of gross depravity, and change their hearts as it pleased Him. Accompanying this, regenerated people began to yearn for greater freedoms to live in a situation where the gospel could flow freely without hindrance from kings, religious oppression, or potentates. The timely invention of the printing press allowed a greater free-flow of information without government controls or religious bias. It was nothing less than a thirst for truth, not just in theological matters, but also in political issues. People began to see the value of liberty in the education of their children.

By means of the Great Awakening, the Founders' Fire was kindled in America, and it inspired in later years a number of Christian initiatives that eventually abolished slavery, advanced the recognition of women's rights, and the establishment of missionary societies that sent missionaries throughout the world.

Ministers during this period saw a transformation in their manner of preaching. Before the Awakening, most sermons were intellectual and dry. However, under the influence of God's Spirit, many found a new boldness, passion, and sensed a new freedom to preach Christ with fervency, touching the emotions of their hearers, and not just their minds and intellects. Preachers and evangelists such as Gilbert Tennent, Jonathan Edwards, and George Whitefield clearly led the way in the First Great Awakening.

Some in our time would seek to mock and dismiss these early Awakenings as merely religious emotionalism. However, I believe we would be wise to remember that God has often shown great mercy in touching the wicked hearts of His elect and drawing them—often kicking and screaming—to His high purposes. From among them, great statesmen, reformers, scientists, political leaders, and ministers were raised up. These leaders shaped the course of nations, even healing many of the national wounds inflicted by the evils done by wicked men.

Another Great Awakening Due?

We are, I believe, at a crucial crossroads, and poised for *another Great Awakening*. As a point of fact, we have *no other hope*. If God does not look upon America with reviving mercy, the alternative will be His judgment, and very likely, the destruction of our nation at the hands of depraved men. Perhaps His chastisement will precede the pouring forth of His mercy, for often people will only turn and seek His mercy when they find themselves broken and humbled. In that regard, I believe God's correction may be an important and compassionate component to the blessings that may follow.

There is a powerful scene in the epic film, *Return of the King*, produced by Peter Jackson, and based on the classic book by J.R.R. Tolkien. In this scene, the armies of Middle Earth are facing overwhelming Orc forces that are streaming out of the Black Gates of Mordor to fight the last battle with a diminished and war-weary small army of men.

Aragorn the King realizes they are vastly outnumbered and surrounded. Without a miracle, they are all doomed. Far away in the distance, on the steep slopes of Mt. Doom, deep in the heart of Mordor, Frodo and Sam are struggling up the last yards of the volcano to throw the ring of power into the lava-fires and destroy the evil power of Mordor over Middle Earth forever. Everything depends on Aragorn's tiny army fighting long enough to distract the attention of Saron away from Frodo so he can accomplish his mission to destroy the ring. (If none of this is familiar, that's okay. You really *should* watch the film.)

The following speech by Aragorn encouraged me, and I hope it does you as well:

> *Hold your ground!*
> *Sons of Gondor, of Rohan, my brothers,*
> *I see in your eyes the same fear*
> *that would take the heart of me.*
> *A day may come*
> *when the courage of men fails,*
> *when we forsake our friends*
> *and break all bonds of fellowship,*

> *but it is not this day.*
> *An hour of wolves and shattered shields,*
> *when the age of men comes crashing down,*
> *but it is not this day!*
> *This day we fight!!*
> *By all that you hold dear*
> *on this good Earth,*
> *I bid you stand, Men of the West!!!*
>
> Aragorn at the Black Gate
> From the Film, *The Return of the King*
> By J.R.R. Tolkien

The Founders Yet Speak

Can we still hear the Founder's voices, calling to us across the corridors of time from our nation's past? Does their wisdom yet whisper to us today from the now-empty seats of Independence Hall in Philadelphia? Can we still discern the voices of Christian Patriots echoing faintly from the now-quiet and midst-laden battlefields where the tocsin alarm of our war for freedom and independence is now silent? The ghosts of those Patriots still beckon to us from the once frigid encampments at Valley Forge, and the smoky and bomb-scarred ramparts of Fort McHenry where brave men and women laid upon the altar of freedom (as President Lincoln once penned in his Gettysburg Address) "their last full measure of devotion." These men and women are still calling us to our duties from the pages of history if we will but listen. I might imagine, if our Founding Fathers could somehow send us a message from the eternal realm, it might read something like this:

> *To our dear fellow Americans, who are now our posterity and who were the objects of all our hopes and dreams. Look kindly upon us, and remember what we sacrificed and painfully labored for in establishing, for your mutual benefit, and for your children's children, a Constitutional Republic. By the grace and providence of God, we bequeathed you a legacy of liberty and freedom, unmatched in all of human history.*
>
> *We were not perfect men by any means, for we were of our times, inheriting the failures and fallen nature of our shared Adamic ancestry. Of ourselves, we were sinners, as all men are, and could wish we might have walked in even greater light than we had at the time. For our many failures,*

we ask your forbearance and forgiveness, even as we have sought and received the same from our Father in heaven through the mercy of Christ. However, we accomplished, by the aid of Providence, the establishment of a government "of the people, by the people, and for the people." It is by no means perfect, and we would make no such claim. We tried, as God gave us light, to infuse within our Constitution and Bill of Rights the ability to amend, revise, and improve our republic while retaining intact its' basic framework.

You have now inherited this Republic, and we trust you will value it and faithfully labor to preserve, protect, and defend the freedoms we made possible by those founding documents. It is a sacred trust you have inherited and will require your constant vigilance and willingness to sacrifice for the sake of liberty, even if necessary, unto death. You will face twisted and selfish men in your time just as we did in ours, who will seek to subvert and destroy the very foundations of freedom, which are ultimately only to be found in the holy Bible and our Savior, Jesus Christ.

Against these antagonists you must, as we also found necessary, be ever ready and willing to rise to the defense of your nation and the Constitution. Most importantly, never forget that despite our labors, or yours in the future, our nation's security depends ultimately upon God's Providence, and it is to Him that we must owe our supreme allegiance over all. Above all, we pray you will not squander the freedoms granted to you by God, and fail to use them to spread the light of His excellent grace through Christ to all men everywhere.

May you find the strength and courage to continue the great adventure which we call the United States of America. May God's grace be upon you and your posterity, and may the flag of freedom ever continue to fly over this land!

Are We At "The End?"

I close this book with a question many have asked in recent times: "Are we at the end?" Many sincere Christians anticipate the soon appearance of Christ, and sadly in some cases, almost seem to rejoice each time evil advances, or a new disaster breaks upon humanity due to teachings that assume that the world *must* go to complete ruin before Christ returns. However, Jesus once asked a question in Luke 18:8 that should concern—and perhaps trouble—each of us.

> *...but when the Son of man cometh,*
> *shall he find faith on the earth?*

Speaking for myself, I certainly hope He will find "faith-full-ness" in me. Is it possible to separate "faith" from the fruit of "faithfulness?" It would not seem so. People who obsess about the "end times" might want to consider readjusting their priorities. While we hope and pray for Christ's soon return, this should *not* be our first concern. I suspect He wants to find us "about our Father's business" and perhaps *so occupied* with His work that we lose ourselves in it. For myself, I'm good with God's perfect timetable for the consummation of all things. It is *far* above our pay-grade to concern ourselves too much with this.

We have a *great opportunity* before us, and there is much to look forward to. *Much more indeed*! The Founders' bright beacon of hope beckons us onward to a higher destiny, yet requires the fuel of obedient dedication and faithful reliance upon God's Providence. For now, *let us brace ourselves to our duties*. Let us each take up the torch of Christ's gospel and grace!

So, are we at "the end?" I do not believe so in any sense of *finality*. This "end" (however it manifests) is only the start of a *new beginning*. We are, however, at a *defining moment*—a pivotal point in history—and a time of impending monumental change orchestrated by God in *every detail*. In this confidence, we can walk with inner peace and serenity no matter *how* crazy this world becomes in the short-term. It is certainly not an "end," or cessation of all further activity. Sir Winston Churchill foreshadowed my assessment of our present struggle with the "Shadow Agenda" of this present world in one of his most memorable World War II speeches, delivered at the Lord Mayor's Luncheon at Mansion House in London on November 10, 1942. Churchill was responding to the news of the decisive Allied victory at the Second Battle of El Alamein in Northern Egypt and sagely stated:

> *Now, this is not the end.*
> *It is not even the beginning of the end.*
> *But it is, perhaps,*
> *the end of the beginning.*

> *And the seventh Angel blew the trumpet,*
> *and there were great voices in heaven, saying,*
> *"The kingdoms of the world*
> *are our Lord's, and His Christ's,*

and He shall reign for evermore."
Revelation 11:15

~~~~~~

POST-TENEBRAS LUX!
(After Darkness, Light)

Notes

1. John Philpot Curran: Speech upon the Right of Election, 1790. (Speeches. Dublin, 1808.) as quoted in the Oxford Dictionary of Quotations, NY, 1953, p167 and also in Bartlett's Familiar Quotations, Boston, 1968, p479

2. https://www.constitutionfacts.com/us-declaration-of-independence/the-five-riders/

3. online.hillsdale.edu

4. http://www.christianlaw.org/cla/

5. http://aclj.org/

6. https://cbmw.org

7. Charles B. Galloway, Christianity and the American Commonwealth (Nashville, TN: Publishing House Methodist Episcopal Church, 1898), p. 114.

8. "History of Revivals of Religion, From the Settlement of the Country to the Present Time," The American Quarterly Register, (Boston: Perkins and Marvin, 1833) Vol. 5, p. 217.

9. Alpheus Packard, "Nationality," Bibliotheca Sacra and American Biblical Repository (London: Andover: Warren F. Draper, 1856), Vol. XIII p.193, Article VI.

10. Benjamin Franklin Morris, Christian Life and Character of the Civil Institutions of the United States (Philadelphia: George W. Childs, 1864), pp. 334-335.

11. Noah Webster, Letters of Noah Webster, Harry R. Warfel, editor (New York: Library Publishers, 1953, p. 455, letter to David McClure, October 25, 1836.

12. The Great Awakening, By Martin Kelly, American History Expert http://americanhistory.about.com/od/colonialamerica/p/great_awakening.htm

13. Great Awakening, From Wikipedia, the free encyclopedia http://en.wikipedia.org/wiki/Great_Awakening

14. http://www.sermonaudio.com/sermoninfo.asp?SID=102702215836

15. A History of the American People By Paul Johnson, Harper Perennial Publishers, Page 83

16. The Great Awakening, By Joseph Tracey, Quinta Press, Chap 1, page 26

About the Author

For over 40 years, Dr. Bruce Porter has served Christ as a church planter, pastor, firefighter, chaplain, and as a Moral Leadership/Disaster Response Officer with the Civil Air Patrol. He has frequently spoken across America and overseas, calling Christians to rise to their highest calling in serving people according to the gifts each have received from God. Bruce received his Doctor of Divinity degree from Promise Christian University in 2004.

Bruce has shared the gospel in over 40 countries, and responded to multiple scenes of disaster around the U.S. and the world, including, (to mention but a few):

- The Columbine High School attack
- Red Lake High School attack
- Ground Zero in NYC after the 9/11 terrorist attack
- Served at the crash site of AA Flt 586 in New York City
- Erfurt, Germany, School attack
- Sri Lanka after the 2004 tsunami devastation
- Beslan, Russia, School terrorist attack
- Bailey, Colorado, High School shooting
- Israel during First Gulf War and most recent war
- Amish schoolhouse slaughter in Pennsylvania

Bruce and his wife Claudia raised three wonderful and godly children, and, as of this publication, have six grandchildren. Together, they pastor *Torch Life Church,* a totally house-based fellowship. They reside in the mountains west of Denver, Colorado. For information on future book releases or to schedule speaking engagements, contact:

bruce@BruceSpeaks.com
   You may also visit the author's blog page at:
   www.brucespeaks.com

Made in the USA
San Bernardino, CA
24 May 2018